Backward Classes and Social Justice

Edited by

M.H. Makwana and Richard Pais

RAWAT PUBLICATIONS

Jaipur | New Delhi | Bangalore | Hyderabad | Guwahati

ISBN 978-81-316-0406-9

Published by
Prem Rawat for **Rawat Publications**
Satyam Apts., Sector 3, Jawahar Nagar, Jaipur 302 004 (India)
Phone: 0141 265 1748 / 7006 Fax: 0141 265 1748
E-mail: info@rawatbooks.com
Website: www.rawatbooks.com

New Delhi Office
4858/24, Ansari Road, Daryaganj, New Delhi 110 002
Phone: 011 2326 3290

Also at *Bangalore, Hyderabad* and *Guwahati*

Typeset by *d'lines* DTP SERVICES, Jaipur
Printed at Chaman Enterprises, New Delhi

Contents

III
Dalits and Development

IV
Caste System: Regional Context

Acknowledgements

Ever since we took over as the Convener and Co-convener respectively of Research Committee (RC)–09: Dalits and Backward Classes of Indian Sociological Society, New Delhi, in 2005, we have been thinking about the ways and means of developing our RC. Immediately we were struck with the idea of starting Prof. C. Parvathamma Memorial Lecture in the memory of Prof. C. Parvathamma, eminent Dalit sociologist from Karnataka during the sessions of All India Conferences of Indian Sociological Society which are held every year. Accordingly, in Chennai Conference in December 2006, we held the First Prof. C. Parvathamma Memorial Lecture, which was delivered by Prof. Nandu Ram, Professor of Sociology, Jawaharlal Nehru University, New Delhi. The paper was later published in a booklet.

After the Second Prof. C. Parvathamma Memorial Lecture, which was delivered by Prof. R. Indira, University of Mysore, Mysore in 2007 during the Dharwad Conference, another idea struck to us was to edit a book on, *Backward Classes and Social Justice*, by including the Prof. Parvathamma Memorial Lectures and some of the important papers presented in our RC. The idea was put before the General Body of RC–09 in Dharwad Conference, which was accepted wholeheartedly. During the 34th All India Sociological Conference at Jaipur we approached Rawat Publications, Jaipur for publishing this volume and they readily agreed to our request. Now, the fruit of the efforts of RC–09 is in your hands.

We would like to thank Indian Sociological Society for giving us an opportunity to serve as Convener and Co-convener respectively of RC–09 and the encouragement given by the office bearers of the Society. We also thank the members and participants of RC–09 for attending and participating in RC deliberations in large numbers and encouraging us in editing this volume.

Our special thanks go to Prof. Nandu Ram, Professor of Sociology, Jawaharlal Nehru University, New Delhi for delivering the First Prof. C. Parvathamma Memorial Lecture during the Chennai Conference in 2006, Prof. R. Indira, University of Mysore, Mysore for delivering the Second Prof. C. Parvathamma Memorial Lecture at Dharwad Conference in 2007 and to Prof. H.M. Vasanthamma, former Professor of Sociology, Maharaja's College, Mysore for delivering the Third Prof. C. Parvathamma Memorial Lecture during the Jaipur Conference in 2008. We are grateful to Prof. Jag Mohan Singh Verma, Dr Rose Veera D'Souza, Prof. K. Gopal, Prof. M. Gurulingaiah, Dr Parthasarathi Mondal, Dr Jagan Karade, Prof. Venkateswarlu, Dr Y. Ravindranath Rao and Dr Vinay Rajath D for their encouragement by contributing articles for this volume.

We would like to thank our family members who had a fair share of all the pleasures and pains during the preparation of this volume.

We are indeed grateful to Rawat Publications for publishing the volume in an elegant manner within a short time.

M.H. Makwana
Richard Pais

I

Introduction

1

Introduction

M.H. MAKWANA AND RICHARD PAIS

Though the social philosophers say that all human beings are born equal, the social reality is that not all human beings are born equal. There are inequalities expressed in terms of age, sex, colour etc. Humankind lives in groups. Among groups too we find differences of origin, structure, development etc. Based on such differences societies have been stratified and low and high statuses accorded to them. Class, estate and caste are the important types of stratification found in societies, though one may also find stratification based on race, religion or language.

The Indian society is a complex society and is characterized by a high degree of social stratification and inequality based on caste, religion, colour, region and social origin. Caste is a unique system of stratification found in India and over centuries it has continued to be of critical importance. It is one of the complex, hierarchical and interrelated systems. It is intimately related to social, economic or religious systems, and in recent years, to political system as well.

System of Inequality

The caste system is basically a system of inequality. It has been described with features, such as hierarchy, occupational specialization, separation (based on the concept of purity and pollution), endogamy and ideology etc. Caste, as a system of social and economic organization, is governed by certain customary rules and norms, which are unique and distinct. In such a system, the occupations are hereditary and compulsory. The organization of the caste system is based on the division of people into sub-castes (*jatis*) in which civil, cultural and economic rights of each individual caste are determined by birth and heredity. As there is hierarchy among castes, there is also hierarchy among the occupations associated with them. The pure castes are associated with pure occupations and the lower or untouchable castes are associated with occupations, which are impure and polluting. The whole system of caste is reinforced with the concepts of *dharma* and *karma* and this makes the system deeply resistant to change.

The origin of caste is attributed to the *varna* system initiated by the Aryans, who invaded India and conquered the natives making them the fourth *varna*—the Shudra *varna*. Not finding sufficient women among the migrants the Aryans started marrying women from the local Shudras resulting in innumerable caste groups. But now scholars are of the opinion that the caste originated from tribe and its clan, within its totemic structure, through switching from exogamy to endogamy and getting legitimated by ideological elaboration at later stage. The tribe-caste continuum can be proved through the fact that various Scheduled Castes in South India live, even today, with certain socio-cultural attributes or characteristics of tribe (Ram, 2007).

The caste system involves, particularly for the low castes, a negation of equality and freedom and the denial of basic human rights. Because of the principle of hierarchy in the caste system, entitlements to various rights become narrower as one goes down the caste ladder. In fact, various castes are artfully interlinked with each other in such a manner that the rights and privileges of the higher castes become the disadvantages and disabilities of the lower castes nay untouchable castes. The castes are governed by a notion of 'humanhood' under which the untouchables are considered as 'inferior human beings' and, therefore, not entitled to any individual rights—social, religious, political and economic—while the high castes are considered to be 'superior human beings' and entitled to more rights and privileges (Thorat, 2009: 5).

Backward Classes

When India became an independent nation, among several other problems, it confronted the problem of social and economic backwardness of some sections of the people. Though the British government tried to develop the Scheduled Castes and Scheduled Tribes, it was the Indian government which provided them with constitutional safeguards for social, economic and political purposes. One of the Directive Principles of State Policy of the Indian Constitution (Article 46) states, "the State shall promote with special care the educational and economic interests of the weaker sections of the people and in particular of the Scheduled Castes and Tribes and shall protect them from social injustices and all forms of exploitation".

The backward classes consisting of Scheduled Castes (SCs), Scheduled Tribes (STs) and Other Backward Classes (OBCs) have been clamouring for equality and social justice.

Tribals, consisting of 8 per cent of India's population and constituting more than 400 groups, have been living since pre-historic times and have survived with their unchanging ways of life for centuries. They suffer from isolation, exclusion and underdevelopment due to the dominance of Hindu social order. Historically, the tribals have been ethnically different from the mainline Indian society with their distinct cultures, languages, social organizations and economies—hunting, food gathering and shifting cultivation and with habitats of their own in the river valleys and forest regions (ibid.: 7). Since the advancement of science and technology, a vast socio-cultural gulf has appeared between tribal groups and the people of neighbouring plains (Rao, 2006: 73). After independence, though most of the tribes have been scheduled, there are also non-scheduled tribes such as Kudubis and Ladakis. Though facilities of reservation are provided to them, most of them suffer from multiple problems as isolation, poverty, unemployment, land alienation, illiteracy and poor health. The problems of the tribals have increased due to the presence of greedy traders, moneylenders, government officials and missionaries.

Backward classes form the bulk of Indian population. Like the terms, Scheduled Castes and Scheduled Tribes, the term 'backward classes' has not been defined by the Constitution of India. This has caused immense difficulties to the executive and the judiciary. Hence, both the bodies evolved their own scales and criteria to measure backwardness. Justice K. Subba Rao, former Chief Justice of India has defined backward classes as an ascertainable and identifiable group of persons based on caste, religion, race, language, occupation and such others with definite characteristics of backwardness in various aspects of human existence—social, cultural, economic, political and such others (quoted by Rao, 2004: 290). Justice Subba Rao further observed, "Unless adventitious aids are given to the under-privileged people, it would be impossible to suggest that they have equal opportunities with the more advanced people. This is the reason and the justification for the demand of social justice that the under-privileged citizens of the country should be given a preferential treatment in order to give them an equal opportunity with other more advanced sections of the community" (Agrawal and Aggarwal, 1991: 47).

Though the first Backward Classes Commission was appointed in 1953 under the chairmanship of Kaka Kalelkar, its recommendations were not accepted by the Central Government. The second Backward Classes Commission was constituted in 1979 under the chairmanship of B.P. Mandal, which submitted its report in 1980. It was only in 1990 that the Government of India under the leadership of V.P. Singh accepted the recommendations of Mandal Commission due to political compulsions. Though V.P. Singh became the 'Messiah of the Backward Classes', the whole country, specially the northern India, burnt due to large-scale protests and self-immolations by youths. Similarly, in 2007, the attempt of UPA government, under the leadership of Arjun Singh as Human Resource Minister reserving seats for OBCs in professional courses at Indian Institutes of Management (IIMs) and Indian Institutes of Technology (IITs), evoked widespread protests. All this is because of the lack of understanding about the conditions of backward classes and the need for reservation.

Social Justice

Social justice is a complex term and its meaning has changed from time to time and from generation to generation. Though the Indian Constitution has accepted this term, nowhere it has been clearly defined. Social justice can be understood as giving every man his due. John Rawls, in his major work, *A Theory of Justice* (1972) conceptualizes justice as fairness. In his analysis fairness refers to desirability of advantage for the marginalized groups. According to him, all social primary goods are to be distributed equally unless an unequal distribution of any or all of these goods is to the advantage of the least favoured. Social justice also refers to doing what is socially right.

Social exclusion is understood as the process through which individuals and groups are wholly or partially excluded from full participation in the society within which they live. Social justice is the balance between the individual's rights and social control ensuring the fulfilment of the legitimate expectation of the individual. The Supreme Court of India regarded the concept of social justice "as a living concept of revolutionary import, it gives sustenance to the rule of law and meaning and significance to the ideal of a welfare state" (cited in Kumar, 2008: 89).

The evolution of the philosophy of social justice in recent years is derived from the ideas of French Revolution of 1789 and is based on the principles of liberty, equality and fraternity. The ideas of liberty, equality and fraternity are inseparable and constitute an integral whole called 'social justice'. The value of liberty involves the 'absence of restraint', the value of equality comprises the 'absence of discrimination' and the value of fraternity is embedded in 'cooperation among fellow human beings' (Jogdand et al., 2008: 163). An attempt on the part of the Indian government to bring about social justice to the backward classes has resulted in the reservation policy which derives its strength and inspiration from the Constitution.

Reservation Policy

The present reservation policy is the result of relentless continuation of the caste inequality and social exclusion of the backward groups. It is also the result of selfless and dedicated service of leaders Jyotiba Phule, Narayan Guru and B.R. Ambedkar. The major breakthrough was accomplished with the promulgation of the 1935 Government of India Act, which provided for reservations. After independence, the Constitution of India prohibited the practice of untouchability (Article 17) and also provided for protective discrimination (Articles 16, 332, 334 and 335) through the reservation of seats in the Parliament and State Legislative Assemblies. Articles 29 and 46 provided for their educational uplift.

Reservation is an attempt to provide opportunities to the neglected sections of the Indian society to take part in the national development process. It is believed that native intelligence has a tendency to be normally distributed and evenly shared by all human groups. Therefore, for the development of the nation's economy, society and polity, the best from all sections of the population, including the SCs, STs and OBCs, should be encouraged to participate in national life (Palatty, 1992: 83). Reservation is constitutionally guaranteed to partly offset the weight of centuries old caste system and discrimination. Though, prima facie, reservation or protective discrimination violates the principle of equality of opportunity enshrined in the Constitution, it is generally perceived as some kind of compensation for past discrimination and an opportunity to attain social mobility in society and thus attain equality with others. Social justice here is ensured through individual mobility and thus leading to group mobility (Kumar, 2008: 2).

Caste, ethnicity, and social, educational and economic backwardness were some of the criteria of reservation. All theoretical formulations recognized that, in its essential form, caste, as a system of social and economic organization, is governed by certain customary rules and norms, which are unique and distinct (Thorat et al., 2009: 3). In India, due to the prevalence of caste system, social justice was denied to a substantial number of its population. Basic amenities that were deemed inevitable for the development of man were rendered virtually inaccessible to them.

Indian Sociological Society, founded in 1952, has been trying to organize itself on the pattern of International Sociological Society. From XX All India Sociological Conference held at St. Aloysius College, Mangalore in December 1993, it has been organizing sociological conferences every year giving opportunities to sociologists, both young and old, to present the fruits of their research. In 2000 it started organizing Research Committees (RCs) giving further opportunity to scholars to present the fruits of their research in their respective research committees. We have been associated with RC–09, Dalits and Backward Classes, right from its inception. RC–09 is the most active research committee.

In 2006 RC–09 started Prof. C. Parvathamma Memorial Lecture in the memory of Prof. C. Parvathamma, eminent Dalit sociologist from Karnataka. First Prof. C. Parvathamma Memorial Lecture was delivered by Prof. Nandu Ram, Professor of Sociology, Jawaharlal Nehru University, New Delhi during the Chennai Conference in 2006. The second lecture was delivered by Prof. R. Indira, University of Mysore, Mysore in 2007 during the Dharwad Conference and the third lecture was delivered by Prof. H.M. Vasanthamma, former Professor of Sociology, Maharaja's College, Mysore during the Jaipur Conference in 2008. All the three lectures are included in this book.

The book is divided into four parts, i.e., Introduction, Backward Classes and Social Justice, Dalits and Development, and Caste System: Regional Context. The first part includes the introduction by the editors about the book and the profile of Prof. C. Parvathamma by Prof. H.M. Vasanthamma. Part two is about Backward Classes and Social Justice, and it consists of five papers. The third part deals with Dalits and Development, which again has five articles and the last part, which contains four articles, examines the caste system nay problems of Dalits in South India, Haryana and Karnataka.

While presenting the profile of Prof. Parvathamma, her student, Prof. Vasanthamma reminds the readers that the achievements of Prof.

Parvathamma were a saga of struggles. Besides being the victim of economic and social deprivations and being the only child added to her problems. All the reverses that she faced in her life only goaded her to achieve success throughout her career. The qualities she possessed are rare phenomena: she is a positive amalgamation of simplicity, feminity, self-sufficiency, loyalty, hospitality and above all she was a hard working lady.

Prof. Parvathamma being a bright student passed B.A. and M.A. examinations with distinction and she received lot of gold medals and cash prizes. With a government scholarship for studies abroad she went to Radcliff College, Massachuset, USA. As she was not satisfied with the academic environment there, she went to Manchester University, United Kingdom and got herself registered for Ph.D. degree. After receiving her Ph.D., she returned to India in 1961 and started her career in teaching at the Maharaja's College, Mysore in January 1962. Since she belonged to the SC community, she had to face a lot of hurdles in her career of nearly four decades. In 1998 she was offered the Vice-Chancellorship of the Karnataka University, which she politely declined to dedicate herself for the noble task of teaching and research.

Prof. Parvathamma not only analyzed the working of political parties but also attempted a sociological analysis of nation building. According to her, post-independent India has given birth to more communal and caste organizations than under colonial rule. Instead of moving towards socialism, coupled with classlessness, we have endeavoured to create class cleavages and a few tycoons can hold the country to ransom. Land reforms, irrigation, the green revolution and all that followed have not improved the lot of the peasants and agricultural labourers. Prof. Parvathamma also expressed her views on education, particularly higher education, professional education and health education, as education was the lever of social change. She considered that the abandoned customs, traditions and values of upper strata had become the burden of the masses. She was perturbed by social inequality, injustice and discrimination, which characterized Indian way of life.

Prof. Parvathamma was of the opinion that 'protective discrimination' should be time-bound for all categories at all levels. But, she was critical of the 'schedule' which was bursting at the seams with the inclusion of more and more groups. She exhorted her caste men to stand on their own feet once they were able to emancipate themselves from the debilitating conditions associated with their birth. Finally, Prof.

Vasanthamma concludes that in spite of her handicap, Prof. Parvathamma established her identity as a great scholar and a great human being.

Part II consists of five contributions from Prof. R. Indira, Prof. Jag Mohan Singh Verma, Dr Rose Veera D'Souza, Prof. K. Gopal and Prof. M. Gurulingaiah. Prof. Indira, with her long association with Prof. Parvathamma, examines the hidden forces which act against the policy of protective discrimination through her paper, *Social Justice: The Hidden Faces*. Prof. Parvathamma unfolded the reality of social inequality and discrimination prevailing in the Indian society in the classrooms to the upper caste students like Prof. Indira—nay, she took Prof. Indira to her department as soon as she completed her Masters' degree and continued to inspire her.

Prof. Parvathamma, a social scientist par excellence, studied and wrote critically over a wide range of issues and addressed questions of immense sociological significance going well beyond the times she wrote. She wrote extensively on protective discrimination and her views often challenged the existing myths about reservation as the panacea for all social inequalities. Reservation was a mechanism for creating a socially just world in which diversity and pluralism existed. The yawning gap between the provision of equal opportunities and the equal utilization of these opportunities runs as an undercurrent theme in all of Prof. Parvathamma's discussions on social justice. The entire discourse surrounding equality rests on the premise that justice must be ensured in the distribution of equal opportunities. Though we have a democratic Constitution, which ideally stands for equality, freedom and justice to all the citizens, it was difficult to bring about equality due to old social structure and sets of values that were wedded to a hierarchical system of caste, which was reinforced through the concepts of *karma* and *dharma*.

There is a big gap between 'being considered equal' and 'being treated equal'. Secondly, many fail to understand that while the history of social justice efforts is only a few decades old, the history of deprivation is centuries old. Thirdly, our society lives under the illusion that once equal opportunities are provided, there is no need for any group receiving preferential treatment. However, the 'open system' is not really open. Finally, since reservation essentially means redistribution of power and advantages that a few groups have enjoyed for thousands of years, there is bound to be unrest and dissatisfaction among many in these groups

Prof. Parvathamma focused on the issue of abuse of the reservation benefits meant for SCs and STs by those who did not even belong to these groups and in this process taking away the benefits from them. According to her, backwardness has become a symbol and an ideal to cherish to reach a bargaining position for privileges. As a result, the reservation policy has come to be misused to the disadvantage of the deserving persons. She pointed out to the abuse of reservation policy by those who did not come under its ambit through organized pressure groups. She also expressed the desire for de-scheduling.

Another important process Prof. Parvathamma observed in the castes is the classes within the castes. Social justice efforts also cannot definitely afford to ignore the existence of a 'creamy layer' within most castes. In this connection, she was critical of SC leadership. The ignorance of the SCs is exploited by their leaders. Political reservation has become redundant and it has and will serve another kind of vested interest. She considered growing caste polarization as a challenge to social justice.

Jag Mohan Singh Verma, in his paper, *Social Justice in India: A Case for Equality through Privilege*, examines whether 'equality through privilege' is a myth or a reality in order to ensure social justice to the backward communities. He argues that though the *varna* system was based on functional considerations, the subsequent system of caste is based on hierarchy and thus exploitation. Though the backward communities were called differently, over the years, the backward classes were divided into three broad categories known as SCs, STs and OBCs. The pitiable plight of these deprived communities in the past and present furnishes a historically unparalleled example of discrimination, exploitation and suppression.

The influence of caste was so great that even alien rulers, including the Mughals and the British, had to depend on it to rule the country. The caste has permeated various sectors of activity, such as politics, administration and the private sector. With the adoption of the Constitution of India, the nation was declared to be democratic socialist welfare state committed to the uplift and welfare of deprived sections of Indian society. Though Dr Ram Manohar Lohia, the Left and Dalit groups continued with the reform perspective, there arose illiberal, casteist prejudices against the underprivileged. Caste violence erupted involving various caste groups to fight for their share in the resources of production and power in society.

Another concept is of 'creamy layer' which tried to take away the elites from amongst the deprived sections of the society. The author is of the opinion that the exclusion of creamy layer from reservation will negate its purpose at two counts—first, they will continue to be oppressed and discriminated against because of the fact that they belong to the backward caste and the other they will not be provided with the reservation cover because of their belonging to the creamy layer. The ultimate result will be that they will slump into the morass of backwardness further. The author concludes that the creamy layer formula is incoherent and irrelevant to the principle and philosophy of reservation and negates its very purpose to improve the lot of the underprivileged as it enunciates economic parameters as its basis. It, therefore, deserves to be rejected outright in order to ensure the ends of social justice to the members of OBCs.

The next article, *Social Justice and Welfare State Agenda in India* by Rose Veera D'Souza traces the development of the welfare state in India from its inception to the present context and throws a cursory look at the making of the philosophy of social justice and welfare state during the colonial regime. India crafted its welfare state in India on to the goals of social justice. The expansion of welfare state evolved as a policy, an institution, with the intellectual consensus that political authorities should be responsible for the provision. The article assesses the impact of globalization on the concerns of welfare and social justice in India and examines the relevance of welfare state in the light of the challenges posed by neo-liberal ideology. It looks into the shift in welfare state agenda in the backdrop of whittling down of the traditional social sector. The re-looking process towards the social sector in particular and welfare state in general explains the goals of social justice embedded in our welfare state.

The welfare state in India is guided by three institutional principles: economic management, provision of services for all citizens and social insurance. The five-year plans aimed at achieving two major objectives: (a) reduction of inequalities in income and wealth by ensuring redistribution of resources; and (b) improvement in income and conditions of living of the deprived sections of the society. The viability of welfare state, which came to the fore to address significant concerns affecting the interests of the marginalized and the disadvantaged, though deeply affected in the context of globalization, the welfare state in India cannot be dismantled given the need of the day. The growth of welfare state in India should be looked in relation to the democratic ethos and socialism because independent India visualized democracy as the best possible way to extend social justice and equality. The vision of a welfare state was put forward through the model of liberal democratic set-up when India got independence and the principles of liberty and equality were underscored.

The welfare state has come a long way from colonial welfare provisions to the present ad hoc welfare state. The welfare state is a form of investment—investment in education, health, nutrition care of the children and increase in social productivity. The welfare philosophy strengthens social justice, equality and liberty—the significant goals of democracy in India.

The welfare state still remains at the level of need in the context of globalization given inequities and marginalization that large masses of people suffer from. Lack of substantive freedom denies people the freedom to secure freedom from hunger, or to achieve sufficient nutrition, or to obtain remedies for treatable diseases or the opportunity for proper clothing and shelter and to enjoy water or sanitary facilities. The welfare state must be pruned and streamlined only to reach greater masses for development and retain democratic faith in India.

In his article, *Backward Classes and Social Justice through Reservation*, Prof. K. Gopal examines the problems associated with reservation to backward communities, nay, Other Backward Castes (OBCs). The architects of modern post-independent India had thought of this vast country to develop into a real socialist, democratic, secular or republic. They gave it one of the best constitutions of the world, which granted all its citizens equality, liberty, freedom and the right to be governed by its own representatives through legislatures duly elected by the electorate on the basis of adult franchise.

India was declared a welfare state which thought of the welfare of all. An ancient traditional society with deep-seated hierarchical caste stratification, the country has a huge population of deprived groups and communities. As such, even at the initial stage, SCs/STs were identified and a constitutional provision of positive discrimination with affirmative action was made. An effort to look into the possibility of reservation for OBCs, was made through Kaka Kalelkar Commission in 1953. The Commission did not approve of caste-based reservations in its report submitted in 1955.

Coming to power the Janata Party notified Mandal Commission on January 5, 1979 to submit its report by 31st December 1979. After three extensions the report was submitted in 1980. It was hurriedly implemented with effect from August 7, 1990. There were large-scale protests, including suicides and self-immolation attempts, throughout the country, but nothing happened.

OBC reservation is a bone of contention. The author is aware that many experts have disowned it. It is being supported by the vested interests—beneficiary individuals and groups, politicians for vote bank and academics doing 'Dalitology'. It is unfortunate that though Jai Prakash Narayan was against reservation in professional courses, Nehru and Congress never favoured it. In the present degenerated polity of opportunism, it is distressing that the HRD Ministry of UPA government has supported it. A new trend of efforts to be associated with 'backwards' is emerging and even agitations have been organized for that. In this background, the author warns the sane citizenry to be awakened, activated and sensitized.

In the article, *Marginalization, Reservation and Social Justice: A Study of a Backward Community in Karnataka,* M. Gurulingaiah examines the struggle of the backward community of Yadavas or Gollas of Karnataka towards social justice through reservation. Though the Yadava category of castes consists of about one-tenth of the total population in India, in Karnataka, they are 1.5 per cent of the total population of the state. Gollas consist of two main divisions Uru Gollas (living in villages) and Kadu Gollas (living in forests) and they are mainly concentrated in Chitradurga and Tumkur districts. As a marginalized community, Gollas are backward socially, economically, educationally and politically. Generally, they live in small settlements consisting of some 30–40 households. Since these settlements are not in revenue records, the Gollas suffer from basic civic amenities.

The Gollas started organizing themselves by forming caste associations in order to overcome their ritual, economic, political and social disabilities and also agitate against inequalities, discrimination and marginalization. This process has led to the social movements. The consciousness among Gollas of Karnataka existed even before independence. However, the systematic organization movement and collective mobilization took place only after independence. The movement for social justice and reservation has brought about far-reaching changes among Gollas in social, economic and political spheres of life. The author is of the opinion that failure to include them in the ST category has not yielded good result.

In Part III five more papers are presented by Dr Parthasarathi Mondal, Prof. M.H. Makwana, Dr Richard Pais, Dr Jagan Karade and Prof. D. Venkateswarlu. Parthasarathi Mondal in his paper, *Development, Dalits and Rawls: Rudimentary Considerations,* argues that the centrality of Dalit and backward classes in 'development discourse' has attained considerable significance so much so the government and development agencies worldwide have challenged the privileged castes contention on reservation and affirmative action policies. He argues how liberal policies are accepted in free and equal societies rather than in the traditional societies structured on hierarchy. The author revisits K.S. Chalam's argument of qualifying the constitutional reservations and welfare of the Dalits and other backward classes as the disadvantaged section of the society applying John Rawls' concept of justice. The efficiency of social institutions should be appreciated in their ability to bring in just conditions, qualifies Chalam's foundational thinking for such a consideration. The base for liberal and non-liberal societies is discussed in terms of their ability to extend development to the less marginalized and disadvantaged based on the concept of fairness, rather than on moral grounds.

The author claims that the development strategy in India becomes operational only if substantial freedom and equality is secured to all citizens. The democratic liberal societies are argued to be qualifiers of justice due to the concrete social practices of justness and fairness being embedded in such societies. The Rawlsian theory is drawing similarities with the 'Kantian ethics' not on ethical grounds, but its claims on fulfilling the notions of autonomy, rationality as politically based principles of public realm are well discussed. The application of Rawls' principle of fairness being discussed in terms of characteristics of peoples, both liberal and non-liberal descent peoples. The Kantian paradigm is distinguished with that of the Rawlsian paradigm of justice. The centrality of the principle of justice is addressed in terms of domestic liberal societies to other liberal non-liberal descent societies in the context of states in international society. The absence of free and equal base becomes the inadequacy of descent society. The author argues that since liberal, rational and moral precepts are dependent on the precepts of free and equal base of the individual, the Rawl's principle of justice cannot be extended to the international arena. Caste discrimination in Indian society eludes the principle of justice, especially poor and Dalits are not free and equal, and therefore they are not in a position to secure rationality, reasonableness and morality and it becomes substantial reason for the eradication of caste discrimination to enhance justice.

M.H. Makwana, in his article, *Cooperatives, Dalits and Social Change*, examines the efforts of the voluntary organizations in the field of cooperatives to bring about social change among the Dalits, through an empirical study conducted on Centre for Rural Development (CRD), Ahmedabad. The study highlights the role of the individual and examines his problems and struggles in dealing with the organization and the social environment. It also examines the factors affecting the individual, which will have an impact on change and on the quality of 'collective action'.

The author concludes that the Dalits, who occupy the lowest status in Indian society, have been helped by individuals and institutions for their upliftment. The social change attained by Dalits through the cooperatives was initiated by CRD. CRD as a catalyst has worked for the development of Dalits, tribals, other backward communities and minorities. These cooperatives have also helped in the empowerment of women, especially Dalit women. Dalit women, who have double disability, one being a Dalit and the other being a woman, have benefitted immensely through these cooperatives.

In his article, *Scheduled Castes, Reservation and Social Mobility*, Richard Pais gets an understanding of the social mobility attained by Scheduled Castes (SCs) by availing the facilities of reservation through education and employment. The importance of education in the life of a SC is assessed. First, the educational experience of the respondents is evaluated. Though for most of the respondents the experience was good, for a few it was a bitter one as they faced discrimination from fellow students, teachers and administrators. It has been part and parcel of their classroom, playground and hostel life. Intense discrimination has been experienced in the centres of higher learning.

There has been a remarkable inter-generational educational mobility. The effect of education is seen in the field of employment and income, in the institutions of marriage and family and in other aspects of life. The higher the education, the higher the class of employment, which has resulted in higher income. Educated persons are also able to get the job faster and utilize government facilities. With the rise in education, family has tended to become nuclear, size of household has decreased, and there is decrease in the number of children and increase in the age at marriage. There had been a remarkable 'inter-generational mobility' in terms of occupation of the respondents. There have been several indicators of changed social status and amicable social relationships they enjoyed with their colleagues at the place of work and with neighbours

An attempt was also made to seek the opinion of respondents towards several measures of affirmative action and welfare favouring SCs. Almost all of them feel that reservation in educational institutions, for employment and in political bodies should continue. As a result of reservation, the employed SCs had reached middle class status.

In the next article, *Eclipsed Affirmative Action in India with Special Reference to Minority Educational Institutions*, Jagan Karade delineates the negative role played by minority educational institutions in the country. Indian Constitution has provided safeguards for protecting the Backward Classes from a variety of social disabilities and to secure equality along with all other citizens welfare measures in the form of reservation and other facilities. One of the reservation facilities is in the area of education which is considered to be the basic.

At the same time, the Constitution has also provided facilities to religious and linguistic minorities under Articles 29 and 30. These articles permit any section of the citizens residing in the territory of India or any part thereof having a distinct language, script or culture of its own the right to conserve the same and all minorities, whether based on religion or language, have the right to establish and administer educational institution of their choice. The author argues that the minority rights come in the way of reservation facilities provided to the Backward Classes in the Constitution and thus eclipse social justice.

In his paper, *Need for Special Focus on Other Backward Classes*, D. Venkateswarlu focuses on Mahatma Jyotiba Phule's pioneering effort in striving for social space for the OBCs in Maharashtra, which had inspired many a movement among the lower castes in different parts of the country. His firm resolve to empower the deprived, first in education and then in other spheres, broke the rigid social segmentation. His leadership, ideology and strategy had created a momentum and thrust which other great leaders like Dr Ambedkar picked up and carried further.

The author is of the opinion that enough sociological analysis has been done on the contributions of Mahatma Phule. In this connection, a comprehensive evaluation of socio-economic status of the OBCs has to be undertaken. Secondly, although the existence of a hierarchy among the OBCs is a social fact, it is to be projected as a case of differentiation and not as an internal stratification. Thirdly, the game of the many vested interests that seek to promote and sustain the internal social differences and contesting claims for higher or equal status among the different OBCs has to be exposed. Fourthly, the sociologists have, by and large, been indifferent to taking up the studies on the OBCs. There are not enough ethnographic studies even. Fifthly, the impact of globalization has been adverse on OBCs as on other marginalized sections. The extent and intensity of such impact has to be taken up as a priority study. Lastly, the inevitability of overriding the differences within and establishing a large unity among all the OBCs has to be realized. Further, the need and necessity of a common political platform to act as a strong pressure group has to be noted and acted upon.

In the last part, Part IV, we have four contributions. They are by Prof. Nandu Ram, Prof. B.K. Nagla, Dr Y. Ravindranath Rao and Dr Vinay Rajath. Nandu Ram, in his paper, *Genesis, Mechanism and Growth of Caste System in South India*, taking cue from various theses on the origin of caste, opines that caste originated from tribe and its clan, within its totemic structure, through switching from exogamy to endogamy and getting legitimated by ideological elaboration at later stage. The tribe-caste continuum can be proved through the fact that various Scheduled Castes in South India live, even today, with certain socio-cultural attributes or characteristics of tribe, in spite of their being an integral part of the Hindu caste society. The author further states that since castes and the caste system originated from the numerous tribes and their social relations over generations got crystallized and revitalized at a later stage due to justification from the Brahminical social order based on the notions of purity-pollution and superior-inferior ranks, adopted from the North India, hence the origins of the untouchables/untouchability.

There are around 295 castes notified separately as Scheduled Castes in South India, although their exact number is only 112 as a large number of them are synonymously nomenclatured. After independence of the country, members of the stigmatized castes have been striving for overcoming the stigma of their collectivity as well as of their own through secular domains like education, caste-free occupations or white-collar jobs and power or authority. But, these, in actuality, do not replace or obliterate their traditionally stigmatized group or caste identity. The second option available to the members of the stigmatized castes is a myth related to the origin of their castes or communities. Though a large majority of the people among the lower castes in northern, western, central and eastern parts of the country hardly believe in the Hindu myth about their origin or that of their castes, a majority of people of the lower castes in South India have adopted several Hinduized myths to trace the origin of their castes.

It is often said that the caste system in South India is more rigid than elsewhere in the country. Due to Land Reforms Act of the 1960s, middle level castes became the owner-cultivators and in turn powerful. As a result, lower castes or Dalits were pitiably forced to change their masters from the Brahmins and other upper castes to the middle level castes.

These landowners became tyrannical to the lower castes agricultural labourers and started practising untouchability and other forms of discrimination. However, their practices did not go unchallenged as the lower castes in rural areas started showing considerable degree of resistance resulting into large-scale caste violence. In urban areas, the educational achievement, employment and political participation, in case of the lower castes or SCs, are mostly state sponsored through its policy of protective discrimination.

Social mobility for backward classes and/or untouchable castes has taken place at the group level through the process of social movements. Secondly, it has been sponsored by the state, through the policy of reservation but such social mobility is confined only to a tiny section of the entire community. Now, contest social mobility is also evident among the upwardly mobile SCs. Social change and mobility among the SCs or Dalits in South India is to be analyzed within the social structure operative at both the micro and macro levels. Within the micro or village level not much significant change has occurred among them over the last hundred years or so as is evident from the large number of caste conflicts between them and the atrocities inflicted on them in rural areas. Even, the modern youth undermine the power of their caste panchayat. However, in urban areas, both intra- and inter-generational social mobility are visible among them.

In the paper, *Scavenging and Scavengers in the State of Haryana*, B.K. Nagla presents the profile of the scavengers in Haryana, such as Valmiki (Balmiki), Chuhra, Bhangi and Lalgegi. Though the community's traditional primary occupation is scavenging, including removal of night soil from the houses and offices, their secondary occupations include manual work, playing the band, petty trade, hawking, vending of fruits and vegetables, and selling of meat and eggs. They are also engaged in animal husbandry, poultry and piggery. Since these occupations are in the unorganized sector, they require more labour, full day's work and the total employment of the family with low returns.

Since the scavengers belong to the lowest strata of society, caste Hindus keep them at bay and do not have close social relationships with them. They are non-vegetarians and accept food from all communities. Men often have the habits of drinking, drug addiction and gambling, which results in bickering and quarrels in the families.

Since the scavengers are Hindus, they share major religious centres and centres of pilgrimages with other Hindu communities. Besides, they have their separate temples—the Balmiki temples. They are an endogamous community having village and *gotra* exogamy. Though adult and negotiated marriage is the norm, there are also a few child marriages. Extended families still exist among them but many breaking into nuclear ones.

The scavengers claim to give equal status to women. They also contribute to the family income by way of doing scavenging work. After independence, caste councils have become less effective whereas service organizations like the Balmiki Harijan Seva Samiti have sprung up. Generally, they are Congress supporters but leaders of every party cajole them for votes during elections.

There have been many efforts by the government to improve the conditions of scavengers. These include education, training, and other means of rehabilitation. Conversion of dry latrines into wet ones has eliminated the practice of carrying the night soil on the head to a great extent. Though facilities of education and health are provided, they are not utilized properly. The National Scheme for Liberation and Rehabilitation of Scavengers has helped them by engaging in alternative and dignified occupations.

The author concludes that programmes for awareness development through personal contacts, involvement of voluntary organizations and the utilization of mass media are necessary to bring about a change among the scavengers.

The paper, *Kudubis of Karnataka: A Case for Reservation* by Y. Ravindranath Rao aims at contributing to the understanding of the most backward non-ST of coastal Karnataka, viz., Kudubis. The objective of the paper is to bring the discussion around the tribal features and dimensions in Kudubi community, their most primitive institutions and practices, existing tribal structure. Based on these empirical facts, the author argues that Kudubi community is a genuine case for reservation. The paper offers a perspective that tribes in India are classified as 'Tribes' and 'Scheduled Tribes'. The tribes, which are not scheduled, are also the weaker sections of India's populations like the Scheduled Castes.

The analysis presented in the paper is a part of the larger study, conducted empirically along with the evaluation of secondary data, in Dakshina Kannada and Udupi districts of coastal Karnataka. The paper shows the extreme backwardness of Kudubis, both economically and educationally, owing to several factors, including non-recognition. The author is particularly concerned with the issues, complexities and challenges in tribal mainstreaming, development and existing conditions of a non-ST in Karnataka. The paper is a contribution to the contemporary policy debates about the role of modern nation-states and the communities. It also contributes to determining the direction of the future trend in the social existence of tribals in India in particular and global society in general.

The last paper by Vinay Rajath D., *Caste, Religion and Social Exclusion*, highlights the discrimination faced by lower castes and recent converts to Catholicism in coastal Karnataka. He is of the opinion that social exclusion and discrimination are the direct consequences of caste practices. Caste system from the very beginning has excluded the lower sections, especially the untouchable castes, commonly referred to as Dalits today, from all the benefits and privileges that a normal citizen would deserve. Exploitation and subjugation were commonly accepted and even justified. The system of religious beliefs justified the existing inequality and exploitation. So, social exclusion is the result of practice of caste and religion.

It is interesting to note that in India we find non-Hindu groups also practising the caste system although they reject the Hindu beliefs. Different studies have observed caste groupings among Muslims as well as among Christians. Christianity that believes in the fatherhood of God and brotherhood of mankind dogmatically denounces inequality in any form. However, in some parts of India, the Christians are stratified by the castes of their predecessors, which has led to segregation, discrimination and even social exclusion. Roman Catholic missions in India, from the beginning, appear to have regarded the caste system as the given social structure of Indian society. Churches in India were largely controlled by upper caste Catholic priests and nuns. Low caste and Dalit Catholics were discriminated against by upper caste Catholics.

The paper focuses on the Konkani-speaking Roman Catholic community of coastal Karnataka. Overtly, this community appears to be a homogeneous community. But, actually, they are not a monolithic block. They have internal caste divisions; the chief castes among Catholics of coastal Karnataka are Bammon, Charodi, Sudir, Gowdi and New Catholics. The study observes categorization and differentiation on the basis of origin of caste and ascription of superior or subordinate social position of a caste. The ascription of a relative lesser position to the Gowdi, Sudir castes and the New Catholics is significant. The study further explores and analyzes how the caste discrimination and segregation are systematically observed in social life.

REFERENCES

Agrawal, S.P. and Aggarwal, J.C., 1991. *Educational and Social Uplift of Backward Classes.* Delhi: Concept Publications.

Jogdand, P.G. et al., 2008. *Globalization and Social Justice*. Jaipur: Rawat Publications.

Kumar, Santhosh V., 2008. *Social Justice and the Politics of Reservation in India.* New Delhi: Mittal Publications.

Palatty, Antony, 1992. "Reservation and its Implications" in *Samaja Shodhana, Journal of Mangalore Sociology Association.* Vol. 1, No.2.

Ram, Nandu, 2007. *Genesis, Mechanism and Growth of Caste System in South India.* New Delhi: Indian Sociological Society.

Rao, Ravindranath Y., 2006. "Tribal Social Organization" in Richard Pais (ed.), *Indian Society: Rural and Urban.* Mangalore: Mangala Publications.

Rao, Shankar C.N., 2004. *Sociology of Indian Society.* New Delhi: S. Chand & Company Ltd.

Rawls, J., 1972. *A Theory of Justice*. Oxford: Clarendon.

Thorat, Sukhadeo et al., 2009. *Social Justice Philanthropy*. Jaipur: Rawat Publications.

2

C. Parvathamma on Politics, Marginalization and Education

H.M. VASANTHAMMA

Some are born great, some achieve greatness by sincerity and hard work and to some greatness is thrust upon. Prof. C. Parvathamma is a great person in every respect and she belongs to the second category. Her achievements were a saga of struggles. Besides being the victim of economic and social deprivations and being the only child added to her problems. All the reverses that she faced in her life only goaded her to achieve success throughout her career. The qualities she possessed are rare phenomena: she is a positive amalgamation of simplicity, feminity, self-sufficiency, loyalty, hospitality and, above all, a hard working lady.

I met Prof. Parvathamma in April 1986 when I went to apply for M.A. course. I was really shocked to see a person so simple, wearing a simple cotton saree and her *pallu* covering three-fourths of the head. The way she called me into her room and enquired about me and my family is still vivid in my mind. When I told her that my father was standing outside, she immediately asked me to call him inside. With folded hands she greeted him by saying *namaskara* and affectionately asked him to be seated. When my father explained to her the problems of educating me, she advised him not to worry about anything. I was so thrilled to talk to her and I felt that I saw goddess Saraswaty's face in Prof. Parvathamma. From that day onwards I felt that I was in the company of a great thinker and scholar.

Prof. Parvathamma was born in a poor, humble and socially backward family. Though her mother was a poor, young widow, she had

Text of the Third Prof. Parvathamma Memorial Lecture delivered in RC–09 during the XXXIV All India Sociological Conference held at Jaipur from 27 to 29 October, 2008.

the will and courage to admit her daughter to a school. In taking this firm decision her mother was determined to ensure that her daughter should not miss what she herself had been denied of in life.

Prof. Parvathamma recalls that the school in which she was enrolled was a single-teacher school in a small building just outside the village. She always used to tell that the village schools have never changed even after 35 to 40 years of India's Independence. Four classes were taught by the same teacher probably in turns. Those days classes were small with only a few students. Though those were the days when caste practices were very rigid, fortunately, she did not experience any discrimination in her early school days. Prof. Parvathamma completed her school education under the guidance of a strict disciplined and authoritarian mother and kind hearted teachers and fellow students.

There was no middle school in the village those days. Being a girl and possibly the only girl student from her village, it was a daring act to commute daily to the school. The worse is that the two villages were separated by a river, which used to be very dangerous during rainy season. In the face of these difficulties her mother was worrying too much. At that time one Brahmin from Lokikere came forward to offer her food and accommodation during the monsoon period. Due to some family problem her mother declined the offer and decided to send her daughter to Davanagere for middle school education. Since she had to stay in a joint family consisting of 15 people, she was required to do household chores. In spite of all her problems she studied well and was awarded a scholarship which in those days was Rs 3 per month. By the time she finished her four years of middle school, her mother decided to settle down at Davanagere itself. A small hut measuring 10' × 12' with country made tiles was built on a site owned by her relatives. For some time her mother worked in a mill and then started selling vegetables and fruits to support her daughter's education.

In 1942 she joined the Government High School at Davanagere and, with lot of hardships, successfully completed her matriculation. Later, she joined Maharani's College for Junior Intermediate. Here too, she struggled a lot. She finally joined Maharani's Ladies Hostel. After passing Intermediate Arts in second class, she joined B.A. Honours at Maharaja's College with Social Philosophy as her subject. Prof. T.A. Purushotham was one of the eminent teachers who taught her in B.A. Honours.

She passed her B.A. Honours with first rank in 1950. This brought her recognition from her classmates, teachers and well-wishers. Though some of her friends advised her to go abroad to continue her education, her economic condition did not allow her to do so. Soon, she was offered a part-time employment to teach B.A. Honours classes in Maharani's College on a monthly salary of Rs 50. In September 1950 she got a permanent job on a monthly salary of Rs 118 per month.

After her M.A. in 1952 she served for five years in Maharani's College. Distinctions and honours came to her right from her school days. She was a scholarship holder in her middle school and high school. She passed her B.A. and M.A. with distinction and also received a number of gold medals and cash prizes.

In 1956 she was awarded a government scholarship for higher studies abroad. However, she was not able to pledge the required security for Rs 20,000. After many unsuccessful attempts a relative from Bangalore arranged to pay this amount through one of his caste Hindu friends. She had secured a seat in Radcliff College at Cambridge, Massachusetts, USA. She left for USA in February 1957. As she was not satisfied with the academic ambience there she decided to go to United Kingdom. The Department of Sociology and Social Anthropology at Manchester University allowed her to register for Ph.D. after passing the qualifying examination. Professor Max Gluckman was her guide. Prof. Gluckman also taught her Durkheim's Rules of Sociological Method. F.G. Bailey was her external examiner. During the fieldwork in India, Prof. M.N. Srinivas was appointed her local supervisor. After receiving the Ph.D., she returned to India in 1961. After some time she was posted in the Maharaja's College in January 1962.

The professional career of Dr Parvathamma spanned nearly four decades. She had to face a lot of hurdles in her career. In 1964 she was appointed the Head of the Department. This heralded the beginning of fresh conflicts and confrontations which persisted till the end of her career.

During her academic career she was associated with a number of government and semi-government and autonomous bodies in various capacities. As early as 1967 she was appointed a member of the Central Advisory Board for Harijan Welfare by Government of India for a period of three years. In 1998 she was offered the Vice-Chancellorship of the Karnataka University. She politely declined this offer as she had a few more years of service and her priority was her commitment to teaching and research.

Views on Indian Politics

If internal bickering and factionalism were rampant in the Congress party, interpersonal rivalry, jealousy, avarice for positions and power, or in short, personality clashes characterized the non-Congress political parties. The whole of South India, North-East and West Bengal and North-West, particularly Punjab, slipped from Congress hold and fell into the hands of regional parties. The rationale behind this is that national interests preponderate during parliamentary elections and regional interests outweighed during assembly elections. Though this was a simple rationalization, there was need to find out how and why this was happening. The average Indian voter carries only personality images, rather than programmes, which are at stake and will probably emerge from realistic empirical background.

Prof. Vasanthamma's interest in Indian politics and science and technological development in India has been deeply shared in one of her speeches connected with nation-building and social process. It was during 40th year of Indian independence that Prof. Parvathamma overtly and inertly felt the pulse of the nation and its different processes. She was not in favour of digressing from the analysis of the political processes in the country, lest it should directly and indirectly figure and colour all national development programmes. According to her, the role of communication has continued to be a one-way process. Traditionally, all communications emanated from the higher caste groups and were directed towards the lower and lowest categories in the caste hierarchy. It was by no means a two-way process; and mutual exchange of views and ideas were not possible. There has been widening of the means of communication through newspapers, radio, television etc. Yet communication and mass media is effectively controlled to a great extent by the government and the powerful. With a negligible minority, educated elite, perhaps nationalist minded people, are occasionally voicing their differences and are being critical of the policies and persons. The controlled mass media is trying to rejuvenate the traditional values, which need to be undone as a last resort by a cultural revolution. In the Indian context, the general public, except for participating in elections, has no opportunity of having a dialogue with the elected leaders. They have been tamed to listen and listen only.

Views on the Marginalized

Indian Constitution speaks of secularism, socialism, casteless and classless society. But, all this is on paper. In the last 40 (i.e., when she spoke) years, as a nation, we have moved miles away from every one of these ideals enshrined in our Constitution. Post-independent India has given birth to more communal and caste organizations than under colonial rule. Instead of moving towards socialism, coupled with classlessness, we have endeavoured to create class cleavages and today a few tycoons can hold the country to ransom. The rich have become richer, and these are essentially a few. A large number has been marginalized and pushed below the poverty line. Most of the policies evolved and programmes implemented by the government to alleviate the poor have been misused, abused, thrown out of gear, thwarted, and circumvented by the vested interests in the country. How can national development come about with the bottom heavy marginalized population? Prof. Parvathamma had very serious concern about the marginalized groups in India.

Land reforms, irrigation, the green revolution and all that followed it have not improved the lot of the agricultural labourers, who traditionally came from the lower and lowest rungs of society. Uneconomic holdings and rising cost of agriculture have added more people to the ranks of landless agricultural labourers in recent years. Yet, the farmers are agitating (often rich peasants) and the government is willing to negotiate to come to an amicable settlement. But, when labourers organize and demand for higher wages—the nation has witnessed only killings. The Kilvenmani massacre decades ago in Tamil Nadu echoed in distant Bihar during 1988. These are usually branded as communist and Naxalite motivated and not as problems of the exploited classes, who are harassed by the rich upper caste employers. The issues are subverted and never faced by the government. This situation is multiplying year after year.

Views on Education

Taking education for instance as one of the major problems, Prof. Parvathamma tried to delineate how and why formal education has not made much headway at initial stages, while higher education has expanded beyond one's imagination. Innumerable issues connected with education have figured or can influence national development and help to bridge the communication gap between the educated and the uneducated and the varied sections of the Indian society. To analyze and find out the pros and cons, one has to refer to the past history and its impact or otherwise on present situation, followed by an examination of the role of government and private agencies.

Regarding college, university and professional education, a majority of the students who complete the schools will knock at this. At this stage the plus-2 or pre-university is very crucial. Diversion to professional courses like medical and engineering as distinct and prestigious courses takes place at this stage. Majority of arts and commerce students will have to settle their future course of study from pre-university stage. But, for a pre-university science student, especially for an aspiring one, it is not the entry to B.Sc. degree or honours course but finding their way to professional courses holds much sway.

There is no manpower planning and surplus numbers of doctors and engineers have turned to make a business of their profession. Government's effort to provide skeleton health services through primary health centres and family welfare programmes, can scarcely meet the health needs of rural communities. So, we are back at square one. In spite of increase in the number of educational institutions and professional colleges, and plenty of doctors and engineers and other qualified graduates, India presents a pathetic picture. There is dearth of service spirit but no dearth of qualified people. Vested interests have gripped the situation. Best education continues to be the monopoly of the rich and the influential in the society. Even today the situation remains the same in at least half of the rural society in India.

Education is the lever of social change. Growth of science and technology can foster secular values. Is this happening or can it happen in Indian society? This is a million-dollar question and there is no answer to it. Though formal education is considered to be the best lever of social change, in the Indian context, unfortunately, too many divisive forces are operating. Lack of opportunities often tends to aggravate the situation and encourage people to become dishonest, subvert and circumvent.

Abuse, misuse, hostility, jealousy and subversion have marked the operation of the scheme. The government and politicians dare not risk incurring the displeasure of demanding groups. The Vanniyars of Tamil Nadu is a case in point. Voting in elections holds the key for its population. Thus vested interests have not only undermined all 'good intentioned' schemes evolved by government but also thwarted and diluted them at the stage of implementation.

In what other ways India can be proud of her past? India has a literary tradition of thousands of years. But bulk of its population was scrupulously kept outside the purview of learning, reading and writing. It was mostly religious learning. Thus acquisition of knowledge became esoteric and confined to groups with ascriptive characteristics only. Whether the tussle between the invading Aryan hordes and the native *Dasyusr,* the differences between the conquerors and the conquered became crystallized and led to social compartmentalization is not just past history, ancient at that.

In free India, elections and political machinery have added new dimensions. It is common knowledge that caste and religious sentiments have found new and fertile ground to flourish. These are encouraged and supported directly and indirectly by political leaders. The political dimension has acquired added strength. Today most of them appear to acquire and act as pressure groups for the benefits it can bring. Convergence of several sub-castes to attain a bargaining position in the name of religion and caste are quite common. The *Akhila Bharata Veerasaiva Mahasabha* of Karnataka is a case in point. This certainly is not India's great past and it should not be allowed to perpetuate.

Similarly, the cultural traditions and values are not uniform or universal. The culture and values cherished by the elitist groups over the centuries have percolated down the hierarchy. The abandoned customs, traditions and values of the upper strata have become the burden of masses today. Female infanticide, child marriage, dowry, low status of woman and other forms of discrimination are only a few to mention. Each one of them and all of them put together hamper national development to a considerable extent. The situation remains almost the same even after 60 years of our Independence.

Prof. Parvathamma further questioned that in a competitive world dominated by science and technology, how India can afford to lose sight of having a window to the rest of the world. Are we not playing with the life and opportunity of our young educated youth by incapacitating them through wrong emphasis and priority? If Russia, China and Japan have achieved a breakthrough and success in all walks of life by sticking to native language policy, it is a wrong analogy. Our past history, the divisive forces and feudal values cannot be replaced by emphasizing 'nativism' as the cure. It will enhance and contaminate rather than act to promote unity and national integration. Karnataka for Kannadigas, Maharashtra for

Maharashtrians and Bihar for Biharis, including job opportunities can hardly function effectively with the rising regional separatism. Once again, these are the political processes and leadership that have fostered and promoted regionalism. In fact, no one seems to bother because the path is beset with agitation, violence, destruction of life and property. Ultimately, governments in the name of democracy succumb to all kinds of organized threats. These processes have become rather the order of the day and are repeated for all and sundry issues.

Social inequality characterized the Indian way of life. Injustice and discrimination in interpersonal relations amongst different caste groups is universal. These cannot be wished away because, it is written in our Constitution. New sets of values have to be created to replace the old and worn out inhuman values. To decry apartheid practised by white rulers of South Africa, we should first set our own house in order. We have a backlog of inhuman values blocking the road to successful secular democracy. There is urgent need to bridge the widening gulf between constitutional guarantees, legislative measures and executive action.

Regarding reservations, Prof. Parvathamma used to say that reservation or what has come to be known as 'protective discrimination' should be time-bound for all categories at all levels. The way it is operating smacks common sense. The Scheduled Castes (SCs), Scheduled Tribes (STs) and others have derived some benefits because of reservation policy is undoubtedly true. But for this it would have been negative had their development would have been at standstill in educational, political and other areas. But, the point is that the 'schedule' is bursting at the seams with the inclusion of more and more groups. There is ever increasing demand by many caste groups all over the country to get included in the list of SCs/STs. Given the political will—not to displease voters—and the mad rush for SC and ST tag, the race is likely to become endless. The principles underlying 'scheduling' originally were based on certain important facts. Reservation is basically to be seen as a means of undoing social wrongs over centuries.

Children and youth of the country should be weaned away from such traditions and values. Education should be reoriented to eschew narrow loyalties of caste, community, religion, region and language. At present, these loyalties drain the strength of Indian youth to a great extent. Conserving the youth's energy and directing it for nation building should be embarked upon systematically and on rational basis. All reservations, if continued, should be evaluated and rationalized to serve the purpose for which they are meant.

Actually, writing about Prof. Parvathamma is a difficult job, as this intellectual giant has been one of the most outstanding women in the history of Mysore University, and her towering personality and the convergence between knowledge and wisdom is simply marvellous. I, as one of her students, had the benefit of her wise counsel for more than 35 years. I used to like her frankness, coupled with compassion and sense of humour.

According to Prof. C. Rajagopal, former Head of the Department of Sociology, Bangalore University, the initial impression Prof. Parvathamma creates on any one who meets her for the first time is that she is a formal, reserved, somewhat withdrawn and not disposed to be friendly. This appearance like most appearances is highly deceptive and is far removed from reality. But, those who have had close contact with her have always discovered a totally different person in her. I always considered her to be friendly, warm, humane, sensitive, unassuming, synthetic, compassionate and with a child-like simplicity. Speaking further about Prof. Parvathamma, Prof. Rajagopal interprets that she was always wedded to her community. She allocated her time to her caste and fellow castemen. It is my understanding, born out of my association with her, that unlike many other scheduled castes, she always preferred to be identified herself as an SC. It is because she believes that she has successfully shaken off the shackles through her own efforts and therefore does not deserve to be treated as inferior to none. It is not a matter of personal conviction but she has converted her personal conviction into a social policy, which is amply reflected in some of her sociological writings. At a time when the forward classes are shamelessly clamouring for the 'backward' label to reap the reservation benefits, Prof. Parvathamma's exhortation to her castemen to stand on their own feet once they are able to emancipate themselves from the debilitating conditions associated with their birth, marks her off from the rest of the people with a profound sense of social and moral commitment. On her side, she would like to see her fellow castemen treated with the same self-respect and dignity, which she claims and commands for herself. But, unfortunately, Prof. Parvathamma's thinking is somewhat ahead of her times and instead of admiring and complementing her for her principled stand, she has been branded as an anti-SC, even by her own fellow castemen.

Prof. Parvathamma was an embodiment of moral and personal integrity. She never used to compromise her cherished values for securing either office or position and power. She was extremely humble and modest. She was very kind hearted and noble. She has dedicated her life and property to the cause of the poor and their upliftment.

REFERENCES

Parvathamma, C. 1984. *Employment Problems of University Graduates*. New Delhi: Ashish Publishers.

——. 1984. *Scheduled Castes and Tribes: A Socio-economic Survey*. New Delhi: Ashish Publishers.

——. 1978. *Under the Impact of Direct Change*. New Delhi: National Publication.

——. 1984. *New Horizons and Scheduled Castes*. New Delhi: Ashish Publishers.

Prof. Parvathamma's Felicitation Volume. 1999. Mysore: Mysore University.

II

Backward Classes and Social Justice

3

Social Justice

The Hidden Faces

R. INDIRA

When I received an invitation from RC–9 (Dalits and Backward Classes) of the Indian Sociological Society to deliver the Second Professor C. Parvathamma Memorial Lecture at the XXXIII All India Sociological Conference to be held at Dharwad, my heart chocked. What better recognition and honour could I have received in my life than being invited to deliver a lecture instituted in the memory of my illustrious *Guru*, who was not just a teacher, but also a guiding beacon in my life? While I felt humbled and touched, I also became immediately conscious of the immense responsibility that I had on my shoulders, as I knew well that living up to the academic standards set by my illustrious teacher was not an easy task.

My association with Professor C. Parvathamma (affectionately called CP) dates back to the year 1970 when I joined the Department of Sociology in the University of Mysore as her student. The most striking quality of her classes was the space she provided to her students for not only dialogue, but also dissent. The lively discussions in her classes mostly centred on issues of social inequality and the various forms it took in our society. As a young student who had little practical knowledge of the myriad ways by which inequalities operated in this society, it was in her classes that I got my first exposure to the forms and degrees of inequality prevailing in the Indian society and how it had persisted in spite of constitutional safeguards and guarantees. As days passed on, her classes removed the veil on many of the myths surrounding the equality debate. To this day, these classes remain evergreen in my memory.

Text of the Second Prof. Parvathamma Memorial Lecture delivered in RC–09 during the XXXIII All India Sociological Conference held at Karnataka University, Dharwad from 29 November to 1 December, 2007.

I was lucky to get the opportunity to serve as a teacher in the same department where I completed my Master's degree. To me CP gave this opportunity immediately after I obtained my M.A. degree in the year 1972, and for the next 16 years, I had the good fortune of working under her leadership. A bitter critic of one-sided interpretations of social phenomena, she was opposed to assumptions that ignored ground realities. This was to be the guiding principle in my life, and it is to her I owe the rational, critical and freethinking spirit that I have tried to imbibe.

Professor Parvathamma was a social scientist with a fine creative mind. Though she wrote during the days when descriptive empirical research was considered the ultimate in social sciences, she was never satisfied with mere narrations. Not only would she raise critical questions about research themes, but also expected and encouraged her students to do so. Her own writings covered a wide range of issues and addressed questions of immense sociological significance going well beyond the times she wrote. Be it her works on castes or tribes and their problems, religion, the play of power dynamics in Indian rural settings or marginalized groups and affirmative action and social movements, CP's sharp pen pierced through those aspects, which only an erudite scholar like her could discern. She wrote in a language that was simple, but scholarly, sharp and critical. She belonged to the rare group of social scientists who could 'take a stand' on an issue, and never deviate from that position, whatever the 'pressures' may be. She looked beyond the visible parameters of events and issues, and in that process created an academic environment, in which her students were encouraged to engage in debate and dialogue that looked for newer knowledge horizons. Perhaps, her training at Manchester under Max Gluckman had a bearing.

CP wrote on a wide range of subjects and I do not claim to do justice to all the ideas that formed part of her thought process. In this talk, I will only make a moderate attempt to present and discuss her key insights on one of the most challenging issues of our times—the struggle for social justice. She wrote and spoke extensively on this theme, especially on the policy of 'protective discrimination' and her views often challenged the existing myths about reservation as the panacea for all social inequalities. The several hidden faces of the system of reservation and the overt and covert ways in which they operate in our society, is a theme on which CP raised and answered very fundamental questions, and my lecture today is mainly attempting to discuss these questions in the background of her work.

In this paper, I have mainly drawn insights from CP's views on the 'what, why and how' of social justice. I have quoted extensively from her select works on this theme, because I believe that her views, always stated in a straight and forthright style, must serve as a model for sociological expressions.

The term 'social justice' as used in this presentation refers to a situation in which justice is achieved in every aspect of society, rather than merely the administration of law. It is generally thought of as a system, which affords individuals and groups fair treatment and an impartial share of the benefits of society. In other words, social justice is a mechanism for creating a socially just world in which diversity and pluralism exist not only in theory, but also in practice.

Did Constitutional Provisions Remove Social Inequality?

The yawning gap between the provision of equal opportunities and the equal utilization of these opportunities runs as an undercurrent theme in all of CP's discussions on social justice. The entire discourse surrounding equality rests on the premise that justice must be ensured in the distribution of equal opportunities. In fact, Aristotle treated justice as a synonym of equality. In Greek, the word 'equality' means justice. To be just is to be equal and to be unjust is to be unequal (Aristotle, 1966).

The Constitution of India no doubt paved the way for the establishment of an egalitarian social order by removing discrimination and ensuring equality of opportunity. Article 14 of the Constitution ensured that the state shall not deny to any person equality before the law or the equal protection of the laws within the territory of India and Article 15 prohibited discrimination on grounds of religion, race, caste, sex or place of birth. If the provisions of these two articles were to be implemented in letter and spirit, there would be no space for inequality in Indian society. However, has it happened that way?

Besides ensuring equal access and prohibiting discrimination, the Constitution also tried to address the question of unequal access by providing reservation to the Scheduled Castes (SCs) and Scheduled Tribes (STs). The constitutional mandate of setting right inequalities inherent in the social system was an attempt at laying a level field for different groups to play the 'equality game' in a more egalitarian set-up. Ambedkar, who was Chairman of the Drafting Committee of the Constitution, had clearly visualized a situation where the advent of political freedom would not automatically usher a reign of social equality. The very idea of 'protective or positive discrimination', which he championed, emanates from the principle that those who have lagged behind in the race for achieving social and economic power, have to be given a 'special push'. This push empowers them to contest the equality race on equal terms with those who have enjoyed all the advantages that their birth or upbringing, or both, have brought them. Ambedkar was of the view that "parliamentary democracy in standing out as a protagonist of liberty has continuously added to the economic wrongs of the poor, the downtrodden and the disinherited class. Political democracy cannot succeed when there is no social or economic democracy" (Parvathamma, 1989: 128).

Reservation is seen as a policy instrument that seeks to "correct the distortions in history and create a civil society. It seeks to restore the democratic right of access to power and wealth to those who were ostracized from the mainstream of yore. For this, however, a mere provision of rule of law won't suffice as equality is not likely to be achieved unless groups that rank in the traditional system of stratification are purposively assisted to leap across the gap that separates them from others" (Galenter, 1948: 41).

The process of achieving equality is thus not as simplistic as it appears. In CP's words, "the contemporary Indian society with a democratic Constitution ideally stands for equality, freedom and justice to all the citizens. These constitutional guarantees, however, are not translated into action and, therefore, there is inequality in practice. A democratic country tagged on to old social structure and sets of values which are wedded to graded hierarchy can hardly strike a balance between the political and social structure and bring about social equality" (Parvathamma, 1989: 27).

Almost all societies are characterized by hierarchies, which have placed different groups on a social scale, and it is this social positioning that determines the pattern of distribution of favours in an unequal society. Our past experiences have shown that "arbitrary differentiation has been made for the characteristics which are beyond the control of individuals and groups and such individuals and groups have been exploited for the purpose of ensuring the dominance of certain groups or class of individuals. Justice requires equitable and just distribution of social goods and resources or burdens and benefits but that has not been the case in the past. A whole lot of people have been discriminated against and slavery and serfdom justified on this or that ground right since the dawn of civilization in the east and the west. Either one talks of the segregation of blacks in the United States of America, apartheid system of South Africa, or the plight of low caste people of India, all have suffered the same fate, i.e., exploited and deprived for the reasons beyond their control" (Bell and Singh, 2003: 5).

CP's main line of argument in her discussions on social inequality was that it was a product of the caste system and that it actually enjoys religious sanctions. Caste-related inequalities are justified in the name of *dharma* and *karma* creating an illusion that one is destined to enjoy or suffer because it is one's birth into a caste that determines what one should do or should not do. The positioning of castes in the hierarchy brought inherent advantages to a few and accrued disadvantages to others.

CP considered ritual status bestowed by caste as a major hurdle to the establishment of an egalitarian social order. In her view, 'ritual status' and notions of 'ritual purity and pollution' are the "central principles of social stratification. These notions pervade everyday life and colour all human relationships. There is very little that is left without being covered by them. There are clean and unclean occupations. Unclean occupations cause pollution and lower the social status of people following them. Even food and drink have differential status and could be hierarchically graded. All these notions are rooted in Hindu beliefs and practices. Thus religious discrimination provides the real hurdle for any kind of modernization. Can secularism and democracy initiate changes in the traditions?" (Parvathamma, 1989: 17–18).

In a society with deep-seated caste-based inequalities, mere provision of equal opportunities does not equalize opportunities for people who continue to face institutional barriers to equal access and treatment. Very few have realized that the constitutional commitment to preferential treatment is only an attempt to undo the effects of centuries of caste-induced deprivation. I would like to quote Bell and Singh (2003: 6), who in my view have described the situation in India vis-à-vis reservations very aptly when they observed that "India, the biggest democratic system of the world, with a thousand million plus population and mind boggling variety, a system which boasts of more than 5000 years history and continued civilization and a hoary past, now mired in the under-development and medieval hierarchical social order, but raring to rise into an economic powerhouse of the world with convincing democratic credentials, have been experimenting with the protective discrimination programmes of unprecedented variety. Reservations in jobs, in educational institutions, legislatures and in the local self-governing institutions, better known as Panchayati Raj Institutions, for Scheduled Castes, Scheduled Tribes, Other Backward Classes and now women, has been a grand experiment by any standard. It may also be noted that Scheduled Castes, Scheduled Tribes and Other Backward Classes are a whole cluster of thousands of castes spread over length and breadth of the country. But has it succeeded in achieving the target it has set before itself 53 years ago?"

Many people in our midst are under the impression that the provision of reservation benefits to those groups in the lower rungs of the socio-economic ladder can automatically set right the inequalities suffered by them in accessing opportunities for upward social mobility. There are also frequent references to the time-bound reservation scheme, which the Constitution had proposed. The critics of reservation vehemently argue that the interest of the upper castes is being hampered, by continuing the provision of reservation beyond the time limit that the Constitution had initially set. However, what these groups fail to understand is that "while the history of social justice efforts is only a few decades old, the history of deprivation is centuries old". Can five or six decades of reservation remove the inherent inequalities embedded in our social set-up like a magic wand? Societies across the world abound with examples to show that it cannot.

There is actually a big gap between 'being considered equal' and 'being treated equal'. There is no challenging the fact that that "the history of apartheid in South Africa, slavery and Jim Crowism in the USA and caste-based discrimination in India violates an understanding of what justice or equality means. The colour of someone's skin or the birth of someone into a lower caste is not and cannot be a morally justifiable reason for treating people differently. The argument then arises that if justice means treating all people equally in all circumstances, then, why is it acceptable to favour some people because of their skin colour" (Argyle, 2002: 397).

Reservation is basically to be seen as a means of undoing social wrongs with a history of centuries. The justification for preferential treatment comes from the fact that those who were in bondage for centuries need to be given a special access if they have to compete on equal terms with those who are placed in situations of social and economic advantages. We may here quote President Lindon B. Johnson of the United States who, while signing the 1964 Voting Rights Act said, "You do not take a person who for years has been hobbled by chains and liberate him, bring him up to the starting line of a race, and then say, 'you are free to compete … .' and still justly believe that you have been completely fair".

Our society lives under the illusion that once equal opportunities are provided, there is no need for any group receiving preferential treatment. However, the 'open system' is not really so open, because 'who gets, what type of opportunity' is determined by several other factors. As Lawrence Blum (1988) has written, "persons can fail to be judged purely on ability because they have not gone to certain colleges or professional schools, because they do not know the right people, because they do not present themselves in a certain way. And, again, sometimes this sort of discrimination takes place without either those doing the discriminating or those being discriminated realizing it … . Often these denials of equal opportunity have a lot to do with class background, as well as race or sex or with a combination of these".

It would not be out of context to quote Luke Charles Harris and Uma Narayan, who, in their paper "Affirmative Action and the Myth of Preferential Treatment: A Transformative Critique of the Terms of the Affirmative Action Debate" (1994: 454–455), had observed, "affirmative action is not a matter of affording 'preferential treatment' to its beneficiaries. Our position is that affirmative action is best understood as an attempt to promote equality of opportunity in a social context marked by pervasive inequalities, one in which many institutional criteria and practices work to impede a fair assessment of the capabilities of those who are working class, women or people of colour. Thus, affirmative action is an attempt to equalize opportunity for people who continue to face institutional obstacles to equal consideration and equal treatment. These obstacles include not only continuing forms of blatant discrimination, but more importantly, a variety of subtle institutional criteria and practices that unwarrantedly circumscribe mobility in contemporary America".

The Constitution of India is only the beginning of a long-drawn struggle against deep-rooted social inequalities. Since reservation essentially means redistribution of power and advantages that a few groups have enjoyed for thousands of years, there is bound to be unrest and dissatisfaction among many in these groups. However, those who have enjoyed advantages for several hundreds of years must make way for others. Those opposing protective discrimination must realize that equality of opportunity must be distinguished from equality of result.

Clamour for Backwardness: The Bane of Reservation?

CP was one of the few sociologists who had the courage to bring to fore issues that were considered 'sensitive' or 'controversial' by others. One such issue was the abuse of the reservation benefits meant for SCs and STs by those who did not even belong to these groups. She was one of the first sociologists who expressed serious concerns nearly two decades ago about new groups trying to get into the 'backward bandwagon' only to garner the benefits of reservation, taking away the rights of the poor among the SCs and STs. Commenting on this phenomenon, CP wrote, "Getting reservation benefits has almost become glamorous. Everybody drawn from across a cross-section of castes have begun clamouring for benefits of reservation" (Parvathamma, 1999: 1).

A proactive academic, who never minced words when it came to taking a stand on issues that were otherwise considered 'contentious', CP came down heavily on the tendency of socially advantaged sections to lay a claim for the backward tag. The following cryptic observation by her lifts the curtain on a hidden face of social justice that often escapes public attention: "Over the years it looks as though the economic, educational and political backwardness has become an end in itself. Today, every section of the Indian people advances some kind of backwardness to plead and claim special care and protection from the government. The ramifications of backwardness on the basis of population, caste, culture and religion, language, region and occupation, are only a few to mention. One wonders why the entire sub-continent and its people could not be declared backward! It is no exaggeration that today no caste group is in a mood to admit that they constitute an advanced section of the population. Backwardness has become a symbol, and an ideal to cherish to reach a bargaining position for privileges. Probably, the original implication of constitutional protection has lost much of its relevance" (Parvathamma, 1989: 129).

The fact that new groups are trying to garner opportunities meant for the 'truly backward' has come into the open many times, yet it is not taken seriously because there is no political or social will to address this issue. That it is possible for anybody to procure a caste or income certificate has been brought to public notice more than once, but what is our response? A Karnataka legislator once produced on the floor of the house a scheduled caste certificate, which he had managed to get from the concerned authorities; there was a hue and cry for some time, but similar incidents continue to happen, and yet people get away. Because of systemic failure, even today people can manage to get multiple caste certificates and use whichever suits them. A classic example is the case of a youth who once appeared in our office with four certificates and demanded that he be allotted a PG seat in any of these categories where there is a vacancy!

One often hears of politicians or those in public service obtaining false caste certificates to either contest elections or gain coveted government posts. It is also not uncommon to find misuse of caste and income certificates by aspirants for higher education. When such manipulations come into the open, a few voices of protest are raised and even the media tend to highlight the issue, but as is usually the case, public memory is short, and the protest peters down. Since persons who indulge in such fraudulent acts generally enjoy a political clout, they mostly tend to escape. Action may be initiated against a few violators, but it does not undo the damage that has been done to a really deserving person. The play of vote bank and caste politics comes in the way of any meaningful action against erring persons. The recent suspension of a college professor for producing a false caste certificate, 21 years after he used it to secure the job, is but one example of official apathy to such a critical issue as misuse of 'positive discrimination' efforts.

As noted by Timmaiah regarding the reservation situation in Karnataka, "the reservation policy has come to be misused to the disadvantage of the deserving SCs/STs and OBCs. As a result of politicization, the benefits of the reservation policy have come to be grossly misused not only by ineligible people but also by those who are eligible. It has become common for ineligible people to get caste-cum-income certificates to gain entry into professional courses. However, this is less common in the context of government jobs. False certificates are used more by candidates from rural areas who are self-employed and, hence, reliable assessment of their income becomes difficult. This practice has degenerated to the legal adoption of children of ineligible parents by their servants from lower castes for consideration, just to get them admission into professional courses" (1993: 166).

Nearly two decades ago, CP had pointed out to the abuse of reservation policy by those who did not come under its ambit. In her later works, she also made extensive references to this phenomenon. Calling groups that were trying to jump into the backward bandwagon as 'organized pressure groups', she showed how they were vying with one another for OBC, SC or ST status. Since the government yielded to these pressure tactics, many more groups had now jumped into the fray. In her work, *Reservation: A Pie in the Sky,* CP wrote about the misuse of a common nomenclature by a Hindu caste group in Karnataka to claim benefits meant for STs. In her own words, "A concerted effort is afoot by the Kurubas (shepherds) of Karnataka to subsume the tribal group of Kadu Kurubas (jungle tribe) which consist of sub-groups like, Jenu-Kurubas,

Betta Kurubas, and Mullu Kurubas (in Tamil Nadu and elsewhere). The Kurubas have a state level organization to pressurize the government; there are a good number of political leaders, MLAs, MPs, Ministers at different levels. Economically and educationally, they can be said to have advanced while Kadu Kurubas will take ages to reach these levels. In recent years, they have even installed a Jagadguru. So, religious organization and overtones are evident. At some point of time, with all the clout that the shepherd castes (Kurubas) have acquired, by a stroke of political will, the tribal groups merely on the basis of nomenclature are included in the main group, which should sound the death-knell of tribal groups. The Kadu Kurubas can never hope even to survive in this competition" (Parvathamma, 1999: 28).

In my view, the primary cause for certain individuals and groups abusing the reservation policy is the prevalence of deep-rooted corruption in official machinery. Corruption has made a mockery of both rules and privileges. The fact that we have been tolerating manipulation and learnt to live with it, is at the root of many social justice efforts going haywire. If reservation policy has to bring forth the desired results, it has "to be more broad based, include a lot more variables. There should be time schedule and not eternity in its operation. Further, with scheduling, the right to de-schedule based on objective evaluation should be incorporated. While demand for reservation facilities is rampant, no beneficiary has aired satisfactory progress, hence descheduling. It is human nature to seek and continue to enjoy benefits for themselves. Seldom they think of the lot of the poor, deprived and more deserving groups without food, proper clothes or shelter" (Parvathamma, 1999: 31).

Should There be a Creamy Layer?

Social justice opportunities have benefitted certain castes disproportionately, and, in the process, widened inequalities between persons within each caste/class. The advantaged sections in each group (classes within castes) continue to march ahead in the competition to garner the limited opportunities and leave those without these advantages behind. Social justice efforts also cannot definitely afford to ignore the existence of a 'creamy layer' within most castes. Though the concept is used in the context of OBCs to refer to sections that are in positions of relative social and economic advantage, there is a growing creamy layer among other groups too.

The existence of intra-group disparity poses a serious challenge to social justice efforts that generally tend to look at groups as 'homogenous entities'. In reality, however, there is a huge difference between the lifestyle of leaders and masses. Often there is no real understanding about the miserable conditions of large sections of the marginalized in their own caste, on the part of their caste leaders. In her paper, *The Crisis of Scheduled Caste Leadership*, CP wrote, "Many of them do not know the utterly dependent conditions of SCs in rural side. For the masses, the SC is as unapproachable as anybody else. The ignorance of the SCs is exploited by the SC political leaders. Given this, the deliverance of the SC is no longer in the hands of SC political leaders. Political reservation has become redundant and it has and will serve another kind of vested interest" (Parvathamma, 1989: 167).

What CP wrote about SC leadership stands true of leadership in every caste. Politicians of all castes internalize party culture. Since retaining political power is a more daunting task than obtaining it, many leaders who have come to power by projecting themselves as the 'voices of the vulnerable', are engaged in a political rigmarole, which gives them little time or space to worry about the problems of the downtrodden. The reservation policy was intended to set right inequalities between different groups, but it did not always happen that way. As Beteille remarked, "The policy of protective discrimination which sets out to decrease the inequalities between castes and communities ends by increasing inequalities between individuals and members of each caste and community" (1987: 30). That there is no homogeneity even among the groups, which have been covered by the reservation benefits, is by now an established fact. The mere provision of reservation does not ensure that different groups within the same caste would have the same access rate. Can the son or daughter of a scheduled caste or a backward caste landless labourer compete for an opportunity on equal terms with the ward of a doctor or a bureaucrat of the same caste? Can we forget the stark reality that the race for equality is not being run among equals?

It is only when we evolve a system in which the "really deserving backward classes are identified through appropriate tests and the benefits of reservation are provided in such a way as to make them use those benefits effectively that intra-group inequalities are reduced" (Timmaiah, 1993: 32).

Growing Caste Polarization: A Challenge to Social Justice?

The Constitution's commitment to social justice notwithstanding, inherent caste and class barriers have remained deep-seated in our society. Social cleavages have become deeper and stronger today because this society has failed to extricate itself from its feudal past. The constitutional challenge to caste and class hegemony is often mitigated by the emergence of new forces that are trying to keep social distances alive. In a society, which has a history of resistance to redistribution of power, groups that have hitherto enjoyed unquestioned control over society's resources will not give up their position so easily.

It is shocking but true that there is openness about creating networks, based on caste or sub-caste identities, among different groups today. In our own university campus there are events organized by caste associations in which one can see the dais being occupied by a row of guests, all of whom are from the same caste. This list normally includes politicians, bureaucrats, heads of '*mutts*' or *swamijis*, as they are popularly referred to, film stars, and even teachers. I wonder what CP would have said if she had seen this development while she was in the university. Such polarizations based exclusively on caste lines are posing a new challenge to the democratization process and are simply encouraging 'others' to create similar groups. Feelings of 'we' and the 'other' are getting entrenched strongly in society's psyche.

The ideals enshrined in our Constitution are becoming a distant dream today because Indian society is being broken into numerous pieces based exclusively on caste and sub-caste identities and loyalties. Nearly two decades ago, CP had written, "Indian Constitution speaks of secularism, socialism, casteless and classless society. But, this is on paper. In the last four decades, we have moved miles away from every one of these ideals enshrined in our Constitution. Post-independent India has given birth to more communal and caste organizations under the colonial rule. Instead of moving towards socialism, coupled with classlessness, we have endeavoured to create class cleavages and today a few tycoons can hold the country to ransom. The rich have become richer, these are essentially few. A large number has been marginalized and pushed below poverty line. Most of the policies evolved and programmes implemented by the government to alleviate the poor have been misused, abused, thrown out of gear by the vested interests in the country. How can national development come about with the bottom heavy marginalized population"? (Parvathamma, 1999: 72).

Conclusion

Social justice thus is not a simple process of granting favours to the deprived with the intention of undoing the wrongs of the past. Law *per se* cannot alter unequal social situations if there is no will to redistribute social and economic resources both on the part of the powers that be, and on the part of the citizenry. India's experience with social justice has shown that both individuals and institutions have often converted it into a 'personal agenda' in the garb of a 'social agenda'. All those who are concerned or involved with the social justice movement must understand and accept the truth that social justice has many hidden faces over which the veil has to be lifted if it has to make any dent into the unequal social order.

REFERENCES

Argyle, Nolan J. 2002. *From Affirmative Action to Diversity: Managing Human Resources for Productivity.* New York: M.E. Sharpe, Inc.

Beteille, Andre. 1987. *The Backward Classes and the New Social Order.* New Delhi: Oxford University Press.

Bell, John and Amarpal Singh. 2002–03. *Affirmative Action Programme: A Comparative Study of India and U.S.* Brussels: European Academy of Legal Theory.

Blum, Lawrence A. 1988. "Opportunity and Equality of Opportunity". *Public Affairs Quarterly,* 2/4.

Ethica Nicomchea, Book V Chapter VI, 1966 Reprint. In *The Works of Aristotle.* Vol. XII Sir David Ross.

Galanter, M. 1948. *Competing Equalities: Law and the Backward Classes in India.* Delhi: Rajkamal.

Harris, Charles Luke and Uma Narayan. 1994. "Affirmative Action and the Myth of Preferential Treatment: A Transformative Critique of the Terms of the Affirmative Action Debate". *Harvard Black Letter Law Journal,* 11/1.

Parvathamma, C. 1989. *Scheduled Castes at the Cross Roads.* New Delhi: Ashish Publishing House.

——. 1999. *Reservation: A Pie in the Sky.* Hunsur: DEED.

——. 1999. "Nation Building and Development Process: A Sociological Perspective" in *Professor Parvathamma's Felicitation Volume.* Mysore: pp. 69–92.

Timmaiah, G. 1993. *Power Politics and Social Justice: Backward Castes in Karnataka.* New Delhi: Sage Publications.

4

Social Justice in India

A Case for Equality through Privilege

JAG MOHAN SINGH VERMA

The liquidation of odious and inhuman social deprivations of the underprivileged sections of Indian society, through social commitments, political proclamations and constitutional provisions, has been engaging the attention of social scientists, political activists, administrators, planners and voluntary organizations in modern times. It is heartening to note that today most of the social forces are rallying round for the attainment of this objective to provide privileges to the deprived communities to rectify the social aberrations, i.e., the achievement of equality through privilege. One may perceive as a ground reality that even the most progressive, enlightened and vociferous advocates of this policy, somewhere in the depths of their traditional psyche, have failed to really believe in what they proclaim by their lips. And then a new danger threatening to undo whatever has been achieved is the new-fangled concept of the so-called 'creamy layer' (limited elites). Therefore, there is an imperative and urgent need to probe this problem in order to determine whether 'equality through privilege' is a myth or a reality in order to ensure social justice.

Societies all over the world, on the basis of the type of system prevailing in them, can be classified into open and closed ones, the main difference between them being the ability of the members to leave the membership of a particular stratum and to join the other one. Indian society in the Vedic period, when the *varna* system formed the basis of social stratification and differentiation, was essentially an open society based mainly on functional considerations. By and by, up to the coming of *Smriti* period, the open form of stratification was converted into the closed one. The closed system of stratification created the present caste system. Again in the course of time it led to the exploitation of those who were previously engaged in the performance of menial jobs. Thus, on the Indian scene, emerged a particular section of society which still is socially suppressed, culturally depressed and politically oppressed.

Various nomenclatures have been ascribed to these underprivileged sections of society, such as depressed classes and backward classes, which calls for elaboration for their proper comprehension. These deprived communities constitute a sizeable proportion of India's population. Dr B.R. Ambedkar had consistently used the term 'the depressed classes' for the people whom Mahatma Gandhi called *'Harijan'* (a term coined by Narasimha Mehta, a Gujarati saint) and Scheduled Castes/Scheduled Tribes (SCs/STs) in the Indian Constitution and now known as Dalits. The tribal people, denotified tribes, the nomadic and semi-nomadic tribes and the depressed classes, as a group, were called backward classes. The Other Backward Classes (OBCs) were also included in this category. The committee headed by O.H.B. Sarte, with B.R. Ambedkar and A.B. Thakkar as members, in 1930 at Bombay province, had classified backward classes into three categorics, viz., depressed classes, aboriginal and hill tribes, and other backward classes. Kaka Kalelkar Commission and Mandal Commission have also given their own classifications. Over the years, the backward classes were divided into three broad categories, known as SCs, STs and OBCs. The Indian Constitution lists the first two, namely, SCs and STs, but the third group has not been specifically defined. Article 15(4) talks about socially and educationally backward classes. Article 16(4) uses the term 'backward classes'. Article 46 mentions the weaker sections. The term 'deprived communities' has been used in the succeeding description to denote all these sections.

The pitiable plight of these deprived communities in the past and present furnishes a historically unparalled example of discrimination, exploitation and suppression. The deprived communities have been victims of age-old caste tyranny and dehumanizing untouchability rooted in the caste system prevalent in the country since innumerable centuries. The sorry plight of the people of this section of the Indian society, the suppression and victimization they have been subjected to, and the trials and tribulation they have been facing will provoke tears in the eyes of those who believe in the dignity of man and respect for human personality. The deprived communities have a simmering past, terribly insecure present and entirely bleak future in the context of Indian culture. They have been deliberately made what they now are by centuries of oppression and serfdom, by living in starvation, squalor and disease for generations. They are the tragic products of an inexorable fate and of a heart-breaking past. And it must be added that they have been held in their shameful plight by all the holy principles of religion and the most sacred laws of society. The sufferings of deprived communities date back to the hoary antiquity of Brahminism of Hinduism.

Among the most fundamental concepts of Brahminism on the level of theory, the distinct concept is that of rebirth and causality, generally known as *karma* and on the level of practice, i.e., the working out of theory in social behaviour, Brahminism becomes even more distinct. To an exceptional degree it is bound up with a specific social order, the prominent institution of which is the caste system. The notions of *dharma* (normative order), *karma* (personal moral commitment) and *jati* (caste), as the hierarchical principles of social stratification, are basic to Hindu culture.

Originally, *karma* simply meant a biological law of causality linked with that of *samsara,* i.e., rebirth. But, with religious development the immortality of soul was intertwined with the dead and its retribution (*karma phala*). The doctrine may be summarized by referring to *Manu Smriti.* All action (*karma*) springs from mind, speech and body and produces either good or bad results. These *karmas* are the causes of various conditions of the life of man. Thus, as a result of mental sins, a person becomes a low caste (*antya jati*) in the next birth. The sins of speech and body result in rebirth as animal and inanimate object, respectively. The transmigration of souls thus occurs in accordance with the good or bad conduct of the individual. *Karma* and *samsara* are the bonds which ideologically weld the social system and the Hindu religion together. *Karma* is the exact accumulation of an individual's actions (sometimes referred to as the exercise of moral law in the universe). *Samsara,* the doctrine of rebirth in a caste is appropriate to the *karmic* legacy. Good and evil deeds will be rewarded either in this life or in the next—the application of the law of causality to human destiny. Nobody can escape from *karma*. It is unfailing. The *karmic* residue is only exhausted by being born repeatedly in different castes. This is where the curious inconsistency of *karma* appears. A man of low caste may hope to appear subsequently in a higher caste on living according to *dharma*, which is largely caste duty. This is visible in the concept of *dharma.* First, it is said that the individual is bound by *karma* to the endless round of *samsara*. Then, it is said that a total release ultimately is possible. This is *moksha,* which cannot be achieved unless it is founded on the *dharma*.

That is, it depends entirely on fulfilling the duties appropriate to a particular caste. Failure to do his caste duty would spoil the individual's spiritual chances. It must be pointed out that 'appropriate action', apart from inhibiting social mobility, may involve the infliction of suffering as a necessary part of it. Ambedkar believed that through the centuries this Brahminic philosophy has performed life-thwarting pathogenic functions. It made us a sick people and our society a sick one.

It is the caste identity that enables the Hindu to get along with his daily life. Even alien rulers, including the Mughals and the British, had to depend on caste to rule the country. All non-Hindu religions, too, succumbed to this ultimate sociological invention.

In Hindu social order, caste contributed to a stratified and compartmentalized society based on status, hierarchy, and ritual purity or pollution. Endogamy, occupational rigidities, and constraints on upward mobility and migration strengthened and perpetuated caste-based inequalities. These inequalities have persisted. They are not only 'historical' but in a large measure current. They have been pervasive over time and space in India. They have permeated various sectors of activity, politics, administration and the private sector. Caste also has been tenacious and self-perpetuating given its ramifications in nepotism, caste fraternity and marriage. The caste Hindus have been and are still treating deprived castes as sub-human creatures having no quality of character and personality. The sufferings of deprived castes vary from caste to caste and religion to religion as also in the time-frame. Culturally and socially, they have been depressed and backward. Performance of holy rites, rituals and ceremonies has been forbidden for them. Economically, they have been exploited and downtrodden, their plight being not very much different from that of the slaves and serfs of the feudal times. They have been living in totally abject conditions of drudgery, bondage, compulsory labour and toil, the fruit of which were expropriated from them by the caste Hindus. The deprived communities, which constitute a sizeable proportion of Indian society, have a large history of social degradation, economic exploitation and cultural depression.

With the spread of democratic, egalitarian and socialist ideology in the country and the adoption of the Constitution of India, the state in India was declared to be democratic socialist welfare state committed to the uplift and welfare of deprived sections of Indian society. The economic amelioration, social rehabilitation and cultural uplift of the deprived sections of the society constitute one of the major aspects of the social and economic policy of the Government of India.

India has adopted the strategy of planned development through democratic framework for social transformation and economic emancipation of its citizens, especially the deprived communities, after the banishment of colonial rule in the country. The need for providing protective discrimination or positive discrimination was felt by the framers of Indian Constitution to afford equal opportunity for advancement of the deprived communities. The relevant provisions in the Constitution of India are included under Articles 15–17, 23, 25, 29, 35, 38, 41, 46, 164, 244A, 275, 320, 330, 332–35, 338–42, 371, 371A, 371B and 371C. The Directive Principles of State Policy have given clear instructions, which are to be adopted by State and Central Governments in the overall governance of the country. Many institutional structures in the form of communities, departments, corporations and commissions have been evolved by the Government of India and State Governments to safeguard the interests of the deprived communities.

Various Five-Year Plans have been formulated and implemented in which the allocation of funds for the development of the deprived communities has been given a priority. Voluntary organizations have also taken a lead by initiating programmes for the welfare of the deprived communities. The citizens of India have agreed through their Constitution to establish egalitarian, secular, socialist, democratic republic of India. Special Component Plan (SCP) and Special Central Assistance (SCA) were introduced in the planning process in 1979–80. As such, from the Sixth Five-Year Plan onwards, the Tribal Sub-Plan (TSP) was introduced for the development of tribals and Special Component Plan (SCP) for the development of SCs. The National Commission for Other Backward Classes has recently been established by the Government of India.

Dr Ram Manohar Lohia, the Left and Dalit groups continued with the reform perspective. But, the momentum of reform was extremely weak by the seventies. The ebbing of reform facilitated the degeneration and a deepening systemic crisis. The result was most clearly revealed in the virulent anti-Mandal agitation and the bursting of illiberal, casteist prejudices against the underprivileged. Caste violence erupted involving various caste groups to fight for their share in the resources of production and power in society. While caste conflicts might have existed for centuries, it has become heavily accentuated and has assumed endemic proportions in contemporary times. The growing politicization of the socially backward, economically aspiring, politically ascendant and traditionally weaker castes of Indian society, especially the scheduled and other backward castes, had led the members of these castes to assert and secure their lawful rights and to resist any oppression by the dominant upper castes. Caste violence is a violence of the caste Hindu to subdue the deprived castes. The retaliatory violence of the oppressed against the oppressor is violence for equality and justice and violence against domination. All these aimed at reducing inequalities among citizens of this country in different walks of life.

Now, one very vital and basic fact which stands marked out is what the Supreme Court of India has discerned and described as the 'creamy layer', albeit newly generated from amongst the deprived sections of the society, is in reality the cumulative response to the working in the society of the democratic compulsions, constitutional and legislative safeguards, social reform movements, allocation in Five-Year Plans for this object and the influence of the Directive Principles of State Policy. The process of the generation of this creamy layer is in nascent stage. It does not require much effort to see that any move to banish this creamy layer from under this umbrella is inevitably fraught with serious negative and counter productive consequences and is terribly premature too. In fact, enough and reasonable time is to be allowed to this creamy layer to stabilize itself and to allow this process to percolate down to other levels where it has not yet started. Of course, a stage is bound to come when this protectionism would be naturally rendered redundant, but not now. To cry halt to it here would definitely be undoing of all the good work done so far. The exclusion of creamy layer from reservation will negate its purpose.

The idea of reservation was mooted by the founding fathers of our Constitution as a device of positive discrimination to ensure an adequate representation of the deprived castes of our society in the places of higher echelons, authority, power and position in order to safeguard their interests and protect them from the onslaught of discrimination and injustice perpetrated on them by the unequal pattern of social order and vested interests of the high ups and the dominant. It must be remembered that no amount of economic prosperity and affluence can erase the scar of social disabilities generated by the Indian hierarchical social order based on caste. Innumerable cases can be cited when the interests of the persons belonging to the economically well-off sections of the deprived communities (the so-called creamy layers) have been ignored and they have been subjected to the heights of discrimination and injustice due to caste prejudices of upper castes. One cannot think of the upliftment of the weaklings of the system through economic criteria, because social backwardness created by unequal social order is a social problem. Since the entire group suffers the brunt of caste prejudices, irrespective of its economic attainments, it needs and deserves equal protection against exploitation and injustice. One of the most important consequences of disentitlement of the creamy layer would be that it will act as a retrograde mechanism for these relatively advanced sections of the OBCs because they will suffer at two counts—first, they will continue to be oppressed and discriminated against because of the fact that they belong to the backward caste and on the other they will not be provided with the reservation cover because of their belonging to the creamy layer. The ultimate results will be that they will slump into the morass of backwardness further.

Another problem, which is likely to emerge out of the principle of creamy layer, is the problem of backlog of unfilled vacancies reserved for OBCs, as it has been observed in the case of SCs and STs, even when there was no principle of creamy layer enforced in their cases. When introduced in the case of the OBCs, it will be extremely difficult to find adequate suitable and qualified candidates from these communities for appointment, particularly for jobs requiring professional, technical and higher academic qualifications.

The creamy layer formula is incoherent and irrelevant to the principle and philosophy of reservation and negates its very purpose to improve the lot of the underprivileged as it enunciates economic parameters as its basis. It, therefore, deserves to be rejected outright in order to ensure the ends of social justice to the members of OBCs, not as a political gimmick but as a commitment to a social cause.

The idea of reservation implies establishment of equality through privilege and it provides privileges to the deprived communities like SCs, STs, OBCs, various religious minorities and other marginal groups to improve their social, cultural, economic, political and educational conditions with ultimate goal of enabling them to come at par with others. The principle of equality through privilege should be adhered to both in letter and spirit in order to build a modern, open, plural, culturally rich, prosperous and egalitarian society out of a fragmented, poverty-stricken, weak, diffident, insular, archaic and conservative social order. In fact, hierarchical system of socio-economic power structure of traditional Indian society has placed the higher caste groups in commanding position of dominance and forced the lower caste groups in submissive silence. Even after the independence this trend continued and whatever socio-economic transformation took place has only been on a limited scale. In order to ensure social justice from Ambedkar's point of view, the entire traditional Indian social structure and social system need to be totally overhauled and replaced by new social order.

REFERENCES

Ambedkar, B.R. 1936. *Annihilation of Caste*. Bombay: Thacker & Co.

——. 1946. *Who Were the Shudras?* Bombay: Thacker & Co.

Aggarwal, P.C. and Ashraf, M.S. 1976. *Equality through Privilege*. New Delhi: Shri Ram Center for Industrial Relations and Human Resources.

Barbar, B. 1965. *Social Stratification.* New York: Harcourt Brace.

Beteille, Andre. 1971. *Caste, Class and Power.* Bombay: Oxford University Press

—— (ed.). 1972. *Social Inequality.* England, Harmondsworth: Penguin Books.

——. 1983. *Equality and Inequality: Theory and Practice*. Delhi: Oxford University Press.

——. 1985. *Inequality and Social Change*. Delhi: Oxford University Press.

——. 1993. "Power and Authority: Courts and the Political Process". *The Times of India*, April 20, Lucknow.

Bailey, F.G. 1957. *Caste and Economic Frontier*. Manchester: Manchester University Press.

Bhagwandas. 1969. *Thus Spoke Ambedkar: Selected Speeches*, Vol. II, Jullandar: Bheem Patrika Publications.

Cohen, Marshall et al. 1977. *Equality and Preferential Treatment*. New Jersey: Princeton University Press.

Dube, S.C. 1980. "Sociology of Violence: Roots in Political Culture". *The Times of India*. August 11.

Dutt, Nripendra Kumar. 1968. *Origin and Growth of Caste in India*. Calcutta: Firma K.L. Mukhopadhyay.

Markandan, K.C. 1966. *Directive Principles of the Indian Constitution*. Bombay: Allied Publishers.

Mehta, Subhash Chandra. 1963. "Persistence of the Caste System: Vested Interest in Backwardness". *Quest* 30 (January), pp. 20–27.

Oommen, T.K. 1985. *Sources of Deprivation and Styles of Protest: The Case of the Dalits in India, Readings on Scheduled Castes*. Hyderabad: National Institute of Rural Development.

Planning Commission, Government of India, Seventh Five-Year Plan (1985–90), Vol. I, New Delhi.

Shukla, V.N. 1964. *The Constitution of India* (4th ed.). Lucknow: Eastern Book Company.

Shyamlal, 1981. *Caste and Political Mobilisation: The Bhangis*. Jaipur: Panchsheel Prakashan.

Sachchidananda and Lal, A.K. 1985. *Elite and Development*. New Delhi: Concept Publishing Company.

Singh, Yogendra. 1973. *The Modernization of Indian Tradition: A Systematic Study of Social Change.* New Delhi: Manohar Publications

Unnithan, T.K.N., Indra Deva and Singh, Yogendra. 1965. *Towards a Sociology of Culture in India.* New Delhi: Prentice-Hall.

Verma, Jag Mohan Singh. 1991. *Democratic Ethos and Developmental Process in India.* New Delhi: Uppal Publishing House.

5

Social Justice and Welfare State Agenda in India

ROSE VEERA D'SOUZA

The idea of welfare has often been discussed as related to justice, equality, freedom and rights and justified in terms of the concept of redistributive justice. Since, these concepts are invariably connected to the idea of substantive ends of political life, the role of the state to achieve individual self-fulfilment achieves significance (Barry, 2002: 1).

The significant goal of the state's social policy in almost all societies is to maximize the well-being or satisfaction of the individual and community. Achieving social justice in the society is linked to the policies and institutions of the contemporary welfare state. Welfare is related to the external material condition of the individual like adequate food, housing, education etc. and the core of welfare state activities encompasses programmes for economic security, health, housing, education and social services. Governments have a wide range of possible actions. Hence, the state through legislations and facilities offers protection to its people. It sets the rules by which companies, charities and other organizations operate. This became almost a central idea of the welfare state in the 20th century.

The welfare state in India is the development of the 20th century that grew in intimacy with contemporary political thought of the West. In this century, welfare ideal came into the political realm with its three basic principles.[1] Consequently, in India too, the national leaders under colonial rule envisaged a welfare state to strive for the well-being of the Indian masses. The very act of securing freedom against the colonial rule symbolized a struggle for an active state and the nationalist discourse significantly articulated such a state.

The Indian national movement gradually and later the Constitution of India laid the foundation for the interventionist state in India.[2] The vision of a welfare state was put forward through the model of liberal democratic set-up when India got independence and the principles of liberty and equality were underscored. Article 39 of Indian Constitution assures "equal justice on the basis of equal opportunity". The preamble to the Constitution enumerates the goals of equality, justice and liberty.[3]

The role of the interventionist state was constantly addressed by the nationalists right from the beginning of the freedom struggle. They addressed the problem of freedom from hunger and want regularly. Besides, employment and industrial and agricultural development became significant aspects of the nationalist discourse.[4]

While addressing the issue of industrial development, the Indian leaders demanded that the Government of India should follow a policy of direct, deliberate and systematic promotion of industrial development by giving up the laissez-faire policy, as they considered it as the *sine qua non* of nation's economic welfare (Uppal, 1984: 2). They also demanded active intervention of the government through policies to achieve agrarian reforms, including protection of land lease arrangements. M.G. Ranade argued that the doctrine of the state, being the guardian of the entire community, is required to be implemented to protect the weak.

In 1930s welfare ideas had a steady growth elsewhere and they influenced British India too. Such developments immediately initiated spiralling concern for the welfare state. The intellectuals of India developed a consistent effort to provide a solution for India's economic and social problems. The Karachi resolution of the Indian National Congress (INC) (1931) expressed it by redefining *'swaraj'*, as 'economic freedom of the starving millions' along with political freedom.

The nationalist struggle had addressed the question of poverty, agriculture, education and industry already in a concrete and a specific manner. The resolution on fundamental rights and economic programme of the Karachi Congress, later in 1931 had similar goals.

The agenda of social justice well figured in the writings of contemporary political and economic thinkers who argued for state intervention and put across several plans and proposals.[5] In 1936, Nehru enunciated a view of the relationship between socialism and development which was shared by several leaders throughout the Third World: "I see no way of ending the poverty, the vast unemployment, the degradation and the subjection of the Indian people except through socialism."[6] The National

Planning Committee was set up in 1938 by the INC which envisaged a comprehensive scheme of national planning.

In June 1944, a Planning and Developmental Department was established making Sri Ardeshir Dalal, who had also been associated with the Bombay Plan, to draw up a Five-Year Plan for the central government. The Second Report on Reconstruction Planning proposed a 15-year 'Perspective Plan', along with a more detailed plan for the first five years. It had the goals of reducing inequalities in income distribution, provision of basic amenities to the poor and promoting cottage industries to promote employment. The industrial policy was also envisaged with more edge towards state intervention.

The Bombay Plan was considered to be significant in the direction of India's economic planning, mixed economy and strengthening an interventionist state. The philosophy of welfare was very evident in the way independent India was constructed as well as in the series of official documents on planning, developed by the national leaders. Though the Bombay Plan was appreciated, it also generated sharp controversies on the issue of the role of the state. It had allotted a gradual control over the basic and key industries only, with the rest of the industries being under the private sector. It was considered to be a weak and ineffective approach to bring about a change in the socio-economic structure of the society. Consequent to this, M.N. Roy presented the essence of 'People's Plan' that brought in the nationalization of agriculture and liquidation of rural indebtedness. The role of the state was streamlined in pursuing the goals of free and compulsory education, minimum scales of wages and assured supply of basic needs, such as food, clothing, shelter and health.

Gandhiji believed in the maximization of social welfare and for this purpose he emphasized on the importance of the welfare of the individuals by reducing inequalities in income and wealth. Gandhi's concept of 'Ramarajya' supported egalitarian, non-violent and democratic social order, wherein moral values pervade all spheres of human life. Politically, it is a form of stateless society; socially, it is a form of classless society where all persons are equally treated, irrespective of differences; and economically, it is a form of socialist society in which inequalities based on possession and non-possession vanish because all wealth belongs to the society as a whole.

Constituent Assembly Debates and the Welfare Ideal

The nationalist Congress party's socio-economic and political agenda for independent India was incorporated into the provisions of the Indian

Constitution after much deliberation and discussion in the Constituent Assembly. When the Constituent Assembly met to discuss the resolution on aims and objectives of the Constitution, the leaders laid down the promise of a welfare state.

The social revolution was considered to be the topmost priority of the national agenda of the Constituent Assembly when it adopted the 'Objectives Resolution', which put across social, economic, and political justice, and equality of law, status and opportunity. The directive principles of state policy were meant to pronounce "the 'socialist' as well as the social revolutionary content of the constitution".[7]

The Constituent Assembly categorically stated that the state shall make efforts to secure, to all workers, by suitable legislation or economic organization or in any other way, agricultural, industrial or otherwise, work ensuring a decent standard of life and full enjoyment of leisure and social and cultural opportunities.

The discussion in the Constituent Assembly significantly dealt to make directive principles of state policy justifiable.[8] The fundamental rights and directive principles of state policy also enumerated minority rights. The Constitution of India provides certain fundamental rights (Articles 15–17, 25–30) and directive principles for the benefit of minorities in India. It has been argued that the debates in the Constituent Assembly had a tolerant rather than an encouraging approach of the state towards the minorities (Jain, 2005). It should not be taken to indicate that the national leaders were not in favour of providing safeguards to the minorities for cultural preservation and secular development, but it was basically on account of the historically developed social distance among certain communities and partition of the nation that had made them weary of assertive minorities, especially when history had proven that such assertion might obstruct the process of nation building (ibid.). In a way the constitution-makers reposed faith in the minorities to assert their demands and not to provide the promised fundamental rights automatically.

Affirmative provisions for the well-being of the marginalized and disadvantaged sections of the society were to become important provisions of fundamental rights and directive principles. Dr Ambedkar played a major role in this regard. He emphasized the need to plan for economic development well before we attained independence. He enunciated the need for equality and social justice while drafting the Constitution of India. The need to create certain special provisions for the disadvantaged groups within the overall liberal framework of the polity was largely considered. He consistently argued that the Indian polity cannot be solely based on the foundation of equal rights and liberties. He proposed a set of principles justifying preferential treatment. He argued for special provisions for the untouchables on grounds of representation, social presence and selfhood. "Representation can help them to seek rights and resources to pursue their aims and objectives otherwise impossible to pursue" (Rodrigues, 2005: 56). Ambedkar gave due consideration to the educational and economic needs of the minorities. These interventions influenced the development and planning process of India. There was extensive discussion on affirmative policies, such as reservation in the Constituent Assembly. India's left parties did not want them to be granted on caste basis. "They argued instead that a more egalitarian social order could be built through property redistribution and the expansion of public sector" (Weiner, 2002: 203). Welfare initiatives, such as land reforms and tenancy reforms, became important elements in Ambedkar's scheme of the welfare state. Land reform was argued to be the key to equality as caste was retained by unequal property relations that allowed the upper castes to maintain their social, political and economic dominance. The government set a quota for Scheduled Castes (SCs) and Scheduled Tribes (STs) for all government appointments, including representation in the public sector. Quotas were also established for admission into elite educational institutions, such as medical colleges and national universities. The directives became the cornerstone of the welfarist orientation in independent India.

The welfare state is not merely a state but a social system. It comprises of liberal values, democratic polity and mixed economy. It maintains the principle that every member of the community is entitled to a set of rights and resources because he is a human being, who should have a minimum standard of living, including universal education and health care. It requires the state to ensure economic stability and progress, when there are violent booms and bursts in economy due to conflicting private interests. The state should ensure full employment, social security and social insurance; a system of taxation properly adjusted to periods of prosperity and adversity; designing public policies in such a way as to redistribute purchasing power in harmony with the best interests of the nation. A few argue that these things have to be provided for in a democratic political set-up without depriving people of their liberty or self-respect (Bava, 2004: 352–73).

Policy Initiatives

Towards the close of 1954 a resolution in this direction in the parliament propounded the goal of socialism, and since then between the sessions of

Congress at Avadi (1955) and Bhuvaneshwar (1964) and in subsequent public statements socialism was endlessly discussed. As welfare and its manifestations were the prominent features in the 20th century, they necessarily had their influence on Indian governance. Along with nationalist zeal, India envisaged the development of the country as free from poverty, ignorance, disease and inequality. The reason behind the setting up of the National Planning Commission in 1950 was to work out design for economic development and formulate economic plans for more balanced and effective utilization of resources and capacities.

The First Five-Year Plan commenced in 1950–51 and it was followed by a series of five-year plans. When India took up the initiative of development and planning, it had a choice between the market-driven path of development as pursued in the West and the centrally planned approach to development as was being followed in the erstwhile Eastern bloc. The welfare state in the West was already taking deep roots. But, none of the existing models were easily compatible with India's requirements. India took the middle path, a distinctive path of its own, which implied a harmonious blend of the market and the state—mix of private and public sectors. The distributional aspects of India's development experience, since independence, throw light on the welfare programmes and policies that India adopted. It pursued a reformist path in order to secure social justice through parliamentary democracy.

The Industrial Policy Resolution of 1948 also made clear that "the equitable distribution of wealth, not the distribution of poverty" should be the criterion for government participation in industry and for "the conditions in which private enterprises should be allowed to operate" (Government of India, 1948).

The Planning Commission was established within a month of the Constitution's inauguration, to determine the machinery for implementing the directive principles of state policy and to allocate national resources in order to achieve better results (Cabinet Secretariat, 1950). The rights not only placed restrictions upon the government but also demanded the intervention of the state to strive for them. Pursuits to make way for development or to implement the directive principles resulted in opposition from all kinds of entrenched interests. Efforts towards the abolition of zamindari system led to legal bottlenecks at various levels (Austin, 1999: 74–98).

Commitment to the poor and the downtrodden found its expression in the nationalist political discourse. Both Gandhi and Nehru shared such a commitment. The socialistic vision and the rhetorics in the sphere of policy often reiterated such goals. The policies such as land distribution and the laws governing employment of urban labour found attention. However, placing high priority on consolidation of democracy encouraged the hopes of the masses by promising egalitarian development of the poor. Under Nehru's leadership, the Constitution, the parliament, the ruling Congress party, and the Planning Commission all formally endorsed egalitarian, secular and socialist goals of national policy that established a consensus at the level of principle on the aim of constructing a 'socialistic pattern of society'. Critics, however, have felt that "the philosophy of welfare adopted by the Indian state adhered to a needs-based conception of justice in theory, but was in practice based on ideas of charity, benevolence, and paternalism".[9]

The Indian Welfare State at Work

The growth of welfare state in India and the realization of social justice should be studied in relation to the democratic ethos and socialism partly because the Indian freedom struggle saw democracy as the best possible way to extend social justice and equality. The first, theoretical chapter of the First Five-Year Plan document entitled *The Problem of Development* enumerated the aspirations of a welfare state in India. The chapter contains quite a few statements about changing "the socio-economic framework" or about "re-adaptations of social institutions and relationships".[10] Referring to the colonial 'cramped', 'partial' and 'limited' development, it sought to change the course of affairs through planning. In the mid-1950s, after the consolidation of political power and the rehabilitation of the economy from the miseries of World War II and partition, India made a sharp break with the inherited colonial policy of laissez-faire. Such a "break in economic policy—with economic planning, autarky and building socialism" are of 'historic importance', to India.[11]

Planning, Policies and the Development of Welfare State

Several characteristics of the welfare state in India came to be spelled out through the five-year plans. They covered six domains: education, health, housing, employment, personal social services and social security. In a way there was a universal agenda of welfarism that was spelled out here. Anti-poverty and social justice issues have figured prominently in the plan pursuits of India.

Socialism and democracy were supposed to be the means to attain equal opportunities of education, health care and employment. In 1970s, the world witnessed increasing awareness in development strategies of previous decades that would not eliminate or even reduce poverty to a large extent. Economists and policy makers in India were also aware that the rate of economic growth was too slow to lift the living standards of the bottom half of the population to acceptable levels. There also developed a debate on the appropriateness of various strategies to alleviate poverty. Even the most ardent protagonists of the 'trickle-down mechanism' accepted that India has been too slow to make any major dent in the poverty problem. This idea had been widely accepted and it has led to the increase in the scale of intervention by the government towards the target group (Dutta, 1996: 101).

Between 1977 and 1991 the most stringent controls on imports and licensing were gradually lifted. The government expanded anti-poverty schemes, especially rural employment schemes, though all this did not considerably reach the targeted group comprising the poor and the marginalized.

The welfare state in India is guided by three institutional principles: economic management, provision of services for all citizens and social insurance. The five-year plans aimed at achieving two major objectives: (a) reduction of inequalities in income and wealth by ensuring redistribution of resources; and (b) improvement in income and conditions of living of the deprived sections of the society.

The foundational thinking of welfare state—"let the rich pay"—was applied in the Indian context as well. Hence, the government sought to reduce inequalities by initiating higher taxation to higher income groups, higher taxes on luxury items and land ceiling both in urban and rural areas to reduce concentration of wealth in a few hands. The consistent emphasis of the plans was on development activities, such as health and education, to improve the quality of life and to generate resources and to foster economic growth.

Welfare State in India and Liberalization

The incapacity of the welfare state to ensure development and growth begot, in a way, the process of liberalization. The World Bank experts since 1958 had advised India against public sector programmes and sought greater role to private enterprises (Frankel, 2005: 179). The neo-liberal interpretation conveyed the impression that India's lackluster performance was due to sluggish economic growth, which followed from the mixed economy and the closed and static model of development.

India embraced the liberalization policy in 1991 that allowed her to enter the trade market dynamics. The reasons for India taking such a decision often raised divergent opinions (Bhaduri and Nayyar, 1996: xi).

In the midst of the grave balance of payments crisis of 1990–91, the government led by Narasimha Rao made the decision to give up the old paradigm and introduced economic liberalization. It sought stabilization and SAP of the IMF and World Bank. There was a significant support, if not eagerness, among Indian policy makers too in shifting over to liberalization (Mooij, 2005: 25). Jagdish Bhagwati and T.N. Srinivasan, who have been important defenders of liberalization in India, argued that the new set of policies would bring in "a successful transition from an essentially inward-looking posture to an outward-oriented economy, exploiting foreign trade and investment opportunities fully; a new policy framework which will promote greater efficiency, growth and therewith a surer and deeper attack on poverty alleviation".[12] The liberalization process in its essentials came to be endorsed by a broad spectrum of political parties.

As integral to the process of globalization, social sector reforms have been introduced in India. Attention was given to PDS (the National Social Safety Net Programmes include the PDS costing Indian tax payers about 0.5% of GDP), Integrated Child Development Services, employment guarantee schemes, the Integrated Rural Development Programme, and other social welfare programmes targeted for the elderly and the disabled. The reforms underlined continued commitment to traditional programmes for poverty alleviation that were practised before the reforms. Such programmes were even expanded from 1993–94 onwards.

Liberalization inaugurated a paradigm change in India's economic policy during the first half of the 1990s. The policy shift was from "high regulation internally and high protection externally to a situation of moderate regulation and moderate protection" (Nayar, 2001: 157). The reforms brought down taxes and slashed customs duties. The licensing and control structure was dismantled. Though there may have been apprehensions on the part of the small-scale industrial sector about the threat to its existence from greater competition, it came to be drowned down by the welcome accorded by big business houses. There was one caveat: while the internal liberalization was accepted wholeheartedly, external liberalization was given a critical approval (Nayar, 2001: 159).

As the reforms progressed, poverty alleviation programmes were also broadened to include programmes on health education and family welfare.[13] Health inequalities were very sharp in India, in comparison with many other countries, even poor ones.[14] To acknowledge the changing health needs and the ability to respond to the changing context the National Health Policy, 2002 was passed. The policy envisaged to maximize the broad-based availability of health services to the citizenry of the country on the basis of realistic considerations of capacity.[15] It suggested a new policy framework for the accelerated achievement of public health goals in the socio-economic circumstances currently prevailing in the country. The priorities pronounced were in terms providing child health care, prevention of diseases and AIDS awareness. It emphasized on improved standard of governance as a prerequisite for the success of health policy. The National Vector Borne Disease Control Programmes (NVBDCP), 2005 is very significant in this regard. The National Rural Health Mission (NRHM) has been launched for nation-wide implementation with effect from April 2005 along with adequate support to implementation.

In 2001 proposals were made to reduce 'labour market rigidities': Firms below 1,000 workers were allowed to function outside the jurisdiction of Industrial Dispute Act, while at the same time contractual labour was sought to be made legal. The thrust of the proposed amendments was to facilitate the process of relieving workers out of existing permanent and secure employment; and to create a redefined framework wherein labour can be engaged for jobs that are flexible, time-bound, and can be easily turned down. Organized labour had enjoyed a distinct position among the prominent stakeholders in the limited welfaristic domain crafted in the post-independence phase and continued to be favoured client of the state in the later years (Roy Chowdhury, 2005: 264). Traditionally, it was taken for granted that MNCs provided better wages and working conditions and hence it does not require a backing of welfaristic measures, whereas, some of the bitter industrial confrontations have taken place today in the MNCs.[16] Thus globalization has brought in significant shifts not only in terms of labour relations, but also in the role of the trade union and management. In this context, the role of state as regulator of labour issues calls for significant attention.

In 2001, the government enacted the 93rd Constitutional Amendment declaring education as a fundamental right. It enabled the citizen to seek the enforcement of the right to education by resorting to writ jurisdiction. For a few years there was a growing awareness regarding India's failure in the field of education. The available data did not show any substantial improvement in the patterns of education expenditure in the 1990s. Critics had even suggested that the growth of education had slowed down, after structural measures were introduced in 1991, and education expenditure in the states also declined (Dreze and Sen, 1995: 123). The literacy campaigns by the states also did not bring considerable results. It is to be noted however that while substantial progress was not achieved in basic education over the past decade, the literacy rates have increased from 52 per cent to 65 per cent over the period 1991–2001 (Ferro et al., 2004: 171) Enrolment at the primary schools has also shown an increase.

The changing relations between the union and states have also experienced considerable change in the context of reforms. One of the important policy reforms that was introduced in the 1990s was the enactment of the 73rd and 74th Constitutional Amendments, which led to decentralization of power to the local bodies in rural and urban areas, respectively. The passing of the 73rd amendment has brought in devolution of power to panchayats in all state governments. Formally, the Panchayat Raj Institutions (PRIs) came into existence all over rural India after the enactment of 73rd Constitutional Amendment. Many substantive provisions of the constitutional amendment, such as reservation for weaker categories to entail active participation, devolution of finances and functions parallel to political authority and responsibility for district planning process, were made although such legislations did not bring in immediate change in all the states.[17] Much of the enthusiasm was built only after the 1998 loan agreement between the few state governments of India and the World Bank, specifying that the devolution of powers to local bodies must be made part of the governance reform.

Economy and Welfare

There has been a mixed response on the impact of globalization to the kind of welfare state crafted in India after independence. Some welcome the changes that have taken place, from a "close economy heavily determined by state intervention, to the present open international market situation", with less dependence on the state. There is a shift from the earlier 'Hindu rate of growth', which was around 3.5 per cent per annum, to the present higher rates of growth, which is around 5.6 per cent per annum achieved since 1980. The share of public investment has declined in the GDP, to the levels of 1970s, whereas private investment has continued to increase steadily although the aggregate investment rates have remained constant.

Economic analysts have argued that the expenditure on social sector schemes, as part of welfare-related programmes, has been increasing in real terms in the era of liberalization. Critics however point out that the public investment in agriculture and irrigation, and the share of agriculture in total capital formation, has declined (Frankel, 2005: 783). As such, employment opportunities have also declined. According to a major study, quoted by Frankel, agriculture almost became stagnant in absorbing labour resulting in economic growth of 1990s as a 'jobless variety' (Dyson et al., 2004: 159–160).

In the 1990s the central government has considerably expanded its activities in the field of elementary education with some help from foreign agencies, but mainly through the schemes of District Primary Education Programme of the state governments. However, the public expenditure on elementary education by the state governments seems to have declined (Dreze and Sen, 2002: 168).

Public health care expenditure in India is expressed in the state and central government's expenditure for various schemes. However, it is established that the states' share in the total revenue expenditure did not increase due to fiscal constraints of the states, whereas the central support has shown a steady increase.[18]

One of the important objectives of welfarism in India has been the reduction of poverty. How has liberalization affected this objective? Acceleration in economic growth is considered to be a great achievement after economic reforms. And economic growth is the leading determinant of poverty reduction and the policies that enable overall economic growth will be the key indicators to improve the income of the poor people in India (Ferro et al., 2004: 153).

The growing inequalities are the significant problem that India faces specially after liberalization. Growing income inequalities have encouraged the privileged groups to perpetuate and reinforce their control over limited resources and channels of income generation in the economy (Kumar, 2005: 1039–40). Poverty levels vary across the states. Due to economic growth, the incidence of poverty as reflected in the proportion of people below poverty line (BPL) has come down in all the states. However, inter-state disparities persist. And, these regional disparities explain much of the inequities that are growing in India (Bagchi and Kurian, 2005: 322–348). Evidence suggests that the significant cause for the widening of regional inequalities is the uneven flow of investment to various states after liberalization, giving rise to North-South divide in India (Mooij, 2005: 31).

In India, the state has played a central role in producing the mixed economy. By replacing the earlier laissez-faire colonial state, the interventionist state provided a direction for the growth of industrialization. It invested in public sector and spent on education and health. Globalization has brought in heavy changes in such a perspective.

There has been growing concern about the capabilities that are considered to be important for the improvement of Human Development Index (HDI). According to the Human Development Reports, published by the UNDP annually since 1991, India has shown consistent improvement on the HDI front. The 2006 UNDP Human Development Report also has shown a progress from the earlier 2005 HDI position. India's position in 2005 was 127 out of 177 countries with 0.602 HDI value whereas it is placed 126th position out of 177 with 0.611 HDI value in 2006. In 2004 India was placed at 127th position with 0.595 HDI value.[19]

The impact of liberalization of the economy on welfare of people has therefore remained mixed. While inequalities have reinforced and the overall role of the public sector has declined, there is no evidence to suggest that social welfare policies have necessarily been affected on the whole.

The Political Domain

Globalization is argued to have affected the preferred role of the state and its autonomy. The erosion of the state autonomy is discussed at three levels: the Indian state vis-à-vis MNCs, the Indian state vis-à-vis the states in India, and the Indian state vis-à-vis politics of inclusion.

Since there are competitors for the economic sovereignty of the state, the retreat of the state seems to have taken place. Such a retreat of the state is linked to the creation of huge economic blocs, within the context of which the economic role of the individual nation-state is being extensively downgraded in favour of supra-national institutions.

However, all these arguments that seem to claim for a constrained role of the state in turn help the state in India to retain its foothold. Though the MNCs are enjoying increasing edge, at the same time, politically, national governments are responsible to their "electorates for levels of employment, rate of growth and performance of the economy in general". By bringing in the growing power of the lower strata of the society against the upper class, the state has placed limits to enterprise solely directed to private profit. Bardhan says, cynics may argue "… that the retreat of State, implied by economic reform, is now more acceptable to the upper classes and castes, not only because the regulatory and interventionist State has become too burdensome for the Indian economy, but also because these classes and castes are now losing their control over state power in the face of the emerging hordes of lower castes, and thus opting for greener pastures in the private sector (and abroad)" (cited in Mooij, 2005: 30–31). The role of the state also seems to have changed in the context of reform as the lower strata of society are also claiming a fair and just share in the state resources.

In the case of the growing strength of the lower strata of the society vis-à-vis the upper classes, the state needs to strengthen its material base on which the marginalized and the disadvantaged rely upon. In the view of Deepak Nayyar, "the rich dominate the economy now more than earlier, but the poor have a strong voice in the polity now more than earlier" (cited in Mooij, 2005: 31). Such a politics of inclusive democracy helps the state to strengthen itself to concentrate on helping improve its human development capabilities and to accommodate the civil society and marginalized and disadvantaged sections of the society who assert their rights for an egalitarian order.

India was first among the major democracies of the world to appreciate cultural rights by establishing the principles of diversity and pluralism in the context of choice, rather than tradition. The Indian approach provides large space for the development of a broad-based democracy by suggesting that people have the right to linguistic and religious identities and it is the only "sustainable approach to development and democracy in diverse societies".[20] Secularism, democracy and federalism promote the political culture of integration of the marginalized, disadvantaged and minority sections of the Indian society. Pluralism guarantees inclusion and autonomy for cultural communities. In the cultural domain, while the threats that liberalization holds are real, there are also assertions of cultural identities which, on the whole, seems to be very positive in India.

The Changing Nature of the Welfare State in India

Under liberalization, the Indian welfare state is not getting dismantled but it is redefining itself to suit the changing context. New concerns seem to be brought before the state as discussed earlier. Competitive federalism, the politics of inclusion and the need for better human development capabilities have brought more challenges to make the welfare state more of outcomes than of rhetoric. It requires to emphasize action-oriented plans rather than stints of populism as the electorate also becomes more alert. The anxiety with regard to certain aspects such as labour, education and languages seem to be real. Affirmative action policies allocate jobs, promotions, business loans for higher education and legislative seats to the disadvantaged sections of the society. Without these policies group inequalities and socio-economic exclusions can be more glaring. There are voices arguing that privatization should be geared to achieve better investment and better solidarity to direct better opportunities to the disadvantaged too. Similarly, it is said that voluntary organizations should be encouraged and monitored so as to achieve better outcomes.

India adopted a democratic Constitution in 1950 and since then it has succeeded in promoting and adhering to the basic structures of democracy. The democratic institutions in India are constantly debated and reassessed. Incorporating the viable suggestions, the democratic structures in India have not changed radically and have retained their significance despite challenges. Economic disparities, social inequality, poverty, illiteracy, secessionist and ethnic tendencies and communal riots have not shaken the democratic foundations in India. On the contrary, democratic precepts evolved mechanisms to manage the society by intervening to suggest and work out remedies. The citizen of India continues to look upon democratic institutions as instruments of popular aspirations and the changing context has rendered more space to caste leaders, social activists, press media and NGOs to be more vocal of the rights of the people and the role of democracy. "Today, in spite of the leaders and elected representatives, it is the environment of public opinion which provides sustenance to democracy, ... one may be quite right in inferring that many a party and their leaders and other representatives are being tolerated because people want democracy" (Alam, 2004: 85).

One of the distinct experiences that the democracy of India shares is that there is no singular set of practices but numerous claims and counter-claims (Alam, 2004: 85). The Dalit movement and political mobilizations have acquired specific space. The Indian welfare state has established a web of institutions for the implementation of policies with regard to disadvantaged groups. Though a few of these institutions were established way back in 1950s, they gained statutory status in 1990s.

In terms of policy measures, in 1990s, the Indian economy moved away from planning and state intervention towards market and competition, or from an interventionist state to a regulatory state. In social policy this shift meant a diminished and reduced role for the state's redistributive agenda and a greater focus on group-based social justice and particularistic institutions. Such a shift in the larger context of the role of the state was also in part a response to the political mobilization and growing clout of the articulate sections of the disadvantaged groups demanding greater recognition and presence in decision-making structures. The National Commission for the Scheduled Castes and National Commission for Minorities work to promote the welfare of the disadvantaged and compelling demands of social equality. As a result, it highlighted, on the one hand, the institutionalized commitment to the protection and welfare of the marginalized and the disadvantaged on the part of the state, and on the other, the creation of an organized mechanism for the representation of their concerns. The prevalence of such institutions helped in promoting the implementation of preferential treatment programme even at a time when powerful economic groups claim greater resources. Cultural and identity politics has displaced the earlier politics of economic and social inequality. The real empowerment and enablement of the disadvantaged sections of the society will take place only in a state and society where concrete strategies for empowerment are geared to achieve larger vision of securing substantive equality.

No doubt, the democracy of India has been facing the marginalization of social groups and communal tensions. Yet it provides enough spaces for the people to assert themselves and the power of dominant groups can never be hegemonic.[21] The rise of backward castes and identity politics can be a democratizing development, making them more participative.

Anomalies and Contradictions of the Welfare State

While the welfare state in India is holding itself against the insinuations of liberalization and re-articulating itself afresh, it may be useful for us to keep in mind certain structural constraints in which it is located.

The Indian state took upon itself several concerns distinctive to itself which was not the case with the modern state in the West at any given time. It was at the vanguard of economic development and the planning process reinforced such a role of the state enormously. The state attempted to play out this role through the bureaucracy in general and developmental bureaucracy in particular. However, in this 'avatar' of the state, it towered above citizens and increasingly tended to be paternalistic.

In India, the state became the agency of extending preferential treatment to low castes and tribes. In pursuit of such an objective opportunities were set aside for these groups in public employment roughly in proportion to their demographic weight. A similar allotment was also made in terms of the resources and services at the command of the state. The limited scope of these benefits and their uneven reach led to the creation of a segment of beneficiaries who stood to gain disproportionately compared to the rest of the community. In fact, the role of the state in preferential considerations of this kind led to the creation of an elite class. The socialist rhetoric was advanced to build political capital, but policies in favour of the poor were seldom pursued vigorously (Kohli, 2002: 2).

The state in India came to extend certain resources and opportunities to groups and communities of innumerable kind on account of certain disadvantages they suffer from. They were women, children, farmers, backward classes, people living in backward regions etc. Some of these groups were targeted for special consideration on account of the explicit constitutional mandate in this regard. Again, resources and opportunities were too scanty and they accrued unevenly to different constituencies. Some of these benefits were employed clearly for electoral gains and were susceptible to be influenced by the electoral arithmetic. Given the diffuse and discretionary nature of some of these benefits, often, bureaucracy and political interests came to entrench themselves claiming to dispense these benefits. In fact, they stood to gain out of them much more than the target population.

Given the hierarchical and segmented nature of the Indian society, extending civil and political rights to certain communities and groups, such as untouchables, elicited from the state extensive interventions of diverse kinds. In the process the role of the state was reinforced affecting adversely the purpose it set out to pursue.

India was and continues to be a deeply diverse society with regard to cultural practices, beliefs and linguistic affinities. Some of them called for extensive support from the state to further their distinctive belonging and in some other cases to ward off and contain conflicts arising from the pursuit of such belonging. The welfare state was called upon to play this role.

The role that the state had to play came to be defined in the context of electoral democracy with universal franchise. The welfare measures that adopted were often dovetailed to the requirements specific to the conditions of such a democracy. Often scarce resources were allotted not on grounds of their optimum utility, considered on dispassionate grounds (if there, are any of the kind) but on the basis of pulls and pressures exerted from the electoral arena.

The Indian state with its claims on welfare came to function in an arena that was federal in nature. Over time this federalism entrenched itself with the convergence of distinct social forces at the level of the union on one hand, and at the level of the states, on the other. Given the division of powers between the union and states, several measures of welfare came under the purview of the states and the others of the union.

Welfare state dispenses welfare through a set of institutions. In India, often such institutions had to be freshly crafted and they came to be fashioned in an ethos that was preceded by a hierarchical and highly rank-conscious bureaucracy. The welfare state in India is a poor delivery device. It has been accused as being incompetent and unable to cater to the needs of the underprivileged and disadvantaged sections of the society. It has to be admitted that given the size and population of India, welfare measures in the country were relatively insufficient. The inability of the state to reach to the marginalized and the disadvantaged sections of the society led to the retreat of the state from social goals that the Planning Commission evinced. The deviation of the Planning Commission from the socialistic objectives planned immediately after independence is not less significant in this regard (Frankel, 2005: 246–92). Among the various aspects of economic liberalization policy, the central issue at stake was the relative role of the state and market in the operation and management of the national economy. Contemporary movement in economic policy reform has involved the retreat of state and giving up of many of its economic functions in favour of the market, which has been accorded a wider and increasingly important role. It is necessary also to question as to what ought to be the appropriate relationship between the state and the market for purposes of effective economic performance (Bhaduri and Nayyar, 1996: 123–55).

Therefore, the welfare state in India has different trajectories of development, distributive justice, sustaining pluralism while wielding them into the bonds of a nation, representative democracy, fragility of public institutions, federal impulses, making it a variant of a kind irreducible to its counterparts elsewhere, particularly in the West.

The Critique of the Welfare State in India

In India, the state was basically a *mai-baap* state responsible for meeting a range of welfare needs of the people. The significant legitimization for state intervention in a wide range of economic and social areas was provided by the ideology of development. The dominant belief was that mass poverty at the root of India's social backwardness and underdevelopment could be removed by such intervention creating conditions for a more egalitarian and just society (Chatterjee, 1998: 8–9). The equal and just society was primarily seen in terms of distribution of goods, rather than rights.

However, despite such a concern being displayed through planning, most of the policies remained at the populist level. Besides, even the Nehruvian model failed to institutionalize its ideological preferences. Indira Gandhi's regime displayed greater interventionism and highlighted a policy of 'uplifting the poor' (*Garibi Hatao*). Yet it did not bring in much change except for the rhetorical deviations. The developmental model only perpetuated marginalization of millions of people and reinforced inequality. As a result, demand groups targeted the state for its failure. It was in 1970s that few marginalized sections of the society grew to be assertive and demanded some or the other provision for their upliftment. The inability of the state to govern becomes the target of the protests alongside the unfulfilled agenda throwing up challenges before the Indian 'socialist' state as was the case with the European welfare states faced with a different set of problems (Rudolph and Rudolph, 1987: 8).[22]

Besides, the welfare policies often put across were not implemented seriously. The socialist commitments often pursued by the Indian leaders turned out to be shallow. The socialistic rhetoric was advanced to build political capital, but policies in favour of the poor were seldom pursued vigorously (Kohli, 2002: 2). Much of the opposition to welfare state in India did not come up through the ideological route but on grounds of 'fiscal crisis' of the state. Since the governments were facing resource crunch, it affected the financial flow to public expenditure, leading to cutback in social services and other welfarist interventions.

Welfare Programmes in India: An Assessment

Among the important goals that India wanted to realize during its independence era was the 'welfare of the society'. This goal remains central even today. "... reform policies cannot tilt too heavily in favour of the wealthier sections of the population and the welfare role of the state can not be done away with" (Mooij, 2005: 38).

The welfare state in India since independence intervened through the domain of planning, policy-making and institution-building (Arora, 2005: 12). Under the democratic polity, it sought to build up a mixed economy committing itself to a wide ranging roles and responsibilities. A regulatory system was acquired to keep the private sector under its control and also to exercise directive, protective, promotional and welfare responsibilities in relation to the economy and society. These responsibilities were carried with direct intervention but also through budgeting, fiscal, monetary and pricing policies etc. and securing outcomes of work by regulating minimum wages, working hours, and social security provisions.

Public provision for education and health services was also considered important and their significance was asserted in various plans. Constitutional safeguards were provided and special measures were taken for the religious and linguistic minorities. Development and social welfare became state priorities. The Children's Act, the Dowry Prohibition Act and the Scheduled Castes and Tribes (Prevention of Atrocities) Act were passed and numerous welfare schemes also were adopted to help specific sections of society—SCs/STs, women, children and the disadvantaged.

With economic reforms India experienced a major shift though the substantive articulation and consequences of it may not be wholly anticipated. Such a shift is yet to find a definite articulation. It provides for a reorganization of relations across the state, market and civil society affecting public domain (Arora, 2005: 16). In the changing context, the role of the state is transformed from a regulator to a facilitator of the market. As such, many regulatory practices are dismantled, though new ones are getting formed to respond to the changing scenario. Reduction of subsidies and privatization is secured along with the changing precepts of the welfare state. The role of international financial institutions is significantly increased even in defining policy and policy framework. At the same time, there is also a significant growth in civil society institutions that argue for rights and justice of people.

There has been a general progress over the years in the provision of public consumption and welfare measures for the poor in the form of health and sanitation, drinking water, nutrition, housing, education, transport, roads, communication and electricity. But, the facilities created are indeed meagre in proportion to the total minimum needs, even though the budget in these years allotted a considerable fraction of the budget to these ends. Jean Dreze says that even if the poverty reduction figures are valid, which many economists dispute, the economy would have to grow at a much faster rate than even the most optimistic estimates if it were to truly improve the lot of the poor (Waldman, 2005).

Indian welfare state was crafted with the multi-fold agenda of providing preferential policy to the lower strata of the society: (i) dispense resources to vulnerable sections of society, such as women, children, backward classes; (ii) extension of civil and political rights to the vulnerable sections of society; (iii) protecting the cultural rights of the linguistic and cultural minorities; (iv) provision for federal structure; (v) caring for the individual security of the citizen; (vi) institutions to protect national security; and (vii) a bureaucracy with developmental priorities. However, in the changed context, many of these assumptions of such a welfare state have undergone significant changes. But, given the nature of democracy in India, it is impossible to whittle down certain provisions of welfare. State is constrained to commit more welfare activities due to political compulsions today.

During the 1990s, Indian economy has fared reasonably well in terms of economic growth and related macro-economic indicators and it ranks among the ten fastest growing economies in the world, in contrast with its earlier image of laggard economy (Dreze and Sen, 2002: vi). The government has also initiated measures to persuade ministries/departments towards a close monitoring of the outcomes of the social sector measures (Arora, 2005: 20). The inadequate health and education facilities can render the best policies hollow. Resource scarcity and inadequate mobilizations of resources can dislocate the best of the social sector measures and safety nets. Hence, a close monitoring is essential to make the social sector benefits reach the target groups.

Economic growth and distributive justice through income transfers help to promote economic and social equality. Equality plays a predominant role in the construction of the welfare state even today and the system has been attuned to the promotion of egalitarian principles by increasing social rights, reducing wage gaps and by developing social benefits. In this respect, the redistributive perspective of the welfare state retains considerable support.

The welfare state has come a long way from colonial welfare provisions to the present ad-hocist 'work-fare state'. The present neo-liberal ideology undermines the welfare state citing the disadvantage it has on human initiative and burdensome effect on the economy. The welfare state is a form of human investment: investment in education, health, nutrition care of the children and increase in social productivity. The welfare philosophy strengthens social justice, equality and liberty. Social justice provides considerable ground for income redistribution and other welfare services (Fulinwider, 1988: 263).

NOTES

1. See Biswas (1985: 14). Firstly, it emphasized that every human being is entitled to a minimum standard of living such as food, clothing and shelter. Secondly, it emphasized on the expansion of living standard with the existing knowledge and physical resources and the third principle held that state has the right and duty to act when private initiative fails.
2. See Jayal (1999: 31–51). Jayal has argued that the Indian state was interventionist with a developmental edge than a welfare state.
3. The point that Alexis de Tocqueville makes in *Democracy in America* (1835) is pertinent here. He states that liberalism calls for liberty, while democracy for equality.
4. Poverty became a central issue of concern in nationalist thought and the role of the state came to be accordingly valorized. In the 1870s, the Indian leaders began a serious inquiry into the economic ills of India under British rule. Dadabhai Naoroji wrote about the existence of absolute poverty in India in 1876 in his essay *Poverty of India* and drew attention towards the issue of health as well. Later, G.K. Gokhale also expressed his concern about it in his keynote address at his famous budget speech of 1902. The Indian National Congress (INC) reiterated this concern session after sessions and the nationalist press highlighted the issue too.
5. See Uppal (1984: 5–6). It is further stated that among such proposals, the *Planned Economy for India* (1934) by M. Visvesvaraya needs special mention. It contained a clear statement of objectives and targets and the method to achieve them within a period of five to ten years. He argued that poverty and unemployment in India are due to lack of reasoned policies and programmes to improve income and wealth of the people. See, *Towards an Approach to the First Plan*, p. 3. He listed 'Ten Urgent Requirements', for the economy to plan: elementary mass education; training in defence; industrialization with special emphasis on heavy industries; balancing occupation and arresting the tendency to ruralization; Indian control of finances, currency and exchange, and of the Reserve Bank and gold reserves; Indian control of railway administration; Indian control of protective tariffs and railway freight; Indian

control of purchase of railway and other stores; and training in the highest branches of administration; commerce and technology.

6. See Mukerjee (1986: 165). Also see, Harry Cleaver. 1990. *Socialism*, March, 1990. http://www.eco.utexas.edu/facstaff/Cleaver/socialismessay.html. For a better understanding on the relation between socialistic and democratic principles after independence see, Granville Austin. 1999. *Working a Democratic Constitution: The Indian Experience*, pp. 99–122.
7. See Austin (1999: 71). Austin writes, that "The Constituent Assembly laboured arduously for the social revolution when drafting the Fundamental Rights, Directive Principles of State Policy and the provisions for the uplift of disadvantaged sections of the society." The members of the provincial government also campaigned for the abolition of zamindari system. (See *Congress Election Manifesto*, AICC, 1945).
8. Dr Ambedkar said, "Surely ... it is not the intention, to introduce in this part these principles as mere pious declarations. It is the intention of this (Constituent) Assembly that in future both the legislature and the executive should not merely pay lip service to these principles but that they should be made the basis of all legislative and executive action ... ." (*Constituent Assembly Debates,* 1948, Vol. VII).
9. See Jayal (1999: 39). It is further established that "The idea of a right to welfare or justice was clearly precluded, possibly on account of the Fabian intellectual influence on early policy-makers and the problem of hunger has thus rarely been articulated in the vocabulary of rights".
10. See Government of India, 1951. http://planningcommission.nic.in/plans/planrel/fiveyr/default.html.
11. See Nayar (2001: 50). Nayar also argues that these three features were the development pattern of India until the beginning of the 1990s.
12. See Byres (1998: 3). For Jagdish Bhagwati's views on globalization see, Bhagwati (2004). However, it is interesting to know that Bhagwati was a proponent of planning till 1960s.
13. Health outcomes had shown improvement in India. Earlier, the life expectancy showed an increase from 50 to 61 years over the 1970–93 period. Infant mortality too declined from 137 to 74 per 1,000 live births over the same period, and to 65 per 1000 by 1996.
14. See, World Bank Report, 2001a, pp. 32–39 and 81–89, and *World* Development Indicators, 2001, Table 2.7, http: //www.worldbank.org.
15. See for details, Government of India, "National Health Policy", http://mohfw.nic.in/np2002.htm.
16. Supriya Roy Chowdhury discusses the recent case studies of three different firms—Pepsi, Bata and Toyota Kirloskars in Bangalore and the

way they were handled against the large interests of the workers. Refer, pp. 269–279.

17. For example, in states like Uttar Pradesh, no governments took in the reform of panchayats apart from passing conformity legislation in 1994 following the 73rd amendment. See, Sudha Pai, "Populism and Economic Reforms", in Jos Mooij (ed.), 2005: 120.
18. To gain clear picture on the public expenditure on health care at the centre and state level, see, Ramesh Bhat and Nishant Jain, "Analysis of Public and Private Healthcare Expenditures", *Economic and Political Weekly,* January 7 (2006: 57–68).
19. See, UNDP, Human Development Report 2006, http://hdr.undp.org.
20. See, "Tokenism or Empowerment? A Comparative Analysis of Public Policies and Institutions of Disadvantaged Communities in India", p. 3, http: //www.hasan.pdf.
21. Suhas Palshikar argues that the hegemonic section of the society itself has internal divisions which block them to achieve hegemony of their group. See, Suhas Palshikar, "Whose Democracy Are We Talking About? Hegemony and Democracy in India", in Vora and Palshikar (eds.), 2004: 127–163.
22. For the reference on the European welfare state see, Offe (1984: Chapter 9).

REFERENCES

AICC. 1945. Congress Election Manifesto. New Delhi.

———. 1948. Report of Economic Programme Committee. New Delhi.

Alam, Javeed. 2004. "What is Happening Inside Indian Democracy", in Rajendra Vora and Suhas Palshikar (eds.), *Indian Democracy: Meanings and Practices*. New Delhi: Sage Publications.

Arora, Dolly. 2005. *Social Sector Development: From 'Outlays' to 'Outcomes'*. New Delhi: Indian Institute of Public Administration.

Austin, Granville. 1999. *Working a Democratic Constitution: The Indian Experience.* New Delhi: Oxford University Press.

Bagchi, Amiya. 2002. "Mechanisms of Exploitation from the Age of Merchant Capital in Europe to the Maturing of Industrial Capitalism", *Economic and Political Weekly,* June 8. http://www.epw.org.in/ howArticles. php?root=2002&leaf=06&filename=455.

Barry, Norman. 2002. *Welfare.* New Delhi: Viva Books.

Basu, Kaushik. 2004. "The Indian Economy: Up to 1991 and Since", in Kaushik Basu (ed.), *India's Emerging Economy: Performance and Prospects in the 1990s and Beyond*. New Delhi: Oxford University Press.

Bava, Noorjahan. 2004. "Evaluating India as a Welfare State", in M.M. Sankhdher and Jain Sharda (eds.), *Social Security, Welfare and Polity: Explorations in Political Science.* New Delhi: Deep & Deep Publications.

Biswas, Oniel. 1985. *From Justice to Welfare*. New Delhi: Intellectual Publishing House.

Bhaduri, Amit and Nayyar, Deepak. 1996. *The Intelligent Person's Guide to Liberalization.* New Delhi: Penguin Books.

Bhagwati, Jagdish. 2004. *In Defense of Globalization*. New Delhi: Oxford University Press.

Byres, Terence J. 1998. *The State, Development Planning and Liberalisation in India.* New Delhi: Oxford University Press.

Cabinet Secretariat. 1950 Resolution (Planning).

Cleaver, Harry. 1990. *Socialism*. Http://www.eco.utexas.edu/facstaff/Cleaver/socialismessay.html

Constituent Assembly Debates. 1948.http://164.100.24.208/ls/condeb/vol7p9.htm

Chatterjee, Partha (ed.) 1998. *State and Politics in India.* New Delhi: Oxford University Press.

——. 1993. *The Nation and Its Fragments: Colonial and Post-colonial Histories*. New Jersey: Princeton University Press.

——. (ed.) 1998. *Wages of Freedom*: *Fifty Years of the Indian Nation-State,* New Delhi: Oxford University Press.

Dhar, P.N. 2003. *The Evolution of Economic Policy in India: Selected Essays*. New Delhi: Oxford University Press.

Dutta, Bhaskar. 1996. "India: Tradition of Poverty Research", in Else Oyen, S.M. Miller and Syed Abdus Samad (eds.), *A Global Review: Handbook on International Poverty Research*. New Delhi: UNESCO Publication.

Dreze Jean and Sen, Amartya. 2002. *India*: *Economic Development and Participation.* New Delhi: Oxford University Press.

——. 1995. *India: Economic Development and Social Opportunity.* New Delhi: Oxford University Press.

Dyson, Tim, Cassen, Robert and Visaria, Leela (eds.). 2004. *Twenty-First Century India, Population, Economy, Human Development and the Environment*. New Delhi: Oxford University Press.

Frankel, R. Francine. 2005. *India's Political Economy 1947–2004*. New Delhi: Oxford University Press.

Fulinwider, Robert K. 1988. "Citizenship and Welfare State" in Amy Gutmann (ed.) *Democracy and the Welfare State*. New Jersey: Princeton University Press.

Government of India.1945. Second Report on Reconstruction Planning. New Delhi.

——. 1951. The First Five Year Plan. New Delhi. http://planning commission. nic.in/plans/planrel/fiveyr/default.html

——. 1948. Resolution on Industrial Policy. New Delhi: Ministry of Information and Broadcasting.

Ferro, Manuela, Rosenblatt, David and Stern, Nicholas. 2004. "Policies for Pro-poor Growth in India", in Kaushik Basu (ed.), *India's Emerging Economy: Performance and Prospects in the 1990s and Beyond*. New Delhi: Oxford University Press.

Ghosh, Jayati. "Neo-liberal Reforms". *South Asian,* Lahore. http: //www.southasianmedia.net.

Jain, Ranu. 2005. "Minority Rights in Education: Reflections on Article 30 of the Indian Constitution". *Economic and Political Weekly,* June 11.

Jayal, Niraja Gopal. 1999. *Democracy and the State: Welfare, Secularism, and Development in Contemporary India,* Delhi: Oxford University Press.

——. 2001. "The State and Democracy in India, or What Happened to Welfare, Secularism and Development", in Vinita Damodaran and Maya Unnithan-Kumar (eds.), *Post Colonial India: History, Politics and Culture.* New Delhi: Oxford University Press.

Kohli, Atul (ed.) 2001. *The Success of India's Democracy*. New Delhi: Cambridge University Press.

Kumar, Dharma (ed.) 2005. *The Cambridge Economic History of India, Vol. II: 1757–2003*. Hyderabad: Orient Longman.

Mooij, Jos. 2005. *The Politics of Economic Reforms in India.* New Delhi: Sage Publications.

Mukerejee, Hiren. 1986. *The Gentle Colossus: A Study of Jawaharlal Nehru.* Delhi: Oxford University Press.

Nayar, Baldev Raj. 2001. *Globalization and Nationalism: The Changing Balance in India's Economic Policy*. London: Sage Publications.

Offe, Clause. 1984. *Contradictions of the Welfare State,* London: Hutchinson.

Rodrigues, Valerian. 2005. "Ambedkar on Preferential Treatment". *Seminar,* 549, May, p.56.

Roy Chowdhury, Supriya. "Labour and Economic Reforms: Disjointed Critiques", in Jos Mooij (ed.), 2005: 264.

Rudolph, Lloyd I. and Rudolph, Susanne Hoeber. 1987. *In Pursuit of Lakshmi: The Political Economy of the Indian State.* Hyderabad: Orient Longman.

UNDP. 2004. Human Development Report. New York: Oxford University Press.

Uppal, J.S. 1984. *Indian Economic Planning: Three Decades of Development.* Delhi: Macmillan India.

Vora, Rajendra and Suhas Palshikar (eds.). 2004. *Indian Democracy: Meanings and Practices*. New Delhi: Sage Publications.

Waldman, Amy. 2005. "Against All Odds, India Casts a Safety Net". *New York Times.*

Weiner, Myron. 2002. "The Struggle for Equality: Caste in Indian Politics", in Atul Kohli (ed.). *The Success of India's Democracy.* New Delhi: Foundation Books.

6

Backward Classes and Social Justice through Reservation

K. GOPAL

India is a big sociological zoo. An ancient civilization constantly struggling to adjust with contemporary modernization, the Indian social order reflects a continuum of past, present and a probable future through its innumerable shades of cultural varieties obtainable anytime at some or the other location in the sub-continent. Various kinds of human groupings—herds, nomadics, tribes, castes, classes and even voyagers without boundaries—are available here. There is so much of cultural mix obtained in India that at times one may be at one's wits end to identify what exactly India is?

The national movement provided India with a common enemy in the British to combine to fight forgetting all their differences. Independence in 1947 ushered in a new era. Democracy generated varied expectations in people according to their perceptions of freedom and equality.

The makers of independent India gave the nation in the name of its people a Constitution that secured justice, liberty, equality and fraternity and constituted it into a sovereign, socialist, secular, democratic, republic.[1] India was declared a welfare state. In spite of all hazards—economic, social and political—the country moved on the path of progress. Old transitional social evils were identified and attempts to combat them initiated. Untouchability and its practice were declared a crime. Some positive affirmative actions were initiated to provide opportunities for the Scheduled Castes (SCs) and Scheduled Tribes (STs) by way of time-bound reservations. But these (the reservations), being extended for many times as a political necessity, have become a right, because privilege once granted can hardly be withdrawn.

The Backward Classes

Indian social structure is complex and complicated. As it continues to exist with several age-old traditional set-ups that try to cope up with contemporary needs, the situation gets more and more woolly. The traditional status and modern role conflict is obvious in social life.

At the cultural levels also contradictions emerge. The isolated tribes have their exclusive social structure. But, the tribes in transition present a conflicting picture.

There are the rural and urban differences at different levels. Rural connectivity is a very important factor. In the post-independence period transportation and communication have developed phenomenally. Increased mobility for any reasons affects social mobility.

Class and caste sometimes are used as synonyms which they are not. Class is a socio-economic flexible category while caste is a rigid variable. While identification of class is difficult but that of the caste is certain and once for all. One can hardly change the caste he or she is born in.

While Articles 341 and 342 of the Constitution of India specify the Scheduled Castes (SCs) and Scheduled Tribes (STs) respectively, "some state governments have also specified other categories of people known as the 'Other Backward Classes' and the denotified, nomadic and semi-nomadic communities. No precise figure of the population of these categories is available".[2] The statement about the figures of Other Backward Classes (OBCs) still holds true.

"Our Constitution enjoins upon the states to ensure justice and equality of status and of opportunity to every citizen. Article 17 of the Constitution abolished untouchability and forbids its practices in any form. Article 38, which forms part of the Directive Principles of State Policy, mentions that the state shall strive to promote the welfare of the people by securing and protecting, as effectively as it may, a social order in which justice, social, economic and political, shall inform all the institutions of the national life. Article 46 of the Constitution requires that the states shall promote with special care the educational and economic interests of the weaker sections of the people in general and the SC and the ST in particular. The rights of the minorities are also specifically mentioned in the Constitution particularly in part III which enshrines the Fundamental Rights ... with a view to providing an integrated thrust to the development of these sections of the population, a new Ministry of Welfare was constituted on 25th September, 1958."[3] The year beginning with 14 April 1990 was observed as the year of social justice and programmes connected with that entrusted to a separate centenary cell.[4]

The centenary celebrations were extended up to 14 April 1992. Implementation of action plan lasted up to 14 April 1992. The government conferred Bharat Ratna on Baba Saheb Dr B.R. Ambedkar. 14 April 1990 was declared a national holiday. It was celebrated with the virat sammelan at Ambedkar Stadium, New Delhi. Article 338 was amended replacing the Special Officer (Commissioner) for SCs and STs with National Commission for SCs and STs with special powers and functions and status of Scheduled Castes given to neo-Buddhists.[5]

The Eighth Plan was dedicated to Baba Saheb, and sub-titled as 'Plan for Socio-Economic Justice'. The plan also called for introduction of economic package for comprehensive economic development of certain extremely backward communities like nomadic, semi-nomadic, *Vimukta Jati* communities and artisans and occupational communities like Barbars, Dhobis, etc.[6]

The First Backward Classes Commission

The state having pledged itself to be a welfare state could not and did not close its eyes from the backward castes and classes. The First Backward Classes Commission, also known as Kaka Kalelkar Commission, was set up on January 29, 1953 and it submitted its report on March 30, 1955.[7] The Commission had set four criteria for identifying backwardness. They were:

(i) Low social position in the traditional caste hierarchy of Hindu society.
(ii) Lack of general educational advancement among the major sections of a caste or community.
(iii) Inadequate or no representation in government service.
(iv) Inadequate representation in the field of trade, commerce or industry.

On the basis of above criteria, the Commission prepared a list of 2,399 backward castes or communities for the entire country, and 837 of these were classified as the 'most backward'. The Registrar General and Census Commissioner of India assisted the Commission in making projections of 930 backward castes or communities.[8]

The following are some important features and recommendations of the Commission:[9]

(i) Understanding caste-wise enumeration of population in the census of 1961.

(ii) Relating social backwardness of the class to its low position in the traditional caste hierarchy of Hindu society.
(iii) Treating all women as a class as 'backward'.
(iv) Reservation of 70 per cent seats in all technical and professional institutions for qualified students of backward classes.
(v) Minimum reservation of vacancies in all governmental services and local bodies for OBCs in the following scale:

Class I	25%
Class II	33.33%
Class III and IV	40%

Not only were the members opposed to caste being the basis of identifying backwardness but the chairman himself felt so. In his 30-page forwarding note to the President, Kaka Kalelkar stated: "I was prepared to recommend to the government that all special help should be given only to the backward classes and even the poor and the deserving among the upper classes may be safely kept out from the benefit of this special help. But my eyes were, however, opened to the dangers of suggesting remedies on the caste basis when I discovered that it is going to have a most unhealthy affect on the Muslim and Christian sections of the nation. It is only when the report was being finalized that I started thinking anew and found that backwardness could be tackled on a basis or number of bases other than that of caste. I only succeeded in raising the suspicion of the majority of my colleagues that I was trying to torpedo the recommendations of the commission."[10]

Kaka Kalelkar further observed: "It cannot be denied that the caste system is the greatest hindrance in the way of our progress towards an egalitarian society, and the recognition of the specified castes as backward may serve to maintain and even perpetuate the existing distinctions on the basis of caste ... if the entire community, barring a few exceptions has thus to be regarded as backward, the really needy would be swapped by the multitude and hardly receive any special attention or adequate assistance nor would such dispensation fulfill conditions laid down in Article 340 of the Constitution."[11]

While discussing the first Backward Classes Commission, one should remember that it was in 1953—the first decade of post-independence—when Indian leadership, both in ruling and opposition benches, comprised leaders having made sacrifices during the freedom struggle. They might have made certain mistakes but their intentions could never be doubted. The political environment of the time can be assessed by this only that "Congress leaders had decided that the past must be put behind the county, and that every one should be engaged in the new tasks before the country. Accordingly, as we have seen, Dr Rajendra Prasad and Sardar Patel instructed the then Chief Minister of Bombay, B.G. Khare, to ensure that Ambedkar was elected to the Constituent Assembly from Bombay, even if this had to be done by getting some others to withdraw".[12] And finally, "Of the seven members who were selected for the Drafting Committee, only one was a Congressman. Ambedkar, who had all along opposed the Congress and denounced the leaders who were now in control, was elected Chairman of the Committee".[13]

Not only that Ambedkar was the chairman of the committee, he was also law minister in Nehru's cabinet, which was a surprise to him even. In Ambedkar's own words, "I was called by the Prime Minister to accept the office of the law minister in the Cabinet. The offer came as a great surprise to me. I was in the opposite camp and had already been condemned as unworthy of association when the interim government was formed in August 1946. I was felt to speculate as to what could have happened to bring about this change in the attitude of the Prime Minister. I had my doubts ... but I kept my doubts at rest and accepted the offer of Prime Minister on the ground that I should not deny my cooperation which it was asked for in the building up of our nation".[14]

Another part of the story is that "Ambedkar had started coming over to Jagjivan Ram's house. One day he told him to put in a word with Gandhiji to have him (Ambedkar) included in the Cabinet. Before, talking to Gandhiji, he (Jagjivan Ram) talked to Sardar Patel. Sardar Patel said, do what you think is appropriate. He (Jagjivan Ram) got into quite a quandary—that Ambedkar had always opposed Gandhiji and the Congress, how could he now recommend his case to Gandhiji? Even so, given his large heartedness, he has surrendered in front of you please request Nehruji so that he may be taken into the first Cabinet".[15]

Later, on 10th October 1951 Ambedkar resigned of his own after four years, one month and 26 days.[16]

Those were trying times for India: "The country was partitioned, almost six million were displaced and had to be rehabilitated, almost six lakhs were killed; the country became independent; almost 560 princely states had to be integrated into the rest of the country; Gandhiji was assassinated … it was but natural that these events affected many of the basic conceptions".[17]

With all these happenings, democracy with universal adult suffrage was introduced in nascent, infant, independent, traditionally caste-ridden and hierarchy-oriented segmented Indian society. In one go almost 50 per cent of the Indian population, i.e., the patently 'weaker section' were granted their right to vote without any struggle… . A society that practised untouchability, and at certain places even unapproachability and unseeability, granted equal vote power to each and every adult man or woman. In spite of various odds India moved on road to development. The early 1950s witnessed "the first general elections in India, first amendment to the Constitution, first 5-year plan implemented, and first Asiad in Delhi".[18]

Due to the charismatic leadership of the Congress at the centre and an ineffective opposition, nothing perceptible happened at the all-India level. At the state level, some of them went to the non-Congress parties. In 1974, a veteran socialist and Sarvodaya leader, Jai Prakash Narayan (fondly known as JP) gave a call for total revolution and led a movement for dissolution of the Bihar Assembly … On April 15, 1975 JP also led a 'People's March' to Parliament.[19]

Seventies was the most troubled decade in independent India. The third war with Pakistan broke out in 1971 and Bangladesh was born. There was chaos and turmoil everywhere. JP made a call to police to revolt. Though the things appeared to be in a somewhat controlled manner during the first six months of emergency. It must be interesting to remember that JP's 'Total Revolution' started from Gujarat in 1974 and it was clearly against reservation in medical and engineering courses. JP and thousands of his supporters were put in jails all along the country. It should not be forgotten that after 19 months the democratic process was restored.[20]

It was the decision of the same people on their own initiative to lift emergency who imposed it in 1975. Those detained in jails were released. Elections declared in February and after full throated electioneering they were held in March. The people of India suitably punished those who clamped emergency. Congress was defeated lock, stock and barrel—virtually reduced to dust.

In 1975 Indira Gandhi's election to Lok Sabha was declared 'void' by the Allahabad High Court. On June 25, 1975 the state of emergency was declared in the country.

The events that followed the emergency are presented in chronological order as under: Censorship introduced on August 5, 1975; RSS, Anand Marg, Jamat-i-Islami and 23 other organizations banned; the Maintenance of Internal Security Act Bill approved by parliament on September 26, 1975; the Constitution (30th Amendment) Bill, placing elections of the President, the Vice President, the Prime Minister and the Speaker of Lok Sabha beyond the scrutiny of the judiciary, approved by the Parliament; President suspends seven freedoms guaranteed by Article 19 of the Constitution on January 9, 1976; Lok Sabha passed the 42nd Constitution Amendment Bill making India a Socialist, Secular, Democratic Republic and laying down the fundamental duties of citizens; President dissolves Lok Sabha on January 18, 1977; government relaxes rules of emergency to permit normal political activity and electioneering on February 3, 1977; sixth general elections held on March 16–20, 1977; emergency withdrawn on March 21, 1977; Janata Party and its allies gained absolute majority in Lok Sabha on March 22, 1977; ban on RSS and other organizations lifted on March 24, 1977; Morarji Desai sworn in as Prime Minister on April 30, 1977; nine Congress-ruled states placed under the President's rule on December 19, 1978; the Lok Sabha expelled Mrs Indira Gandhi from the House and sentenced her to imprisonment for a term lasting its prorogation till December 26, 1978; Morarji Desai resigned as Prime Minister and Charan Singh took over on July 17, 1979, heading Janata (S)-Congress coalition; President dissolves Lok Sabha on August 21, 1979 and ordered year-end general elections; JP died on October 8, 1979; Indira Gandhi's Congress (I) won two-thirds majority in Lok Sabha on January 10, 1980; Raj Narayan expelled from Lok Dal and forms Janata (S) party; and Janata Party split again and members with RSS links form BJP (Bhartiya Janata Party) with Atal Bihari Vajpayee as its president.[21]

The old icon JP was the brightest star in post-emergency. The entire opposition combined to make 'Janata Party'. But it was the same old folks, who were aspiring for power since 1947, were now seeking their pound of flash. Some more drifted from Congress to try their luck, most prominent among them was Babu Jagjivan Ram who too ditched Congress (I) to form Congress (J) and probably believed that the Bihari affinity with JP might bring him good fortune. But there were many contenders—most prominently Morarji Bhai, Chaudhari Charan Singh and may be some more. 'Janata' was not an ideology; it was an opportunity. JP had to struggle very hard to somehow get Morarji Bhai the 'biggest cake piece' prime ministership of India. He was the first non-Congress Prime

Minister of India—an old Congressman. The inner battle for chair continued. Though others were also tipped but they remained dissatisfied. Morarji Bhai had to resign on July 15, 1979 and Chaudhari Charan Singh took over as PM on July 17. The President dissolved the parliament on August 21. Chaudhary Charan Singh has the dubious distinction of being the only Prime Minister of India, who never faced the parliament.

Two Commissions appointed by the Janata regime are quite significant—both socially and politically. The State Commission to enquire into 'Emergency Excesses' and the Mandal Commission for 'OBCs' Reservations' are more relevant for the present issue.

"The Deputy Registrar General was asked to conduct a pilot survey to see if backwardness could be linked to occupational communities instead of caste. Such survey was undertaken but it failed to throw up the desired criteria ... the central government ultimately took a decision that no all India list of backward classes should be drawn up nor any reservation made in the central government service for any group of backward classes other than the Scheduled Castes and Scheduled Tribes."[22] Consequently, on August 14, 1961, the Ministry of Home affairs addressed all the state governments stating "while the State Governments have the discretion to choose their own criteria for defining of backwardness, in the view of the Government of India it would be better to apply economic tests than to go by caste".[23]

It had been a general perception that Congress was voted to power mainly due to SC/ST and Muslim support. Those in the opposition therefore, eyed on distracting these groups away from Congress. Janata Party, in order to attract OBCs towards them, notified the Mandal Commission on January 5, 1979. It was an all-OBC Commission chaired by B.P. Mandal, with L.R. Naik (MP) as the only Scheduled Caste (SC) member, who joined after the resignation of Deen Bandhu Sahu on November 5, 1980. "During the visits of the Commission or any sub-committee appointed by them to any state and during any sittings held by the Commission or the sub-committee in any state, the Commission may co-opt two persons, who belong to the state and who are members of backward classes to be additional members of the Commission or the sub-committee as the case may be".[24]

So, largely, it was the Commission of the OBCs, by the OBCs and for the OBCs. Initially, the Commission was supposed to submit its report in a year's time, i.e., on 31st December 1979. It was later extended up to 31st

December 1980 through three extensions. It may be recalled that the Commission got its two extensions—1st April to 30th September 1980 and 1st October to 31st December 1980—by the Congress government at the centre. In toto the Commission identified 3,743 communities as OBCs. The Commission recommended a reservation of only 27 per cent although their population is 52 per cent of the total.[25]

It may be noted that the work started after the inaugural speech of Morarji Desai on 21st March 1979 and ended with the valedictory address by Smt. Indira Gandhi on 12th December 1980. In its preface Mandal writes: "Technically speaking, the Commission has taken 24 months to complete its work. In actual effect, the working time available to us was much shorter .... It became fully operational in the middle of 1979 .... By the time the Commission's work got into full swing, the Parliament was dissolved in August 1979 and states got busy with preparations for the next general elections. By the time these elections were over, nine state assemblies were dissolved .... The above developments had an unsetting effect on the work of the Commission, specially so far as its tour to various states was concerned. The progress of the country-wide socio-educational field survey, which commenced in February 1980, was also seriously hampered. Owing to paucity of time and some what disturbed conditions in the seven north-eastern states, the Commission could not undertake the tour of this region."[26]

The Commission based its caste/community-wise data estimates on the basis of 1891 and 1931 censuses. The Commission also undertook visits of different states and union territories for ascertaining the ground social reality. The detailed tour programme is given in Table 1, which indicates that the Commission toured the country in two phases. Phase I from 14th May 1979 to 19th October 1979 for 32 days and phase II from April 9, 1980 to October, 17 1980 for 62 days. It may be remembered that the only SC member L.R. Naik joined after the 1st phase visit was over. The table also reveals that the Commission felt the necessity of revisiting two states, viz., Bihar (Mandals's home state) and Madhya Pradesh, thus spending 13 days in Bihar and 11 days in Madhya Pradesh. Three union territories, viz., Chandigarh, Delhi and Pondicherry, were allotted only one day and the three distant places Goa, Daman and Diu too were covered only in one day.

The Mandal Report was submitted in 1980. Initially it had the same fate as that of Kaka Kalelkar Report—eating dust. "The governments'

Table 1
States and Union Territories Visited by Backward Castes Commission, 1979–80

Name of the State/UT	***Duration***		***No. of Days***
	From	***To***	
Chandigarh (U.T.)	14–05–79	—	1
Haryana	15–05–79	16–05–79	2
Delhi (U.T.)	18–05–79	—	1
Bihar	26–05–79	30–05–79	5
Kerala	23–06–79	25–06–79	3
Tamil Nadu	26–06–79	30–06–79	5
Pondicherry (U.T.)	28–06–79	—	1
Bihar*	11–09–79	18–09–79	8
Jammu & Kashmir	14–10–79	19–10–79	6
Karnataka	09–04–80	13–04–80	5
Sikkim	21–05–80	23–05–80	3
Orissa	20–06–80	22–06–80	3
West Bengal	23–06–80	26–06–80	4
Maharashtra	20–07–80	23–07–80	4
Goa, Daman and Diu (U.T.)	25–07–80	—	1
Andhra Pradesh	26–07–80	30–07–80	5
Madhya Pradesh	15–08–80	20–08–80	6
Rajasthan	26–08–80	30–08–80	5
Uttar Pradesh	06–09–80	12–09–80	7
Gujarat	18–09–80	21–09–80	4
Dadra & Nagar Haveli (U.T.)	22–09–80	23–09–80	2
Himachal Pradesh	29–09–80	02–10–80	4
Madhya Pradesh*	04–10–80	08–10–80	5
Punjab	14–10–80	17–10–80	4
Total Number of Days			94

*Revisited

foot dragging on the Mandal Report is wholly understandable. To reject it is to court political disaster. To accept it is to perpetuate local dissension and fragmentation, to regress historically. It is a terrible dilemma, and it is not the government's alone."[27] Although the Congress government had granted two extensions to complete its work, the Mandal Commission Report had to wait till August 7, 1990 when the then non-Congress Prime Minister "V.P. Singh announces in both Houses of Parliament the Government's decision to reserve 27 per cent jobs for socially and educationally backward classes in services under the Central Government and public undertakings in pursuance of the Mandal Commission Recommendations".[28]

The report was treated as a vote catching device to attract the OBC vote bank by the then Prime Minister V.P. Singh. "He played this card after sacking the then Deputy Prime Minister, Jat patriarch, Tau Chaudhari Devi Lal of Haryana to consolidate his position. To display his popularity among the masses, Chaudhari Devi Lal had announced a rally in Delhi on August 9, 1990 and to counter the same. V.P. Singh announced the implementation of Mandal Commission recommendations with effect from August 7, 1990."[29]

Students of Delhi University protested against the implementation on the 10th August just after three days of the announcement.[30] "... Anti-reservation rally by the students disrupts normal life in the Capital. Finance Minister, Madhu Dandvate declares in the Lok Sabha that there is no question of any dilution of the decision to earmark 27 per cent of government jobs for socially and educationally backward classes. Delhi Administration decides to close all schools, industrial training institutions and polytechnics for 30 days as a precaution against the growing anti- and pro-Mandal Report agitation."[31]

The discontent continued. On September 16, Prime Minister V.P. Singh, while addressing a rally in Madras, declares that he is prepared to sacrifice his government but will not go back on the reservation decision on the basis of Mandal Commission recommendations. On September 19, anti-reservation agitation in the capital takes a turn for the worse as a student (Subhash Goswami) suffers serious burn injuries when he sets himself on fire in protest against the implementation of the Mandal Commission Report.[32]

Goswami's bid on self-immolation became a trendsetter. *Amar Ujala,* a Hindi daily from Meerut, reported the following figures in connection with anti-Mandal agitation quoted by the Minister of State for Home in reply to a question in the parliament:

Table 2

Loss of Life in Anti-Mandal Agitation in 1990[33]

Place	*Killed in Police Firing*	*Suicide*	*Immolation*	*Total*
Uttar Pradesh	16	28	25	69
Haryana	6	32	22	60
M.P.	—	5	27	32
Bihar	12	12	8	32
Rest of India	24	76	70	170
Total	58	153	152	363

V.P. Singh's bid to project himself as the 'Messiah' of the backwards backfired on 23rd of October when Bhartiya Janata Party withdrew its support to the National Front government and on 24th the President asks the Prime Minister to prove his majority in the Lok Sabha on 7 November, 1990.[34] This was a split in Janata Dal and on November 7, 1990 Prime Minister V.P. Singh submitted his resignation to the President after "the confidence motion was defeated in Lok Sabha by 346 votes to 142. The Congress (I), the Bhartiya Janata Party and 56 members of the breakaway Janata Dal voted against the motion".[35] But, the damage had been done. The already divided and fractured Indian society was further put on way to smaller and smaller factions. None of the two prime ministers could complete a year in office, on both the occasions, i.e., December 2, 1989 and November 10, 1990 the Congress as largest single party declined to form the government and decided to sit in the opposition. Leader of the party, Rajiv Gandhi, declared that Congress would form the government only when it is in majority. Rajiv Gandhi was assassinated on May 21, 1991. A weak Congress forms the government on June 21, 1991. In fact, an era of coalition descended at the national level after December 1989. The political ethos had declined. The attempt by all parties was to capture power by any means—fair or foul. The question of fairness did not arise as none of the parties was given a clear mandate. To acquire a majority a combination of parties and individuals from amongst independents stacked their claim to form the government. It continued till their interest was served. They broke away as and when it suited them. Between 2nd December 1989 and 19th March 1998 India had six prime ministers. One can simply imagine the political chaos in a huge country like India if 13 or 24 parties combine to form the government. The polity was communalized and criminalized. In one Lok Sabha after the other the number of criminal MPs increased. Politics ceased to be a gentleman's pastime. It became a criminalized profession. There was a sharp educational decline. Universities became dens for the criminal youth waiting to be initiated into politics. It is only during this period that *Hindutva* (majoritarianism) got the upper hand in this secular country.

The OBC Reservation Syndrome

Identification of OBC has always been tricky and problematic. Several landowning, artisan, professional castes could be identified as backward on one or the other count but the same could be advanced in other ways. It differed from location to location or with change of profession as well. In several cases, some names, new or changed ones, created problem of identification. Even the commissions criteria to work out OBC differed significantly. "While the Kaka Kalelkar Commission identified 2,399 backward castes, those identified by Mandal were 3,743—an increase of 1,344 after about 25 years."[36] The Anthropological Survey of India in October, 1985 identified 1,051 classes as backward. In the project at least 394 scholars participated in the data collection, of which 197 were from 26 different institutions. They were able to identity, locate and write about 4,384 communities including 443 Scheduled Castes, 426 Scheduled Tribes and 1,051 backward classes.[37]

How Kaka Kalelkar in 1955 identified 2,399 backward castes but did not find it worth reservation? Mandal, 25 years later, found 3,743 OBCs—an increase of 1,344 more totalling 3,743 and recommended 27 per cent reservation in government jobs and five years later the ASI project found only 1,051 classes as backward. The answer lies in the socio-political dispersion, climate and intension. After the violent reactions against Mandal's implementation in 1990 the three reputed sociologists of India who were associated with the Mandal Commission expressed their opinions in the following words: "It will only ignite discussion in the society and reinforce casteism. The report does not take into account the internal differences between the so called backward castes and treats them as a homogenous category. The fact is that some of them are quite well off and constitute the dominant sections in some areas."[38] The remarks of Prof. B.K. Roy Burman were quite damaging for the Commission. He lamented: "The report is without scientific basis. It exaggerates the number of other backward classes. It ignores every suggestion that the experts associated with it made … . They associated our names with the report without listening us or even consulting us on the basis for their ultimate findings. We don't know whether the findings were based on survey or personal impression or plain imagination. To start with, the experts did not even want caste to be the basis for identifying backward classes. The literacy level among Jats, this way, is not very different from Dhobies. But Jats have many more postgraduates. The system that the Panel adopted is unscientific. It multiplies the number of backward classes."[39] The association of the third expert is a mere formality. Similarly, Prof. M.N. Srinivas mentioned: "I wish to make it clear in this context that all I did was to attend a one-day workshop conducted by the Commission in New Delhi, when they were about to start their inquiries. That was the only occasion I met them on professional basis. Subsequently some members of the Commission paid a courtesy visit to me in Bangalore. I gave them a cup of coffee."[40]

Not only the experts, even one of the panelists, the non-OBC, SC member L.R. Naik had his reservations. He said, "During the course of my extension tours throughout the length and breadth of India I observed that a tendency is fast developing among 'Intermediate Backward Classes' to repeat the treatments or rather ill-treatments, they themselves have received from time immemorial at the hands of the upper castes, against their brethren, I mean 'the Depressed Backward Classes'. In an unequal society like ours, it is necessary that the Commission takes all precautions so that the more helpless and needy segments are not deprived of the benefits of the various safeguards by avoiding cut-throat competition among unequals … . In fact, several observers feel that the logic of democratic politics and mass mobilization has brought casteism to the centre of the stage. It is with regret. I affirm that political leaders belonging to intermediate backward classes are not immune from such aberration … . All that they (leaders) seem to be doing is to emulate some disgruntled upper castes in usurping economic and political power in the name of backward classes. This is a mental aberration which deserves outright condemnation from whatever quarters it may emanate—whether from upper castes or intermediate backward classes."[41] Mandal himself puts a question mark on the validity of his report when he laments "hardly any State was able to give the desired information".[42]

The Pandora's box of social divisiveness was opened. It did not stop there only.[43] The recent Gujarat quota movement is just one illustration. Pro- and anti-quota movements are natural by-product of Mandalization.

What is most disgusting was that working for its implementation at the higher levels in professional courses like Medicine and Engineering through the Human Resources Development Minister at the Centre, Mr Arjun Singh in the UPA government. The attempt is to force 27 per cent reservation at any and all cost, even in spite of clear verdict by the judiciary. Though "the Supreme Court has upheld 27 per cent reservation for the OBC's in the government-run higher education institutions … . The court has however, finally denied the benefit of reservation to the creamy layer of the economically privileged classes among the OBC's with an annual income of Rs 2.5 lakh or more. And it has also made the 27 per cent quota inapplicable to privately-owned institutions … . Besides directing the exclusion of the creamy layer from among the OBC's the court has suggested that there should be a periodic review by the government after 5 years whether the system of reservation has worked well."[44]

Further, "the Chief Justice said that unless the creamy layer is excluded from the caste group, there could not be a proper identification of the backward classes … he also advocated that without excluding the creamy layer, the SEBC list would not be valid".[45]

Before winding up a slightly detailed reference of the latest Gujjar quota stir in Rajasthan is very relevant.

Gujjar Quota Stir

"The Gujjars, estimated to number 1.6 crore nationwide, are already included in the other backward caste (OBC) category. They are gunning for ST status ever since Jats were declared OBCs. The other source of contention for the Gujjars is the perception that the Meenas—a community that had comparable socio-economic status—have forged ahead by virtue of being declared STs."[46]

"Being on the list of 'disadvantaged' groups, brings significant advantages in modern India … . Not only do the lists of Scheduled Castes and Tribes still exist, their membership has continually expanded since 1950 … . All this is testimony to the biggest public policy failure since our Constitution came into being."[47]

In May 2007, the Gujjar protesters virtually cut off Rajasthan from the rest of the country for almost a week. Not only the public property worth crores was damaged, 26 persons were also killed.[48] At some places there were also violent clashes between Gujjars and Meenas. Ten thousand Meenas surrounded about 200 Gujjars.[49] The Gujjars have been dealt a setback by a panel appointed by the Rajasthan government which rejected their demands. It, however, recommended an incentive package of Rs 282 crore for the 25 lakh Gujjars in Rajasthan.[50]

In May 2008, the *Gujjar Arakshan Sangharsh Samiti* (GASS) leader Col. Kirori Singh Bainsla assured the government that nothing untoward would happen as I am in complete control of the situation.[51] However, "on May 23, at around 7 am a few hundred people had assembled near Dumria railway station. Bainsla started addressing the crowd. But within hours the crowd started growing bigger, as Gujjars from nearby villages began flocking there. Suddenly a youngman from the crowd hit Bhanmal with *lathi*. As he fell down, another youth fired from a country made revolver, killing the policeman on the spot. The police first used tear gas, which was followed by the firing of rubber bullets. Around this time some one from the crowd started firing. Now, the police opened fire indiscriminately killing 16 persons ... . The assembled people did not allow the police to take the dead bodies. When Bainsla came to know that four dead bodies have been handed over to their relatives by the police, he immediately dispatched a group of people to bring back the bodies. At Sikandra in Dausa district. Suddenly the crowd of over five thousand started moving towards the police station and attacked the policemen. The police station was set on fire. This was enough for the police to open fire in which 22 persons were killed."[52] This was between 23rd and 28th of May in Bayana and Sikandra. One person was killed in Panipat on 29th of May and one policeman and two Gujjars were killed at Sawai Madhopur on 30th.

Colonel Syam Singh Raja of Bharatpur, in a TV interview, declared that Gujjars prefer to serve the forces as their priority. Their next priority is other security organizations. If these are not available then they become dacoits. They are a determined people. Once they decide to get something, they must get that. Another youngman in the interview declared we must get ST status.[53]

Between May 23 and June 18, 2008, Col. Kirori Singh Bainsla was able to keep the rail traffic away from Rajasthan for 27 days. The Mumbai-Delhi route was paralyzed. On 29th May entry into Delhi was obstructed for several hours. On these days 'the Colonel' was in full command. He was the law unto himself. The dead in police firing are not cremated. The dead bodies are kept on stir sites in Bayana and Sikandra. The government would talk to him on his will and venue. His "only unsatisfied will" was the post-mortem to be done by All India Institute of Medical Sciences doctors.

In the words of the Colonel himself, "the 5 per cent reservation given to them under a special category was more than what we were actually looking forward to".[54] Addressing a joint press conference with Gujjar leader Kirori Singh Bainsla in Jaipur, Chief Minister Vasundhara Raje announced five per cent quota for Gujjars as also Rabaris and Banjaras.[55]

Gujjar stir in Rajasthan is currently over.* What about Gujjars living in other states? The Haryana, U.P., J&K and Uttaranchal Gujjars have sympathized with the Rajasthan stir. Why should they be deprived of the benefit which Rajasthan Gujjars have been provided? There is no dearth of Bainsla's there. They too have their 'KHAP' panchayat. They could be equally aggressive. And then what about Jats and Ahirs or Yadavas? All the three—the JAG—Jat, Ahir and Gujjar have almost similar traits. They are dominant aggressive landowning castes, who share common socio-economic, political and educational traits. They cannot be treated separately. Jats and Yadavas have also contributed in their own way in Indian polity. The polity of "reservation underlines a trend of downward—as opposed to upward—mobility. Reservations have though very partially and a symmetrically—turned the ladder of caste hierarchy upside down: The further down the rings you go, the more the reserve goodies you supposedly get".[56] It is obviously a trend towards the 'political desanskritization' for material social gains.

But for the strange hypothesis of Ravinder Kaur projecting the Gujjar agitation as anti-caste and for modern democratic ideals, "where nearly hundred deaths have taken place since the agitation first came out into the open".[57] A very large majority of academics, unless they themselves are doing Dalitology or 'Dalit Sociology', are not supportive of reservations the way they have been politically superimposed. Since the implementation of Mandal recommendations in 1990 intermittently pro- and anti-reservation agitations have surfaced. The judiciary too has been involved. Had the political powers been allowed to have their way complete quota of 27 per cent would have been implemented even at the highest (post-graduate) level much earlier. But, due to anti-reservationists' strong resistance and judicial intervention, this has been delayed so far. The government is trying to implement it in round about way—creating more seats in existing colleges and opening new IITs and IIMs. The Human Resources Minister Arjun Singh, in particular, has turned the IITs and IIMs into a tool of his political ambitions. A 27 per cent OBC quota is being rammed down their throats, yet the number of open, non-quota seats has to be preserved. It was decreed, after doing the math, that the total number of IIT seats have to be expanded by 54 per cent, with next year's Lok Sabha elections setting the general dead line.[58]

* Another episode of Gujjar stir in Rajasthan has just concluded with the same fanfare.

The government is setting up six new IITs, but without campus. IIT-Rajasthan, it appears, will debut from IIT-Kanpur. That's because they have not even decided which city in Rajasthan will eventually host an IIT. Likewise, IIT, Chandigarh, Hyderabad, Ahmedabad, Patna and Bhubaneshwar will be admitting students this year, but with no infrastructure, faculty or even buildings in place. They will instead, have ghost presences in existing IITs.[59]

However, a silverlining is that "the Union Government has set up a commission for fixing reservation criteria for the economically backward classes. The commission will elicit the views of the state governments on the subject, suggest criteria for identification of economically backward classes and recommend welfare measures and quantum of reservation in education and government employment. It will also suggest the necessary constitutional, legal and administrative modalities for implementing the recommendations. The government has also formed a group of ministers to initiate a dialogue with industry and other associations to fulfil the aspirations of the SC/ST youth".[60]

Andre Beteille has analyzed the caste and class phenomena in the present context. "Nehru and his generation genuinely believed that democracy and development would bring in a new social order that would free Indians for the shackles of caste … . In many fields of activity, caste has been in decline … but there is one field, that of politics, in which caste has held its ground or even increased its hold.

The mobilization of support on the basis of caste and community has now become a universal feature of our political life. All parties engage in the practice and they all seek to defend it by the appeal to equity and justice … . This has come to be described as identity politics."[61]

In the post-independence India of 21st century with Nehruvian democracy and development have emerged '*avarna* neo-middle class' which "is now in the forefront of a political movement whose inevitable outcome will be to strengthen the consciousness of caste. If this sounds like a paradox, let me say that it will be naïve to expect democracy in India to be free from paradox".[62] However, paradoxical it might appear, but it is the ground reality, which cannot be ignored if someone is interested in understanding contemporary India. The entire 'reservation quota scenario' is a part of it.

Conclusion

Everyone seeks the services of a meritorious person in the required field at all times. Everyone needs a good driver, mechanic, electrician, doctor, teacher, lawyer, and of course politician. The emergence of middle class in general and '*avarna* and OBC middle classes' in particular has created a social crisis. In the name of equity and justice this neo-middle class wants to grab all comforts of life with scant respect for values. 'Politics' has degenerated the most. Obviously, people get the leaders they deserve or in democracy they elect the people of their own kind. That is why, MPs could be charging money for asking questions in Parliament. The Vice-President of India said that the legislatures are no longer capable of "delivering public good and contributing to effective public policy"... The number of Lok Sabha sittings has come down from a yearly average of 124 in the first decade of 1952–61 to 81 between 1992–2001—a decline of 34 per cent. For the same period, the decline for Rajya Sabha was 20 per cent. The picture in the state assemblies is no different with an average of 20 to 50 sittings a year... the annual average of the number of bills passed has come down from 68 in the first decade to 50 between 1992–2001 .... In 2007, Parliament worked for the least number of days is non-election years during the last eight years".[63] The Speaker of the then Lok Sabha Mr Som Nath Chatterjee "made an anguished cry that MPs were 'working overtime to finish democracy'... figures compiled for the Budget session alone for the past seven years show that the time lost to interruptions has varied from 13 hours to shocking 74 hours".[64]

Between December 2, 1989 and March 18, 1998 a period of about eight years and three months India had six Prime Ministers of which five did not complete a year in office and the BJP's Atal Bihari Vajpai had a shortest term of 13 days and relinquished his office after discussion on vote of confidence which he never sought as he resigned without voting. The foundation for coalition government at the Centre had been laid. It has come to stay now.

The OBC quota reservation is eating into the vitals of the higher education. The quota recipients are always conscious that they were not up to the mark. But for the quota they would not have been there. If their performance is poor or below expectation, it is taken as vengeance or prejudice of the teachers, if they do not belong to their social category.

The author, on the basis of his own long experience of teaching and communication with a large number of teachers in medical colleges and technical institutes, is convinced that a very large majority of quota/reservation students find it difficult to cope with the pressure. Of course, some of them are really brilliant and they can compare favourably with anyone.

So far it was with the students only. Unfortunately, the HRD Minister Arjun Singh was hell bent to demolish the IITs' academic structure through the latest order, signed by the Director, Technical Education in the Union Human Resource Development Ministry, which reads that the matter relating to reservation of SC, ST, OBC categories in recruitment to teaching (faculty) posts in the IITs was considered in the second meeting of SCIC (Standing Committee of IIT Council) held on 11 February, 2008. The recommendations made by the SCIC have been accepted by the Chairman of the IIT Council. Accordingly, it has been decided to implement reservation for SCs, STs, OBCs in recruitment of teaching (faculty) posts in IITs with immediate effect.[65]

The government diktat of June 9, which has been sent to all IITs, lays down 15 per cent, 7.5 per cent and 27 per cent quota in teaching positions for the SC, ST, and OBC respectively ... for subjects in Science and Technology, posts will be reserved for lecturers and assistant professors. In other areas, like management, social sciences and humanities, reservation will be applicable upto the professor level. The government ruling allows the IITs to de-reserve the posts after a year, if they do not get filled 'despite all efforts'.[66]

It may be recalled that "IITs currently have reservations for backward category candidates for administrative posts—from attendants to the level of deputy register".[67]

Obviously, this ill-conceived, unfortunate, ill-timed government order is a populist gesture as crude, cruel and criminal as the implementation of the Mandal recommendations in 1990. It is rather childish in the sense that it will not serve the purpose of vote catching for the Congress. At the ground level how many persons would be affected or benefited, and why at all the beneficiaries feel obliged to the government and why not their caste and the parties—the opposition—that has done it for them.

There is and has to be sharp reaction among the IIT academics and some of them have openly come out with their reactions. Former IIT-Madras Director, P.V. Indiresan said that "Arjun Singh has injected AIDS into IITs".[68] And Delhi IIT Professor Pankaj Jalote said that "if selection of faculty is done on anything else but merit, it will affect education".[69]

Caste-based reservation leads to injustice to the meritocracy of the entire society. So ultimately mediocrity dominates meritocracy and the society suffers. This is the scenario in contemporary India. "Indians today are more conscious of their caste identity than at independence. Caste is as salient a determinant of life choices based on public policy in modern India as it was in ancient India based on religious and social reality. And it threatens long term economic prosperity. Social cohesion and political unity alike."[70] "Because of this only Rabri Devi governed Bihar for a number of years and Mayawati is not only the U.P. Chief Minister for the fourth time, a former government school teacher is ranked a few notches below Shah Rukh Khan in the advance tax list. Not only is Mayawati's income more than that of any politician, she ranks higher than the Ambani brothers, Birlas, Bachchans, Ratan Tata and Infosys' Nandan Nilekani."[71] How strange the leader of the deprived masses is so rich, and that too, on the basis of only birthday gifts by admirers.

In a nutshell, India had enough of reservations. It now needs mass education. Mandatory education should be implemented. On economic basis all those belonging to any caste, creed, sex or any other categories, who cannot support their education, be taken care of by the government. The brighter among them be supported to the highest levels. Let merit not suffer at the bands of economic deprivation. Let professions be not the victim of reservation. Of course, Indian politicians may not support it because a really educated India would not tolerate the existing breed, but of course the politicians of the then emerging India would be like the highly educated politicians of the pre-independent India who brought freedom from slavery and for some decades led the country march on the path of social development.

NOTES

1. *Manorama Year Book.* 2000, p. 520.
2. *India 1980,* p. 122.
3. *India 1991,* p. 257.
4. Ibid., p. 258.
5. Ibid., pp. 278–279.
6. Ibid., p. 279.
7. Report of the Backward Classes Commission, 1980, p. 1.
8. Ibid.
9. Ibid.

10. Arun Shourie. *The Mandal Report the Stench of Casteism*. August 1990, op. cit.
11. Report of the Backward Classes Commission. p. 2.
12. Arun Shourie. 1997. *Worshipping False Gods*. p. 402.
13. Ibid., p. 148.
14. *Dr Baba Saheb Ambedkar: Writings and Speeches*. Vol. XIV, Part II. p. 1318.
15. Indrani Jagjivan Ram. 1995. *Dekhi Suni Beeti Batten*. Jagjivan Vidhya Bhavan, Vol. II, p. 15.
16. Arun Shourie, op. cit. p. 56.
17. Ibid., p. 523
18. *Manorama Year Book. 2000*, p. 68
19. Ibid., p. 609.
20. Ibid.
21. Ibid.
22. K. Gopal. 1991. *India on Flames*. p. 95.
23. Report of the Backward Classes Commission. p. 2.
24. Ibid., pp. 7–8.
25. K. Gopal. op. cit. See Mandalisation of Reservation. p. 106.
26. Report of the Backward Classes Commission, Preface, op. cit., p. ix.
27. A.S. Abraham. "Backwards or Forwards? Implications of Mandal Report". *The Times of India*, July 5, 1983.
28. *India 1991*, p. 1000.
29. K. Gopal. op. cit., p. 114.
30. *India 1991*, p. 1000.
31. Ibid., pp. 1000–1002.
32. Ibid., pp. 1002–1004.
33. *Amar Ujala*. Meerut. January 10, 1991.
34. *India 1991*, p. 1000.
35. Ibid., p. 1009.
36. K. Gopal. op. cit, p. 113.
37. *Hindustan Times*. Delhi. September 30, 1990.
38. Rahul Phatak. "Mandals Experts Disown Report". *Indian Express*. August 31, 1990.
39. Ibid.
40. Ibid.
41. Chandran E. Reservation for OBC.

42. Arun Shourie. "Three Sets of Facts on Mandal". *Indian Express*. September 2, 1990.
43. Pandora's Box *ToI*. Surat. May 27, 2008
44. K.V. Venugopal. "OBC Reservation: What it Holds for Future" "Alive". June 2008. pp. 10–11.
45. Ibid.
46. Pandora's Box, op. cit.
47. Ramesh Thakur. "Breaking the Race Barrier: Obama did not require quotas to reach where he has". *ToI*. Surat, June 18, 2008.
48. Sanjai Gupta. *Dainik Jagran*. June 1, 2008.
49. TV Channel Report in June, 2008.
50. Pandora's Box, op. cit.
51. S. Santosh. "On the Boil Again", *Sahara Time*. June 7, 2008.
52. Ibid.
53. TV Interview.
54. *ToI*. Surat, June 21, 2008.
55. *ToI*. Surat, June 19, 2008.
56. Jag Suraiya. "Mobs and Marriages", *ToI*. Surat, June 2, 2008.
57. Ravindar Kaur. "A Case for Inclusion", *ToI*. Surat, June 5, 2008.
58. Swagato Ganguly. "Politics Could Ruin a Once Great Institution", *ToI*, Surat, June 11, 2008.
59. Ibid.
60. IIPA Newsletter. Vol. LII, No. 6, June 2008, p. 8.
61. Andre Beteille. "The Paradox of Democracy". *ToI*. June 27, 2008.
62. Ibid.
63. *ToI*. February 6, 2008.
64. *ToI*. March 1, 2008.
65. Hemali Chhapia. 'Government Orders Quota for IIT Teachers too'. *ToI*. June 29, 2008.
66. Ibid.
67. Ibid.
68. 'HRD min Injects AIDS into IIT's', *ToI*. June 30, 2008.
69. Ibid.
70. Ramesh Thakur, op. cit. *ToI*. June 18, 2008.
71. Pradeep Thakur. 'Maya's Annual Income, jumps to Rs 60 crore'. *ToI*, February 6, 2008.

7

Marginalization, Reservation and Social Justice

A Study of a Backward Community in Karnataka

M. GURULINGAIAH

The Yadavas or Gollas is one of the backward communities in India. The Yadava category consists of about one-tenth of the total population in India. "The castes coming under this category are to be found in different parts of India, Burma, Nepal and Sri Lanka and are known as the *Ahir* in Punjab, Haryana, Himachal Pradesh, Delhi, Uttar Pradesh, Madhya Pradesh, Bihar, Gujarat and Rajasthan, the *Gopalas* and *Sadagopa* in Bengal and Orissa, *Govali* and *Gopala* in Maharashtra, *Golla* in Andhra Pradesh and Karnataka and *Idayan* and *Konar* in Tamil Nadu … ." (Rao, 1987: 124).

Two things are common to these cognate castes. First, they claim to be the descendants of the Yadu dynasty (Yadava) to which Lord Krishna belonged. Furthermore, many castes in this category have a set of occupations centering on cattle. The Krishna mythology lends a kind of legitimacy to these pastoral occupations relating to cattle, and the castes following these occupations are to be found in almost all parts of India. The present paper tries to examine reservation and social justice among Gollas of Karnataka and their role in the Yadava movement in Karnataka.

Gollas of Karnataka

Yadavas or Gollas are the backward and nomadic communities of Karnataka. They are dispersed throughout Karnataka but relatively large concentrations of them are found in Chitradurga, Tumkur and Bangalore districts. According to the Third Backward Classes Commission's Report (1988), the total population of Gollas in Karnataka was 5,85,314. They constitute about 1.5 per cent of the total population of the state. According to Stuart (1918), there are two main divisions among Gollas, i.e., Uru Gollas and Kadu Gollas (Hatti Gollas). Gollas, who live with other caste groups in the villages, are called Uru Gollas and Gollas living in exclusive settlements *(hatties)* are known as Kadu Gollas. In this context, Rao stated that "Golla is the name of another sub-caste found in Dharwad, and it suggests that the Gollas of Karnataka might have been incorporated into the Govali and the name of Lingayat Govali in Belgaum and Dharwad suggests that the Karnataka Gollas, who were converted to Veerasaivism, were retained as a separate sub-caste among the Govali" (1987: 129).

Traditionally, all the castes included in the category of the Yadavas were above the line of pollution but the rank of each caste or sub-caste varied from one region to another and within a region, from one locality to another. For instance, Kadu Gollas occupied a position lower than that of the Uru Gollas in Karnataka and they were designated as Sudras. Though bearing a common name, Kadu Gollas differ very widely in habits and customs from Uru Gollas. Nanjundaiah (1908) is of the opinion that Uru Gollas have accepted most of the customs of the caste Hindus, whereas Kadu Gollas are still following their own customs and traditions. Ethnographic studies on Kadu Gollas, such as Sherring (1974), Thurston (1909) and Iyer (1988), have revealed their typical social structure and political organization. According to them, Gollas, an offshoot of Yadavas, have migrated from northern India and settled down in the forests of the South, having their own colonies called *Gollara Hatties*. These *hatties* are not found in revenue records. In this regard, Thurston (1909) stated that "the Gollas are said to have originally migrated from northern India and are still a nomadic tribe, living in thatched huts on the outskirts of villages. Some of their social customs are akin to those of the 'Kadu Kurubas', a backward tribe of Karnataka. Iyer (1988: 219) referred to Kadu Gollas as Kalli Gollas, as their hamlets are usually surrounded by a hedge of the milk-bush (Eugenie Thirukalli). Shankaranarayana (1982: 20) and Paramashivaiah (1979: 202) endorse this view. Kadu Gollas are so called because their dwellings are always erected outside the village or jungle land, capable of affording pasture to their cattle. Iyer viewed that the names which they use 'Yadava *Kuladavaru*' (Yadava dynasty) or 'Krishna *Kuladavaru*' (Krishna dynasty) is because they believe that Krishna, who was of the Yadava race, was brought up by the women of their caste, known as *Gopis*. They also style themselves as people of *Gokula* (low tribe), either because they trace their origin to a cow or because they are professional cowherds. The caste titles they affix to their names are Golla, Gollas Gouda, etc."(Gurulingaiah, 2007 : 46).

There are several popular legends regarding the origin of the Kadu Gollas. According to a legend Gollas originally came from forests near Delhi. They were looking after the cattle and were leading a happy life. Ambe Raya and Thumbe Raya were their ancient leaders. They lived like sages. There was a lady in their clan called Chandana Gandhi. She fell in love with Moon God and got a son. His name was Chandra Murthy (later called Chandamuthi). As this child was born before marriage, elders of clan pressurized Chandana Gandhi to come out with the person responsible for her motherhood. She said the child is the son of Moon God. All the members were not ready to believe it. She challenged them and asked them to verify. According to her suggestion, a cow was exposed to sun rays and to their astonishment it became pregnant. Through the rays of the sun, the cow gave birth to a child. It was named Chithamutti. When Ambe Raya and Thumbe Raya were dying, Chithamutti and Chandramutti were young. During that time, Chandana Gandhi had a daughter from a mortal husband whom she married later and Chithamutti married this daughter. Chandamutti married Balanagamma, daughter of Adishesha. They had many daughters. Once daughters of Chandamutti and Balanagamma were carrying vessels containing ghee and the Nawab of Delhi was attracted towards them. He wanted to marry them. But he did not succeed. He troubled Chandamutti and Chithamutti. Chandamutti and Chithamutti, with their children and cattle, migrated from the river banks of Thungabhadra to Vijayanagara. They led a happy life there for some time.

Once, the cattle of Chandamutti and Chithamutti grazed crops in the land of the Vijayanagara king, so the king got angry with them and imprisoned them. The two young women belonging to barber community, who were taking food to them in prison known as Ghali and Dhooli, married them. When the king was asleep, Ghali and Dhooli diplomatically succeeded to take them out of the prison. Then, Chithamutti and Chandamutti married and took Ghali and Dhooli into their clan. As days passed, their tribe increased. They came down to Chitradurga and Tumkur areas of Karnataka and built their abodes. From here, some people went to the forest and some others went to various villages. This event led to the emergence of two separate groups called—Kadu Gollas and Uru Gollas.

According to another legend, Kadu Gollas' original place was Delhi and its surrounding areas. As they were unable to suffer the prosecution of the Muslim rulers, their chiefs migrated to the South. Two of them, Arimere *Gouda* and Mere Rame *Gowda*, remained together for a long time at a place called Ramanahalli, after which the former separated and went to a place called Uttaragutti. He had seven strong limbed sons and an equal number of beautiful daughters and had amassed considerable amount of wealth. His daughters attracted the attention of the chief of the place, Ramasulivarha, who failing to obtain them by fair means, seized them by force when they had gone to sell milk and butter. Six of the damsels however escaped to their relatives, who then migrated further South; but their cousins, the descendants of Mere Rame Gowda, who had settled near Monadihalli, did not associate with them, as they had been separated for more than two hundred years. They had to move still further South, and after a weary time of wandering, they settled in Magadi (outskirts of Bangalore), Tumkur and Chitradurga districts.

They brought an idol of their deity called Chitradevaru from Delhi and consecrated it, after holding an elaborate feast in its honour at Magadi. They spread to Ratnagiri, when one of their girls was married to the king of the place. (The descendants of this union are called Kambera Gollaru, and are looked upon as inferior to other Gollas). All this is stated to have occurred before 1271 of the Salivahana era. There were further migrations, and they mingled with various local tribes in the course of their wanderings and gave rise to many sub-divisions. Two of the sub-divisions (Arinavaru and Merenavaru) are said to be the descendants of Golla girls, who married two brothers of the 'Beda' caste—Areraya and Mereraya. There is yet another story. Their father, who was a free-booter, was taken prisoner by a Beda chieftain, and the girls, who were sent to carry food to him by stealth, were prevailed upon to marry these lieutenants of the chief in consideration of their father's release.

Stratification

There are more than 28 divisions (sub-sects) among the Gollas and they are called Kadu Golla, Hava Golla, Handi Golla, Dasa Golla, Vidya Golla, Bajanthri Golla, Helava Golla, Peddathi Golla, Uru Golla, Kuri Golla, Ganga Golla, Karama Golla, Kanchi Golla, Gowda Golla, Puja Golla, Hanuma Golla, Hasu Golla, Kettahatti Golla etc. Among these divisions, Kadu Golla is one of the dominant groups and they differ from other communities in custom, rituals and pollutions. They do not mingle with other communities, especially the Uru Gollas, nor do they intermarry. In this regard, it is stated that, "... though bearing a common name, they differ very widely in habits and customs from Uru Gollas and merit separate treatment" (Iyer, 1988: 219).

Among the Kadu Gollas, primarily, there are three exogamous clans, viz., Chandamutti, Chithamutti and Ramegowdana Kuladavaru. Every clan has a story of its origin. The clan for its existence is further divided into many sub-sects. The names of these sects are derived from those of articles in common use or from the names of the patron deities. These family names are generally known only to the headman of each village, which often consists of families belonging to a single exogamous division.

According to Iyer (1988: 22–24), the Kadu Gollas comprise of three primary exogamous clans known as Chithamuttaru also as Karadi Gollaru (Bear tribe), Chandranavaru (Moon tribe) and Ramegowdana Kuladavaru (Rame Gowda's descendants). Each of these is divided into one primary division and is prohibited from marrying within the same sect or clan. These sub-groups are called 'Bedagu'.

Iyer (1988: 223–24) has listed exogamous clans among the Kadu Gollas as follows:

Chithamuttaru		***Chandinavaru***		***Ramegowdana-Kuladavaru***	
Clan	***Symbol***	***Clan***	***Symbol***	***Clan***	***Symbol***
Karadiyavaru	Bear	Ajjaru	—	Areraya	Person
Kamberu	Pot	Arisinaka-lliyavaru	Milk-hedge	Arenavaru	A Plant
		Konanavaru	He-Buffalo	Marenavaru	Flay
		Polanavaru	—	Belloru	Joe
		Somanavaru	Moon	Bellurvaru	Place
		Yagadinavaru	—	Chiranavaru	—
				Huruliyavaru	Gram
				Masinavaru	Deity
				N. Halliyavaru	Deity
				Onakeyavar	Pestle

Another study conducted by Shankaranarayana (1982: 24–25) has also listed exogamous clans among the Kadu Gollas. They are:

Chithamuttaru	***Chandinavaru***	***Ramegowdana-Kuladavaru***
Karadi Gollaru	Ajjaru Gollaru	Arenavara gollaru
Maranavaru	Sannara	Merenavaru
	Somanavaru	Kamberu
	Bommanavaru	Kahaleyaavaru
	Konanavaru	Odeyavaru
	Polanavaru	Onakeyavaru
	Yagadinavaru	Masinavaru
		Chinanavaru
		Belloru
		Bellurunavaru

There are two sub-divisions among Chithamutti. Both of them belong to the Karadi Gollas. Karadi Gollas tie the *tali* (mangalya) at the time of marriage and they say that they belong to *'Bevinahalli Gudikattu'* and Karadi clan. Those who belong to Maranavaru Gollas do not tie the *tali* at the time of marriage and they belong to *'Nandihalli Gudikattu'*. Due to regional differences, there are sub-divisions among the Karadi Gollas and Maranavaru Gollas. For instance, Kareobanahalli and Balenahalli Karadi Gollas have separate divisions. Similarly, Kaluvarahali and Hagalavadi Maranavaru Gollas have separate divisions.

Settlement Pattern and Housing

The impact of socio-economic, cultural and geographical environment on the Kadu Gollas can be easily seen by observing their settlement pattern. According to Hoebel, "the spatial arrangement of the subgroups of a society in relation to each other, to their environmental resources, and to other societies, is called the settlement pattern" (1976: 120). Hoebel also notes, "house types are variable in their structure, depending upon the nature of the local climate and materials, the kind of subsistence economy indulged in and the nature of the social organization of the society and the kind of aggressive threats it must face from the enemies" (ibid.: 126). Similarly, Christensen (1975 : 68) notes that, "we may regard buildings as messenger from past generations, from owners and users who have left them behind as the material relics of varying ways of life. Modern buildings represent information and stability" (Gurulingaiah, 2007 : 49). Thus, the settlement pattern and housing powerfully represent the past and present life.

Kadu Gollas live in the middle region of Karnataka (particularly in the districts of Chitradurga and Tumkur) The important crops and fruits in this region are ragi, rice, coconut, groundnut, arecanut, mango and vegetables which are grown in large quantity.

Iyer says, "the Kadu Gollas live in village neighborhood lands offering abundant pasturage and facilities for cultivation. Their villages are hedged with prickly-pears, or thorns of jail, or with milk-bushes. They were probably once nomadic, but are now settled in villages of their own, though they change to new spots once every four or five years or whenever their cattle die in large numbers or some pollution is suspected to have affected. Their huts are supported by pillars. Mud walls are sometimes constructed to support the thatch, the passage is closed with thorns. The shape of the roof may be gabled or rounded, but that of the temple-house is always of the latter type. The roof consists of clay or leaves. Each *hatti* is generally composed of a number of families of the same exogamous group" (1988: 221).

Generally, Kadu Gollas live in small settlements (*hatties*) consisting of 30–40 households. There is a headman for each settlement. Every settlement generally consists of families belonging to single exogamous divisions. The houses are built of walls plastered with clay. The flooring is done with mud and doubled with cow dung and the roofs are constructed with bamboo and coconut leaves. Structurally, the houses are of two types: circular or rectangular. With one or two rooms. There is no separate allocation of rooms for cooking, dining, sleeping or storing. Today, tiled and RCC houses are indicators of their enhanced status, but most of them still live collectively.

Society and Culture

Kadu Gollas have their own unique social and cultural life. Theirs is a well-structured society. Their ultimate abode is *hatti*. While a *'kanathi'* is a cluster of many *hatties* a group of *kanathis* is called *'ambu'*. When many *ambus* are put together, it becomes a *'gudikattu'*, and when many *gudikattus* join together, it becomes a *'kattemane'*. *Kattemanes* are centres, where discussions take place, disputes heard and judgments given. They are also places where they worship the souls of their dead. These are called *'amavasye'* centres. Kadu Gollas have three *kattemanes— kareobanahalli, talavatti* and *ramanahalli*. The community leader of the Kadu Gollas has all the powers. In this regard, Nanjundaiah and Iyer (1988: 230) say that in each *hatti* or hamlet, they have a *'yajamana'* (headman) who wields extensive powers. He settles all their secular disputes and they rarely resort to courts. He is the *pujari* (priest) and conducts worship in their temples on Mondays and the oracles of the deity are manifested through him. He cures snakebites and cattle diseases by medicines and charms and whenever there is an epidemic or other serious calamity, he exhibits his practical good sense by ordering the removal of the settlement en bloc to a new site. In his caste functions, he is assisted by a Kolkar of his own caste, and a Halemaga of the Beda caste. Their tribal councils are held in places known as *kattemane,* where questions affecting the whole tribe, such as breaches of caste rules, are enquired into and settled. Such councils consist of *yajamanas* of various *hatties* and the friends of the appellate jurisdiction over the decision of smaller councils. Parties testifying before their tribal council swear by Junjappa, or the sacred sheep and they believe that if they tell lies they will be afflicted with blindness. Persons accused of adultery were sometimes subjected to ordeal of fire, being required to hold a red hot bar of iron in the hand, their innocence being established if they were not scalded. But with increasing infidelity, this has become absolute. If a person eats forbidden food, he will be required to pay a fine of 24 *anas*, and will have to purify himself by shaving his face clean, and having his tongue slightly branded. If a woman does this act, she will be ousted from the caste. For a general assault, a fine of thirteen *anas* is imposed.

Elderly men among the Kadu Gollas wear a piece of cloth round their waist and cover themselves with a blanket. Some of them also wear trousers. Traditional women do not wear blouse and ascribe the omission to Lord Krishna's act of tearing off this part of their dress in her sports with *Gopis* (maidens). They regard Krishna as their husband. Usually, they like colorful *saris*. They wear bangles of bronze. They tie their hair without combing. Widows apply some ashes on the forehead, and wear glass bangles. In this context, Thurston states that "the females don't wear the bodice *(ravike)* usually put on by the women of the country. Nor do they, in their widowhood, remove or break the glass bangles worn on the wrists, as is done in other castes" (1909: 287). Kadu Gollas are either dark or dark-brown in complexion and are of average height. The dress of males consists of a waist cloth, turban and an upper cloth, which may be either a blanket or of thick cotton stuff. Their women generally wear a white cloth, bordered with red fringe either of lines or flowers, or a coloured *sari*. The male members wear gold earrings, shaped like cobra, and use silver wristbands. Women before marriage wear silver wristlets, but after marriage it is replaced by *gollakadaga* on the left wrist. They tie their hair into a knot, and adorn it with a silver crest or flowers. These days, young girls wear *kumkuma*. Even after the death of the husband, they continue wearing it. It is also observed that, married women wear various types of modern ornaments and dresses. A black blanket is their favourite dress. Almost all the Gollas chew beetle leaves and nuts.

When a child is born, both mother and child have to spend three months outside the *hatti*. At the end of the period, the naming ceremony takes place. The mother and the child bathe and go to the village temple where the *pujari* puts into their mouth a few drops of milk of the dedicated sheep *(jennige kuri)*. Names of the Kadu Gollas are quite amusing like Karadi, Kairya, Huliya, Jadiya, Giriya, Junjappa, Kendaiah etc. Women have the following names: Rangamma, Chittamma, Kariyamma, Chinnamma, Maramma, Sannamma, Thimmakka, Jaditanna etc. According to Iyer, "Kadu Gollas observe no ceremonies for giving names to children. The *yajamana* of the caste, in communication with the patron deity, directs that the child be named after the grandmother or by any other name. But today like many other castes, they consult an astrologer and *panchanga* (calendar) and choose the day and time of celebration for naming the child"(1988). Now they use the modern names like Siddalingam, Prakash, Nataraj, Krishna, Manjunath, Shankara, Basavaraja, Deexith, Achutha, Naveena, etc., for males, and Lakshmi, Parvati, Shruti, Padma, Bagya, Leela, Sumitha, Akshata, Ashitha etc. for females.

With regard to their diet, Iyer states that "their staple food is ragi, and they are allowed to eat flesh, fish, fowl, hare, sheep and rabbit. It is, however, considered pious to avoid all animal food, and when they partake it, they never cook it in their houses, but resort to a tank, or water-course, outside and carefully cleanse and purify all the utensils used in the process" (1988: 240). Kadu Gollas eat various types of vegetables grown in the fields. They like grams very much. They eat mutton, chicken and bandicoots. Since they have their own cows, they also consume milk, curds, butter and ghee.

Reservation and Social Justice

Kadu Gollas in Karnataka have suffered from economic, political, ritual and civic disabilities. As herdsmen, milk-sellers, labourers, palanquin bearers and tenants, they are economically dependent and politically subservient to the locally dominant landowning castes. Devaraj Urs, former Chief Minister of Karnataka, opined that the economic and social conditions of the Gollas are worst and they are similar to that of the Scheduled Castes (SCs) and Scheduled Tribes (STs). Hence, they belong to the exploited and oppressed category. The Gollas in Karnataka started organizing themselves by forming caste associations in order to overcome their ritual, economic and political disabilities and also to agitate against inequalities, discrimination and deprivation. This process has led to widespread collective mobilization and in turn to social movements. The emergence of awareness among the Gollas was a gradual process, with different degrees of intensity. The Yadava consciousness among Gollas of Karnataka existed even before Independence. However, systematic organizations, movements and collective mobilization took place only after Independence.

Around the turn of the 20th century the Gollas were aware of the benefits of modern education and employment opportunities and organized themselves into caste associations. Consequently, the Yadavas of Karnataka organized themselves under the leadership of Dr B. Abbayya Naidu. They built a hostel for students in Gandhi Nagar—a central locality in Bangalore. Sriram Reddy, an ex-MP from Bangalore, who is a Yadava, is taking active interest in the welfare of the Yadavas in Karnataka. Another important leader of the community is Munivenkatappa Yadava, a businessman, who has made liberal financial contributions for the establishment of a hostel for Yadava students.

The Mysore Yadava Sangha established a scholarship fund for which Dharma Prakash Rao Bahadur K. Kuppuswami Naidu contributed one lakh rupees. The other leaders of the community who have contributed for the fund are Dr B. Jayaram, with a medical degree from Wales, Dodi Kunte Ramakrishnappa, M.V. Veerappa and B.V. Hanumanthappa. Every year, about 150 scholarships are given to students from middle school to the post-graduate levels. Most of the above mentioned leaders belong to the Uru Golla community and none of them belongs to Kadu Gollas. In organizational activities of the community, Kadu Gollas have neither the required capacity nor the courage to do so. Kadu Gollas suffered from educational, civic, ritual and communicational disabilities. However, with the advent of Independence, Kadu Gollas became aware of the benefits of education and non-traditional occupations and also got courage to establish caste association along with Uru Gollas. Most of them are keenly associated with specially the educated Kadu Gollas. The aim of the caste association is to gain educational and economic advantages and organize cultural activities. Uru Gollas and Kadu Gollas jointly started the Karnataka State Yadava Sangha in 1942 at Bangalore. Thereafter, Gollas started organizing themselves and established caste associations and hostels in various districts of Karnataka.

In the 1920s English-educated Yadavas emerged from different parts of the country, provided leadership and established the All-India Yadava Mahasabha (AIYM) in 1923, which was later (30 June 1951) changed to All-India Yadava Sangha (AIYS). Dr V.R. Khedekar, one of the founding fathers of the Mahasabha, was a notable leader during this period. The establishment of the AIYM was a great event in the history of the Yadava movement. It gave expression to the national identity of several regional Yadava associations. These regional associations then brought about awareness among people belonging to Yadava caste to realize their mythical descent from Krishna, their political supremacy and the necessity of exploiting modern educational and employment opportunities in order to make progress.

The Mysore State Yadava Sangha was affiliated to AIYS, which organized its 12th Annual Conference in 1950 in Bangalore that was attended by many delegates from South India. Speeches were delivered in Telugu, Kannada, Tamil and Malayalam, in addition to Hindi and English, and the conference created a general awakening among the Yadavas of South India, particularly Karnataka. The 52nd session of the AIYM was held in Bangalore from May 12 to 14, 1989 in Glass House, Lalbagh under the presidentship of Sri Shyamlal Yadava, State Minister for Agriculture, Government of India. Delegates from almost all the states attended the conference. The conference resolved to urge the government to extend facilities to the Yadava caste to raise good breed of cattle by providing adequate grazing land and also demanded that Gollas be given the ST tag immediately. In this process, the Karnataka Yadava Association did not lose its identity but was linked to the AIYM within a federal type of framework.

An analysis of the various resolutions passed by the AIYS at its conferences and annual meetings indicates that there were five major points of focus. First, a number of resolutions were concerned with reformatory measures, such as the abolition of dowry, abolition of the ban on widow remarriages in certain sections where this was practiced, and a strong plea for inter-sub-caste and inter-regional marriages among the Yadava castes. Secondly, there was a concern for the programme adopted by the Indian National Congress, particularly the programme to remove untouchability. Thirdly, they supported the Hindi movement and the adoption of Hindi as the national language. At the same time, they also encouraged regional languages. The AIYS also supported the anti-cow slaughter movement. Fourthly, they supported those issues about which the regional *sanghas* were interested in, for instance, the problem of inadequate grazing land for cattle which concerned the Yadava caste in different parts of India. Lastly, the resolution urged the Government of India to adopt the recommendations of the Backward Classes Commission.

The Yadavas in different districts of Karnataka have started organizing themselves for welfare activities. Thus, the Raichur District Yadava Sangha, which was established in 1954 under the leadership of H. Govindappa, a progressive farmer, is affiliated to the Mysore State Yadava Sangha. Similarly, Yadavas in Chitradurga district organized themselves under the leadership of S. Siddappa, an advocate in Karnataka High Court, and in Shimoga under Narayanappa. After Independence, Gollas of Tumkur district started organizing themselves under the leadership of L.T. Govindappa, who had been a government officer, D. Kariyappa, G.M. Naganna and other notable leaders. They established caste association in Tumkur and all talukas of the district. Further, through the caste association, they started a Yadava hostel for college students in Tumkur. Later, various Yadava *sanghas* at taluka level also started emerging. The registered Yadava associations at taluka level bear names like Taluk Yadava Sangha, Gubbi, Tiptur Taluk Yadava Sangha, Turuvekere Taluk Yadava Sangha, Chikkanayakanahally Yadava Sangha, Tumkur Taluk Yadava Sangha, Pavagada Taluk Yadava Sangha, Sira Taluk Yadava Sangha and Kortagere Taluk Yadava Sangha. Besides, the Yadavas also started associations at village level. In Madhugiri and Sira, Gollas established Yadava hostels for students under the umbrella of their taluka associations. Today, a large number of educated youths are coming forward to organize and mobilize Yadavas in the state.

The Yadavas of Karnataka also organized state and district-level conferences in various districts of the state. For example, the Mysore State

Yadava Sangha organized a conference on 3 September, 1972 at Turuvekere, Tumkur district. It also organized similar conferences in every district of the state. Meanwhile, taking the cue from their elders, the Yadava students also started organizing themselves in the state in order to fight educational problems they faced. Consequently, the First Akhila Karnataka Golla (Yadava) Students' Conference was held on 25th February, 1973 in Bangalore under the leadership of S. Siddappa. During the conference numerous problems pertaining to education and reservation in educational institutions were discussed. Another state-level conference was held at Hiriyur on 26 October, 1980 under the auspices of the Chitradurga District Gollara Sangha. This was a commendable venture in mobilizing the Yadavas from all over the state and unite them to fight for a common cause. In this conference, the members of Golla community submitted a memorandum to B.P. Mandal, who was the chairman of All India Backward Classes Commission, requesting that the Golla community should be included in the list of Scheduled Tribes (STs) so that they should be able to get all the benefits and assistance on par with STs. The Karnataka State Yadava Conference was held on 13 February, 1982 at Madhugiri in Tumkur district under the leadership of S. Siddappa, Secretary of Karnataka Yadava Sangha. During this conference, a number of resolutions such as the inclusion of Gollas in the list of STs, scholarship for the Golla students etc. were passed. The conference also urged the Government of India to implement the Mandal Commission report as soon as possible.

Soon after the national conference, which was held in May 1989 in Bangalore, an emergency conference was held on 3 September, 1989 in Bangalore again to urge the government to continue the facilities that have been provided by the Havanur Commission.

Movement for Scheduled Tribe Tag and Reservation

The Government of Karnataka in 1966 issued an order treating the Gollas as nomadic and semi-nomadic tribes granting free education and scholarships to the Golla students and reservation in admissions to technical schools and colleges and also in appointments, allotment of house sites, janatha houses and economic benefits like subsidies in the purchase of milking cattle, bullocks and agricultural implements on par with SCs and STs. These communities were granted the above said benefits without any income limit (Gurulingaiah, 2007 : 132).

Subsequently, the first Backward Classes Commission was appointed by Devaraj Urs, the then Chief Minister of Karnataka, under the chairmanship of L.G. Havanur. The Havanur Commission submitted its report in 1975, and the state government accepted its recommendations in spirit. The Commission added seven more communities, including Gollas, to the nomadic and semi-nomadic tribes' list and named them as 'Backward Tribes'. However, the Havanur Commission, while classifying Gollas under the Backward Tribes, imposed income restrictions for the benefit of reservation in admission to technical schools and colleges and other educational facilities like free-ship, scholarship and economic benefits like subsidy for purchasing bullocks, cattle and also allotment of housesites and lands. Subsequently, due to the representation made by the Karnataka Yadava Sangha, the restrictions were removed by the Chief Minister, making Gollas be able to enjoy the benefits that were enjoyed by the nomadic and semi-nomadic tribes. The government had already issued an order to the effect that the economic and social conditions of the Gollas are as worst as the conditions of SCs and STs. Hence, the Gollas were to be treated at par with SCs and STs so far as filling up the lower posts like class 'D' officials and other economic benefits.

In 1979, the order was questioned by the Veerasaiva Mahasabha in the Supreme Court. Subsequently, the state government appointed the second Backward Classes Commission, under the chairmanship of a retired Secretary of Karnataka Legislature, T. Venkataswamy, on 18 April, 1983 to suggest appropriate criteria for preparing the list of socially and educationally backward classes.

When the Venkataswamy Commission submitted its report on 31 March 1986, there was widespread rage and agitation by the Lingayats and Vokkaligas in the state against the report. Actually, the Commission had eliminated 13 castes, including the two dominant communities, the Lingayats and Vokkaligas, from the list of Socially and Economically Backward Classes (SEBCs). As a result of this, the state government, headed by Ramakrishna Hegde, was forced to reject the report and issue an adhoc order on 13 October, 1986 on reservation for a period of two years or until the next Commission is appointed and submitted its report.

The order included virtually every caste/community in the list of backward classes, thus bringing back all sections of Lingayats into the list of backward classes. The order also included certain other communities in the list of backward tribes and renamed them as Group 'A'. The Gollas were included in Group 'A'. Later, when the Congress party was elected to power, Chief Minister Veerendra Patil extended this order for another year. The succeeding government headed by S. Bangarappa continued to extend the order without taking any decision on the Chinnappa Reddy Commission's report.

After the Venkataswamy Commission's report was rejected, the Janata government, headed by Ramakrishna Hedge, had appointed the third Backward Classes Commission on 9 March 1988, under the chairmanship of a retired Supreme Court judge, M. Chinnappa Reddy, to identify socially and educationally backward classes and provide reservation for them. The Commission classified various castes/communities into three categories: category I consisting of 52 castes, category II consisting 14 castes, including Gollas, and category III consisting all other comparable SEBCs. The Commission recommended 5 per cent reservation for category I castes/communities, 28 per cent for category II castes/communities and 5 per cent for category III castes/communities. This made the magnitude of reservation for SEBCs 38 per cent thereby taking the total reservation to about 56 per cent inclusive of reservation for SCs and STs. The Commission submitted its report to the government headed by M. Veerappa Moily, who implemented it on 20 April, 1994. After the implementation, various communities, belonging to backward castes, strongly opposed and agitated against the report. Gollas also launched a strong agitation against the recommendations of the Chinnappa Reddy Commission. Actually, the Havanur Commission had treated them as a backward tribe and they were enjoying the benefits provided to the nomadic and semi-nomadic tribes, without any income restrictions. But, the Chinnappa Reddy Commission placed the Gollas in the list of backward castes, instead of placing them in most backward castes (Cat. I). Consequently, Gollas were denied all facilities, such as reservation in admission to technical schools and colleges and also other educational facilities, like free scholarship, and economic benefits like subsidy to purchase bullocks, cattle, etc. The Gollas of different districts in the state then collectively mobilized and organized themselves under the leadership of S. Siddappa, Dwarkinath and others to protest against the report and urged the government to withdraw it and continue reservation facilities to them which they were earlier enjoying under the government order of 13 October, 1986.

The strongest movement of the Yadavas in Karnataka started on 18 July, 1994 in Bangalore. They protested against the implementation of

Chinnappa Reddy Commissions Report and also against the government, which was headed by Veerappa Moily. In their protest, the Yadavas alleged that the government, by placing them in the backward caste category, had deprived them of all the benefits in various fields. In addition, the Gollas accused that the category II had many communities, which were economically and socially stronger and placing the Yadavas in that category was 'unscientific and unfair'. The agitators were of the opinion, as quoted by the *Hindu* daily newspaper of 19 July, 1994 that "Government decision came as a surprise and it had even affected the admission of Golla children in schools".

Further, they said the Gollas had been deprived of all benefits available under category 'A' as most of them lived in villages and *hutties* and remained highly backward. About 80 per cent of them lived below the poverty line and the government's move would seriously affect them with regard to various concessions and privileges.

As a result of the agitation by the Yadavas, the Government of Karnataka issued an order on 17 September, 1994, placing the Gollas in Category I (Most Backward Castes), with all the benefits. The percentage of reservation, according to the order, for the Other Backward Castes of Karnataka, under Article 15(4) and Article 16(4) of the Constitution, in education and appointments, is fixed at 50 per cent as follows:

Backward Classes	***Education***	***Appointments***
Category I	4 per cent	4 per cent
Category II A	15 per cent	15 per cent
Category II B	4 per cent	4 per cent
Category III A	4 per cent	4 per cent
Category III B	5 per cent	5 per cent
SC	15 per cent	15 per cent
ST	3 per cent	3 per cent
Total	50 per cent	50 per cent

Now, Gollas are treated as most backward castes and are placed in the most backward category (Category I). Today, they are claiming reservation in educational institutions, especially medical and technical institutions, and in appointments in various government services, without income restrictions on par with SCs and STs.

As we look back, the life of Gollas has been a path of struggle for equality. The struggle for reservation has brought about far-reaching changes among them in various spheres of their life. It is solely because of the educational progress made by some of them, social movements initiated with the help of national and district level associations and due to the efforts of the community leaders.

REFERENCES

Gurulingaiah, M. 2007. *Tribal Culture, Change and Mobility*. New Delhi: Anmol Publication.

Hoebel, Admson. 1976, *Cultural and Social Anthropology*, New Delhi: McGraw Hill Book Co.

Iyer, L.K.A. 1988. *The Mysore Tribes and Castes* (5 volumes). Vol. 3, Delhi: Mittal Publications.

Nanjundaiah. 1908. *Ethnographic Survey of Mysore*, Bangalore: Government Press.

Rao, M.S.A. 1987. *Social Movements and Social Transformation*. New Delhi: Manohar Publications.

Rowe, William L. 1967. "The New Cauhans: A Caste Mobility Movement in North India", in James Silverberg (ed.), *Social Mobility in the Caste System in India*. Hague: Mouton Publishers.

Shankarnarayana, T.N. 1982, Kadu Gollara Sampradoyagalu Mattu Namkikegalu, Mysore, Prasaranga, University of Mysore.

Sherring, M.A. 1974. *Hindu Tribes and Castes*. Vol. III, Delhi: Cosmo Publishing.

Smelser, Neil. 1962. *Theory of Collective Behaviour*. London: Routledge and Kegan Paul.

Stuart, H.A. 1918. *Manual of North Acrcot District*. Madras: Madras Census Report.

The Hindu. 19th July, 1994. Bangalore.

Thimmaiah, G. 1993. *Power Politics and Social Justice: Backward Castes in Karnataka*. New Delhi: Sage Publications.

Thurston, Edgar. 1909. *Castes and Tribes of South India*. Vol. III, Madras: Governmental Press.

Venkataswamy, T. 1986. Report of the Second Backward Class Commission. Vol. III, Bangalore, Government Press.

III

Dalits and Development

8

Development, Dalits and Rawls

Rudimentary Considerations

PARTHASARATHI MONDAL

There is an increasing awareness in the development discourse worldwide regarding the centrality and importance of Dalits and other backward classes. The growing tide of consciousness and activism, ranging from the boardrooms of international human rights and development agencies to central and state governments in India, has challenged the never-ending clamour of the historically privileged castes to oppose reservations and other affirmative action policies for the downtrodden castes. Bereft of the mask of the official Left in India, today, there is recognition, as in the colonial times, that the enlightenment, liberalism and capitalism penetrate better with citizens in nations that are free and equal rather than with those that continue to remain enthralled by the charms of hierarchy and tradition. The support for modernity in India's development strategy is therefore increasingly sought for and supported by the Dalits and other backward classes (OBCs). Noted economist and educationist K.S. Chalam has been at the forefront of taking forward the debate on the relationship between the liberal capitalism of contemporary India and the development of Dalits (Chalam, 2007). In this context, he has been eager to explore the political and ethical framework, which would ensure a greater participation of Dalits in a liberalizing India.

This essay, therefore, is an attempt to revisit Chalam's suggestion that contemporary India being a liberal capitalist society it is worthwhile to explore the applicability of John Rawls' notion of justice as fairness and Amartya Sen's concepts of entitlements and capabilities in the case of constitutional reservations and welfare of the Dalit and OBC people, which are identified as the worst off sections of Indian society. Chalam recommends that these works "... need to be articulated through the works of B.R. Ambedkar to find out solutions to the reservation problem. The question of justice is to be examined from the point of view of Dalits and the circumstances in which they live" (2007: 177). Rawls' insight that laws and social institutions however efficient and organized must be replaced if they are found to be unjust is the beginning point of Chalam's appreciation. Democracy, state and the market can therefore be guiding principles and institutions of India's development only if their parameters of justice are at tolerably acceptable levels.

Chalam goes on to commend another contention of Rawls, namely, the principles of justice which state that inequities in society are just and acceptable only if they result in benefits to all and especially to the most disadvantaged sections (the difference principle). Here, it is seen that the compensatory reservation policy of the post-independence Indian state has not been able to adequately provide the benefits of society to the least disadvantaged. Chalam however argues that it is Sen's extension of the Rawlsian primary goods to entitlements and capabilities which is more likely to make reservations effective. As entitlements of primary goods may not necessarily generate capacities in people to ensure justice, it is profitable to build the capability of individuals to make effective choices by removing obstacles to their development and freedom. Caste-based reservation system must be sensitive to the impact of current socio-economic system on people's capabilities (say, through education, health and income) and formulate policy accordingly.

In the following pages, I discuss one aspect of Chalam's suggestion, namely, the broad relevance of Rawls' thinking for understanding the Dalit situation in India. Although Rawls formulates the principles of justice as fairness in his major work *A Theory of Justice* (1972) (hereafter *TJ*), it is in his later book *The Law of Peoples* (1999) (hereafter *LP*) that he tries to extend justice as fairness to other liberal and non-liberal societies. According to him, although many non-liberal societies are blatant violators of human rights, there are some non-liberal societies which, although not exactly and fully liberal democracies, can be considered to be progressive and amenable to principles of justice as fairness. It is the latter societies which are considered to be 'decent' by Rawls, which thus become worthy of consideration for a discussion on the principles of justice in the arena of international relations. Accordingly, when Rawls is trying—in *LP*—to extend beyond borders the principles of justice, it is these decent non-liberal societies, which become the main type of society, which is the 'significant other' or foil to liberal societies.

Now, although India is not liberal in the Rawlsian or American sense because of democratic deficits which are rooted in historically structured inequities (leading to many of its citizens suffering from multiple vulnerabilities), it has a constitution and it is acknowledged to be the largest democracy in the world. It may thus well qualify to be a decent non-liberal society. There is a possibility then that the principles of justice could govern the relations between India and other liberal societies and between India's people and their government. In this sense, Chalam is not too far off the mark in claiming that the applicability of Rawls' justice as fairness merits consideration.

I argue however that an exploration of the notion of 'peoples' in Rawls raises obstacles to the extension of the principles of justice beyond the borders of liberal societies. The way in which Rawls specifies and formulates the principles of justice may well not allow him to extend their operation in a consideration of relations between liberal peoples and non-liberal decent peoples. The application of justice as fairness to non-liberal decent peoples is thus dependent on their meeting fully the characteristic features of liberal peoples. In the Indian context, this means that the eradication of casteism and oppression of the Dalits and OBCs is a *sine qua non* for the flowering of liberal capitalism.

I proceed then by discussing how the principles of justice as fairness are not based on comprehensive moral doctrines and how they obtain only in liberal democratic societies and the social practices of justice which are operational therein. The next section surveys Rawls' effort to turn these specific principles of justice towards other liberal and non-liberal societies. His exposition of international justice is marked by a movement from domestic liberal society to liberal and non-liberal nation-states and then back to liberal and non-liberal 'peoples' in terms of the arena of the principles of justice. This is crucial because it hinges on the notion of 'peoples' which further opens up the space—as we see in the following sections—for a close look at the relationship between peoples and individuals and at the central features of peoples. Rawls contends that the principles of justice are applicable in liberal societies only if the people therein are free and equal besides being moral and reasonable. However, he feels that societies wherein people are moral and reasonable without being free and equal can be considered to be non-liberal but decent societies. In this manner, they are therefore acceptable and accordingly the international relations business between liberal and such non-liberal decent societies can be established.

I argue here how it is difficult to separate the requirements of reasonableness and morality from the freedom and equality of citizens and peoples and consequently how Rawls' distinction of liberal and decent non-liberal peoples is imperilled. It does not follow that the principles of justice can be exported to non-liberal decent peoples and govern the relations between them and liberal peoples. The concluding section offers a few remarks on the implication of this for Dalits and India's development. India's development strategy would have to be such that it makes all its citizens and peoples free and equal if the principles of justice are to be operational. Irrespective of economic growth and capitalist development in India, caste discrimination against Dalits cannot go hand in hand with justice as fairness.

Justice as Fairness and Liberal Democratic Societies

There are, amongst others, two intertwined features of Rawls' elaboration of justice as fairness, which are germane to the discussion here. First, the principles of justice guiding justice as fairness are not based on metaphysical or comprehensive moral doctrine. Second, the principles of justice pertain only to liberal democratic societies. These principles are however not derived from abstractions existent in liberal democratic societies but from specific and concrete social practices of justness and fairness, which are already embedded in such societies.

In *Justice and Fairness* Rawls states that the "fundamental idea in the concept of justice is fairness ..." (1958: 47) and the two principles of justice are the ones which specify justice as fairness. The two principles of justice, which are considered to be only a *part* of a comprehensive vision of the good society and are derived from the original position under conditions of the veil of ignorance, are "... first, each person participating in a practice, or affected by it, has an equal right to the most extensive liberty compatible with a like liberty for all; and second, inequalities are arbitrary unless it is reasonable to expect that they will work out for everyone's advantage, and provided the positions and offices to which they attach, or from which they may be gained, are open to all" (ibid.: 48).

However, these principles of justice become most effective only under conditions of fairness. When free persons, having clear ideas of what are their legitimate claims, having no greater power over each other and engaged in a joint activity with competing claims, agree to these principles as being mutually acceptable, does this particular conception of justice appear fair. "It is this notion of the possibility of mutual acknowledgement of principles by free persons who have no authority over one another which makes the concept of fairness fundamental to justice" (ibid.: 59). Justice and its principles therefore make sense only when it is perceived as fair.

Now, one of the central assumptions here is that a person is acting on the basis of his self-interest. Rawls is nonetheless at pains here to distinguish between a general theory of a person being self-interested from a person being self-interested in contexts of justice (ibid.: 55–59). That is, he is trying to say that the issue of justice arises mainly when arbitrations of competing claims have to be made and in such situations it is but natural to expect a person to argue from the point of protecting his self-interest only. This however does not mean that a person acts in all instances in his life from self-interest.

However, as Brian Barry notes, there is a significant shift in the understanding of personhood by the time Rawls writes *TJ*: "… emphasis now rests on the desire to act justly being a central aspect of human development, a natural (and reflectively supported) extension of love for particular people and loyalty to particular associations. The desire to be just and cooperate in the maintenance of a just society is something that a man cannot frustrate except at the cost of stunting his moral nature, which is the most important part of himself" (1975: 2–3). The shift comes close on the heels of a growing importance of Kant in Rawls' work, viz., in *TJ*.

Rawls' main statement on the importance of Kant to his work in *TJ* is in §40 which he titles "The Kantian Interpretation of Justice as Fairness" (Rawls, 1972: 251–57). Justice as fairness is considered to be in consonance with the ethics of Kant, especially as they pertain to the notions of autonomy, rationality and categorical imperative. Now, Rawls seems to be saying that these ethical principles of Kant are not to be understood as being based solely on universal or metaphysical assumptions. Care must be taken to read his ethics not from his works on moral philosophy but mainly from the works on politics and political theory (ibid.: 251).

When Rawls is pointing towards Kant's political works, he is usually read as hinting that metaphysical principles may be allowed to subtend any notion of justice but even these metaphysical principles need to be restrained by moving them away from comprehensive doctrines of the traditional metaphysical sort or even those of moral philosophy. The grounds for justice as fairness can be argued in metaphysical terms but in a much restrained way. This also means that although comprehensive metaphysical doctrines do not form the grounds of justice as fairness, the principles of justice are nevertheless derived from some metaphysical assumptions.

Rawls brings in Kant in the context of autonomy whilst discussing the nature of decision-making in the original position. The principles of justice as fairness constitute freedom because they are arrived at by individuals who in the original position have no idea of the consequences of their decisions. The decisions are taken autonomously and not heteronomously (ibid.: 252). The Kantian spirit is furthered by Rawls, when he relates justice as fairness to the public sphere. The principles of justice are not principles of the inner recesses of one's emotions or morals but principles in the public realm. "For once we think of moral principles as legislation for a kingdom of ends, it is clear that these principles must not only be acceptable to all but public as well" (ibid.). Justice as fairness and its principles are more political than moral. This is roughly the manner in which Kant discusses how the realm of politics constitutes only the outer shell of the metaphysics of morality. Rawls can thus be read as using Kant to state that metaphysical principles do form the foundation of justice as fairness but barely so. The conditions of freedom are minimally metaphysical. Freedom is political.

The spirit of Rawls' enterprise is to make justice universal but by keeping, as much as possible, one's feet on the ground as it were. This is apparent later on in *TJ* when he discusses the categorical imperative and distinguishes it from hypothetical imperative:

> The principles of justice are also categorical imperatives in Kant's sense. For by a categorical imperative Kant understands a principle of conduct that applies to a person in virtue of his nature as a free and equal rational being. The validity of the principle does not presuppose that one has a particular desire or aim. Whereas a hypothetical imperative by contrast does assume this … . The argument for the two principles of justice does not assume that the parties have particular ends, but only that they desire certain primary goods. These are things that it is rational to want whatever else one wants … . The preference for primary goods is derived, then, from only the most general assumptions about rationality and the conditions of human life. To act from the principles of justice is to act from categorical imperatives in the sense that they apply to us whatever our aims are. (ibid.: 253)

The desires of the individuals in the original position behind the veil of ignorance are in consonance with the categorical imperative because they represent what every one of these individual wants and not what this or that individual wants. Individual desires represent hypothetical imperatives. Freedom is there in following the commands of the categorical imperative rather than hypothetical imperative. Rawls contends that the thing desired by all the individuals—all rational beings—is considered to be certain primary goods. The universal here is not the entire universe of society which is so abstract that it is difficult to state. That which is wanted by all rational beings is considered to be the universal. These desires seem to be primary goods. Primary good is not something which is desired and known only by the desiring and knowing individual in the original position but it is something which is desired and known by all the parties in the original position. The categorical imperative is thus limited to only the public. Primary goods become then more a part and parcel of the metaphysics of politics than of the metaphysics of morality. In arguing this way, Rawls is, on the one hand, limiting the operation of the categorical imperative, as the foundation of principles of justice, by preventing the universal from being extended infinitely and being located in the depths of the moral sphere. On the other hand, Rawls can be read as stating that although comprehensive doctrines do not subtend justice as fairness it is nevertheless grounded in metaphysical assumptions.

Therefore, it can be argued that Rawls is saying in *TJ* that justice as fairness is not metaphysical at all because it is obtainable only in liberal democratic societies. Rawls continues this argument in his writings of the middle and later periods in a fresh manner when he discusses justice as fairness being a 'political and not metaphysical' conception. But he gradually turns more specific or more inwards—from a society which is liberal to constitutional democracies like America [in 'Kantian Constructivism in Moral Theory' (1980)] to existing intuitive social practices in modern liberal democracies [in 'Justice as Fairness: Political not Metaphysical' (1985) and in *LP*]. This is movement is best captured through his 'political' conception of justice. In 'The Priority of Right and Ideas of the Good' (1988) Rawls says: "The distinguishing features of a political conception of justice are, first, that it is a moral conception worked out for a specific subject, namely, the basic structure of a constitutional democratic regime, second, that accepting the political conception does not presuppose accepting any particular comprehensive religious, philosophical, or moral doctrine; rather, the political conception presents itself as a reasonable conception for the basic structure alone; and third, that it is formulated not in terms of any comprehensive doctrine but in terms of certain fundamental intuitive ideas viewed as latent in the public political culture of a democratic society" (1988: 450).

Rawls is now saying that the principles of justice are to be found in practices already existing covertly in liberal democratic states which are geared towards working out 'overlapping consensus' between divergent beliefs systems. The meaning of justice is somehow linked to the way it is practised. It remains a moral doctrine because it does not represent a temporary or expedient cessation of war between natural enemies, but because it evolves out of how modern citizens negotiate their lives in the face of competing claims to the good in the public sphere and is therefore not universal or metaphysical at all. The principles of justice are moral because they aim at securing a consensus across a broad bandwidth of people who are holding on to their religious or cosmological beliefs but the principles are not metaphysical because they are not aimed at establishing any one comprehensive doctrine as the ground for justice as fairness.

In trying to understand the bases of principles which govern justice, Rawls speaks of the social practices already existing in liberal democratic societies. Accordingly, he directs our attention—in 'The Idea of an Overlapping Consensus' (1987)—to at least five social practices of interpersonal and societal negotiation in liberal democratic states, which should and can form the legitimate basis for evolving workable principles of justice (Rawls, 1987: 421). The first fact is that society is pluralistic, and secondly that this pluralism is likely to abide if normality prevails. Next, such pluralism can be overcome only through an excess of coercive power by the state. Further, the context for this persistent pluralism is of course scarcity of resources and this implies that the principles of justice should aim towards a distribution of these scarce resources in such a way that the plurality of worldviews is maintained to the greatest possible extent. The fifth practice is that is that there is well-organized system of cooperation between citizens, which enables most people to overcome the constraints of context and achieve most of their individual desires.

Two more 'basic intuitive ideas' subtend these practices of liberal democratic societies, which are elaborated in 'Justice as Fairness: Political not Metaphysical' (1985). First, the "overarching fundamental intuitive idea, within which other basic intuitive ideas are systematically connected, is that of a society as a fair system of cooperation between free and equal persons" (Rawls, 1985: 395–96). The second intuitive idea is explained thus:

> Since we start within the tradition of democratic thought, we also think of citizens as free and equal persons. The basic intuitive idea is that in virtue of what we may call their moral powers, and the powers of reason,

> thought, and judgment connected with those powers, we say that persons are free. And in virtue of their having these powers to the requisite degree to be fully cooperating members of society, we say that persons are equal. (ibid.: 397)

Therefore, given the need to construct principles which would guide in a fair manner the distribution of scarce resources in a plural society, it is only principles which are evolved out of these existent social practices or facts of life in liberal democratic societies which can work feasibly. Such principles would assume a specification of basic rights and liberties, prioritize these rights and liberties, and provide equal opportunities to citizens in order to actualize these privileges. Needless to say, as these principles are being evolved and not thrust upon, the citizens by the political philosopher, shared *modus operandi* for discussion and verification and shared virtues of tolerance are assumed (Rawls, 1987: 429 and 439).

Justice as fairness is thus not a metaphysical or theoretical task but very much a practical one. It is to be constructed out of the commonly observed practices in which citizens of the liberal democratic societies are engaged in whilst negotiating the achievement of their individual desires. These practices relate to social cooperation obtaining between free and equal persons engaged in the distribution of scare resources in society on an equal opportunity basis, with the goal to ensure that the diversity and plurality of moral beliefs and worldviews is respected and maintained. What we see here then in Rawls—noticeable very early on in his *oeuvre* but more marked later—is the effort to locate the principles of justice as fairness in the social practices of liberal democratic societies as a part of the enterprise of avoiding the question of metaphysical or comprehensive moral doctrine.

From the Nation-State to Peoples

In *LP* Rawls explores the extension of the principles of justice obtaining in liberal democratic societies to non-liberal and other types of societies. This is unavoidable, Rawls thinks, in a closely interconnected world and so the aim should be to find out the principles of international justice, which would guide the governance of relations between different societies and governments across the globe. To be sure, this project begins in *TJ* (Rawls, 1972: 377–78) when Rawls briefly shifts his attention from the principles of justice in domestic society to a consideration of the principles which should adhere in a relationship between liberal domestic society and other liberal societies and between liberal societies and non-liberal societies.

In this movement Rawls considers the principles of justice in the context of 'nations' or 'states', that is, his unit of analysis now becomes states or nations and not societies. The effort is therefore to extend the contractarian framework beyond societies to nations. Having said this, the 'law of nations' is to be based on a hypothetical contract not between nations but between their representatives who would devise principles of justice from behind a veil of ignorance regarding themselves, their societies and their nations. The pursuits therefore of the representatives would be moral because they would be keeping the interests of their nations in mind and not their own economic and other interests. Interestingly, Rawls does not talk here of individual rights and justice, and mutual assistance and respect because nations are expected to take care of these matters for their citizens.

However, by the time Rawls gets to write *LP*, he has shifted his focus of international justice back from nations to societies or 'peoples'. It is now peoples, who have moral character, rather than the nation or the state. Accordingly, nations are now characterized by their societies or peoples and not by their states (Rawls, 1999: 4). The first type of society is 'reasonable liberal peoples' whereas the second type of society is 'decent peoples'. The first can relatively safely be taken to mean liberal democratic societies or constitutional democracies. The second refers to "... non-liberal societies whose basic institutions meet certain specified conditions of political right and justice (including the right of citizens to play a substantial role, say through associations and groups, in making political decisions) and lead their citizens to honor a reasonably just law for the Society of Peoples" (Rawls, 1999: 3, fn. 2). Liberal peoples and decent peoples are together taken to be 'well-ordered peoples'. The third type of society is 'outlaw states' wherein fair terms of cooperation do not or cannot obtain. The fourth type is 'burdened societies' or societies burdened with unfavourable conditions. These societies do not provide its peoples, for material or cultural reasons, the minimum institutional embodiment (e.g., a nation or a state) which could secure for them grounds for living as moral agents. Lastly, one has 'benevolent absolutisms' which respect human rights but, do not permit its peoples political participation and hence cannot be considered a well-ordered society.

The focus of the typology is on arguing out the parameters for achieving a just world mainly between liberal and decent peoples. The faith is that most of the vicious crises of the earth (e.g., war, mass migration, and weapons of mass destruction) arise because of political injustice. Hence, once these injustices are removed and politically just social policies and institutions are put in place, most of the most intransigent difficulties are likely to give away (ibid.: 6–7). Rawls is firm that the law of peoples is derived form and an extension of political liberalism. Whereas, however, in the law of nations diversity of nations was permitted, in the law of peoples diversity of meanings in constitutional liberalism or diversity of cultures and traditions is allowed.

Clearly, Rawls' concern is to chalk out the grounds for interaction between liberal peoples and non-liberal peoples which are decent (i.e., decent peoples). However, the principles are guided from the vantage point which consists of an extension of the principles operating within a closed domestic liberal society to the principles which are to be obtained between liberal societies. The 'law of peoples' therefore resembles more the principles operational in liberal societies. The superiority and desirability of liberalism is taken for granted as well as advocated. Rawls thus retains the hope that in this manner the non-liberal decent peoples would be encouraged to move towards liberalism eventually: "... if a liberal constitutional democracy is, in fact, superior to other forms of society, as I believe it to be, a liberal people should have confidence in their convictions and suppose that a decent society, when offered due respect by liberal peoples, may be more likely, over time, to recognize the advantages of liberal institutions and take steps toward becoming liberal on its own" (ibid.: 62). Accordingly, the principles of the law of peoples are:

- Peoples are free and independent, and their freedom and independence are to be respected by other peoples.
- Peoples are to observe treaties and undertakings.
- Peoples are equal and are parties to the agreements that bind them.
- Peoples are to observe a duty of non-intervention.
- Peoples have the right of self-defense but no right to instigate war for reasons other than self-defence.
- Peoples are to honour human rights.
- Peoples are to observe certain specified restrictions in the conduct of war.
- Peoples have a duty to assist other peoples living under unfavourable conditions that prevent their having a just or decent political and social regime (Rawls, 1999: 37).

However, the shift to the concept of peoples is central to the extension of the principles of justice in domestic liberal society to other liberal and non-liberal decent societies and so it would be fruitful to get a grip over this transition. In explaining this movement, Freeman (2007: 419) contends that Rawls was responding to criticism from theorists of cosmopolitanism. Cosmopolitanists have argued that Rawls should have posited a global original position between individuals across all nations instead of only between their representatives. This would have provided greater possibilities of justice because it assumes equal respect for persons. As equal respect for persons is the basis for social justice in Rawls, it could also provide the basis for relations among everyone in the world. "Liberal cosmopolitanism is defined by its main proponents as a moral ideal grounded in the equal moral status of all persons and the justifiability of social arrangements to everyone in the world. These moral values are said to imply the recognition of equal basic rights and liberties for all persons in the world and a global egalitarian principle of distributive justice" (ibid.).

Secondly, and in a somewhat similar vein, Graham (2007: 152) notes that one of the main reasons for Rawls' shift from nations to peoples is to overcome the challenges thrown by the Westphalian approach to international relations wherein nation-states have a right to wage war to what is perceived as threats to its borders even when not provoked and also to organize their domestic institutional, legal and social arrangements even at the cost of violating the rights of their own citizens (if thought necessary). According to Rawls, a person who is a citizen has, if required, moral claims against the nation or state.

Rawls' own account of the shift is enunciated in §2 of *LP*, entitled "Why Peoples and Not States?" (Rawls, 1999: 23–30). According to him, states or nations are identified with a rational pursuit of power and self-interest and are thus perceived with evident dislike from the point of view of justice as fairness:

> How far states differ from peoples rests on how rationality, the concern with power, and a state's basic interests are filled in. If rationality excludes the reasonable (that is, if a state is moved by the aims it has and ignores the criterion of reciprocity in dealing with other societies); if a state's concern with power is predominant; and if its interests include such things as converting other societies to the state's religion, enlarging its empire and winning territory, gaining dynastic or imperial or national prestige and glory, and increasing its relative economic strength—then the difference between states and peoples is enormous. Such interests as these tend to put a state at odds with other states and peoples, and to

> threaten their safety and security, whether they are expansionist or not. The background conditions also threaten hegemonic war. (ibid.: 28–29)

States also have a right to act independently of the interest of its citizens and Rawls thinks this is a pretty rotten thing to happen. The police, the judiciary and other cognate institutions are adequate to deal with matters of justice and so there are no grounds for a government to call in the armed forces against its own citizens. Even the nation-state's right to war is qualified. These are, Rawls says, in line with development in international law wherein human rights have gained tremendous prominence in national and international governance.

(Liberal) peoples, on the other hand, have a reasonably just constitutional government, citizens with common sympathies and a moral nature. The institution of constitutional government means that the government is under the political and electoral control of the people, that is, it takes care of their basic or fundamental interests. In addition, the peoples are not subject to the hidden or otherwise machinations of "private economic and corporate power". The shared sympathies between citizens are dependent on their common culture, language and history which have evolved out of their intermingling down the ages. Liberal peoples are also moral in the sense that their rational behaviour is often constrained by their sense of what is reasonable. Moreover, liberal peoples operate within fair terms of cooperation and try to sustain this ethos from one generation to the next. Therefore, for Rawls, the "… difference between liberal peoples and states is that just liberal peoples limit their basic interests as required by the reasonable" and all hopes of "… reaching a realistic utopia rests on there being reasonable liberal constitutional (and decent) regimes sufficiently established and effective to yield a viable Society of Peoples."

The derivation of the principles of justice for the international arena (i.e., the law of peoples) as distinguished from the principles of justice for domestic societies depends on an original interpretation of the 'original position' (ibid.: 30–34). This second original position is much like the one in the law of nations wherein representatives of different societies gather to discuss the terms of the cooperation between their societies. Sheltered behind a thick veil of ignorance regarding their own societies and themselves (in terms of resources and desires), they arbitrate on principles of justice, knowing only that their societies are held together by democratic conceptions and norms of justice. They are solely concerned with promoting justice in their own societies and therefore they ignore all other peoples and their interests.

Accordingly, the law of peoples brooks no consideration of global distributive justice or a world-state or global legal body which would have an original right to specify global property or terms of contract. The relationships between peoples are to be practically governed by agreements and treaties between these peoples which shall have jurisdiction secondarily derived from the principles of the law of peoples. Thus peoples rather than states or other supra-national bodies are the pivot for international justice. What is the nature of the relationship then between peoples and individuals? What are the basic features of liberal peoples? How do they compare with those of the decent peoples?

Peoples, Personhood and Liberal Democracies

Rawls' understanding of the individual in the context of justice begins at two levels, namely, in 'real' or 'actual' society and in the original position. In actual life there are certain goods—'social primary goods' (e.g., rights and liberties, powers and opportunities, income and wealth, and the bases of self-respect)—which are ways and means of meeting a very wide range of desires of the individual in a liberal society (Rawls, 1972: 62). The individual citizen, who is presented by Rawls, is a rational being, that is, someone for whom it is rational to desire the maximization of the social primary goods in the pursuit of his plans for life. Each person is therefore seen to maximize his or her share of the primary goods. As Steven Smith says:

> There are at least four presuppositions concerning the nature of rationality and action that underlie (Rawls' framework). First, rationality is, on this account, exclusively a predicate of individual actors and actions; this is the principle of methodological individualism. Second, rationality is concerned with means and not ends. It is a form of calculation that allows the agent to acquire the objects of his desire, rather than prescribing what kinds of objects he ought to desire; this is the principle of value-neutrality. Third, the natural goal of each agent is to maximize the number of pleasures and minimize the number of pains; this is the principle of psychological hedonism. And fourth, the problem of politics is conceived as finding ways of limiting the infinity of human desires so that each can coexist with all under the rule of universal law. This is the principle of the social contract or the 'natural condition', which is in turn said to generate the conditions of political legitimacy (1986: 121–22).

The nature of such an individual becomes further evident from *TJ* when Rawls elaborates on "the circumstances of justice" (Rawls, 1972:

126–30). According to him, the issue of justice arises in societies where people are born into arrangements of voluntary association which are in need of rules of fair play. "The circumstances of justice may be described as the normal conditions under which human cooperation is both possible and necessary" (ibid.: 126). The society which Rawls has in mind whilst discussing justice is a society which is marked by "cooperative venture for mutual advantage" (ibid.: 126) and which is characterized by conflict and identity of interests. People cooperate because they are aware of the benefits which cooperation accrue to them whilst, on the other hand, they vie with each other for a greater share of the pie. The objective circumstance which makes cooperation possible and necessary is that "... many individuals coexist together at the same time on a definite geographical territory" (ibid.).

These individuals are roughly homogenous in physical, intellectual and social terms. They also live under conditions of scarcity of natural resource endowments. The subjective conditions, which make cooperation between these people possible and necessary, are the differences in their plans and strategies for the good life which leads to conflicting situations under circumstances of scarcity. This situation is complicated by people having limited knowledge of affairs of the world and by the "diversity of philosophical and religious belief, and of political and social doctrines" (ibid.: 127). "Thus, one can say, in brief, that the circumstances of justice obtain whenever mutually disinterested persons put forward conflicting claims to the division of social advantages under conditions of moderate scarcity" (ibid.: 128). Now, in order to bring about a resolution of this situation, certain principles of justice are necessary. "Thus principles are needed for choosing among the various social arrangements which determine this division of advantages and for underwriting an agreement on the proper distributive shares" (ibid.: 126).

Rawls does say that this situation is "... simply a part of men's natural situation" (ibid.: 127) that is, the conditions of cooperation and conflict are universal to human society and that "the account of these conditions involves no particular theory of human motivation" (ibid.: 130). But he also says that the self-oriented plans of the good life are 'rational long-term plans' (ibid.: 129). Rational individualistic strategies of behaviour are therefore characteristic of individuals in modern liberal societies.

The situation is more or less the same with individuals in the original position. Representatives of individual citizens cluster together to discuss and choose between alternative principles of justice which would most likely be agreed upon by real citizens as grounds for a fair system of cooperation between them. The "parties are modelled as rational, in that their aim is to do the best they can for citizens whose basic interests they represent, as specified by the primary goods, which cover their basic needs as citizens" (Rawls, 1999: 31). However, there is at least one important modification. The "original position with a veil of ignorance is a model of representation for liberal societies" (ibid.: 30). The individual representatives in the original position are, unlike citizens of the real world, prevented from holding on to comprehensive notions of the good or any other idea of themselves or their societies. They are aware only of the most general primary goods on which they must arbitrate. This alters the nature of rationality to an extent.

Recall that Rawls wrote earlier to *TJ*, in the 'Outline of a Decision Procedure for Ethics', that he is concerned with "... a reasonable decision procedure which is sufficiently strong, at least in some cases, to determine the manner in which competing interests should be adjudicated, and, in instances of conflict, one interest given preference over another ..." (Rawls, 1951: 1). In other words, the procedure which is followed in order to arrive at the principles of justice is rational. That is, individuals in the original position behind the veil of ignorance follow a rational procedure to arrive at the principles of justice. These persons are then rational beings. Only such rational beings constitute the parties in the original position. Now, there is no doubt that Rawls understands rationality as a process whereby individuals, in the furtherance of their ends or desires, weigh their options carefully before coming to a decision on the most effective option for each of them. However, the rational process is slightly modified in the original position.

Rational choice procedures seem to have two components: one, individuals weigh options carefully in order to select the most effective means to their ends and two, the choice is guided by their specific desires. Now Rawls takes care to limit this instrumentality by making it blind by dropping the veil of ignorance over the desires of individuals. Desiring individuals without knowing the consequences of their specific desires from the principles of justice to be formulated in effect formulate principles, which do not have connection to their specific ends as motivations. They have to now take decisions on the principles on the basis of the most general information about society. In such a situation they have to weigh the options amongst this general information and choose the best possible course of action.

In doing this, therefore, the individuals in the original position are following the first component of a rational choice method. They are acting as rational agents because they are taking decisions on the basis of an instrumental and 'optimal-effectiveness' procedure. This instrumentality is nonetheless disconnected from the individuals' specific desires and connected only to the most general features or characteristics of society. In this sense, the individuals do not satisfy the second component of a rational choice procedure. In other words, it is only with the most general knowledge of society and not with the knowledge of the specific desires or ends of individuals that the rational choice process is followed.

The rational individual citizens and their representatives in the original position are also reasonable people. Reasonable citizens are those who are "... characterized by their willingness to offer fair terms of social cooperation among equals and by their recognition of the burdens of judgment. In addition, they are said to affirm only reasonable comprehensive doctrines. In turn, such doctrines are reasonable provided they recognize the essentials of a liberal democratic regime and exhibit a reasoned ordering of the many values of life (whether religious or nonreligious) in a coherent and consistent manner. Though these doctrines should be relatively stable, they may evolve in the light of what, given the development of their tradition, are accepted as good and sufficient reasons" (Rawls, 1999: 87).

Rationality is however different from reasonableness. Rationality is tied with the individual's conception of the good—his good "... for Rawls is the rational plan of life he/she would choose under conditions of deliberative rationality" (Freeman, 2007: 150). Reasonableness, on the other hand, has to do with 'right'—"including individual moral duties and moral requirements of right and justice applying to institutions and society" (ibid.). A reasonable individual is "... one who is cooperative and fair-minded, who respects others and their position and is sensitive to the reasons and purposes they have, and who is willing to moderate his demands and meet others halfway when conflicts arise" (ibid.). Thus, both rationality and reasonableness are independent and different aspects of practical reason. Even if a person is perfectly rational, he is still unreasonable if he violates reasonable moral requirements.

Being reasonable also means having a sense of justice (ibid.: 150–51). The sense of justice is the willingness to voluntarily submit to duties and obligations of justice. Rawls contends that this is characteristic of all human beings and thus individuals are neither motivated only by self-interest nor do they submit to justice only when it benefits them.

Certain claims are made by Rawls in favour of the sense of justice (ibid.: 254). Humanity is flawed if it does not have the primary motivational basis in the form of a sense of justice. This develops as a part of the normal process of growing up and living life and thus becomes an extension of our affective and moral life in our familial and social circles. The sense of justice is oriented towards philosophical principles as much as social norms and values. Consequently, the sense of justice develops along with the sharpening of the individual's capacity to reason, think and understand. Lastly, as the sense of justice is at its origin social in nature, most social constraints are in consonance with it and do not cause it injury.

The sense of justice therefore gives us a clue as to how individuals are moral agents. Rawls devotes a large part of Chapter 8 of *TJ* to the morality of personhood after the discussion on the sense of justice. According to Rawls, "... each citizen is regarded as having ... the two moral powers—a capacity for a sense of justice and a capacity for a conception of the good. It is also assumed that each citizen has, at any time, a conception of the good compatible with a comprehensive religious, philosophical, or moral doctrine. These capacities enable citizens to fulfill their role as citizens and underwrite their political and civic autonomy. The principles of justice protect citizens' higher-order interests; these are guaranteed within the framework of the liberal constitution and the basic structure of society" (1999: 92).

Reciprocity is very important to Rawls in the case of the two moral powers. For instance, individuals treated with a sense of justice tend to reciprocate with a sense of justice. Thereafter, Rawls develops three stages of morality in persons, namely 'morality of authority', 'morality of association' and 'morality of principles'. The morality of authority refers to the sense of justness which develops in individuals when they are brought up in a family which is just. The love, trust and fair play of the parents inculcates in the child love for the parents and an internalization of these principles of justice. In morality of association a similar phenomenon of internalization takes place but this time it is from just practices within an individual's colleagues, friends and professional associations to which one belongs. Accordingly, feelings of trust and friendship arise and duties and obligations are learnt. At the third stage morality develops as a result of adherence to principles of justice rather than any adherence to persons—friends/colleagues or kith and kin.

When we move from individual citizens to their representatives in the original position to peoples, we learn that peoples are also imbibed with a sense of the rational, the reasonable and the moral. David Reidy notes that by 'peoples' Rawls means those bodies politic which are able to conceive of themselves as 'corporate artificial moral agents or persons':

> A corporate artificial moral person, a people, must first possess an institutional 'body' minimally sufficient to enable it to act on the global stage. This need not but often will be a government operative within a fixed territory. It must also possess to the requisite minimum degree the capacities essential to moral agency. On Rawls's view, these are, as is well known, the capacity to form, revise, and pursue a determinate conception of its good, what Rawls calls the capacity for rationality, and the capacity to propose and honor fair terms of cooperative interaction, or the capacity to be reasonable. A people secures the former through its internal culture and deliberative practices when these are sufficiently unified and stable to enable it to form, revise, and pursue rationally a determinate conception of its good. It secures the latter through institutional arrangements and cultural commitments sufficient to enable and incline it to subordinate to the demands of justice the rational pursuit of its own interests in its relations with other persons, whether corporate and artificial or natural. (2004: 295)

Therefore, individual citizens in liberal societies, individuals in the original position and liberal peoples are rational, reasonable and moral. A people is thus an aggregate of individual citizens, who form a corporate body, which is (like individual citizens) moral in nature. Peoples are moral because as corporate agents they have the capacity for rationality and capacity to propose and honour fair terms of cooperation. It is on these grounds that people warrant respect as equals and as deserving of equal justice (Freeman, 2007: 294). As seen above, these grounds develop as a part of the normal process of living life and thus become the natural qualities of a human being. Hence, equality is natural to a person. Such moral persons are equal because they consider themselves and others to have an equal right to determine the foundational principles of justice. These individuals also share the capacity to form and interrogate their notions of the good, participate in fair systems of cooperation, and comprehend and follow a public conception of justice.

Peoples are also free persons (ibid.: 294–95). This is so because they have the capacity to revise formulated notions of the good and thereby change their plans and strategies in life. Secondly, people are self-authenticating units and as such they are entitled to make claims on social and political institutions in terms of their own interests. The ends and goals of life are to a large extent formulated by them and are always open to voluntary revision. This is done in a manner which takes into consideration the resource base of society—people are held responsible for the extent and type of demands being made in their own interest on other people and on institutions. Accordingly, therefore, persons can themselves assume responsibility for their life goals without interference from the outside. As such, they are free (in a third sense). As this freedom is contextual to the society and people in which the individual resides, it cannot be considered to be metaphysical (i.e., 'free-will') in nature.

The Rawlsian individual citizen, person in the original position and a people are all therefore free and equal beings. However, these free and equal beings are weaved into rational and reasonable persons by Rawls with the help of the concept of 'rational autonomy' devised by Immanuel Kant. This is done most strikingly, as we have seen earlier, in §40 of *TJ*, entitled "The Kantian Interpretation of Justice as Fairness" (Rawls, 1972: 251–57). The main Kantian conceptions used by Rawls are autonomy, rationality, and the categorical imperative. A well-ordered society is peopled by autonomous citizens. This is the autonomy emulated from the rationally autonomous parties in the original position. When these citizens act according to the principles, which the parties in the original position would choose under what Rawls calls 'fair terms of cooperation' the citizens enjoy the autonomy, which was prized by Kant as the moral ideal. Further interaction is based not only on mutual self-respect and reciprocity with a clear idea of benefits and burdens but also on a public conception of this mutuality.

The parties in the original position also act rationally. This is because they accept the principles of justice knowing well that even though they have to reach at their decision from behind the veil of ignorance, they have chosen such principles which would lead to the best possible deal for themselves, irrespective of what is revealed about their socio-political and economic background after the veil is lifted. On this basis, Rawls contends, citizens who take themselves to be rational can adopt these principles of justice.

Kant makes a distinction between categorical imperative and hypothetical imperative. When one acts on the desire for a specific end, he is said to be motivated by hypothetical imperative but when he is spurred on by goals which concern the whole of humanity he is taken to be motivated by the categorical imperative. In other words, when one is acting under categorical imperative, he or she is willing a moral law as a principle governing the actions of all rational beings. It is possible thus to do this and move away from hypothetical imperative only when we abstract ourselves away from our interpersonal differences.

So here we have a person who is a free and equal rational being and who is careful enough to will as principles which can be willed by all.

Clearly, Rawls is making an effort to mould his social contract on a Kantian understanding. *TJ* was followed by a series of writings which, while constituting a response to the many critics of *TJ*, also gave Rawls the opportunity to elaborate his linkages with Kant. For instance, in 'A Kantian Conception of Equality' (1975), Rawls contends that the veil of ignorance could be seen as an incorporation of a Kantian idea in his scheme in the sense that the requirement of the parties to deliberate on the principles of justice without any knowledge of the parties' background is similar to Kant's notion of negative freedom which meant the freedom to act independently of contingencies. Thus, in the original position, knowledge of only the most general laws governing nature and society is permitted. Rawls also draws a parallel with Kant's conception of positive freedom. Positive freedom is possible because the parties in the original position deliberating on principles of justice are free and equal moral persons. Secondly, the principles of justice have a content consonant with the view of free and equal moral persons because "... these principles express, on their public face as it were, the conception of the person that is realized in a well-ordered society. They give priority to the basic liberties, regard individuals as free and responsible masters of their aims and desires, and all are to share equally in the means for the attainment of ends unless the situation of everyone can be improved, taking equal division as the starting point. A society that realizes these principles would attain positive freedom, for these principles reflect the features of persons that determined their selection and so express a conception they give to themselves" (Rawls, 1975: 265–66).

In 'Kantian Constructivism in Moral Theory' (1980) Rawls finds the Kantian understanding of the person as appropriate to his present concerns. The concern is that in liberal democracies like America there is no agreement on how to organize institutional arrangements such that they would conform to the freedom and equality of citizens (Rawls, 1980: 305). In this search, the Kantian notion of the person is helpful. This is so because such a person is both free and equal. In addition, he is capable of ensuring the best bargains for himself in any situation of negotiation and at the same time he wills those first principles of justice which can also be willed by other rational persons like him. The former is called the rational and the latter the reasonable by Rawls. The sense of mutuality and reciprocity of the reasonable forms the context of the rational and thereby subsumes it. Without conceptions of the good persons would not know why they should cooperate. In this manner, the free, equal, rational and moral person becomes the means and ends of social cooperation (ibid.: 306). The aim of a theory of justice here should be to formulate or construct the principles of justice from the common sense manifest in social cooperation between such persons.

It is fairly clear therefore that the Rawlsian person is free, equal, moral and rational in an integrated manner. The rational and reasonable cannot be separated from the free and equal citizen, individual or people. As Freeman notes, "Moral persons are persons who have the two moral powers and who consequently regard themselves as free and as equal. Having the moral powers means that moral persons are rational since they have a capacity to form, revise, and pursue a conception of the good; and also they are reasonable since they have a capacity for a sense of justice, including the abilities to understand, apply, and follow requirements of principles of justice" (2007: 293–94).

Decent Peoples and Personhood

We have seen earlier how Rawls, in trying to extend the operation of the principles of justice as fairness to other liberal societies and non-liberal societies, focuses attention on non-liberal decent peoples. Decent peoples and liberal peoples are admitted into the club of 'well-ordered societies'. Of particular relevance and interest to Rawls is decent peoples whose basic structure has a 'decent consultation hierarchy' and whom he calls 'decent hierarchical peoples' (Rawls, 1999: 63). In §8.2 of *LP* (1999: 64–67) Rawls lays down some criteria for designating decent hierarchical peoples. Such societies should not have aggressive aims against other peoples and must accept diplomatic or other peaceful means to meet its legitimate goals or ends. Even if it seeks wider influence, it must maintain the independence of other peoples. Secondly, the legal system of such societies must give respect and primacy to human rights—if it fails to protect rights to life and property, freedom of speech, religion and thought, and equality before law, then such peoples end up lacking the idea of social cooperation. However, many of these rights are derived from a "... associationist social form which sees persons first as members of groups—associations, corporations, and estates. As such members, persons have rights and liberties enabling them to meet their duties and obligations and to engage in a decent system of social cooperation" (ibid.: 68).

Moreover, such peoples must have a common good idea of justice and therefore follow certain moral duties and obligations, which are in line with this notion of justice (ibid.: 77). Belief—sincere and not unreasonable—in these duties and obligations, arising from the common good idea of justice, must especially be held by the administrators of the legal system. Most importantly, these peoples must have a consultation hierarchy which gives adequate representation to all segments of society. This means that dissent is permitted although it must be confined "... within the basic framework of the common good idea of justice" (ibid.: 72). The consultative mechanism here must meet the following six guidelines: (i) all groups are consulted, (ii) each member of a society must belong to a group, (iii) each group must be represented by a body which contains at least some of the group's own members, (iv) the rulers must weigh the views of each group, (v) the decisions should be based on a consideration of the common good (or, in the absence of common good) special priorities of such societies, and (vi) the special priorities must match a general scheme of cooperation which is made explicit (ibid.: 77).

Decent peoples thus are guided by a common good idea of justice and provide space for religious freedom to multiple sects. They admit a measure of liberty of conscience and freedom of thought and do not violate human rights. They also honour the law of peoples. Hence, although they are not as reasonable, rational and free as liberal peoples, they deserve the respect and interaction of liberal peoples. How then do these stipulated characteristics compare with those of liberal peoples? Rawls says that even though "... all persons in a decent hierarchical society are not regarded as free and equal citizens, nor as separate individuals deserving equal representation (according to the maxim: one citizen, one vote), they are seen as decent and rational and as capable of moral learning as recognized in their society" (ibid.: 71). Therefore, decent peoples have rationality, reasonableness and morality although they are more in tune with their associationist societies rather than the more austere requirements of liberal peoples.

Rawls again clarifies and elaborates these crucial observations: "To repeat, I am not saying that a decent hierarchical society is as reasonable and just as a liberal society. For judged by the principles of a liberal democratic society, a decent hierarchical society clearly does not treat its members equally. A decent society does, however, have a common good political conception of justice ..., and this conception is honoured in its decent consultation hierarchy ... . Moreover, it honors a reasonable and just Law of Peoples, the same that liberal peoples do ... . A decent hierarchical society honors a reasonable and just Law of Peoples even though it does not treat its own members reasonably or justly as free and equal citizens, since it lacks the liberal idea of citizenship" (ibid.: 83).

It is clear then that what decent peoples share with liberal peoples are rationality, reasonableness and morality. These are the common meeting grounds, which should encourage liberal peoples to tolerate, interact and gradually draw towards full-blown liberalism the decent peoples. Although not at the highest-order levels, decent peoples do encourage citizens to pursue their interests—the only requirement is that they be in tune with the people's idea of the common good. Similarly, such peoples have a sense of justice as is evident from the consultation hierarchy. These two parameters shape the morality of decent peoples. However, decent peoples are not free and equal and this, according to Rawls, is the source of inadequacy or weakness of decent societies. Nonetheless, Rawls says it is enough if the decent peoples of non-liberal societies are reasonable and moral—they need not be free and equal.

Therefore, what becomes apparent is that Rawls marks off freedom and equality as the main features, which distinguish liberal from decent peoples. Although decent peoples do not have the 'strong' version of rationality, reasonableness and morality, they have *some* version of it. Accordingly, therefore, it is possible to consider as decent peoples those peoples who have rationality, reasonableness and morality even if they are not free and equal. Here, it is not clear as to how one can one be moral, rational and reasonable in the Rawlsian sense without being free and equal? It has been brought to our notice by Rawls' own formulation that the rationality and reasonableness of moral peoples are integral to them being free and equal. Personhood *per se* can be granted to an individual only when it is in his or her nature to be equal and morality is granted to a person when he or she rationally maximizes his or her desires with a plan of life which he or she can voluntarily revise and when this plan is imbibed with a sense of justice. Hence, whether at the individual level or at the (national or international) representative level, these parameters have to be present if Rawls' definition and understanding of liberal peoples itself is to hold. In other words, the rationality, reasonableness and morality of decent peoples which Rawls conceptualizes in a minimal way cannot be in any way Rawlsian rationality, reasonableness and morality. If we are to be guided by Rawls' understanding of liberal rationality, reasonableness and morality, then, peoples at all levels have to be free and equal. The 'watered-down' rationality, reasonableness and morality of decent peoples are not Rawlsian at all. Therefore, Rawls cannot postulate a certain framework for liberal peoples and then use the same framework to define decent peoples when that framework clearly does not obtain in those other peoples. There can be a law of peoples only between liberal peoples.

Concluding Remarks

I began by noting the possibility of extending Rawls' principles of justice as fairness to the context of India's development with special reference to the Dalit population. In this regard, the essay noted the non-metaphysical, practical and liberal nature of the principles. Against this background, the law of peoples was discussed. This led us to carefully look at the characteristics of peoples, both liberal and non-liberal decent peoples. Rawls' parameters of decent peoples were then scrutinized and this led to the realization that there are basic conceptual problems in extending justice as fairness to outside liberal peoples.

The difficulty lies in trying to characterize other societies wherein the Rawlsian precepts do not hold. If you are not free and equal then, according to Rawls' understanding of liberalism, you cannot be a moral, rational and liberal person or people. It is therefore not possible to extend Rawls' liberal principles of justice to the international arena, especially to non-liberal peoples. Justice as fairness will do fine with liberal peoples but the grounds for its application, according to its own understanding, do not obtain with non-liberal peoples. It now becomes possible to see the difficulty of going ahead with Chalam's suggestion of applying Rawlsian theory to an understanding of India's development with special reference to Dalits. Although India has a constitutional democracy, according to Chalam's own admission, the affirmative action policies have failed because they have been continuously hijacked by the caste system. Liberal capitalism, which has today gained ground with liberalization and globalization, has by the same process eluded a majority of the Dalits and other backward classes. The complicity of international capital itself, in this process of exclusion, especially with reference to the poor in the Third World (and the consequent problems created for Rawls' theory which skirts this issue), has also been noted by Thomas Pogge (1994) and other commentators. This means that Indian people, especially the poor and Dalits, are not free and equal and therefore are not in position to become embodiments of rationality, reasonableness and morality. The eager quest for modernization and liberal personhood, especially on the part of these sections of Indian society, can be enhanced by the eradication of caste discrimination against them.

Acknowledgement

This paper represents initial thoughts on Rawls, Dalits and development and draws on earlier presentations made at seminars in Madras, 2001, London, 2007 and Ahmedabad, 2008. I am grateful to all the participants for their comments. I have been particularly helped by discussions with Prof. Valerian Rodrigues, who has encouraged me to re-think some of my assumptions.

REFERENCES

Barry, B. 1975. "The Liberal Theory of Justice: A Critical Examination of the Principal Doctrines". In John Rawls (ed.), *A Theory of Justice*. Oxford: Clarendon.

Chalam, K.S. 2007. *Caste-based Reservations and Human Development in India*. New Delhi: Sage Publications.

Freeman, S. 2007. *Rawls*. London: Routledge.

Graham, P. 2007. *Rawls*. Oxford: Oneworld.

Pogge, T.W. 1994. "An Egalitarian Law of Peoples", *Philosophy and Public Affairs* 23(3): 195–224.

Rawls, J. (1951) 1999. "Outline of a Decision Procedure for Ethics". In S. Freeman, ed. *Collected Papers: John Rawls*. New Delhi: OUP.

———. (1958) 1999. "Justice as Fairness". In S. Freeman (ed.), *Collected Papers: John Rawls*. New Delhi: OUP.

———. 1972. *A Theory of Justice*. Oxford: Clarendon.

———. (1975) 1999. "A Kantian Conception of Equality". In S. Freeman (ed.), *Collected Papers: John Rawls*. New Delhi: OUP.

———. (1980) 1999. "Kantian Constructivism in Moral Theory". In S. Freeman (ed.) *Collected Papers: John Rawls*. New Delhi: OUP.

———. (1985) 1999. "Justice as Fairness: Political not Metaphysical". In S. Freeman (ed.) *Collected Papers: John Rawls*. New Delhi: OUP.

———. (1987) 1999. "The Idea of an Overlapping Consensus". In S. Freeman (ed.) *Collected Papers: John Rawls*. New Delhi: OUP.

———. (1988) 1999. "The Priority of Right and Ideas of the Good". In S. Freeman (ed.) *Collected Papers: John Rawls*. New Delhi: OUP.

———. 1993. *Political Liberalism*. New York: Columbia University Press.

———. 1999. *The Law of Peoples*. Cambridge, MA: Harvard University Press.

Reidy, D.A. 2004. "Rawls on International Justice: A Defense", *Political Theory* 32(3): 291–319.

Smith, S.B. 1986. "Hegel's Critique of Liberalism", *The American Political Science Review*, 80(1): 121–39.

9

Cooperatives, Dalits and Social Change

M.H. MAKWANA

Though the voluntary sector has been playing a key role in the emancipation of the depressed and suppressed people of the society since ancient times, it has gained momentum during the last few decades all over the world. This process is evident in India too for more than half a century. It is very clear from the history of the world in general and of a nation in particular that a number of enlightened people have made serious efforts to change the economic and socio-political conditions of the people.

The history of reform movements in the world and particularly in India reveals that reformist activities were basically philanthropic in nature and aimed at the elevation of the suppressed. These were neither based on any rational method nor it aimed at establishing any legitimate position for the suppressed. This kind of approach was mainly initiated under the influence of religious and humanistic ideology. However, the movements for organizing people, based on rational and scientific methods were started in 19th century by Jyotiba Phule and Raja Ram Mohan Roy. These movements became popular through the works of Gandhi and Ambedkar and their life mission to fight for the socio-economic and political rights of the downtrodden. Their efforts through their constant struggle and through the constitutional guarantees have made ever lasting impact.

In fact, after independence, a number of voluntary organizations also started working all over India for the emancipation of the depressed with the support of individuals, governments as well as international agencies. In spite of several plans and programmes for the development of the society in general and Dalits in particular by successive national and state governments for almost half a century, poverty and sufferings of the people have been increasing. As a result, people are losing faith in the sincerity of the governmental bureaucratic machinery. Hence, voluntary organizations working in different fields such as tribal, rural and urban are gaining more importance than the governmental machinery. However, in spite of the best efforts of these organizations, they are criticized on various counts. This article examines the efforts of the voluntary organizations in the field of cooperatives in bringing about social change among the Dalits.

Social Change

The term 'social change' denotes the development and historical transition of people and various dimensions of their collective life, ranging from their lifestyles, habits, dress codes, cultural traits and mores to social thinking and spiritual belief. Every society that takes up innovations in its group life naturally passes through a dynamic but painful process of attitudinal change, which often takes a long span of time. Just like an individual, the social mind also feels a sense of detachment and a pain of evolution while it passes through transition since it always shows a strong instinct to stick on to tradition. This makes the process complex and tedious and often incomplete and lingering. MacIver and Page (1979: 508) stressed this phenomenon in their writings on social change. According to them, the term 'social change' conveys the adoption of certain new attitudes appropriate to the context of modernity, but retaining the old identity. This implies that various sections feel the need to appropriate a space which would benefit them in the fast changing scenario.

Identifying significant changes involves examining the extent and depth of changes that have taken place in the underlying structure of a situation over a period of time. In case of human societies, measuring the extent of change in the system is a complex process since it demands comprehensive explanation regarding the change that has occurred in the basic institutions during a specific period and also it requires examination of elements that have not unchanged and the reasons for it.

For the past two centuries, social theorists have been trying to develop an acceptable theory that can explain the basic nature of social change. But, so far, no single theory has been developed that can give us a complete explanation of the diversity of social change. In this context, we can only identify the major factors that have consistently been influencing social change.

"Social change is a process responsive to many types of changes, to change in the man-made conditions of living, to change in the aptitudes and beliefs of man and to change that go back beyond human control to the biological and physical nature of things" (ibid.). Thus, MacIver and

Page try to investigate the trends of social change in relation to the three great orders, i.e., the biological, the cultural and the technological.

Changes that are taking place in the world today are producing different cultures and societies more interdependent than ever before. Secondly, these are faster compared to earlier times. Due to this process, changes taking place at one place can directly affect others. The social, political and economic changes, which go beyond the geographical borders of countries, decisively condition the fate of the societies outside.

Sociologist James H. Laue stresses 'power' as a key factor in social change. He says, "social change may be defined as the continuous process of re-distribution of power. Power is the control over decision—the decision that affects people's lives. The more the people affected in significant ways by a particular decision, the greater the power of the decision maker" (Laue, 1971: 219). According to Harry M. Johnson, "There are two kinds of processes going on in a social system, i.e., process that maintains or tends to maintain the structure of the system and process that tends to change it" (1969: 625).

Throughout the recorded social history, men have apparently considered that change per se is undesirable and that the ideal social condition is stability. Whether society, as they have known, has been stable or whether it has been undergoing rapid change, they have sought to maintain or to achieve continuity of social life—to preserve for their descendants what they have inherited from their ancestors. Folklore, myth, legend, theology, social philosophy, ethical and aesthetic standards and other symbolic constructs have, for the most part, reflected the traditional modes of social conduct and have operated as social controls, subtly or overtly, coercing the individual members of society to conform to the traditional ways of life.

Although the study of social change centres upon the rise, adoption and establishment of new social elements in a social system, the new is significant only in terms of its consequences. A new tool, a new idea, a new procedure, technological or otherwise, or a new pattern of human relationship becomes socially significant only through the way in which and the extent to which it functions differently from the old and this difference depends not only on the new element itself, but also upon the context in which it operates.

Theories of Social Change

The theories of social change can be grouped into four main categories: evolutionary, cyclical, conflict and functional. The evolutionary view of social change was highly influenced by Charles Darwin's theory of biological evolution. This theory fascinated many sociologists like Herbert Spencer, Walter White, Ralph Linton, etc. Spencer was of the opinion that societies have been gradually progressing towards a better stage. It always evolves from a military society to an industrial society. His view was known as Social Darwinism. Contemporary cultural evolutionists like White argue that "culture is an independent force that involves towards ever greater use of physical power, sources and ever greater control of environment" (cited in Biesanz and Biesanz, 1978: 430–31). Similarly, Linton says that "changes in culture have been directed towards a better adjustment of the social organism to its environment" (ibid.). Emile Durkheim identified the cause of social evolution as a society's increasing 'moral density'. He explains this idea by using the concept 'solidarity'. Durkheim viewed society as changing in the direction of the greater differentiation, interdependence and formal control under the pressure of increasing moral density.

The early evolutionary doctrines were conducive to the colonial interests of Europeans, as they provided justifications for colonial rule over primitive people and for the enforced spread of western culture. Those who supported this theory had not taken cultural relativity into consideration and hence judged and evaluated other cultures solely on the basis of their own standard culture.

Ian Robertson thinks that "cyclical theories of social change focus on the rise and fall of the civilizations attempting to discover and account for these patterns of growth and decay" (ibid.: 496). The famous cyclic theorists Pitrim A. Sorokin and Oswald Spengler experienced shorter range of ups and downs. Spengler, in his book, *The Decline of the West* pointed out that the fate of civilization was a matter of destiny. Each civilization has a life cycle similar to living organism. His theory has many limitations to explain the phenomenon of social change since the biological analogy he used is too unrealistic. According to Spengler, "It is not possible for societies to rejuvenate themselves. Change leads to extinction, not to perfection" (ibid.: 430–31).

Pitrim A. Sorokin, in his book, *Social and Cultural Dynamics* proposed that the society alternates between two cultural extremes: 'the sensate' and 'the ideational'. He felt that a certain amount of development in either direction is bound to be followed by its opposite. He detected this pattern in painting, law, war and revolution (ibid.: 431). Arnold Toynbee, in his book, *A Study of History* (1988) used 'challenges' and 'responses' as the key concepts to explain social change. Every society faces challenges—at first, challenges posed by the environment; later challenges from internal and external enemies. The nature of the responses determines the society's fate. The achievement of a civilization consists of its successful responses to challenges; if it cannot mount an effective response, it dies.

The major proponents of functionalism like Robert K. Merton and Talcott Parsons stressed that functioning of every social system has equilibrium in its goal. Parsons stressed the importance of cultural patterns in controlling the stability of society. He considered change, not as something that disturbs the social equilibrium, but something that alters the state of the equilibrium so that a qualitatively new equilibrium results. Merton believed that since a socio-cultural order is complex, interdependent, even fragile, system, you can never 'do just one thing'. Many plans have unexpected and unintended consequences which may or may not be desirable (Biesanz and Biesanz, 1978: 432).

The conflict theories highlight the forces producing instability, struggle and social disorganization. According to Ralf Dahrendorf, the major assumptions of conflict theories are: (1) every society is subjected to change at every moment, hence, social change is ubiquitous; (2) every society experiences social conflict at every moment; (3) every element in the society contributes to change; and (4) every society rests on constraints of some of its members by others. There is no society, changing or unchanging, which does not have conflict of one or the other kind. It is so obvious that there is no case of social change, which is not associated with conflict, some way or other. Dahrendorf further says, though conflict produces social change all the time, the change is not always revolutionary. We cannot change our laws, our bureaucracy, or even our families in many cases. Likewise, David Lockwood says, there are mechanisms in societies that make conflict inevitable and inexorable (cited in Kornblum, 1988: 581–82). According to R.L. Coser, conflict and disagreement are integral parts of people's relationships, not necessarily signs of instability and break up. In his analysis, the results of the social conflicts lead to change or they can stimulate innovation. Thus, Coser analyzes the role of conflict in maintaining group cohesion (cited in Wallace and Wolf, 1980: 134–36).

Social Change in Indian Society

A major part of Indian society consists of villages. An analysis of change with a focus on rural society is, therefore, important to understand the trends and directions of social change in the country. Change in any aspect of rural society can be seen only by understanding the totality. The economists who focused attention on rural society, did not give any importance to social relationships in their analyses. Their concern was only economic categorization of the agrarian society. They debated about the direction and pattern of change in India. One section of these economists focused on change based on village economy and supported decentralized planning. There are a large number of sociological studies which, in a similar manner, totally ignored the economic aspect of village life organization or dealt with it only at surface level. Most of such studies of rural change are mainly concerned with the changes in the structure and functions of one or a few villages. They are incomplete in many other respects. The analysis of factors in the process and sequence of change in the stages of modernization has not received the attention it deserves. In the study of social impact, the dimensions of time and rate are necessary to the system as structure and function. Moreover, all dimensions of structure and functions are to be given due treatment, not only the economic, social, psychological or any single dimension of the system. They all are closely related.

In order to understand the forces behind the process of change in rural society, it is important to examine the major strategies adopted by social scientists for the analysis of social change and then find out the proper way of understanding it. Two main ways of looking at social change are: One that tries to understand rural social change through macro-level analysis and generalizations. The village is seen as a part of the total structure, and uniformity in the various parts of the system is assumed in this perspective as it ignores inter-village and intra-village variations. The other is the one which focuses on the social and ideological autonomy of the village and assumes that the changes in rural society are mainly through a natural, gradual, evolutionary process. A village is a unique independent entity in this approach. The change is therefore to be studied at micro level.

While in the first view the major sources considered responsible for change in a village are exogenous, the second emphasizes endogenous sources of change. A close examination of the two lines of study shows the incompleteness of each for grasping the reality of rural social change as we find it today. A congruence of the two may provide a more appropriate way of looking at rural social change. The contention in upholding an integrated strategy is to emphasize that though the change in rural society in India is being induced from outside the context, the nature of responses is indigenously determined.

Dalits

The term 'Dalit' has come into vogue in the last 75 years. It is Sanskrit in origin, meaning to develop, to get damaged with pieces, get injured. The term also means deserted, impaired, crushed, suppressed and oppressed persons. In Gujarat, the world 'Dalit' was first used by Kanaiyalal Munshi in his presidential speech at 13th convention of Gujarat Sahitya Parishad in 1937–38. The renowned national poet Zaverchand Meghani has also used this in his poem 'Yug Vanddana'. Before Independence, in Maharashtra, poet Keshavasut also used this term long before the inception of Dalit literature in 1960. During the Dalit Panther movement, all depressed, oppressed, weaker sections and minorities, women and tribals were considered as Dalits.

Dalits (mostly referring to Scheduled Castes) form the neglected strata of Indian society. Before independence they were considered untouchables and used to do low-paid, unskilled and dirty jobs. They lived on the outskirts of villages. Dalits do not form homogeneous groups. In reality, there are many sub-castes under the Scheduled Castes (SCs). These castes vary from State to State. Since the beginning of *varna vyavastha* they have been given different names such as *Shudras, Atishudras, Parias, Panchamas, Namashudras, Antyajas* and *Avarnas*. Mahatma Gandhi called them—*Harijan*—a term coined by Narasimha Mehta, a Gujarati saint. Dr B.R. Ambedkar called them 'depressed class'. They were categorized as Scheduled Castes in Indian Constitution. In Gujarat, Urmilaben Patel has identified this community as a 'developing community'.

Cooperatives

Cooperation is not new to India. A close study of the present village life in any part of the country makes us think about the spirit of cooperation permeating all socio-economic activities in some way or the other. From the beginning cooperatives have been regarded by the government as a means to create a more equitable form of society. For instance, the State of Gujarat has taken the lead in setting up of milk cooperatives through the National Dairy Development Board in Anand. Eventually, the non-governmental organizations (NGOs) have played a crucial role in making cooperation available to the rural sector, especially to the poor and landless.

An organization is one of the possible structures through which the power of collective action can be materialized in order to bring about changes in society. Collective action implies a group of people acting together for a purpose. In this study, the organization includes NGOs and cooperative societies. People, however, are the actors and targets of those changes which will take place ultimately in them, for them and by them.

In this context, social practitioners influenced by the theories of entrepreneurial management tend to consider the deals with their organizations as mere enterprises. Various perspectives are utilized in order to bring a greater understanding and efficacy to the operations of these organizations. For instance, the very expression 'human resources' may treat people as mere resources for the organizations—a resource at the service of the goals of that organization. In a way, human nature may be lost somewhere in the process of becoming a means for the organization at the service of social change. Each person, however, is more than a man or woman for the organization. People's lives, their ups and downs are also factors influencing the objectives of these organizations. Hence, understanding organizations does not always imply that the people belonging to these organizations are also being understood. In other words, the organizations must understand people as much as the people must understand the organization. So, for this reason, this study proposes to consider and analyze effective action for social change. It is because there has been an undervaluation of the person and a lack of concern and interest regarding the interactions between the multiple dimensions of the person and his environment

The objective of this study is, therefore, to highlight the role of the individual and to examine his problems and struggles in dealing with the organization and the social environment. It also examines those factors affecting the individual which will have an impact on change and on the quality of collective action.

For this study three organizations have been selected. They are: Centre for Rural Development (CRD) located in Ahmedabad, Federation of Agricultural Cooperatives (FAC), and Women's Credit Cooperative (WCC) in Bhal, Khambat taluka, Kheda district in Gujarat.

CRD is a registered trust working for the development of Dalits, tribals, other backward communities, minorities, and especially women. In 1970, it was invited by a group of college teachers who wanted to apply behavioural methods and techniques to motivate a group of Vankars, Dalits in Bhal of Khambat taluka. It was founded on the conviction that a change in behaviour, motivation and bargaining power was inseparable from a gain in the economic bargaining power of the community. CRD started some economic afforestation projects through the establishment of a number of agricultural cooperatives managed by the Vankars. In course of time, it extended its activities to other areas and other communities. First, it was started, in Dhandhuka, it started work with the Vankars and Koli Patels and later in Danta taluka with the tribals of the area. The organization has attempted to establish various types of local organizations to raise the bargaining power of these communities. By 1987, CRD had also integrated a gender perspective into its approach.

FAC is a local organization operating from the Bhal village of Khambat taluka. It was created by federating the various village cooperatives established in Bhal. The members of these cooperatives were mostly Vankars. Each village cooperative developed forest plantation on degraded land leased out to the community by the government. Later, when the FAC was established, the cooperatives diversified their activities into fisheries and started an integrated agricultural programme to improve the productivity of Vankar farmers in the cultivation of rice. FAC also provided seeds and fertilizers at low prices and set up a rice mill to process the produce of farmers.

WCC was promoted again by the CRD as an attempt to redress the imbalance, in favour of women and a commitment to include women in the effort to correct the injustices inherent in the social structures of caste and gender. As in many other cases, the movement started around various village groups of women, which decided to collect the women's savings and address their problems. Once the cooperative was registered, its growth was remarkable. After an initial period in which the committee decided to collect savings and increased capital, they decided to frame some regulations and by-laws for the credit. Lately, there have been various attempts to diversify their operations so as to take care of the consumption needs of the community.

A number of people belonging to three organizations were interviewed to get the plurality of experiences and perspectives. Sixty respondents were selected for formal interviews and many more were interviewed informally. The information furnished in this way was cross-examined with the attendance at meetings and camps. Examination of archival material, reports and informal observations was also done. The study is focused on personal and collective ups and downs in people's interactions within and outside the organization. Here, an attempt has been made to explain: (i) the interaction between the CRD members and their environment in the process of change; (ii) the effects of those interactions on the individuals as members of the CRD; and (iii) the influence of (i) and (ii) on collective action.

Interface between the Person and Organization

The main function of the CRD is to act as a catalyst. This organization brings isolated people together around common ideas and needs. The organization contextualizes what they have previously experienced as personal and individual problems within structural and community perspectives. It has brought about awareness of the social, economic and cultural structures responsible for perpetration of injustices against Dalits, tribals and women. The organization provides to its members a conceptual framework, a vision which is liberating and a kind of formation that regards people's experiences as the foundation for understanding and critical reflection. It is a means of development at the personal and community spheres under conditions of relative social support away from the authority of tradition.

Education is understood not in the sense of transmission of knowledge but in the sense of learning by posing questions and stimulating dialogue. A new experience of acceptance and a relatively safe setting are provided where necessary behavioural changes can take place. Unconventional modes of formation are adopted to learn symmetrical relations of connectedness and equality with others. The use of non-biased language for communication and the fact that men and women use the feminine grammatical form to refer to both male and female is just one example of the importance given to gender awareness.

The organization has adopted the means of conscientization, a concept popularized by Paulo Friere. Dialogue acts as a means for fostering critical consciousness about social reality. The aim of this kind of formation is a living knowledge that gets translated into action. The process of conscientization becomes part of an empowering strategy, which develops an awareness of the personal and structural dimensions of oppression, which is suppressed by the dominant knowledge system. Formation is a means to balance unequal relations of knowledge, which are critical in perpetuating class, caste and elite domination. Formation enables people to identify themselves as knowing actors, defining their reality, shaping their new identity and transforming their lives. It is a means of preventing an elite group from exclusively determining the interests of others. In a Dalit member's own words, "I did my MA in Economics and I came to know about so many things through books, about poverty and all that but what is real poverty? The books say one thing, the reality is completely different. I told a hundred of SC and ST students that I had sat on a bench and I had been taught what poverty was but that when I joined CRD I found out that it was actually a different thing". One Dalit woman said, "The development course has helped me to organize not only my work but my ideas and reality. It is not only to work as charity but understanding people's movements and culture. It helps you to see things more critically and analytically". Gradually, the members feel motivated by a sense of commitment rather than job, directed towards meaning and the purpose of justice. Another Dalit person said, "I am a Dalit, I fought for my rights, for equality in my community, for my people ... the course on development has made me understand a lot because what earlier I believed, I now know is not true". People working with one another realise the growing awareness of previously common unrecognized needs. The staff are social beings coming from different religious faiths such as Hindu, Muslim, Parsi, Christian; different castes and classes; and men and women, who are the subjects and objects of their change and development.

The organization based on shared values, collective action and commitment is discovered at the intersection of one's growing commitment and new powers achieved through the social self. This set of values can guide anyone, no matter what their position in societies. This is the context for impulses towards group identity, social consciousness and collective action. Collective actors emerge and people develop their own specific lifestyles and culture. People's commitment is preserved by a continuous identification with the organization's collective experiences of injustice.

The organization has created spaces where Dalits can break the stereotypes of 'being good for nothing' or 'rice Christians' and 'illiterate'. The way to disprove this stereotype is to actuate behaviour that contradicts it, that is, by taking the initiative, developing skills and qualities and responding actively and positively to any kind of human problem. But, at the deeper level of their being, some realize constantly that there are other forces that compel them to feel that they are not as good as others. They are aware of certain personal inner dynamics which control their thinking and behaviour. This situation creates a kind of inner conflict, a duality between what the organization proclaims and what it feels deep down. Ideas internalized from childhood influence feelings and behaviour and limit the Dalits' capacities of being fully aware of themselves.

Learning also involves examining the self from a new and critical standpoint. It is a way of seeing how life experiences one's understanding of self. People can collectively explore the real commitments that define their lives as human beings and create a vision of self-actualization in their social environments—a new way of expressing what their world should be.

Through the actions of the CRD members feel inwardly empowered. This gives them a feeling of emotional and intellectual vitality. Justice and equality are the values most people identify with. These shared values help them to overcome differences among themselves so as to generate the group's identity which becomes social power.

Knowledge and skills in management and team work dynamics are quite high on the whole. This helps the group to understand the functioning of the organization as well as its own dynamics. The members acknowledge the need for a more professional attitude towards work. Although this is a necessary input at the organizational level, a majority of the interviewed members said, "our relationships are professionally alright but we do not go beyond that" or "no one cares about my life after working here for so many years". The absence of empathetic relationships of support may give an impression of replicating the style of business management in what is actually a non-profit organization. According to another member, "CRD applies managerial concepts and skills but it also should take care of emotional and physical aspects".

The emphasis of professionalism or leadership has a dual impact on the members. On the one hand, they understand the necessity of leadership for mobilization and so on, and on the other, leadership often becomes the reference point to evaluate their performance. The leader appears as a role model with full potential and qualities. The notion of leader in organization is related to 'superiority' and power. As power is something needed and wanted, everyone wants to be a leader. As a result, all the interviewed members, except one, are considered to be leaders. It seems that people feel somehow forced to say that they are leaders when in fact they are not because otherwise they could feel inferior. People are not nearly as incompetent or incapable, relative to leaders, as we seem to feel. Dependence on leaders does not allow people to feel responsible and give their best because it is assumed that only leaders can do so. People should be motivated and trained to give their best as persons. There is no need to be a leader to bring about changes.

Conceptual myths like 'intellectual' as a person with bookish knowledge along with the concept of 'field worker' as a practical person divide the organization into these two categories. The problem is the value of superiority-inferiority attached to each term. Each feels simultaneously superior and inferior to the other. It is again one of those ways of categorizing and stereotyping people, which hinders the integration of the two dimensions of change and the establishment of the necessary healthy relations for a joint action.

Interface between the Person and Society

The members, who identify with the CRD and are committed to its cause, also live in a society that is fundamentally different from and possibly at odds with the values of the organization. These practitioners do not easily fit into the dominant culture of a society where gender, class, caste, race and religious discrimination are the predominant norms.

Family and community in India are very strong support systems for the individual. These traditional norms of coping with insecurity do not fully lose meaning. That is why, changes affecting those support systems must take place gradually or at the back of the family relations so that those family relationships are not seriously affected.

Family and community influence and pressure to maintain traditional values which go against the practitioner's personal convictions, are very high. According to one respondent, "I hold views opposed to theirs, they know, but I do not trumpet it around, to keep the peace. To put family before self is the area of internal turmoil". The stereotype of women as unassertive leads society to see particular, moderately assertive women as extremely assertive and provocative at home. Adjustments take place continuously as a way of surviving. These women also find it difficult to find a meaningful and supportive environment besides the family and community where they belong to and where most of their social relationships have to be established. They find it wrong with a society that does not integrate a person's social worth into their right to be herself. Being a living model is more important and it is the only way.

Non-Dalit women face family opposition for working in an organization which does not provide the necessary status to them. Their values are rarely shared by families. The women have to pay the price of following practices and ideas which go against their beliefs for the sake of peace and family acceptance. In other words, they have to be 'good' in order to gain acceptance, love and support. Support outside the family is almost non-existent.

It is the women who face the dilemma between how they have to live outside and how they have to live at home. They are pulled back and forth by contradictory values and styles of life. They continue to bear the burden of domestic work. They must follow the traditional roles of mother, wife and daughter-in-law in the expected stereotyped manner and in opposition to what they work for and believe in. After marriage the workload of women staff members increased considerably affecting work at their workplace.

The women's feelings and struggle are hidden behind smiling faces. Their troubles are born in solitude. Men's situation is quite different. They definitely 'help' their wives at home but none of them is responsible for running the house and looking after the children. On top of that the wives 'kindly' adjust to their schedules and agendas without any complaint.

The traditional role of a son, a husband or a father does not create any problem of identity or discomfort as it reinforces the already existing role. The comment, "I never tell my wife what she has to do" reveals the way a husband takes advantage of a situation which favours him.

Consumerism and the desire for higher standards of living also play an important role in pulling back the individual from the organization. "The world is changing and other factors have to be considered. The media is influencing us to change our ideology, our commitment. The organization may not be able to change accordingly. Then clashes between the individual and the organization ... then the problem of dysfunctionality."

Interface between the Person, Organization and Society

Any change brings about conflict. Conflict emerges when power is at stake. Power is also intimately attached to identity. Dalit community, women and Christianity are sectors of society seeking power, justice and respect. They see new structures coming up—local organizations, cooperatives—strong enough to fight discrimination and inequality. Upper castes, men and at times the Catholic clergy retaliate strongly. There are too many fronts to fight on at the same time. The practitioners' own beliefs are challenged by the influence of new liberating ideas, provided by the new environment, the organization, and by the shock of the clashes with social reality. Practitioners consciously challenge the status quo, both through their individual and collective actions. These individuals must continuously handle the tension between the personal and professional lives at odds with one another. They struggle to reconcile conflicting identities fostered in different but, in this case, overlapping social networks. This is the area of negotiations for the sake of change.

A variety of powerful emotions contribute to the difficulty of sustaining change. The pulls on each of these three stakeholders, e.g., the person, the organization and society, are painful and threatening. Loneliness, silence and tiredness may contribute to the temptation to abandon the fight.

The more radical the person is, the higher is the price to be paid. The social consequence is isolation, misunderstanding and the constant need to explain to other social institutions and organizations what one does and why and how one functions. Those who are more radical are actual leaders in most cases and independent of family or societal opposition and support. A radical approach to things brings about losses of emotional support of the closest ones.

Social identity and self-identity become gradually antagonistic. There has been selective change in self-perception, but two or more levels of identity are functioning antagonistically. Thus, remarked a person, "somehow I find myself a victim of my own demons". These demons are the product of socialization and cultural environment. These are man-made. So, one needs to look at them and decide if he or she wants to keep them in his or her head or not. If people do not become aware of themselves, it is because of these demons only.

Society consists of Dalit members and their status vis-à-vis other castes considered. In this situation, one has to invest a lot of energy in counteracting external powerful influences. Even today external structures must be fought as much as internal ones in the voluntary sector. Being a Dalit has its own consequences. To a question, "Do you still feel the pain of being a Dalit?" the answer would be "I definitely feel the pain of being a Dalit. Just because I am a Dalit they (upper caste people) do not want me to reach to their status or power. Right now I am doing so much work in the organization that I can guarantee that not a single director in any NGO will be able to do so much work with so much professionalism and intellectual capacity. The moment they see that you are a Dalit they will claim that your intellectual capacity is very low."

In this context, the non-Dalit members also get the feedback from observers and they are confused about what they really stand for. The ambivalence of non-Dalits as sensed by Dalit members may result in guilt, self-defeat and a sense of dual identity. The non-Dalits focus their attention on understanding the rights of both Dalits and non-Dalits. Practitioners also feel the incongruities between their own values and beliefs about social justice and the values and beliefs enacted in society. Their survival depends on an ongoing public awareness of the separation between society and the organization and an ongoing private acknowledgement that both are vital parts of their lives.

There is also the tendency towards individualized forms of change. The individual becomes gradually the centre of his or her own decisions and conduct in life opposing the thinking behind the traditional lifestyle of his or her community. For instance, these changes affect patterns of interaction dependent upon housing and living arrangements. These individuals chose their own separate relationships and live on their own. It implies that the ascriptively organized joint family starts losing control over the individual.

Surprisingly, the men's awareness of, and commitment to fighting gender discrimination is very high. They help in household work doing activities as child rearing, cooking and washing utensils or clothes. On the other hand, not only women's willingness to work is common, they are also ready to fight against injustices done to women. All these activities have also been promoted by male members of the NGO with a genuine aim to promoting women's liberation.

The women's history is marked by their struggle with multiple injustices. They are struggling to go ahead in a castiest patriarchal society and are also to develop Dalit identity in their organization. They also face the fear of being ineffective at work because of their Dalit status. The struggle may be invisible to their other caste members.

Conclusion

Dalits who occupy the lowest status in society have been helped by individuals and institutions in their upliftment. This paper examines the social change attained by Dalits through the cooperatives, initiated by CRD. CRD as a catalyst has worked for the development of Dalits, tribals, other backward communities, minorities and women. The cooperatives have helped in the empowerment of Dalits, specially women. Dalit women who have double disability, one being a Dalit and the other being a woman, have benefitted through these cooperatives.

REFERENCES

Biesanz, J. and Biesanz, M.H. 1978. *Introductory Sociology.* New Jersey: Prentice Hall.

Buchanan, Francis.1990. *Land of Perumals of Cochin: Its Past and Present.* New Delhi: Asian Educational Services.

Johnson, Harry M. 1969. *Society: A Systematic Introduction.* New Delhi: Allied Publishers.

Kornblum, William.1988. *Sociology in a Changing World.* New York: Holt Rinehart and Winston Inc.

Laue, James H. 1971. *Sociology for the Seventies: A Comparative Perspective.* New York: John Wiley & Sons Inc.

MacIver, R.M. and Page, C.H. 1979. *Society: An Introduction.* Madras: Macmillan Company.

Wallace, Ruth A. and Wolf, Alison. 1980. *Sociology.* New Jersey: Prentice Hall.

Worsley, Peter. 1982. *Contemporary Sociological Theory.* New Jersey: Prentice Hall.

10

Scheduled Castes, Reservation and Social Mobility

RICHARD PAIS

Caste system is a unique system of stratification found in India and over centuries it has continued to be of critical importance. It is one of the complex, hierarchical and interrelated systems. It is intimately related to social, economic and religious systems and, in the recent years, to political system as well. Any person desirous of knowing the Indian social structure should have the knowledge of caste system. Untouchables occupy the lowest strata in the caste system. This paper examines the social mobility attained by Scheduled Castes (SCs) as a result of reservation in education and employment. It is based on the research done by the author on 220 SCs employed in government and semi-government organizations in Mangalore. For the purpose of analysis, their class of employment, i.e., Class I to IV, was taken as the basis of employment.

Origin of Untouchability

Though the caste system is more than 2,000 years old, untouchability is of a later origin. Till about the second century AD, certain castes like the Ayogava, Paulkasas and the Nishads were despised, but were not considered to be untouchables (Gupta, 1993: 139). The notion of purity and pollution, as Dumont (1972) observed, is integrally linked with the practice of untouchability. Gradually, this notion of purity and pollution freed itself from its specific and original task of separating untouchables from the others but began to be operative at different planes of the caste system. Imputed with maximum degree of ritual and social impurity, the occupations of these castes were held to be the lowest in the hierarchy. Being outside the fourfold classification of society, they were known as

Panchamas (the fifth *varna*). With the emergence of castes *(jatis)* there also arose many castes among the untouchables.

The untouchables were involved in occupations, which were usually considered to be polluting or defiling. These included occupations like scavenging, removing carcasses from the village, etc. Though the untouchables were related to other castes through the *jajmani* relations, they themselves were not eligible to receive several services, particularly by the other upper caste service providers. They were even not allowed to own land and houses. The untouchables of Kerala were not allowed to carry umbrellas, to wear shoes or gold ornaments, to milk the cows or even to use the ordinary language of the country. Both men and women were forbidden from covering their bodies above the waist (Ghurye, 1990: 13).

The untouchables suffered many religious disabilities too as no Brahmin performed any ceremony for them. Being debarred from entering temples, they sought to propitiate the local deities and demons by sacrificing 'unclean' animals as pigs and cocks. Education and learning of sacred scriptures were denied to them. In the laws of Manu, it is ordered that molten lead be poured into the ears of any Shudra who dared to listen to a reading of the Vedas (Isaacs, 1965: 65). Despite all these deprivations the untouchables were an integral part of the village, town or city. According to Srinivas, "the fact that they are denied privileges which the higher castes enjoy does not mean that they are not an integral part of the society" (1989: 65).

At different times in history these castes were designated as Chandalas, Panchamas, Atishudras, Dalits, etc. Mahatma Gandhi used to call them 'Harijan', a term coined by Narasimha Mehta, a Gujarati saint. 'Dalit' is a recent coinage and came into vogue in the 1970s in Maharashtra with the formation of a distinct political party, Dalit Panthers. This term is now used all over India. "Dalit identity is primarily political and hence its orientation is militant and rebellious" (Oommen, 1994).

'Scheduled Caste' is the most widely prevalent classificatory term used to designate these classes. In 1936, for purposes of giving effect to the provisions for special electoral representation in the Government of India Act, 1935, some untouchable castes were listed (i.e., scheduled). From then onwards the term 'Scheduled Castes' has been in vogue and the Constitution of India has accepted it. But nowhere in the Constitution have they been defined. "The terms 'Scheduled Caste' and 'Scheduled

Tribe' are only legal fiction and a constitutional myth" (Parvathamma, 1989: 4). Articles 341 and 342 of the Constitution of India empower the President of India after consulting the head of the particular state to notify by an order the castes, races or tribes or parts of or groups within castes, races or tribes which shall for the purposes of the Constitution be deemed to be Scheduled Castes/Scheduled Tribes in relation to that state. Ghurye (1990: 306) defines Scheduled Castes as those groups, which are named in the Scheduled Castes Order in force from time to time. "The Scheduled Caste category is intended to comprise those groups isolated and is disadvantaged by their 'untouchability', i.e., their low status in the traditional Hindu caste hierarchy which exposed them to invidious treatment, severe disabilities, and deprivation of economic, social, cultural, and political opportunities" (Galanter, 1984: 122).

Scheduled Castes' Welfare

Although there has been a general impression that the caste system is resistant to change, there have been several attempts to change by way of reforms and legislations. The earliest attempt towards a reform can be traced to Buddhism. Though Buddhism was not primarily concerned with caste or with the practice of untouchability, it developed as a protest against ritualism, traditional and Brahminic Hinduism. It provided a rational scheme to recover from the ritual-stricken and caste-ridden society. Another such attempt was through Jainism. Unlike Buddhism, it never posed a serious threat to Hinduism. People were attracted towards Jainism for its principle of *ahimsa* (non-violence) but in actuality it had little influence over the caste system. Veerasaivism in the 12th century condemned caste differences and the practice of untouchability. But, like most of other religion-based reforms, it also had to succumb to the pressures of caste system and eventually became a caste.

Islam, during the 13th century and later, appealed to many among the low castes and outcastes, especially when it was the religion of the ruling class. Christianity, another casteless creed, tried to impress on the natives in the Indian sub-continent. Christian missionaries converted quite a large number of untouchable castes and tribes, and provided educational and health facilities. In the 18th century several social reform movements, such as Arya Samaj, Brahma Samaj and Ramakrishna Mission, preached against the inequality based on caste. Saints like Gyaneshwar and Tukaram, and social reformers like M.G. Ranade, Mahatma Jyotiba Phule, B.R. Ambedkar and Mahatma Gandhi, also tried to put an end to the evil of untouchability.

The contributions of Dr Ambedkar and Mahatma Gandhi for the eradication of untouchability are very significant. Though both were very staunch in their cause of eradicating untouchability, they differed in the ways of solving the problem. Mahatma Gandhi described untouchability as the black spot on Indian society. Despite his belief in *varnashrama dharma*, he pioneered in myriad ways to awaken the conscience of Hindu India to ameliorate the lot of untouchables. In his profound love for the untouchables, he declared, "I do not want to be reborn. But if I have to be reborn, I should be born an Untouchable" (Mahar, 1969: 72). Dr Ambedkar, a Mahar from Maharashtra,[1] tried to attack the very root of the problem, i.e., the caste system. For him, the institution of untouchability was an integral part of Hinduism since caste was a major tenet of Hindu religious beliefs. Hence untouchability was not merely a social or economic problem but religious problem as well. He asserted that there would be outcastes as long as there are castes. Therefore, according to him, nothing can emancipate the outcastes except the destruction of the caste system. Having failed to improve the conditions of untouchables in the caste structure of Hindu society, he renounced the Hindu religion. In October 1956, Ambedkar along with two lakh Mahar followers, embraced Buddhism. Addressing a large gathering after the conversion, Ambedkar proclaimed, "The Hindu religion offered no opportunity for the Untouchables to improve their lot, for it is based on inequality … . On the other hand, Buddhism is based on equality and justice … . I would like to see all India become Buddhist" (Mahar, 1969: XVIII).

Though the British government followed a policy of non-interference in caste, it tried to discourage caste exclusiveness. Because of the pressures from a few social reformers and the protests by a few untouchable castes, the British governments had to enact several legislations. The Government of Madras, for instance, passed the Madras Removal of Civil Disabilities Act in 1938. According to this Act, it was a penal offence to discriminate against the castes in regard to publicly supported facilities such as roads, wells and transportation, as well as privately run establishments such as restaurants, teashops, hotels, shops etc. In 1858, the Government of Bombay also announced that all schools maintained at the government cost would be open to all castes and classes.

After independence, the Constitution of India prohibited the practice of untouchability in any form. Article 17 states that untouchability is abolished and its practice in any form is forbidden, and that the enforcement of any disability arising out of untouchability shall be an offence punishable in accordance with law. Articles 15, 25, 29(2), 38 and 46 deal with untouchability, and prohibit all forms of discrimination against any group of people. The Constitution also provides for the adoption of positive measures to put an end to untouchability, and helps to promote the educational and economic interests of the weaker sections of people. Though the Constitution was framed in 1950, it was only in 1955 that the Indian Parliament passed the Untouchability (Offences) Act. Repeated demands for stronger protective legislation forced the government to change the legislation into Protection of Civil Rights Act in 1976.

The Indian government is following the policy of 'protective discrimination'. The Constitution (Articles 16, 332, 334 and 335) provides for the reservation of seats for them in the Parliament and State Legislative Assemblies. Articles 29 and 46 provide for their educational uplift.

Thus, for nearly 60 years, there have been consistent efforts to safeguard the interests of the SCs. Consequently, several social and economic changes are evident among them. Though the changes were slow before independence, they have been accelerated after independence, in particular during the last 20 years. It is true that legal provisions have not helped much in raising their social and economic status; the protective discrimination of the government in the areas of employment, education and politics has substantially contributed to the enhancement of their status.

Education and Social Mobility

Education is an important social process, which has an important bearing on the lives of people. It is a consciously controlled process whereby changes in behaviour are produced in the person. In this process changes are brought about by external control. The aim of education is not mere acquisition of knowledge but helping the individual to make proper adjustment in his or her social environment. So, with education, the individuals become able members of society.

In the modern world education is one of the important factors of social mobility. It is a source of social status in society. It is an elevator of social progress. In a free society the individuals are able to acquire education and increase their status in society. The developed countries of the world have progressed today because of the progress they have made in the field of education. Education not only determines one's occupation but also improves it and in turn leads to improved income. In general, better-educated person is in a better position to deal with problems of everyday life.

When India became an independent nation, among several other problems, it confronted the problem of social and economic backwardness of some sections of people. Such backwardness was primarily due to lack of education among them. It was believed that with the spread of education, not only would several social evils eventually disappear, but also would enable the backward and the SC people to get better employment opportunities. The Government of India tried to impart education and create such facilities for their social and economic upliftment. SCs were one of the groups, which were most backward. An attempt is made here to trace the progress made in the field of education and its consequence upon social mobility for the SCs in India.

Though education is mainly the concern of the state governments, the Government of India has not only made liberal allocation of funds but also special provisions in all the five year plans for the education of SCs and STs. Besides, governments both the central and state levels have also initiated a number of measures to bring these communities on par with general population. Important amongst them are: (1) reservation of seats in schools and colleges and other educational institutions; (2) relaxation in age limits and lowering of minimum marks for admission to various institutions; (3) exemption from payment of admission fees, tuition fees, examination fees and special fees like medical, library etc.; (4) various types of scholarships and stipends provided by the Department of Education and Social Welfare; (5) free distribution of books, uniforms etc.; and (6) free hostels for the students.

In spite of the earnest efforts of the government and other non-governmental agencies, the SCs still lag behind the rest of the population in their educational achievement. Among the SCs themselves, some groups have made more progress than others. These are usually the urban-based, castes/groups and some who were not formerly untouchables. Rural-based SCs, by and large, continue to be educationally and economically backward.

Discrimination Faced

Discrimination based on caste has been a part of most SC people's life experience. A question was asked whether the respondents experienced any discrimination because of their caste background during schooling. It was reported that the fellow students, teachers, administrators and the public used to discriminate them. It used to take place in the class rooms, hostels, games field, camps etc. Discrimination was of various types. The most common type of discrimination reported was that they were given a separate bench. Even teachers were no exception in discriminating the students of the SC community. They used to abuse and cane them for coming in physical contact with them. A few other respondents narrated how many of their fellow caste students had to discontinue studies as a result of teachers' caste prejudices. If these respondents could finish their schooling, it was largely because of the perseverance and relatively better economic status with which they could withstand prejudice and punishments.

Discrimination was also found in hostels where such students were allotted separate rooms, utensils etc. and they were often asked to clean the hostels. Many of the talented students were not allowed to represent the school or college in sports and games because of their caste background. It was also the case in National Cadet Corps or National Service Scheme and in such other extra-curricular activities. At least four respondents were prevented from entering the Hindu temples by the teachers when they were taken to educational camps and tours.

One of the important features of this discrimination was that the respondents did not feel much discrimination when they were in primary and high schools. They felt it more when they were in pre-university classes and in colleges. In other words, it implies that caste-based discrimination seems to have been less severe in rural schools than in urban colleges. Discrimination has been intense in universities and almost all the respondents who have completed their post-graduation reported about this. Here discrimination was reported to be in subtle forms, such as avoidance behaviour, awarding fewer marks by teachers, passing sarcastic remarks etc. It thus appears that discrimination of SC students was much more in the college and university campuses than the schools located in villages and small towns.

Inter-generational Educational Mobility

Taking into consideration the backwardness of the SCs historically in the field of education, it is but natural to find a gradual improvement in the educational accomplishments among them in every subsequent generation. In this connection, the educational achievements of three generations were compared as shown in Table 1:

Table 1
Inter-generational Educational Mobility

Educational level	*Education of*					
	Grandfathers		*Fathers*		*Respondents*	
Illiterate	205	(93.2)	101	(45.9)	6	(2.8)
Lower Primary	7	(3.2)	30	(13.6)	8	(3.6)
Higher Primary	5	(2.3)	44	(20.0)	17	(7.8)
High School	3	(1.3)	16	(7.4)	39	(17.7)
SSLC	—	—	22	(10.4)	41	(18.6)
PUC/Inter	—	—	3	(1.3)	36	(16.3)
Degree	—	—	4	(1.8)	42	(19.1)
PG	—	—	—	—	16	(7.3)
Diploma	—	—	—	—	15	(6.8)
Total	220		220		220	

Note: Figures in parentheses are percentages.

As may have been anticipated, there is an impressive inter-generational educational mobility among the respondents. Illiteracy, which was as high as 93 per cent among the grandfathers, comes down by half to 46 per cent among the fathers of the respondents. Correspondingly, the proportion of those with education up to high school gradually goes up in the subsequent generations. Examining the inter-generational educational mobility between the father and the son, we see a high level of mobility. Illiteracy, which was present among 101 fathers of respondents, has reduced and is found among six respondents only. Similarly, the education has increased in all levels among the respondents compared to their fathers and grandfathers.

Education and Employment

One important disability among the SCs was that traditionally they were engaged in occupations, which were ritually polluting and with low economic status. An important means to overcome this problem was to change the occupation.[2] In order to encourage them to take up occupations in the nearby developing industrial and administrative sectors, the government provided reservations for them in public sector employment proportionate to the size of their population. While there is a gradual shift from rural-based menial occupations over the years, we can still find them in low status and low-paid jobs even in the modern occupations. Thus, for instance, it is mainly the SCs who are employed as sweepers or cleaners (*bhangis* or *poura karmikas*) in the municipal corporations, government offices, banks, etc. One of the reasons for such a phenomenon is that members of other castes do not seem to be as willing as the SCs to take up such menial occupations. Besides, many SCs seeking employment in organized sectors do not have the educational qualifications higher than that required for such menial jobs. For, the type of employment taken up by workers is usually related to the kind and extent of education they have had (Nandu Ram, 1988; Prakash, 1989). Table 2 shows the relationship between education and the type of employment.

As may be seen from Table 2, there is a near perfect fit between the status of employment and one's educational qualifications, particularly at the two extremes. All the illiterates are employed in occupations designated as Class IV and those with higher levels of education in occupations of high social and economic status. However, some notable anomalous instances are also to be found, for whom education has not necessarily resulted in any significantly higher status occupations. For instance, a person with a Diploma in Engineering, and 12 per cent respondents with SSLC, are engaged in occupations grouped as Class IV. In fact, 46 per cent of respondents engaged in this category of employment are with educational qualifications of high school level or above. The next category of employment, namely, Class III, consists of clerks, typists, etc. Usually, for these posts the minimum prescribed qualification is SSLC. In this category, we find nearly 45.9 per cent of persons with more than the minimum qualifications prescribed for the posts. In other words, they are overqualified for jobs they are engaged in. Indeed, a majority of the Bachelor's degree holders work as Class III employees. Two persons even have post-graduate degree, working as clerks and were hopeful that they will get a promotion, and were willing to change employment for better prospects.[3] Statistically, we can infer that as the 'p' value of the test procedure is negligibly small (< 0.005) the null hypothesis that the two attributes 'education' and 'type of employment' are independent, is rejected. Thus, we conclude that the educational level seems to strongly influence the respondents' type of employment.

Table 2
Education and Class of Employment

Education	*I*	*II*	*III*	*IV*	*Total*
Illiterate	—	—	—	100.00	6
Primary	—	—	8.00	92.00	25
High School	—	—	46.15	53.85	39
SSLC	—	9.76	78.05	12.19	41
Diploma	—	13.33	80.00	6.67	15
PUC/Inter	2.78	5.56	91.66	—	36
Degree	21.43	16.67	61.90	—	42
PG	37.50	50.00	12.50	—	16
Total	7.27	10.45	56.81	25.46	100
Number	16	23	125	56	220

Notes: Figures indicate percentages.
Computed value of chi-square = 63.33993
Degrees of freedom = 2
'p' value of the test = < 0.000001
To make the chi-square test valid, the rows and columns were merged appropriately.

Education and Type of Family

Since family is an important institution in society, it will be influenced by education. Table 3 gives the relationship between education and type of family. Four aspects of family are taken, i.e., individuals living alone in rooms and hostels, nuclear, extended and joint family. Nuclear family consists of a married couple with unmarried children. Extended family is one in which the nuclear family lives with one or two relatives. Joint family is one where two or more nuclear families live together.

The number of nuclear families is 113 (51%) and that of joint families is 26 (12%). Except in the case of diploma holders, those people who have studied SSLC and above mostly live in nuclear families. Among post-graduates 11 (69%) are living in nuclear families and nobody is living in joint families. Statistically, we can infer that the 'p' value of the test procedure is negligibly low (< 0.05). Therefore, the Null hypothesis that the two attributes 'education' and 'type of family' are independent, is rejected. Thus, we conclude that the educational level seems to strongly influence the type of family the SC people live in.

Table 3
Education and Type of Family

Education	*Type of Family*				
	Single	*Nuclear*	*Extended*	*Joint*	*Total*
Illiterate	—	50.0	50.0	—	6
Primary	4.0	40.0	48.0	8.0	25
High School	5.1	38.5	43.6	12.8	39
SSLC	4.9	51.2	31.7	12.2	41
PUC/Inter	11.1	55.6	19.4	13.9	36
Diploma	—	40.0	40.0	20.0	15
Degree	7.1	64.3	14.3	14.3	42
PG	18.8	68.7	12.5	—	16
Total	6.8	51.4	30.0	11.8	100
Number	15	113	66	26	220

Notes: Figures indicate percentages.
Computed value of chi-square = 12.972
Degrees of freedom = 6
'p' value of the test = 0.04347
To make the chi-square test valid, the rows and columns were merged appropriately.

Education and Number of Children

Education has an important bearing on the number of children a person has. With increasing urbanization, women working outside the homes and the cost of educating and upbringing the children, people prefer to have less number of children. Table 4 gives the relationship between education and the number of children. There are considerable number of persons, i.e., 24 (13.1%), who are childless. This also includes persons who are recently married. There is a significant change in the average number of children from 3.3 among illiterates to 1.4 among post-graduates. The average rate of children for illiterates is above 3, from primary school learners to matriculates it is around 2–3 and those who are educated up to the degree level and above, it is 2. Thus, we can conclude that the educational level does seem to strongly influence the number of children.

Table 4
Education and Number of Children

Education	Number of Children					
	0	1–2	3–4	5+	Average	Total
Illiterate	—	2	2	2	3.3	6
	(33.3)	(33.3)	(33.4)			
Primary	2	6	12	3	2.9	23
	(8.7)	(26.1)	(52.2)	(13.0)		
High School	5	14	10	4	2.6	33
	(15.2)	(42.4)	(30.3)	(12.1)		
SSLC	4	15	15	3	2.4	37
	(10.8)	(40.5)	(40.5)	(8.1)		
PUC/Diploma	5	13	19	1	1.8	38
	(13.2)	(34.2)	(50.0)	(2.6)		
Degree	6	14	14	—	2.1	34
	(17.6)	(41.2)	(41.2)			
PG	2	10	1	—	1.4	13
	(15.4)	(76.9)	(7.7)			
Total	24	74	73	13		184
	(13.1)	(40.2)	(39.7)	(7.0)	2.2	100

Note: Figures in parentheses are percentages.

Education and Age at Marriage

Education also alters the age at marriage. Educational process itself takes time and getting a job before marriage, specially for male members, delays marriage. The correlation between education and age at marriage is shown in Table 5. In the sample there were 172 male members, of whom 28 were not married and of the total 48 female members eight were not married. The average age at marriage for male members is 27.5 and for female members is 22.1.

There is thus a rise in the average age at marriage from 21.3 years among the illiterates to 30.3 years among post-graduates. We can thus infer that as the 'p' value of the test procedure is negligibly low (< 0.05), the null hypothesis that the two attributes 'education' and 'age at marriage' are independent, is rejected. We may, therefore, conclude that the educational level seems strongly influencing the age at marriage among SCs.

Table 5
Education and Age at Marriage

Education	*Age at marriage*						
	Below 20	*21–25*	*26–30*	*31–35*	*36–40*	*Average*	*Total*
Illiterate	50.0	33.3	16.67	—	—	21.3	6
Primary	39.1	21.7	30.4	4.4	4.4	23.7	23
High School	11.3	45.7	20.0	14.3	5.7	25.8	35
SSLC	11.1	33.3	36.2	13.8	5.6	26.5	36
PUC/Diploma	18.9	21.6	48.7	10.8	—	25.5	37
Degree	2.9	14.3	57.1	14.3	11.4	28.9	37
PG	—	7.6	46.2	7.6	7.6	30.3	13
Total	15.2	26.6	39.2	13.6	5.4	26.4	100
Number	28	49	72	25	10		184

Notes: Figures indicate percentages.
Computed value of chi-square = 21.0076
Degrees of freedom = 6
'p' value of the test = 0.00182
To make the chi-square test valid, the rows and columns were merged appropriately.

Employment and Social Mobility

Among the theories of the origin of the caste system (Ghurye, 1969; Hutton, 1963; Ketkar, 1990) the racial theory and the occupational theory are significant. When the Aryans first came to India, they were divided into three classes, viz., Brahmins, Kshatriyas and Vaishyas.[4] The Brahmins were priests, the Kshatriyas warriors and the Vaishya cultivators. This consisted of the economic organization of Aryans. The first step in the direction of the *varna vyavastha* came into existence when the Aryans conquered the natives and made them the servants (*dasas*). Further, each of these *varnas* was sub-divided into a number of sub-groups or *jatis* (castes). These groups came to be generally associated with certain occupations and many of them have names indicative of their main economic activities. So, *jatis* became more relevant for the day-to-day working of society and *varna* remained an overall theoretical framework explaining and legitimizing a set of fundamental principles governing the relationships among *jatis* and the discriminating exclusion of the outcastes.

In ancient India, to follow one's own hereditary occupation was regarded an ordained duty and the Shastras (scriptures) reinforced this. Manu prescribed for Shudra to meekly serve the upper castes. If a man of low caste follows an occupation of a higher *varna*, Manu laid down injunction that the king shall deprive of his property and banish. Ghurye considered lack of unrestricted choice of occupation as the important feature of the caste system. A caste or group of allied castes considered some of the callings as its hereditary occupation, to abandon which in pursuit of another, though it might be more lucrative, was thought not to be right (ibid.). It was not only the moral restraint and the social check of one's caste fellows that acted as a restraint on the choice of occupation, but also the restriction put by other castes, which did not allow members other than those of their own castes to follow their callings. Later, the inexorable law of *karma* and *dharma* reinforced this idea.

Hierarchy is another important feature of caste system. The castes were ranked and this ranking was dependent on the occupations associated with castes. The occupations involving intellectual skills were regarded as superior to manual labour. The outcastes or the *avarnas* were engaged in occupations, which had the lowest rank. The occupations like skinning of hides, tanning, manufacture of leather goods, sweeping, scavenging etc. were considered to be degrading. So, the groups associated with these occupations were regarded as unclean or polluting and were relegated to the lowest positions in the social hierarchy. In the course of time, 'pollution' became to be determined by birth. Members of these groups were regarded as polluting even when they were not actually engaged in occupations considered as defiling.

Due to centuries of suppression and prevention from taking up other occupations, the SCs not only resigned to their low status but also developed an attitude that changes for them were neither possible nor desirable. As a result, they have remained both economically poor and socially backward. Though occasionally these groups were challenged and some efforts were made by social reformers to improve their lot, structurally, no substantial change was achieved.

After independence the Government of India has gone a long way to help the SCs. While Article 15 of the Constitution of India prohibits discrimination on the basis of caste, Article 17 abolishes the practice of untouchability. Article 16 creates equality of opportunity in matters of public employment. Clause 4 states that nothing in this Article prevents the state from making any provision for the reservation of appointments or posts in favour of any backward class of citizens which in the opinion of the state is not adequately represented in the services of the state. In addition, with the passing of Untouchability (Offences) Act in 1955[5] the stigma attached to the occupations like tanning, sweeping, scavenging etc. was removed. Now, no higher caste person could compel the SCs to pursue these occupations against their will nor can they prevent the them from following other occupations of their choice.

With the provision in the Constitution there is reservation for SCs up to 15 per cent of the vacancies for which recruitment is made by open competition on all-India basis and 16.11 per cent of the vacancies for which recruitment is made otherwise, by open competition (direct recruitment). Reservations is also made at 15 per cent in promotions on the result of competitive examinations limited to departmental candidates in Class II to IV and in promotion in selection in Class II to IV and to junior Class I grades. Other concessions include relaxation of age limits, relaxation in the standard of suitability, eligibility, age, experience etc. Other facilities include separate interviews, carrying forward reserved vacancies for three years, advertising reserved post twice, minimum qualification to posts for Class III and IV, adhoc appointment pending regular appointment, reduction of fees to one-fourth, travelling allowance to attend interviews, pre-examination coaching etc.

Due to legislative measures and through other means as industrialization, urbanization, education, communication, transport, migration etc., there is a change in the occupational pattern of the SCs. Even in rural areas where occupational pattern is close to traditional system changes are found. Parvathamma (1984: 117), in her study on Karnataka Scheduled Castes/Scheduled Tribes, concludes that the glaring absence of occupations like night soil carrying and tanning is not to mean that these people do not follow them. This is due to the fact that not many families among these communities can depend on their traditional caste occupation. As the number of people performing such traditional occupations swell in course of time, they have to look for alternate employment opportunities, while one or two families would be enough to meet the required traditional services in the village. In the absence of skill and sources of achieving new occupations, they had to adopt what was immediately available, i.e., agriculture and manual labour.

While there is change in occupational structure in rural areas, there is greater change in towns and cities. Industrialization and urbanization reduce social distance between castes. People of different castes work together in factories and in other work places without any social inhibitions. Many a time an oppressed and persecuted SC prefers to leave the village and come to a city.

Development of modern administration and industrial systems had adverse effects on the occupations of SCs. Dahiwale (1988: 16–17), who studied entrepreneurship among the SCs in Kolhapur city, mentions the effects upon Mahars, Mangs, Dhors and Bhangis. Modern postal and police departments have put Mahars out of traditional employments that were engaged in communication and crime prevention. Modern industries producing ropes and electrical sound system have withdrawn the services of Mangs of making ropes and drumming. Modern tanning and leather industries made many Chamars and Dhors unemployed. Drainage and use of flush latrines reduced the services of Bhangis.

Government is regarded, not as just another employer, but as the one that affords a degree of security, prestige, and authority not obtainable elsewhere (Galanter, 1984: 84–85). For a broad sector of India's population, including both established middle classes and many aspiring groups, government employment is the prime focus of ambition. In Galanter's view, because the government has been their benefactor and because of their access to employment in the private sector has been severely limited, dependence upon government for employment opportunities is especially pronounced among the SCs. Government employment is a matter of not only of private ambition but also of group advancement SC leaders see in government employment not only career opportunities, but also relief from unsympathetic and oppressive administration, facilitation of the utilization of opportunities and readier implementation for their benefit. Further, the government job is also regarded as a source of prestige for both the individual and the group.

Inter-generational Occupational Mobility

Though it is difficult to compare the employment of the respondents with that of their fathers and grandfathers to evaluate intergenerational occupational mobility, an attempt is made to group the employment of fathers and grandfathers into Class I to IV and it is presented below in Table 6:

Table 6
Intergenerational Occupational Mobility

(in percentage)

Class of Employment	*Occupation of*		
	Grandfather	*Father*	*Respondent*
Class I	—	—	7.28
Class II	—	2.73	10.45
Class III	5.00	22.73	56.82
Class IV	1.82	10.00	25.45
Coolie	78.64	44.09	—
Mason/Carpenter	—	10.90	—
Agriculture	5.90	5.00	—
Crafts	1.82	0.91	—
Others	6.82	3.64	—
Total	100.00	100.00	100.00
Number	220	220	220

From the above table we observe a remarkable intergenerational occupational mobility. The proportion of coolie workers has come down from 78 per cent in grandfathers' generation to 44 per cent in the fathers' generation. A significant factor is that fathers of 24 (10.9%) respondents had taken up masonry or carpentry work, which was not found in grandfathers' generation. It is also a clear indication that even in rural areas SCs have changed their occupation.

Interpersonal Relationships at the Workplace

Considering that caste identities of persons play an important role even in formal organizations, the SC employees are likely to face situations, which are hostile. The hostility would come not merely because of the perceptions of their caste status as low by their fellow colleagues but also because of the prejudices the upper castes may have towards their favoured status (such as reservation in education and employment). Indeed, on account of such hostile, atmosphere at the workplace, newly employed SC persons tend to seek the cooperation of other SC employees.

With a view to assess whether the experience of the SC respondents in this study was any different from the above, the nature of work atmosphere was enquired. This is done in at least two ways: first by asking them to describe the interpersonal relationships at workplace and secondly, outside the workplace.

Nearly 89 per cent of the respondents thought that their colleagues knew their identity quite well. To that extent the kind of interrelationships that existed between them was with the knowledge of the respondent's caste identity.[6] The respondents were also asked to describe their relations with their colleagues as experienced in the beginning of their service and at present, which were grouped under three categories: good, fair and caste-biased.

'Good' here means that they enjoyed the confidence of fellow workers, received and rendered help and advice when needed. The important criterion here is that such a relationship obtained in spite of different caste backgrounds of the persons involved. In other words, it implies that they experienced no caste-based discrimination at workplace. 'Fair' implies that there was occasional caste-based discrimination although within tolerable limits. The third category 'caste-biased' indicates a high degree of discrimination resulting in unpleasant relation ships.

Table 7

Relations with Colleagues in the Beginning and at Present

Relations in the beginning	***Relations now***			
	Good	***Fair***	***Caste-bias***	***Total***
Good	91.30	4.97	3.73	161
Fair	46.34	46.34	7.32	41
Caste-biased	27.78	16.66	55.56	18
Total	77.73	13.64	8.63	100
Number	171	30	19	220

Notes: Figures indicate percentages.
Computed value of chi-square = 106.403
Degrees of freedom = 4
'p' value of the test = < 0.000001
To make the chi-square test valid, the rows and columns were merged appropriately.

It may be seen from Table 7 that there is an evidence of improvement in the relationship over a period of time. In the first place, nearly 161 (73%) found the relationship to have been good at the beginning, which is quite high a proportion, and this increased to 77 per cent at present. Those subjected to 'caste-biased' relationships are small in proportion. Only 8 per cent experienced such a relationship at the beginning of their service. Here too, there was a marginal increase from the past to the present. Interestingly enough, it was observed that there was a uniform consistency in describing the kinds of relationships experienced at two different points of time. Thus, a person having had a good relationship at the beginning of his service tended to find it to be the same at present also. From the point of view of understanding the process of social mobility among the SCs, there are some interesting insights here. In the first place, as much as 77 per cent found interpersonal relationships at the workplace 'good' and another 14 per cent 'fair'. Considering that a vast majority of them described caste-biased relationships that their family members had experienced earlier. This indicates a smooth entry into work life. In contrast to their social life prior to employment and of their parents in early times, these people have an opportunity to experience a work life not solely determined by their caste status. Thus, one may view 'good' and 'fair' relationships with colleagues as an indication of upward social mobility.

While thus generalizing, a note also should be taken concerning those who have viewed the relationships at the workplace subjected to caste bias. These are the people who experienced hostility and peer suspicion towards them. Even if they had no strong sense of their own caste identity and commitment to the cause of SCs as such, many of them were forced to harden the attitude towards other castes. It does not, however, imply that these persons have not achieved any social mobility. Many of them have indeed a better economic status than their parents and the others in their own caste. What they have not been able to achieve is an acceptance by the colleagues as fellow workers independent of their caste identity. As a consequence, even if others consider that such persons have now a better status on account of their employment, they themselves feel that they have not achieved a full social mobility in which their caste identity plays no role.

In contrast, there were also those who experienced peer discrimination right from the beginning. Their selection and employment seems to have been the bones of contention. The performance and the impression left behind by the SCs earlier in the same place of work tend also to be the basis of judging a new entrant to the service. Thus, for instance, a new recruit may find the work atmosphere to be hostile if in the same office or branch several of the SCs had been promoted from lower to higher cadres. So much so that a beginner may find it difficult to learn the work when posted to such an office. One respondent narrated his experience wherein from the day one none of his colleagues were willing to help him. When he wanted to know how to proceed in dealing with office matters, his boss was reported to have chided for his ignorance and was asked to approach the person who appointed him. Many of those who reported 'fair' and 'caste-biased' interrelationships had experienced avoidance by their colleagues. One of them remarked that through such avoidance a new form of 'untouchability' came into being, which was experienced in the past by his forefathers. At least two respondents were compelled to seek legal aid when promotions were denied to them.

Another feature of the nature of interpersonal relationships seems to be that the latter is determined by the cadre of employment. Thus, by and large, persons belonging to Class I and II expressed the relationship to be 'good', while it is usually in the lower cadre that it was reported to be 'fair' or 'caste-biased'. It is necessary, however, to recognize that by the nature of bureaucratic organization itself, the higher cadre officials tend to enjoy greater power and authority as well as relative isolation from the fellow workers. Consequently, they may not encounter opposition as frequently as the others. Thus, we can infer that as the 'p' value of the test procedure is negligibly low (< 0.05), the null hypothesis that the two attributes 'relation with the colleagues in the beginning' and 'relations with the colleagues now' are independent, is rejected. Thus, we may conclude that the relations with the colleagues in the beginning and now are strongly related.

Social Relationships Beyond the Workplace

Social relationships at the workplace usually go beyond the formal place of work. Colleagues may frequently visit each other, families may meet or have common interest. There may be invitations for special occasions, family outings etc. Here, there may be a process of selection based on, among other factors, caste, region and language identities. To assess these dimensions, the respondents were asked whether other caste colleagues visited them in their houses, and if they accepted lunch, dinner or tea. Only 22 per cent of the respondents reported that their colleagues including from other castes do not visit them whereas the rest 78 per cent did confirm that their colleagues visited their houses. However, not all such visitors are offered food or beverages especially because of the kind of dilemma pointed out above. The usual practice however, seems to be that if the visitors were non-SCs, tender coconut water and bakery products are offered. It is rarely that cooked food is offered or accepted. On special occasions, such as house warming, childbirth or marriages, cooked food may be offered if prepared and sold by professional cooks of upper castes. It is not uncommon that a separate dining arrangement is made for such occasions.

Table 8

Occasions for Colleagues Visiting Respondents

Class of Employment	*Occasions for visit*			
	Invitation	*Casual*	*Work*	*Total*
I	14.29	78.57	7.14	14
II	23.81	66.67	9.52	21
III	43.88	41.84	14.28	98
IV	69.23	20.51	10.26	39
Total	44.77	43.02	12.21	100
Number	77	74	21	172

Notes: Computed value of chi-square = 18.461
Degrees of freedom = 3
'p' value of the test = 0.000353
To make the chi-square test valid, the rows and columns were merged appropriately.

In the light of the fact that not all visitors accept food on normal occasions, we find that caste-based factors play an important role involving the SC employees. However, as they admitted, a majority of social visiting involves other SC employees from within the place of work or elsewhere rather than members of upper castes. This gives rise to a question as to the occasion on which fellow colleagues visit SC employees. Three types of visits may be identified, namely, on invitation for special occasions, casual visits and to discuss work-related matters.

As is clear from Table 8 above 48 (21.8%) respondents reported that none of their colleagues visited them at home. Among those who did receive colleagues at home, it is found that majority of visits are in response to special invitations (45%). However, 12 per cent of respondents reported that their colleagues visited only to discuss work-related matters. In a way these two represent a certain non-voluntary nature of visits, as against a casual social visit, which is reported by 43 per cent of the respondents. Thus, one may find less casual or informal occasions when colleagues visit SC employees.

In terms of class of employment, there are some interesting patterns. Casual visits by colleagues is highest (79%) among the SC employees in Class I cadre and this proportion goes down steadily in each successive cadre to 21 per cent among Class IV employees. Reverse is the case with respect to those visiting on invitation, wherein the lowest is among Class I and the highest among Class IV employees. The implication of this pattern is that higher the official status of an employee, the more incidence of casual visits by colleagues. In contrast, the lower class of employees gets visitors on special invitations and as such enjoys less of social calling by their colleagues. So, we can infer that as 'p' value of the test procedure is negligibly low (< 0.05), the null hypothesis that the two attributes 'class of employment' and 'occasions of visit of colleagues' are independent, is rejected. Thus, we may conclude that the class of employment and occasions of visit of colleagues are strongly related.

Why colleagues do not visit some SC employees at home? The main reason is that many of them do not invite or show interest in extending the social relationship at workplace to their families due to a sense of inferiority. About 41 (18.6%) of them have not invited colleagues even if there were special occasions; they feel invitations may not be accepted. The rest had either no opportunity to invite or their houses were far off. Some of the respondents were of the opinion that colleagues of the upper castes, particularly Brahmins, may not visit them, whereas other castes (e.g., Kulals and Billavas) may visit. One respondent mentioned that even if Brahmins visited, they do not eat food cooked by them. Instead, if the food is supplied from a restaurant, it may be accepted. Another respondent said that they give Brahmin visitors tender coconut water and plantains so that they are not obliged to eat what is cooked at home. Yet another respondent concluded that discrimination in visiting colleagues is conspicuous when a person is in a lower position. If a person is high-ranking officer, all caste persons interact with him.

Given this situation, how often do SC employees visit their colleagues of other castes in their houses? On what occasions they visit?

What is their experience? More than 80 per cent of respondents said that they too visited the houses of their colleagues (see Table 9).

Table 9
Occasions for Respondents Visiting the Colleagues

Class of Employment	Occasions			
	Invitation	Casually	Work	Total
I	46.15	46.15	7.70	13
II	47.83	43.48	8.69	23
III	55.36	33.93	10.71	112
IV	68.18	22.73	9.09	44
Total	56.77	33.33	9.09	100
Number	109	64	19	192

Notes: Computed value of chi-square = 10.45
Degrees of freedom = 3
'p' value of the test = 0.0015
To make the chi-square test valid, the rows and columns were merged appropriately.

As in the earlier query, here also, the responses were categorized in terms of the class of employment and occasions for visiting other colleagues. The pattern of response indicates that most SC employees visit their friends only on invitations (57%), and only a very small proportion (10%) to discuss work-related matters. Casual visits, implying voluntary calling on friends, is higher among the higher class of employees and low among the low class of employees. The implication of this pattern is that only a small proportion of employees has been able to go on their own to visit their friends casually while majority still feel constrained and wait for an invitation. Thus we can infer that as the 'p' value of the test procedure is negligibly low (< 0.05), the null hypothesis that the two attributes 'class of employment' and 'occasions of visiting the colleagues' are independent, is rejected. Thus, we may conclude that the class of employment and occasions of visiting the colleagues are strongly related.

Concerning those who do not visit their other caste colleagues (21.8%), it was found that a majority do not visit because they are not invited. An equal number of respondents do not feel like visiting their colleagues either because they do not feel so close to each other or because they wish to remain by themselves. The rest said that they do not like to mix with other caste colleagues. One respondent stated that he does not feel comfortable to go to other caste colleagues' houses because he does not know how they would treat him. Another respondent of Class IV said that she is called only to do some menial work in the houses of other caste colleagues, which she takes up to earn some additional income. Another respondent is very cautious, and goes only to those who do not discriminate.

Interestingly enough, many of those who do visit colleagues report that they had been subjected to discrimination. Discrimination is of various types, such as serving food and beverages in apparently different utensils, not allowing to enter inner parts of the house, serving meals in a separate place, serving food either early or late and along with other guests making sarcastic remarks about SCs and on reservation policy etc. At times even if the colleague does not discriminate, his or her relatives do. Even one respondent was asked to clean the place with cow dung where he ate meals in a Brahmin colleague's house after having been invited to partake food in the house.

Social Mobility as Evident Outside the Workplace

Studies in Urban Human Geography and Urban Sociology have demonstrated that there exists caste and class selectivity with respect to housing patterns (Rao, 1989). In keeping with the traditionally ascribed social status of the SCs, it is possible to find even now in several cities and towns a separate locality inhabited by them. Their existence as a distinct locality in the context of present-day urbanization is also a result of government's housing policy earmarked for the benefits of Scheduled Castes. The result of such a policy is the birth of such new localities.

Civil servants who get posted from place to place every three years usually look for official accommodation to which they are eligible. Invariably, the supply is shorter than demand compelling them to seek rented accommodation. It is not uncommon for the land/house owners even in urban contexts to be selective about the caste and class of their prospective tenants. The concern for class is readily explainable: ability to pay the rent. House owners usually prefer their tenants to be of 'clean' caste implying that they are vegetarians and teetotalers. Such a concern is often notwithstanding the low caste status of the landowners themselves. At best every landowner may prefer to rent out the house to a member of his own caste if not to that of upper caste. Given this tendency, the Scheduled Castes are at a considerable disadvantage.

As a consequence, the SC employees who are not natives or property owners in the town or city where they work are at a severe disadvantage. Notwithstanding their employment status, they may be often compelled to live in localities that are inhabited by the people lower in economic and social status than themselves.

Most of the municipalities and corporations in India have come to employ persons categorized as SCs, who have over a period of time migrated from rural areas. They are engaged in menial jobs as scavenging, sweeping the streets, carrying the city waste, etc. Usually, they live in colonies meant for SCs. In Mangalore too most SC people working in the municipal corporation live in such colonies. Some colonies are located in the centre of the city and some in the periphery.[7] In the present study too, we observe a similar pattern. While about 41 per cent of the respondents are found to be living in SC colonies, about 51 per cent in localities where people of all castes and religions live and the remaining 8 per cent are living in predominantly Christian, Muslim or Hindu localities. As may be expected, the residential pattern of the SCs differs in terms of the cadre of employment of the respondents (see Table 10).

Table 10

Type of Residential Locality

Class of employment	Type of locality			
	Scheduled caste locality	Mixed locality	Other caste/religious areas	Total
I	12.50	87.50	—	16
II	13.04	82.60	4.38	23
III	39.20	50.00	8.80	125
IV	66.07	26.79	7.14	56
Total	41.36	51.36	7.28	100
Number	91	113	16	220

Notes: Computed value of chi-square = 27.436
Degrees of freedom = 3
'p' value of the test =< 0.00001
To make the chi-square test valid, the rows and columns were merged appropriately.

Class I and II employees are found to be residing predominantly in 'mixed' residential localities where people of different castes inhabited.

This suggests that they prefer to live and mix with members of other castes whereas Class IV employees are found to be living in predominantly the SC colonies. In some instances, due to migration and urban growth, SC colonies around Mangalore have become residential areas for several caste communities, including those of non-SCs. However, the recent SC migrants to the city, specially belonging to lower class, prefer to stay in SC localities because land price and house rent are relatively cheaper there as compared to the other areas. Many respondents who had built their own houses with modern amenities in these localities had to feel contended of building their houses there than elsewhere because of the high cost of land in the latter areas.

One interesting feature of the location of residences needs to be elaborated here. As seen in Table 10, a few Class I and II employees have reported to be living in the areas that are known to be SC colonies. This seems to be a departure from the pattern wherein higher class employees tend to reside in the socially and economically better localities. One may ask as to why these officials have been living in such areas as SC colonies. At least three reasons may be found for such a phenomenon. First, many SC employees who were living in such a locality may have now moved up in their cadres, but having built their houses they may now find it difficult to move residences elsewhere. Secondly, some of them may prefer to live there either because of a sense of identity with the caste and kin who may be living there or may feel comfortable there. Lastly, such persons may have found it difficult to find rented accommodation in the other localities because of their own caste status. Thus, we can infer that as the 'p' value of the test procedure is negligibly low (< 0.05), the null hypothesis that the two attributes 'class of employment' and 'type of residential facility' are independent, is rejected. It is, therefore, concluded that the class of employment and type of residential facility are strongly related.

A comment may also be made of many other lower ranking employees living in better social and economic status localities. This is because of their ability to succeed in getting rented accommodation or because the residential accommodation provided by the department is located in such areas.

A general conception in the matter of urban housing is that there is usually a greater anonymity particularly concerning caste and class identities of people. Unlike in rural areas, an urban resident may not be concerned with such details of his neighbours, or even may not be aware of them. Once the caste particulars are known to each other, social discrimination of varying degrees may be found to be in operation.

Members of SCs, particularly those belonging to the former untouchable castes, may face this prospect much more severely in the hands of upper castes in a mixed caste locality than the other lower castes.

The neighbours of more than 90 per cent respondents knew the caste background of the respondents whereas of the remaining 10 per cent respondents did not know it. The reasons for lack of knowledge of caste background were that some respondents had moved in recently, while a few had not deliberately revealed their caste background to their neighbours. Some pointed out that nobody asked about their caste since they were not interactive with the neighbours. However, in one instance, a Class III employee was to be interviewed at his residence. The employee, knowing the purpose of the study and why he was chosen as a respondent, requested not to visit his residence lest his neighbours know his caste background. Instead, he suggested a different venue for the interview.

Perception of Social Status

A multiplicity of criteria, such as landholding, education, income and power, determine the status of individuals and groups in society. Conceptually, social status is that which is ascribed by a group of people for an individual or a group. In this sense social status is something that a person or group comes to 'attain' from other people in a community. However, in recent years, attempts have been made by sociologists and social anthropologists to assess the social status as perceived by people for themselves, i.e., subjective assessment of social status. This is useful because status groups have come to be typical in character in such a way that symbols of status groups could be attained by people to pass off as members of such a reference group.

In the present study, the respondents were asked what they thought of social status expressed in terms of being a member of different social class. Implicit in this was not merely an economic class position but also 'the social position of such a class'. Further, it was also implicit that such a class position was sought to be identified among persons belonging to a lower position in a caste based system of hierarchy. Under such a situation, one may anticipate that their employment status would determine their identification with a higher class status.

As shown in Table 11, a majority of the respondents (62%) have claimed that their household/family enjoyed a status of 'lower-middle class'.[8] About 21 per cent of them claimed to belong to 'upper-middle class'. Not surprisingly, it is the high-ranking employees (Class I and II), who have claimed to be enjoying upper-middle and upper social status and it is the Class III and IV employees who have claimed lower and lower-middle class social status. What is the basis on which these respondents ascribe their own social status? Among 214 educated respondents, it was education, whereas about 54 per cent of the educated respondents believe that their status was determined solely by their being employed in various government jobs, which in turn was a result of their educational attainment. In other words, crucial to their social status was seen to be their educational attainment, through which they were able to get employment. As one person pointed out that whenever he was introduced to his kinsmen, friends and relatives in his native village or elsewhere, were highlighting his bachelor's degree first and later his employment status.

Table 11
Employment and Status of Family

Class of employment	*Status of family*				
	Lower	*Lower-middle*	*Upper*	*Upper-middle*	*Total*
I	—	19.75	68.75	12.5	16
II	—	56.52	39.13	4.35	23
III	4.80	76.00	19.20	—	125
IV	46.43	46.43	7.14	—	56
Total	14.54	62.27	21.83	1.36	100
Number	32	137	48	3	220

Notes: Computed value of chi-square = 44.81
Degrees of freedom = 3
'p' value of the test = < 0.000001
To make the chi-square test valid, the rows and columns were merged appropriately.

The point that is being made here is that although employment has enhanced their social status in their own community as well as in the wider society, they recognized that it is education, which has enabled them to have the employment rather than employment in itself. Indeed, more than 92 per cent of respondents were of the opinion that there had been a significant change in their social status as a consequence of their employment. It is employment, which, they claimed had given them an improved economic status and markedly improved social respectability.

It is not only that the individual has been able to attain a better social and economic status through education and employment but also the entire household/family as a social unit. Thus, it was claimed by the respondents that the social respectability and the class position enjoyed by the household in the neighbourhood was a reflection of the employment status of the individual. So much so that a person's wife well educated or not enjoyed more or less the same social respectability as that of the person in question by virtue of his employment. The same was true in most cases for the wider family as a social unit. For instance, a respondent is employed as a Class I or II officer in government department brought an improved social status to the members of his family as a whole back to the village of his origin. The parents of his siblings derived a much better social position within the village than among several other SC family members.[9]

The basic purpose of reservation in education and employment is to provide adequate opportunities to the socially and economically deprived sections of society. Thereby it was intended to raise the social status of SCs and other backward castes. It was done through various protective and developmental measures. How far this ideal of egalitarian society has been achieved? The respondents were asked whether they considered themselves to be socially and economically equal to the other castes.

Table 12
Attainment of Equality

Criterion	***Equality***	
	Yes	***No***
Socially	140 (64)	80 (36)
Economically	115 (52)	105 (48)

Figures in parentheses are percentages.

The responses are presented separately in terms of social and economic equality. In respect of social equality, as can be seen in Table 12, 64 per cent considered themselves to be equal to the other castes. The reasons for considering themselves equal to any other castes were stated as: that they were equally or better educated as the others (27%); do their work as good as the others (20%); keep themselves as clean in appearance as the others (11%); not discriminated by the others (10%); also human beings like the others (40%); have improved their own social status (10%); and have as good conduct as the others (25%).

It may be pointed out that not only do the employed SC members hold themselves in comparable social positions with other castes, the reasons for such opinion reflect socially a high self-esteem. Some of the reasons such as 'also human beings like the others' or 'not discriminated against by others' suggest a notion of basic human rights and civic liberty among them. We can therefore, infer that as the 'p' value of the test procedure is negligibly low (< 0.05), the null hypothesis that the two attributes 'class of employment' and 'status of the family' are independent, is rejected. Thus, it is concluded that the class of employment and status of the family are strongly related.

It thus needs to explain why 36 per cent of respondents considered themselves socially not equal to the other castes. It is not enough if they themselves claimed to be equal, what is important, according to them, was that the other castes should also consider them to be equal. It was felt that such an attitude was yet to develop. Many others (38%) felt that they belonged to lower castes, while 33 per cent were of the opinion that untouchability still existed, and 14 per cent felt that due to low income they could not be equated with people of other castes, who generally had a better income.

In terms of economic comparability with other castes, a lower proportion of respondents (52%) felt that they were equal to members of other castes. This was because they felt their income to be as good as of the others. In the cases of 10 persons their income was indeed high because their spouses were also employed. About 48 per cent of respondents, who did not consider equal to others, felt thus because either they had low salaried income or their income was through salary alone.

Views Regarding Reservation

In the present study, an attempt was also made to find out if the educated and employed SCs desired the continuation of the policy of reservation. Their opinion was sought separately for education, employment and in political bodies. With regard to education, all the respondents, with the exception of two, were of the opinion that it should be continued. With regard to employment, all except four felt it necessary and with regard to political bodies 16 were against it. Whether for employment or education the reason for desiring the policy to continue was more or less the same: that as members of SCs, particularly of former untouchable castes, they had continued to face social and economic discrimination even after 60 years of independence and pursuing a policy of affirmative action. Those who felt that there was no need for reservation (both in education and employment) argued that the SCs should now be independent and not expect any special status for them to be given by the state.

Those who expressed the need for a continued reservation policy in political sphere argued that the SCs also should get representation in political process. Such a policy gives an opportunity for SCs not only to develop leadership among them but also helps to solve peculiar social and economic problems faced by them. A few respondents went further to suggest a refinement in the system in such a way that there should be a separate electorate in all the constituencies to elect SC representatives. Those who were opposed to the idea of continued reservation policy expressed their reasons with a sense of bitterness. In their view elected SC leaders failed to protect the interests of SCs but tend to become puppets in the hands of political parties of which they are members. They sacrifice the SC interests for petty personal gains within the party. "Eventually none cares for the Scheduled Castes", one of the respondents said.

While SCs are recipients of various benefits provided by the government, it also results in their alienation from the other communities. The other people are not very happy about such a treatment given to SCs. How do the SCs view the opinion of non-SCs towards the benefits given to the former? The perception of the respondents was wide ranging. More than two-thirds of them (67%) attributed the reason to be borne out of jealousy by the upper castes. It was pointed out that because the upper caste people themselves cannot achieve what is being achieved by the SCs, they are opposed to the SCs succeeding in life. A few argued that with the SCs improving their social, economic and political conditions, they no longer be subjected to the kind of suppression as in the past. Therefore, the upper castes' opposition to such social change is seen. About 22 per cent felt that the others do not understand the purpose of reservation policy. They pointed out that it was largely due to the ignorance of the upper castes about the social and economic conditions of the SCs. Neither were they aware nor sympathetic. Hence, their opposition. However, four persons did not find any opposition from upper castes. Even, five respondents were sympathetic to the upper castes' opposition stating that there are poor people in other castes also and they also should be given the benefits of reservation.

Who opposes the policies of welfare and protective discrimination? Nearly 15 per cent of the respondents could not pinpoint who were opposed to these policies. Among those who had responded about 21 per cent thought that practically all the other castes were opposed to it. About 27 per cent of them held the upper castes to be opposed to these policies while an equal proportion of them felt that all caste Hindus to be opposed. A few even held specifically the lower castes to be opposed in this regard.

A second set of questions pertains to seek their suggestions to improve the policies of uplifting the SCs. There was more or less unanimous view that the implementation of the existing policies was not satisfactory. One notable suggestion that a majority of them made was that honest and committed SC persons should be made responsible for implementing all the policies concerning the SCs. It was also suggested that implementation of programmes should not be left merely to the politicians or to the individuals, but it should be entrusted to responsible committees. Some called for severe punishment to the officials who failed to implement the policies. Another important suggestion that came was to improve the means of communication and dissemination of information to help the SCs in rural areas.

Some respondents used this opportunity to critically look at the existing policies and their implementation. One respondent elaborated how there had been inadequate support to education beyond the provision of reservation. It was pointed out that the attention given to the education in rural areas, particularly to the SC education, was inadequate and did not bear potential of emancipating them. It is not enough if hostel facilities are given, but parents should be given economic support so as to afford education of their children. A few respondents also pointed out that the only way to improve the social and economic conditions of the SCs is by providing a government employment to at least one person in every such household.

Another important suggestion made was to restrict the facilities only to the former untouchable castes, and remove from the list of SCs all other castes. This is because the others are economically advanced and did not suffer the stigma of untouchability in the past.

Conclusions

In the present study, the importance of education in the life of an SC is assessed. First, the educational experience of the respondents is evaluated. Though for most of the respondents educational experience was good, for a few it was a bitter one of discrimination from fellow students, teachers and administrators. It has been part and parcel of their classroom, playground and hostel experience. Intense discrimination has been experienced even in the centres of higher learning.

There has been a remarkable inter-generational educational mobility. The effect of education is seen in the field of employment and income, in the institutions of marriage and family and in other aspects of life. The higher the education, the higher the class of employment, which has in turn resulted in higher income. Educated persons are also able to get the job faster and utilize government facilities. With the rise in education, family has tended to become nuclear, size of household has decreased and one can also see decrease in the number of children and increase in the age at marriage.

Secondly, an attempt was made to assess the implications for social mobility among members of SCs as a consequence of their employment. There had been a remarkable intergenerational mobility in terms of occupation of the respondents. Among a majority of them, the respondents were the first in the two or three generations to have held urban employment in the government sector. It has brought about major change in the social and economic conditions of their life.

There have been several indicators of changed social status and therefore of social mobility as the consequence of employment. These are evident, for instance, by the amicable social relationships they enjoyed with their colleagues at the place of work and neighbours in the place of residence. There have also been instances of caste-biased relationships indicating social discrimination but that has been the experience of a few only, while a large section reported relationships to be good.

Social mobility was also assessed by analyzing the type of locality in which they lived and their relationships with the neighbours. The pattern regarding the types of locality has come out very clearly. Those in higher positions of employment reside in 'mixed' caste localities, whereas those in lower positions are found to be living in areas known to be SC localities. Most respondents also reported to be enjoying amicable or good social relationships with their neighbours. An outstanding observation is that most of them ascribe an upper-middle or middle class status to themselves. They no longer meekly accept lower status based on their caste identity.

Finally, an attempt was also made to seek the opinion of respondents towards several measures of affirmative action and welfare favouring them. Almost all of them feel that reservation in educational institutions, for employment and in political bodies should continue. The general opinion among them is that caste Hindus and particularly upper castes are opposed to such benefits being given to SC peoples for a variety of reasons. They believe that such an opposition is because they are jealous, or afraid that improvement in the social and economic conditions of SCs would adversely affect their status in society.

NOTES

1. Though the parents of Dr Ambedkar hailed from Maharashtra, at the time of the birth of Dr Ambedkar, his father was serving the British army at Mhow, Madhya Pradesh.
2. The conditions of work were also changed. For instance, Karnataka was the first state in the country where carrying of night soil on the head was banned by the government—an occupation in which most Scheduled Castes in small towns and cities were engaged in.
3. Mere passing a Bachelor's degree is not adequate for in service mobility. In order to get an internal promotion, a government employee has to pass 'departmental examinations' in accounts, business correspondence, English, government rules and regulations, etc.
4. There are also other theories about the origin of Aryans.
5. The Untouchability Offences Act, 1955 was later amended and renamed as The Scheduled Castes and Scheduled Tribes (Prevention of Atrocities Act), 1989.
6. However, in the course of research, the caste identity of the remaining respondents was established among the colleagues.
7. The colonies, which are in the city at present, were in the periphery before the Mangalore city had it's the nominal growth.
8. Although no specific definition of the different classes was made explicit, it was clear that the respondents uniformly and consistently perceived each of these categories. It is in this respect that each of these classes has come to have pre-determined but unspecified attributes.
9. This is not, however, to claim that members of such families in the village were able to overcome all the social discriminations, which the family may have faced prior to the 'employment' of the person in question. What is being pointed out is that the respondents are referring to a relative improvement in social status for the family, in relation to the members of the community.

REFERENCES

Dahiwale, S.M. 1988. *Emerging Entrepreneurship among Scheduled Castes of Contemporary India.* New Delhi: Concept Publishing Company.

Dumont, Louis. 1972. *Homo Hierarchies: The Caste System and Its Implications.* Chicago: The University of Chicago Press.

Galanter, Marc. 1984. *Competing Equalities.* Delhi: Oxford University Press.

Ghurye, G.S. 1969. *Caste and Race in India.* Bombay: Popular Prakashan.

——. 1990. *Caste, Class and Occupation*. Bombay: Popular Prakashan.

Gupta, Dipankar (ed.), 1993. *Social Stratification.* Delhi: Oxford University Press.

Hutton, J.H. 1963. *Caste in India: Its Nature, Function and Origin.* Bombay: Oxford University Press.

Isaacs, H. 1965. *India's Ex-Untouchables.* Bombay: Asia Publishing House.

Ketkar, S.V. 1990. *History of Caste in India.* Delhi: Low Price Publication.

Mahar, Michael J. 1969. *Untouchables in Contemporary India.* Tucson: The University of Arizona Press.

Oommen, T.K. 1994. 'Panchamas to Dalits: The Context and Content of Identity', *Times of India,* May 11.

Parvathamma. 1984. *Scheduled Castes and Tribes: A Socio-Economic Survey.* New Delhi: Ashish Publishers.

Parvathamma. 1989. *Scheduled Castes at the Cross Roads.* New Delhi: Ashish Publishing House.

Prakash, Nirupama. 1989. *Scheduled Castes: Socio-Economic Changes.* Allahabad: Chugh Publications.

Ram, Nandu. 1988. *The Mobile Scheduled Castes: Rise of a New Middle Class.* Delhi: Hindustan Publishing Corporation.

Rao Ranga, A.V.P. 1989. *Urbanization, Occupational Mobility and Social Integration.* New Delhi: Deep and Deep Publications.

Srinivas, M.N. 1989. *Cohesive Role of Sanskritisation and Other Essays.* Delhi: Oxford University Press.

11

Eclipsed Affirmative Action in India with Special Reference to Minority Educational Institutions

JAGAN KARADE

The backward classes have been discriminated for centuries in India. Hopes and expectations for these sections of citizens were practically non-existent. After Independence the Constitution of India categorically laid down that it is the duty of the State to ensure the welfare of the backward classes.

Affirmative action refers to policies intended to promote access to education or employment to historically and socio-politically non-dominant groups. Many thinkers defined the term 'affirmative action' as "the positive steps designed for the elimination of existing and continuing discrimination". Affirmative action involves a set of public policies and initiatives designed to eliminate discrimination based on caste, religion, sex and region.

When India became independent in 1947 and turned into a Democratic Republic in 1950, the Constitution entitled equal rights and special opportunities to backward classes to be free from social bondage. In India, some groups who are targeted for affirmative actions are characterized by race, gender, ethnicity and disability status. Here, reservation is mostly focused on undoing caste discrimination. Affirmative action or reservation aims at compensating the victims of past discrimination and redistribute opportunities. According to A.K. Shiva Kumar, the adviser of UNICEF, "Reservation is a subset of affirmative action. As far as affirmative action is concerned, the amount of representation to be given to underrepresented group is the discretion of the individual organizations whereas in case of the reservation system, the quota or the amount of representation to be given to each group is fixed generally by the government and has to be abided".

The Government of India decided that liberty, equality and fraternity, including social, economic and political justice, the golden goals set out in the Preamble of the Constitution of India, are to be achieved. Therefore, bringing reservation policy in the educational sector means that education is the basic instrument of social and economic change and it transmits the culture of one generation to another. It is also linked with individual and social mobility. It also boosts continued growth of personality, steady development of character and the qualitative improvement of life. A trained mind has the capacity to draw spiritual nourishment from every experience—may it be defeat or victory, sorrow or joy. Education is the training of mind and not straining the brain. Since Independence, welfare measures were taken up by policy makers to expand the education system far and wide. Several commissions and committees have been set up from time to time, such as the University Education Commission (1948), Secondary Education Commission (1952), Education Commission (1966), Teacher Education Commission (1985) and National Knowledge Commission (2005).

The government has been constantly claiming that the conditions of the Scheduled Castes (SCs) and Scheduled Tribes (STs) have been improving since Independence. It has been ascertained that the reservation policy has been a tool for the liberation of those who were considered untouchables and backward classes, viz., SCs, STs and Other Backward Classes (OBCs). The reservation policy considers social justice, enunciated in the Constitution, Article 15 (4), which says,

> to make special provisions for the advancement of socially and educationally backward classes of citizens and for the Scheduled Castes and Scheduled Tribes, it envisages such special provisions of the advancement of all members of such backward classes of citizens. If any discrimination is exercised between the members of a Scheduled Caste on the ground of religion only so as to promote the welfare of one group of members and deny it to the others, the denial will be invalid.

However, Gaikwad (1999) said that, the constitutional protection was provided to the backward classes, in particular SCs and STs, to get them rid of all forms of exploitation, including social injustice. From this point of view, the provisions in the Constitution may be classified into two categories:

1. The measures, which are mandatory, include the provisions laid down in Part III of the Constitution under the heading of 'Fundamental Rights' protecting these people from a variety of social disabilities to secure equality along with all other citizens. Articles 14, 15, 16, 19, 25, 29, 30 and 44 are some of the important ones that are aimed at equality
2. The article and clauses, which safeguard the interests of these communities by providing certain measures, which may be considered under the category of 'welfare measures'.

Clause (4) in Article 15 was added in 1951. The purpose was to bring Articles 15 and 29 in line with Article 16 (4), 46 and 340 to enable the state to reserve seats for the SCs, STs and OBCs in educational institutions and also to undertake special measures for their overall development.

When Kalelkar Commission's report was discussed in the parliament in 1959, the Central Government took a decision that no all-India lists of backward classes should be drawn up, nor any reservation made in Central Government services for any group of backward classes other than SCs and STs. Consequently, on 14th August, 1961, the Ministry of Home Affairs addressed all the State Governments stating, "while the State Governments have the discretion to choose their own criteria for defining backwardness, in the view of the Government of India it would be better to apply economic tests than to go by caste".

This decision has created an anti-reservation stir in the country. At that time some States, being so much confused, did not draw the list of backward classes and preferred to constitute the Backward Classes Commissions. The Gujarat government set up Bakshi Backward Commission in 1972 and later implemented its recommendations. St. Xavier's College Group of Institutions filed a case against the Gujarat government. Meanwhile, this group of institutions protected its right related to Article 29.

After two years, the Janata Party gave assurance about the setting up of the Second Central Backward Class Commission. As a result, it was able to achieve political power in Bihar. In this state, the Karpuri Thakur's government declared 26 per cent reservation for OBCs. Meanwhile, strong anti-reservation movement was built up in Bihar and Uttar Pradesh. Meanwhile, the Janata Party at the Centre constituted the Mandal Commission on 20th December, 1978. The report of the Mandal

Commission was submitted in December 1980. On August 7, 1990 the then Prime Minister, V.P. Singh announced in both the houses of parliament the decision to implement the Mandal Commission recommendations. The government decided to give 27 per cent job reservation to socially and educationally backward communities (SEBCs) in the Central Government and public sector undertakings. With this the ratio of reservation peaked to 49.5 per cent: SCs 15 per cent, STs 7.5 per cent and OBCs 27 per cent.

Afterwards a series of cases were filed against the government's in the Supreme Court and other High Courts such as St. Stephen's College versus University of Delhi regarding religious minority rights and T.M.A. Pai Foundation versus State of Karnataka regarding linguistic minority rights.

After globalization many private professional institutions were opened in India. Though these institutions were reluctant to provide reservation they did not manifest overtly their feelings and took recourse to the Articles 29 and 30 of the Constitution. Now, the time has come for evaluating the rights of minorities regarding educational institutions. This paper focuses on the minority rights and conceptual problems and analyzes the role played by professional minority educational institutions.

Minority Group

A minority or subordinate group is a sociological group, which does not constitute a politically, dominant plurality of the total population of a given society. A sociological minority is not necessarily a numerical minority—it may include any group that is disadvantaged with respect to the dominant group in terms of social status, education, employment, wealth and political power. According to Ambedkar, who explained the term 'minority' in the Constitutional Assembly debates "the word is used not merely to indicate the minority in the technical sense of the word: it is also used to cover minorities, which are nonetheless minorities in the cultural and linguistic sense".

J.A. Laponce, in his book, *The Protection to Minority* describes 'minority' as "a group of persons having different race, language or religion from that of majority of inhabitants". In the *Yearbook of Human Rights* (U.N., 1950) minority has been described as a non-dominant group, having different religious or linguistic traditions than the majority population. Articles 29 and 30 of the Constitution of India guarantee the following privileges to minority groups:

Article 29

1. Any section of the citizens residing in the territory of India or any part thereof having a distinct language, script or culture of its own shall have right to conserve the same.
2. No citizen shall be denied admission into any educational institution maintained by the state or receiving aid out of state funds on grounds of religion, race, caste, language or any of them.

Article 30

1. All minorities, whether based on religion or language, shall have the right to establish and administer educational institutions of their choice.
2. In making any law providing for the compulsory acquisition of any property of an educational institution established and administered by a minority, referred to in clause, the state shall ensure that the amount fixed by or determined under such law for the acquisition of such property is such as would not restrict or abrogate the right guaranteed under the management of a minority whether based on religion or language.

Categories of Minority Communities

In India, the minority communities can be broadly classified as religious and linguistic.

Religious

Before 1993, there were only five noted religious minorities, viz., Muslims, Christians, Sikhs, Buddhists and Zoroastrians (Parsis). When A.R. Antulay was Minister for Minority Affairs, he tried to include the Jains in the religious minorities. It was the policy of the Congress party to appease the minorities which triggered the debate.

Linguistic

According to the 38th report of the National Commission of Linguistic Minority (NCLM), "in each state there is a language which is spoken by the majority of the residents of that state. All others who do not speak that language belong to linguistic minority". In India, 18 major and 1,600 minor languages are spoken and each language can be considered as a minority language.

From the point of view of Article 30, all minorities, if they are based on religion or language, shall have the right to establish and administer educational institutions of their choice. So, many educational institutions are established, of which some are recognized and some are unrecognized, some aided and some unaided.

Aided colleges are privately managed but the government funds them. Section 3(b) of the Private Professional Educational Institutions (Regulation of Admission and Fixation of Fee) Bill, 2005 defines an aided institution as "a private professional educational institution, receiving recurring financial aid or assistance in whole or in part from the Central Government or the State Government or from any body, under the control of Central or State Government disbursing grants-in-aid or financial assistance and shall include a minority institution".

Unaided colleges are privately managed and raise their own funds. The Supreme Court has held that the admission of students is an essential facet of the right to administer educational institutions of their choice, as contemplated in Article 30 of the Constitution. The State Government or the University may not be entitled to interfere with that right, the admission to the unaided educational institutions is on the transparent basis and the merit is adequately taken care of, the right to administer, not being absolute, there could be regulatory measures for ensuring educational standards and maintaining excellence thereof and it is more so in the matter of admissions to professional institutions.

Minority Educational Institutions

According to a survey, conducted by the All India Association of Christian Higher Education (AIACHE) in early 1990s, there were 230 Christian colleges in the country, in which they had a membership of 226 colleges. Table 1 and 2 show the type and number of the institutions of Christian and Muslim communities, respectively. Similarly, according to Federation of Jain Educational Institutions, there are 3,599 Jain minority institutions in India.

As a result of the Supreme Court judgment of 12th August 2005, the Lok Sabha members demanded legislation to reverse the setback caused to the social justice philosophy of the Constitution. The hearing of this

Table 1
Christian Higher Educational Institutions (1994)

Type of colleges	***No. of institutions***
Medical Colleges*	3
Engineering Colleges	2
Arts, Science and Commerce Colleges	175
Educational Colleges	31
Physical Educational College	1
Agriculture College	1
Home Science Colleges	6
Law College	1
Social Work Colleges	5

*Inclusive of dental and nursing colleges.
Source: Vempeny Sebastian, *Minorities in Contemporary India*.

Table 2
Muslim Educational Institutions (1980–81)

Type of education	***Total institutions***
Primary education	12 States, 45 Districts
Secondary education	12 States, 38 Districts
S.S.C. Boards	8
Higher Secondary Boards	5
Engineering Colleges	9
Other Colleges	12

Source: As in Table 1.

case was concerned with religious and linguistic minorities' institutions. According to these institutions, there was unnecessary and unproductive load on their back in the form of government's control, by way of rules and regulations. Therefore, they filed cases against State Governments in the Supreme Court. Some of them were as follows:

1. St. Xavier's College Society, Ahmedabad vs State of Gujarat, 1975(1) SCR 173
2. St. Stephen's College vs University of Delhi (1992) SCR 558–7 Bench
3. Islamic Academy of Education vs State of Karnataka and Others (Writ Petition No. 350 of 1993)—5 Bench
4. Unni Krishnan, J.P. vs State of Andhra Pradesh (1993) 1 SCC 645.
5. T.M.A. Pai Foundation and Others vs State of Karnataka and Others (2002) INSC 491 (31 October 2002)—11 Bench
6. P.A. Inamdar vs Government of Maharashtra (2005)

In these cases, the Supreme Court held that enforcing the state reservation policy on unaided institutions constitutes a serious encroachment on the right and autonomy of the institution. It adds that the government could fix different percentages for minority and non-minority institutions. It could also apply the same principles to non-professional unaided educational institutions. The Bench held that "such appropriation of seats cannot be held to be a regulatory measure in the interest of minority within the meaning of Article 30 (1), in the sight of the political class".

However, if the private institutions are given too much independence, it may invariably lead to the monopolization of higher education. Besides, problems, such as high fee structure, capitation fee, exploitation of teachers, etc., may also come up. In the recent cases, there was a hike in fees in some colleges nay the government gave into pressure.

This rapid growth has, no doubt, contributed to a quantitative increase in the number of colleges providing higher education but this has been at the cost of quality as the government does not exercise sufficient control over unaided colleges. Further, the purpose of these colleges seems to be more profit-making and not to ease the burden of the government or improve the quality of higher education.

The National Commission of Minority Educational Institutions received just 380 applications, before the Supreme Court case of P.A. Inamdar vs Government of Maharashtra and others (2005), seeking minority status. In 2007, with the decision of Central Government to reserve an additional 27 per cent seats for OBCs in all centrally funded educational institutions, the number of applications rose to more than 2,000.

However, after the implementation of the report of Mandal Commission, minority educational institutions have increased in number.

These institutions are taking advantage of Articles 29 and 30, but they are not following them in their real spirit. The reality of minority educational institutions is following:

1. Some educational institutions are aided but they do not implement the reservation policy.
2. The number of professional colleges or institutions run by the non-minority community in the state are increasing.
3. The syllabus of any course is not different from other educational institutions or also not related to Articles 29 and 30, i.e., conserving their religious culture, script and their language

To conclude, in recent times, both developed and developing countries are implementing the affirmative action policies for the weaker sections of society. Indian Constitution is also bound to the development of the weaker sections by providing safeguards to them. The reservation policy helped bring the Dalits into mainstream social order, particularly in the field of education and employment, which enhanced their economic status and thus brought an end their social and economic hardships. Another channel of development is the affirmative action towards the minorities and educational institutions run by them. These minority institutions basking under the facilities of Articles 29 and 30 of the Constitution refuse to admit students of backward classes and thus eclipse social justice.

REFERENCES

Bakshi, P.M. 2007. *The Constitution of India*. New Delhi: Universal Law Publishing Co.

Eternal Values for a Changing Society, Vol. III, *Education for Human Excellence*. Bombay: Bharatiya Vidya Bhavan.

Frontline, September 9 2005. Chennai: Kasturi & Sons Ltd.

Gaikwad, Shankar L. 1999. *Protective Discrimination Policy and Social Change*. Jaipur: Rawat Publications.

Galanter, Marc. 1984. *Competing Equalities.* New Delhi: Oxford University Press.

Kale, R.K. 2008. "Enrolling or Rolling Out: SC and ST Students in Central Universities", *University News*, 46(21), May 26–June 01.

Molishree. 2006. "Minority Educational Institutions: A Critical Analysis". CCS Working Paper No. 154.

Mungekar, B.L. 2001. "Globalisation and Dalits", *Radical Humanist,* April, Vol. 65, No. 1.

Naidu, R.V.K. 2004. *Empowerment of Scheduled Castes*. New Delhi: Kalpaz Publications.

Sharma, Premlata. 2002. *The Problems of Dalits and OBCs.* Jaipur: Book Enclave.

The Radial Humanist, January 2000.

Vempeny, Sebastian. 2003. *Minorities in Contemporary India*. New Delhi: Kanishka Publishers.

Court Cases

P.A. Inamdar and others vs Maharashtra State and others (2005) SCC 5041.

T.M.A. Pai Foundation and others vs State of Karnataka (2002) 8 SCC 481.

St. Stephen's College vs University of Delhi (1992) 1 SCC 558.

St. Xavier's College Society, Ahmedabad vs State of Gujarat (1974) 1 SCC 717.

Unni Krishnan vs State of Andhra Pradesh, (1993) 1 SCC 645.

12

Need for Special Focus on Other Backward Classes

D. VENKATESWARLU

No other stratification system is perhaps as rigid, exclusive, oppressive and exploitative as the caste system in India. It belies all other forms of stratification not only in terms of strict regimentation of castes but also in the range, expanse and intensity of the system. At the one extreme are the '*dwija*' castes and the 'dominant castes' who are endowed with all privileges—ritual, social, economic and political—and at the other are the castes whose very touch is a sin, who are reconciled with the most 'polluted' occupation, whose habitations are separate, who are most dependent on other castes for sustenance and survival and who suffer from such ignominies.

Although religious and social reform attempts, either as sporadic or continuous that lasted some decades, had been initiated at the group or mass level, very few have succeeded in leading to structural or cultural modifications in respect of the lower castes. The movements led by Mahatma Jyotiba Phule, Shri Narayana Guru and Dr B.R. Ambedkar are such movements which could make a dent in the social and cultural scenario of Indian society to a significant extent in most parts of the country.

Phule's attempts were unparalleled in the respect that he strived for the education and general uplift of not only the backward classes, in general, but also the women of these castes, in particular. His bold venture

This is the paper presented in *RC–09, Dalits and Backward Classes* of the XXXIII All India Sociological Conference held at Karnataka University, Dharwad, Karnataka, November 29–December 01, 2007.

through *Satya Shodhak Samaj* (Truth Seekers Society), unflinching against aggressive social hostility combined with family opposition, in empowering the women and lower castes, in education and other fields, showed a path to the later-day reformers and fighters like Ambedkar. His method, that of education, is still seen as the most powerful method of empowering the most deprived in any society. The various publicity brochures, brought out during the launching of National Literacy Mission and during the current running of *Sarva Siksha Abhayan,* also emphasize that education is a 'gateway' to the development process.

It is not the intention of the paper to recount the work of Phule among the women and the lower castes. Enough literature exists on this. The objective of this paper is to carry forward the work of Phule and a call to academics to finish the unfinished agenda he set before himself to focus on the problems of Other Backward Classes (OBCs). For this, certain prerequisites are inevitable.

The first of these is that a comprehensive assessment of the socio-economic status of all the OBCs in the country has to be undertaken and a list of OBCs published at different national-level commissions had given different figures in the past. For instance, Kaka Kalekar Commission (1955) named 2,399 communities and Mandal Commission (1981) identified 3,743 communities as OBCs by following different criteria. If we consider state-level commissions, the lists get more complicated. The only scientific estimation of their population in the present times is based on extrapolation of their population registered in 1931 Census. The debate before 2001 Census for such an exercise was stiffly opposed on the ground that it would sustain the caste system which is weakening due to modernization and that there would be a plethora of false claims. Undoubtedly, the exercise, if undertaken, would be fraught with a variety of problems. But, is there a better way of assessment of the socio-economic status of all the OBCs in the country than the census method? For this, the present lists of OBCs at the Centre and in the states, where they exist, may be followed. Further, a contingency exists as the OBCs are not yet accorded adequate space in the social sphere. Their basic socio-economic deprivations result in low-level aspiration and achievement in education, public employment, economy, politics and other such spheres which suffer from vacuum(s) that rightfully belongs to them but, by default, has been cornered by others.

An objective assessment of the socio-economic status of OBCs alone can help in establishing a 'social class consciousness' to foster unity among all of them. The political parties and some vested interests have always sought to sustain on the divisions within the OBCs and, although, frequent efforts have been made to foster among them, they were pre-empted by raising the bogey of 'casteism' of the leadership of the OBCs or the former tried to usurp this initiative to scuttle such moves. That there are numerous castes among the OBCs can be explained from a historical perspective. There is an unstable and flexible hierarchy of the castes among the OBCs. But they are to be understood only as a horizontal stratification and not as a vertical one. Rather, only differentiation exists among the OBCs and not a hierarchy. This is our second prerequisite.

Thirdly, all organizations representing the OBCs should demand that the term 'backward castes' be adopted in place of the words/phrases like OBCs/LBCs/SEBCs, which have been used in different contexts—constitutional, judicial, general and specialized literature leading to an avoidable confusion (Verma, 2002; Sujatha, 2002; Rao, 2002). Usage of such different names have only led to confusion both among the OBCs and others, especially the media, which has always been unsympathetic, indifferent and hostile towards them more than one occasion. Therefore, such confusion needs to be avoided. Further, there should be no objection for the use of 'castes' in the name as it exists in the case of Scheduled Castes (SCs).

The study of OBCs has also been, by and large, ignored by the sociologists and social anthropologists. There are not many studies about their socio-economic status, political participation, problems or deprivations as are on the SCs and STs, whose combined population is less than half of that of the OBCs. There has not been a single article on OBCs appeared in the *Sociological Bulletin*, the journal of the Indian Sociological Society, for the last eight years. Even ethnographic studies do not exist in a substantial number on them. Few that focus on OBCs smack of "blatant partisanship, class bias, and remarkable casualness" (Verma, 2002: 111). Therefore, there is a need to undertake comprehensive study of different dimensions of OBCs. This is the fourth requisite.

Then, there are many vested interests that are active in the society who sustain and flare up the internal differentiation as irreconcilable stratification has to be exposed. Such interests thrive on wedging deeper cleavages among the OBCs, creating a 'false' ego among the supposedly 'developed' castes among the OBCs and a feeling of 'more relative deprivation' among the other OBCs. This has delayed the 'unification' process amidst the OBCs leaving them more backward and unable to realize the game of the vested interests to subject them to continuous exploitation. Further, especially in the debate over reservation policy, their crocodile tears for the less privileged among the OBCs in matters of educational and employment opportunities and fierce and sustained struggle to deny the constitutional benefits to the 'creamy layer' are to be laid bare and naked. This was evident in the post-Mandal agitations nationwide and in Gujarat, Delhi and a few other states in the recent years. That is not to ignore the different levels of progress and development achieved by the different OBC castes. The priorities and allocations of development must change in the case of different OBC castes depending on the parameters of achievements.

The sixth prerequisite is that a study to assess the impact of globalization on the OBCs has also to be done as there is a general feeling that the process has adversely affected only the marginal groups. They are certainly in a position of disadvantage as they remain backward, compared to the forward castes, in the fields of education, health, economic development and political mobilization. This has to be probed and studied in detail.

Lastly, a call and a message have to be conveyed to all the OBC castes:

- to suppress the differences within and forge a horizontal unity by developing a 'federative consciousness' (Rao, 2002);
- to initiate an internal reform to improve educational and vocational skills among all the castes, many of which are occupational castes, any way;
- to build strong pressure groups for a better bargaining power with the state and dominant sections of the society to obtain even the constitutionally guaranteed privileges;
- to launch a political organization/party to voice their demands as most of the communities have taken recourse to in post-independent India; and
- to shed any social ego vis-à-vis the SCs, STs and minorities as the need of the hour is to forge a larger unity of all the deprived and marginalized communities and sections who have usurped social privileges, property, wealth and power, which has sustained their superiority and will continue to do so for generations to come and, in addition, to initiate corrective steps in this regard.

REFERENCES

Beteille, Andre. 1981. *The Backward Classes and the New Social Order*. Delhi: Oxford University Press.

Keer, Dhananjay. 1964. *Mahatma Jyoti Rao Phooley: Father of the Indian Social Revolution*. Bombay: Popular Prakashan.

Rao, J.V. Raghavendra. 2002. 'Backward Class Mobilization: Marxist and Non-Marxist Paradigms', *Eastern Anthropologist*, Vol. 55, No. 2–3, pp. 177–206.

Rao, M.S.A. (ed.). 1979. *Social Movements in India,* Vol. I, *Peasant and Backward Classes Movements*. New Delhi: Manohar Publications.

Rao, M.S.A. 1979. *Social Movements and Social Transformation: A Study of Two Backward Classes Movements in India*. Delhi: The MacMillan Company of India Ltd.

Shah, A.M., Baviskar, R.S. and Ramaswamy, E.A.(eds.). 1997. *Social Structure and Changes,* Vol. 4, *Development and Ethnicity*. New Delhi: Sage Publications.

Singh, S.N. 1996. *Reservation Policy for Backward Classes*. Jaipur: Rawat Publications.

Sujatha, V.S. 2002. 'The Other Backward Classes: Composition, Characteristics and Empowerment', *Eastern Anthropologist,* Vol. 55, No. 2–3, pp. 133–44.

Verma, H.S. 2002. 'This Special Number', *Eastern Anthropologist,* Vol. 55, Nos. 2–3, pp. 111–14.

IV

Caste System: Regional Context

13

Genesis, Mechanism and Growth of Caste System in South India

NANDU RAM

I am honoured in getting invited by RC–09: Dalits and Backward Classes of the Indian Sociological Society to deliver the First Professor C. Parvathamma Memorial Lecture at its 32nd annual conference held at Chennai, Tamil Nadu during 27–29 December 2006. My first acquaintance of late Prof. Parvathamma goes back to 1973 when I read her research paper on "Dr Ambedkar and After: The Scheduled Caste Classes and Masses", published in the *Eastern Anthropologist*. Then, I met her at IIT Kanpur in 1978 and at Meerut in 1980, and discussed a number of academic issues, especially pertaining to caste system and location of the Dalits or the Scheduled Castes (SCs) in it. Subsequently, we also met at least twice during 1990s at her residence, in some selection committee meeting. Through these meetings and reading her publications, I had found in her a fine brain, brilliant scholar and a very meticulous researcher, endowed with straightforwardness, elderly affection and fine personality. Prof. Parvathamma proved herself to be a lone crusader, after Baba Saheb Ambedkar, against the vulnerable position of Dalits through her academic pursuits. This lecture is a modest tribute to her unforgotten memory and an inspiration to young social scientists, specially sociologists and social anthropologists, pursuing the theme presented forthwith.

Indian society is said to be caste-ridden in whatsoever form caste exists, whether in old or new or even newer. The sociological and social anthropological studies undertaken so far testify that the caste exists as a

This is the First Prof. Parvathamma Memorial Lecture delivered in RC–09 during the XXXII All India Sociological Conference held at Loyala College, Chennai, from 27 to 29 December, 2006.

major social structural and cultural institution (Weber, 1958), with its well-knit organization or system. It exists not only among the Hindus but even the non-Hindu communities in India have also adopted this system at least at the level of social interaction and commensal relations, though they reject its adoption as an ideological basis of their social structure and belief system. Hence, a few sociologists and social anthropologists (e.g., Dumont, 1970) have accepted it as a pan-Indian phenomenon like the *varna* system. Contrary to it is the view of a few scholars that caste system, in their reckoning, persists in India not only as a cultural organization and social structural system but remains a purely localized structural reality (Mencher, 1974) or at least an adaptive structure (Berreman, 1979) where it has necessarily imbibed in itself the characteristics of other non-Hindu communities, including the tribal communities. In the same vein, there is lack of unanimity among the indologists, historians, ethnographers, and sociologists and social anthropologists on the *varna/jati* model of the Hindu society or system, i.e., of the two—*varna* and *jati*—which came first in its social formation. Also, there seems to be lack of unanimity among scholars about the *varna* model being structural reality at all at any point of time in Indian society. In fact, the *varna* system, in their opinion, never existed as a social structural reality; instead, it was an ideal or ideational construct in which the numerous castes and sub-castes were hierarchized and ranked as superior and inferior, along with ranking in superiority and inferiority of the four *varnas*.

Genesis of Caste System

Some are of the view that during the Vedic and later-Vedic periods, the Aryans (who later got identified as Hindus) were divided into four *varnas*. In fact, the *varna* was a technical term used for the then existed four major castes (Muller, 1883; Ambedkar, 1979; Weber, 1958) or classes or social categories, which split later into numerous *jatis* and *up-jatis* or castes and sub-castes or sub-sub-castes, due to multiple reasons. Some of these were imposing or superimposing endogamy over exogamy, the Brahmin's initially adopting a policy of closing their doors of commensality or commensal relations, including marital alliance, with others, which subsequently was followed by the latter groups or *varnas* (Ambedkar, 1979), pursuing specific types of occupations as well as customs and belief systems by different groups of people, and so on and so forth. Opposed to this is the view heralded by a number of social scientists and foreign travellers who had visited India before the first millennium AD. Such view accepts the presence of numerous groups, not *varnas* or castes, of the people pursuing different types of occupations, customs, belief systems and also having heterogeneous types of social organizations, interaction patterns, commensal relations, etc. Then, the extended view is that the four-fold *varna* model was, as mentioned above, an ideal devise or scheme of the Aryans under which the already existed numerous groups of the people were supposedly or notionally fitted. It is a well-accepted fact that quite a few groups did not strictly fit in that, and yet others were either forcefully kept out or they themselves refused to get fitted in and opted out of the scheme. Such groups of people have obviously been termed either indigenous or aborigines or tribals, Dravidians, *Antyajas*, *Antyavasins* (Ati-Shudras or untouchables), etc. In other words, the *varna* system was an idealized version of social organization or social structural arrangement of the then existed population of the Aryans, but in reality the people at large were living in numerous well-organized or loosely organized groups or social categories.

Not going here into further details of historiography of origin of caste or the caste system and also its major characteristics or attributes like hierarchy, separation or repulsion and interdependence (see Bougle, 1971), we may buy the argument, for the time being, that the impressionistic view about the *varna* system being the pan-Indian phenomenon or accepting the four-fold *varna* scheme at all-India level prevalent during the ancient period gets falsified by the facts that are available through the archaeological excavations, historiographic interpretations of inscriptions, interpretations of and inferences drawn from the scriptures written or complied in vernacular languages of different regions, and the ethnographic surveys done about the structural arrangements of almost all groups of people, including their customs, belief systems, commensal relations and occupations practiced in different parts of the country. This then simply means that the ideal devise of the four-fold *varna* scheme was conceived of by the ancient sage-scholars and was ideationally or notionally operative within the Indo-Gangetic basin, though the exerting connived power did try, in some cases successfully but in many cases unsuccessfully, to instal the scheme or system by transplanting the people of some *varnas* from the Indo-Gangetic basin to the other regions of the country as they were indigenously not available there.

Contrary to this, the caste system, either in the form of collectivity of the numerous occupational groups or a well-structured system of social groups, as erroneously projected by some social scientists, has had ever existed at the pan-Indian level though its structural arrangement varied from locale to locale or region to region. It may also be stated that the caste system as a unitary structure or a well-bounded social organization never existed as a static entity; instead, numerous permutations and combinations have ever been in operation within it, making the system relatively complex and yet a dynamic one. Hence, the caste system is not only a localized social structure but the latter has evolved several types of caste systems (and thus there are caste systems) in India, though all of these supposedly operate within the frame of an idealized version of uniform hierarchy of caste system (see Dumont, 1970). Needless to say, such version of the caste system projects its resemblance with the *varna* system, though the numerous castes and sub-castes are not uniformally well categorized and are unqualifyingly accepted within either of four *varnas* in the *varna* system, or there exist even more caste categories placed in altogether different type of hierarchy of castes operative at the local or regional level. Yet, it cannot be denied that the numerous castes and sub-castes have been trying both successfully and unsuccessfully, especially since the colonial period, to get them accepted in the higher ranked castes within the *varna* scheme. In other words, the process of synchronization of the discrete caste categories (caste and sub-castes) has been going on in a continuous hierarchy of the caste system (Gupta, 1993: 110–42), though the continuous hierarchy or continuity of hierarchy is not of traditional ranking of all castes and sub-castes in the descending order to the Brahmin, Kshatriya or Rajput, Vaishya, Shudra and the untouchables.

There is, however, no dearth or empirical evidences to suggest that in their day-to-day life people in different regions have not only downgraded but even denied the ritual or religious supremacy of the Brahmins or of their numerous castes or sub-castes. Contrary to it, it has been said that a Brahmin in a village is considered the superior most, irrespective of whether he possesses the traditional (ideal) attributes prescribed in the scriptures (Mandelbaum, 1972: 24). In certain areas, even the traditional supremacy or dominance of the Kshatriya or Rajput caste, with its sub-castes, has been challenged by the people of the economically, politically and numerically middle level dominant castes. Thus, one finds the earlier formulations easily contestable on the basis of the emergent empirical social realities in different parts of the country. A few such contestable formulations are like, sanskritization leading to positional change or change in the social position or social status of the lower castes but leaving their ranked position vis-à-vis the hierarchical structure of the caste system intact (Srinivas, 1966), the top (Brahmin) and the bottom (the Shudra castes and by extension the untouchables) ranks of the hierarchical caste system remaining intact or immobile and all permutations and combinations or changes occurring only in the middle ranks or orders (Bailey, 1964), and, as stated above, villager knowing fully well about the men of the Brahmin *jati* (caste including its sub-castes) of his village as being neither scholars nor trained priests yet accepting their highest ritual status or rank traditionally decreed on them (Mandelbaum, 1972: 24).

Mechanism and Growth of Castes

There are five main theses on the mechanism(s) and the consequent growth of caste system in a region and from one region to the other over a period of time. Its growth is to be understood in terms of growing its number and consolidation of attributes prescribed to it in a given hierarchy of castes found in a region. How and by whom these attributes were evolved and prescribed to a caste and how were these accepted or contested by its members are not our immediate concerns here. Rather, we wish to state briefly the basic tenets of these theses and examine critically their being valid ones on the mechanism for the growth of castes and the caste system.

The first thesis is of the policy of exclusion which means exclusion or throwing away or boycotting permanently members from a caste. Such policy has remained in operation since the early period of the Indo-Aryan and later Hindu society in India. This operates even today, especially among the lower castes in rural society, though it is applied generally on temporary and not permanent basis. As stated earlier, Ambedkar formulated his thesis in 1916 (published in 1917), about the genesis of caste as an outcome of the superimposition of endogamy over exogamy (as form of marriage) which he considered as one of the mechanisms for the genesis as well as growth of caste. As part of his thesis, he referred to marriage of surplus men (widowers) and surplus women (widows) outside their group or caste as growth of and one of the mechanisms for the genesis of caste into numerous other castes. The final point that he made in his thesis is the closing door policy. In his conceded opinion, Brahmin, Kshatriya, Vaishya and Shudra were initially four classes and not castes, and the *varna*, with the Aryan origin, happened to be a technical term given to each class. The Brahmin, according him, was a class and its members first became a caste through coining and implementing the policy of closing their door for members of the other classes. In other words, the Brahmins adopted endogamy and closed their door of marriage and commensal relations for members of the other three classes. Thus, they first became closed in and then closed for others. "... while making themselves into a caste, the Brahmins, by virtue of this, created non-Brahmin caste; or, to express it in my way (says Ambedkar), while closing themselves in they closed others out" (Ambedkar, 1979: 20). Being guided by the notion of 'pure self and impure other', they might have done this to make themselves as of pure blood and distinctive from others. Later, others imitated them and closed their own door still for others; and, hence, became endogamous. In the words of Ambedkar, "It is 'infection of imitation' that caught all these sub-divisions (non-Brahmins) on their onward march of differentiation and had turned them into castes" (ibid.: 18). Ambedkar's thesis, though not widely acknowledged in sociological and social anthropological analysis of caste in India, stands on its own merit of logical argumentation and empirical verification even in the present time as numerous castes and sub-castes are said to have originated and grown through such mechanisms.

The second thesis on the origin and growth of castes and sub-castes is about the mechanism or process of inclusion which, as the face of it, appears to be contradictory to the above stated thesis. Notwithstanding the invalidated contradiction between the two, the thesis of inclusion explains numerical strengthening and consolidation of castes and sub-castes since the early times in the history of genesis and growth of castes in India. It is evident from the socio-anthropological and historiographical analysis of the various segments of population of the indigenous and Indo-Aryan society of the ancient period that the people, as a whole, including Aryans, classified into Brahmin, Kshatriya, Vaishya and Shudra *varnas*, were tribal in their beliefs, customs, taboos and totems, etc. (see, Risley, 1908; Weber, 1958; Kosambi, 1956; Dutt, 1986). More precisely, they were mixture of both Aryans and non-Aryans or native people (Kosambi, 1953, 1956, 1962, 1965). This was found not only in North India but also in South India where there was a total absence of such classification of people of the Indo-Aryan society. In fact, some people, especially with the nomenclature of Brahmin and Kshatriya or Rajanya from north, were transported and inducted in the south, besides recruitment of the local people to these classes or *varnas*. Anyway, without going into details of their induction process and recruitment patterns, we wish to reiterate here that the policy or process of inclusion of outsiders, especially tribals (Kosambi, 1956; Dutt 1986), into a class and later caste, was approved and legitimized by the then existed power and authority for the purpose of organizing and regulating society of a sort with its own ongoing tradition and civilization of procreation as well as orientation.

It is, however, worth noting that as the system of caste happens to be a system of graded inequality (Ambedkar, 1979), wherein each caste is ranked higher or lower with unequal ranked status and with cumulative social and ritual inequality with the other, the inclusion mechanism was operative in the vertical and not horizontal fashion. This means, the newcomers—both individuals and groups—were included in a particular class or *varna* with lower ranked status (sub-caste) yet with the nomenclature of the same class or *varna* or with the independent ranked status (caste) in the hierarchically arranged system and thereby spreading at length and breadth of the caste system. However, there continued to be asymmetrical relationship among all of them, especially in terms of marriage and commensal relations, ritual purity, etc. It is also true that the independent ranked statuses or castes, not being satisfied with such partial or differential inclusion in the caste system, had all along been contesting for their complete inclusion in the idealized yet socially and religiously accepted system of distinctively ranked upper classes or *varnas*. Thus, this thesis stands valid as the mechanism of inclusion and the resultant contest can easily be seen even in the present time.

The third thesis is of the transformation and spread of clans into castes which we will be discussing, in detail, in the following section. Here, we shall look briefly at the nature and composition of clan and the mechanism it adopted to get transformed into caste by changing its tenets or attributes and switching over to that of the caste. This thesis was initially formulated by Kosambi (1962) as a part of his larger explanation of formation of society and culture as well as of civilization in Indian sub-continent, especially in the peninsular India. He has done this on the basis of the archaeological and historical evidences. Since the people of different stocks or groups observed clan (*gotra*) exogamy and married people of the other clans within the group, this gave birth to caste, and the clan subsided through the passage of time. This thesis has, in recent years, been discussed, in details, by Morton Klass (1998), who has explained how, in the past, clan got transformed into caste. Referring to Levi-Strauss' (1963) two structural type words 'bear' (totem) and 'barber' (caste system), Klass has accepted totemic groups as clans practising rule of exogamy opposed to caste rule of endogamy. "Each 'clan', however, obeys the rule of exogamy: a male and a female of the same clan may not marry each other (as they are treated as brother and sister because of their supposed origin from the same descent), and so the spouse for each member of the society (clan) must be sought in a 'clan' or 'section' other than his or her own' (Klass, 1998: 139). This, in a way, supports Kosambi's thesis of 'marriage commune', consisting of a number of clans living in a single region or circle or caste (ibid.), though he has not specified whether such 'marriage circle' is territorially confined among the members of the same commune living in a single region or outside it. He has further added two more characteristics to his propositional thesis: 'equalitarian clans' and 'absolute surplus'. In the case of equalitarian clans, he says that, "the galaxy of societies and social groups making up the precaste (clan based) South Asian milieu exhibited, to a significant degree, endogamous clusters of exogamous, unstratified, stipulated-decent, 'equalitarian clans', and that it was this galaxy—this total social and economic milieu – that was transformed into the stratified socio-economic system we know of as 'caste system' (ibid.: 158).

Similarly, Klass' thesis or sub-thesis of 'absolute surplus' meant the continuous production of surplus, rather absolute production of food grains, which was obviously more than that required for subsistence. Compared to those whose food production or items produced from hunting and gathering was for the bare subsistence, the producers of 'absolute surplus' emerged as separate castes, though their clan affiliation remained the same (Klass, 1998: 155–56; see also, Jaiswal, 1998: 4–6). This does not mean that castes originated only among those who had 'absolute surplus', rather those being less fortunate with bare subsistence production and rendering services, especially labour, to the fortunate ones as well as those being hunters and gatherers of the forest produces and living in the adjoining eco-zones also formed castes through their interaction with the former. Interestingly, this thesis subscribes to the view that the mechanism of clans to castes, within different eco-zones, was operative simultaneously throughout the whole South Asia, including India. Needless to say, all these castes were neither placed horizontally nor had equalitarian relations among them due to their differential position in the economic structure with whatsoever meagre form it existed. Then, at a much later stage, these castes vis-à-vis their system got legitimized with the introduction of ritual purity and impurity or pollution as well as ranking assigned to each one.

Still another thesis, related to origin and growth of castes, is that of the occupational affiliation or division of labour which has been greatly emphasized in sociological and social anthropological studies on the subject, though Ambedkar (1979: 47–48) considered it, with his substantive argument, as division of labourers. In a simplistic sense, as there existed differential forms of occupations, both skilled and unskilled, pure and impure, the labourers or the people performing these occupations either voluntarily or by traditions or birth were treated as separate castes, or were ranked higher and lower in the order or system. This thesis, not being convincing one, was criticized by Ambedkar (ibid.) on the ground that had the division of labour been the source as well as mechanism of origin and growth of castes and caste system, these could have equally been found in all the civilized societies of the world wherein division of labour is a necessary feature, but this is not the case as the castes, with their system, are found only in India and nowhere else. Secondly, since a person changes his occupation at one time or the other (in most of the cases, the people have changed their traditional or caste specific occupations in the present time), his caste affiliation could also be changed but this has never happened. Hence, the division of labour or occupational pursuit could never be the basis and mechanism of genesis and growth of castes and the caste system as well.

The last thesis about the genesis, mechanism and growth of castes in India is related to the religious Sanskritic texts which subscribe to the view that all the four *varnas* of Brahmin, Kshatriya, Vaishya and Shudra—the four categories or classes of Aryans—were of the divine origin, of meeting of the Purusha (male) and Prakiti-nature (female), or of the four organs—body parts of the Purusha himself. All the four *varnas* had to perform four distinct functions and were assigned specific ranks or status—higher and lower or superior and inferior—and any violation of these was subjected to punishment specially in the form of ex-communication. In the idiom of *varna*, if a male and a female of two different *varnas* had intimate relation and produced a child considered *varnashankar* mixed breed, they as well as their progeny were thrown out of the either *varnas*. Such persons, with their progenies, formed caste or castes, which could not be fitted in the *varna* scheme. As a critique of this thesis, it may be said that it does not stand on the logical argument as no creation of a living being is possible through the body organs other than the particular one. Then, this may be accepted as an ideological legitimacy to the classification of population, in India, into various social categories or classes or *varnas* being higher and lower or pure and impure in the hierarchical scheme. Since the miscegenation or intimate sexual relation between males and females of two different classes or *varnas* has all along been discouraged and punished appropriately by the system, the condemnation of such persons, along with their progeny, and their formation of separate caste, can be accepted as a valid part of this thesis.

Anyway, it may be said here that there is no unanimity among the theses, cited above, on the mechanisms and growth of castes and caste system in India as each thesis emphasizes one mechanism and does not take cognisance of the other. Yet, one may agree that castes originated from tribe and its clan, within its totemic structure, through switching from exogamy to endogamy and getting legitimated by ideological elaboration at later stage. Such ideological elaboration was anchored in the divinity for the universal acceptance of castes and the caste system with the double check through enactment of specific rules and regulations relating to rewards and punishments to the adherents or practitioners and violators respectively. Such rewards and punishments were directed to the upward and downward movements as well as excommunications, in certain cases, of the persons and the groups concerned, within the status scheme that ranked higher and lower along the attributes or *guna* of quality, fate, rebirth, purity and impurity, superior and inferior occupation, etc. One thing is clear that the scheme was evolved by keeping in view the privation of some and deprivation of many in the matrix of the existing ranked statuses, and social interaction and social relations covered under it.

Caste System in South India: From Clan to Caste

In view of the traditional aspect of the caste system, one is generally informed about its rigidity, both in its structural and cultural forms, lived with by the people in South India. Such impression is not merely based on the heresay but is well substantiated by the scriptural texts as well as similar literature written, in local languages, about the local folk-traditions, historiographic interpretations, ethnographic surveys, census monographs and a few independent monographs, and research articles published by historians, and sociologists and social anthropologists, on the society of the South Indian states. But, the more important issue is to know briefly whether the caste system originated indigenously there or had travelled all the way from north to south India and got rigidified there with all its structural attributes as well as cultural practices with firm ideological grounding among the indigenous groups of the people. In doing this, it is also obliquely necessary to probe the possible reasons for the later.

We have stated above that the castes originated simultaneously throughout India. There are, however, four distinctive views about the origin, mechanism and growth of castes and caste system in South India. The first view speaks of origin of caste or castes simultaneously in different parts of the country, including the peninsular India. For instance, Kosambi (1956: 25) accepts the rules of endogamy as survival of the pre-Aryan or non-Aryan tribal practices in the Harappan civilization (around 2000 BC) and finds their fusion as the foundation of the caste system, specially after the developed form of division of labour among the people, as mentioned above. But Kosambi is silent on whether that had happened simultaneously in all or only in specific parts of the country. It is, however, clear from his elaborate narratives about what he spoke more or exclusively of that in the northern India, and he covered, for the purpose, utmost the central and western India. Here, his arguments are inclusive of both the materialist and textual analyses of archaeological as well as living evidences found in these regions. The second view is of Klass (1998) who provides, on the contrary, an exclusive material basis for the origin of caste. As already stated, he speaks of a number of 'equalitarian' endogamous social groups (like those described by Kosambi) in the hunting and food gathering stage (pre-historic times) living in the numerous eco-zones, but he does not call them tribals. Later, these groups or at least some of these succeeded in producing 'absolute surplus' of the food grains and, thus, were 'prosperous' compared to those engaged in producing or collecting food grains, forest produces, or hunted animals for their subsistence. These groups were also having equalitarian exogamous clans, constituting of a single 'marriage circle', and sharing together both prosperity and misfortune. But, with the development of new agricultural technology, those groups which possessed cultivable land turned to be in advantageous position and the deprived ones became labourers to them at the communitarian (group) level. Thus, there emerged a hierarchical ranking of both the advantaged and the disadvantaged endogamous groups, with their exogamous clans, leading from 'clans to castes'.

But treating Kosambi's thesis as a tentative probing, Jaiswal (1998: 3) is of the view that the entry of the tribal groups into the 'general society' is a racial explanation of caste. According to her, if we accept this formulation that the different endogamous tribal groups (with their supposedly racial origin) formed castes or caste system, then it would have formed race or racial system and not the castes or caste system. Notwithstanding the tribe as a race, the origin of caste has also been attributed to tribe by Dutt who says:

> In this matter the aborigines (tribals) contributed more than the Aryans … . The Aryans when they came into India had outgrown this stage of tribal economy, … From what we find among non-Aryanized aborigines of India we can believe that the practices of totemistic exogamy and tribal endogamy were practically strong among the Dravidian peoples of India, which kept the various tribes asunder like so many castes … . Again, even before the coming of the Indo-Aryans, there had been great cultural differences among the natives of India, probably between the civilized Dravidians and the savages pre-Dravidians, between men who dwelt in towns and forts and had well-developed political organization and systematized creeds, and men who still dwelt in forest and caves, and had not advanced beyond the hunting and fishing stage of culture. These differences had raised a wall of separation between the two types, and each avoided contact with the other. These tribal and cultural divisions of society could not be shaken off by the natives even after their conquest by the Aryans, and under the changed circumstances, they became hardened into caste divisions. Hence, the curious fact that the caste rules are more rigid among the Dravidians of the south, not only between the Brahmans and non-Brahmans but between the various sections of the non-Brahmans, between the touchables and the untouchables, than among the more Aryan peoples of northern India. Thus, the practices of the conquered aborigines (tribals) contributed as much to the development of caste as the racial class prejudices of the Aryan conquerors. (1986: 18–19)

It is, thus, clear from the above lengthy quotation that prior to the origin of castes and the caste system, the various types of differences existed among the native or aboriginal or tribal people which supplemented and complemented to the origin and growth of the institution of caste introduced and legitimized by the Aryans in India over a period of time.

Similarly, Klass' formulation, as stated above, also does not hold ground as in many regions the tribals had a well-developed peasantry but, at the same time, retained their distinct tribal social structure and identity, and had not transformed it into that of a caste. But, in certain cases, some tribal groups transformed themselves into caste only after introduction of the Brahmanical culture and ideology (Jaiswal, 1998: 5–6). We shall come to this a little later. We may, however, be tempted to accept, for the time being, Klass' general formulation but this applies largely to the latter part of the colonial period up to the country's political independence, though the study of Nagaraju (1995: 8–23) supports, in a way, this formulation as the tribals of the Rayalseema of south-western Andhra Pradesh gained tribal chieftaincies through their role in the wars between the Chalukyas and Pallavas in the 8th-9th century AD. Later, they adopted the *varna/jati* (caste) model either at the middle or mostly at the lower level in the local caste hierarchy. But it has also been said that a few castes found in the early South Indian society were both structurally and culturally different from the Brahmanical institution of caste—with differential ranking and system of hierarchy based on the notion of purity and impurity or pollution. According to Gurukul (1995: 245), "Most of the views in early historiography of South India confused the problem of caste by taking clan surnames for caste suffixes and juxtaposing them with the *varna* system. It has been clarified that the institution of caste was yet to characterize early Tamil (South Indian) society and what has been listed as castes by scholars in the past are clan names". Yet, like Kosambi, Klass also talks about the general process and ignores the regional specifications, including those found in the South Indian society.

But, the most pertinent question may be raised about the authenticity of the thesis of the tribal endogamy, emphatically emphasized in both the above mentioned formulations. In fact, in absence of any authentication, these are either conjectural probings or extrapolations in view of the well-accepted fact that at the initial stage of the societal evolution, human groups the world over were living a primitive life or, even during the later ancient period, were not only exogamous but also matriarchal, though the matriarchy practised among them was qualitatively different from that practised till recently in the society of some south as well as north-eastern Indian states. It is also a fact that over a period of time matriarchy has been replaced by patriarchy and exogamy by endogamy. Even then, the reminiscences of the earlier practised exogamy are strictly adhered to both among the castes and the tribes throughout the country as the marital alliance within the same *gotra* (clan) is a taboo and totally prohibited in both the cases. In fact, the remnants of clan are also found among most of the Dalits or SCs in South India even in the forms of their avoidance of eating flesh of some reptiles such as tortoise, snakes and birds like crows, fowls, and revering and worshipping them. They also avoid cutting of a few trees, creepers, etc. All these are totems for them and they are supposedly originated from those, or these are treated as their siblings. The tribes and castes, including SCs, are discrete social segments and are originated from various clans which are "named after or otherwise identified with a particular animal, plant or insect. They claim to be descended or otherwise derived from it (clan), and are customarily forbidden to eat the totemic object, although they are free to eat the totemic objects of sister groups of their own society" (Klass, 1998: 138–39).

The third view about the origin and development of caste in South India relies again on clan but derives its strength exclusively from the ancient texts composed and compiled during the contemporary period. More precisely, most part of South India, i.e., *Tamilakam* was divided, during the ancient period, into five ecological or eco-zones, which were known as *tinai*. These five *tinais* were the *Kurunchi* (hilly backwoods or forests) inhabited by the *vetars* and *kuruvars* or hunters and shifting cultivators, the *Palai* (parched areas) lived in by the *marwars* or warriors, the *Mullai* (pastoral tracks) occupied by the *itayars* or pastorialists, the *Marutam* (wetland) occupied and cultivated by the *ulavars* or ploughmen or agriculturists, and the *Neital* (the littoral or ponds) settled in by the *paratavar* or fishing community. But, in those areas where two *tinais* merged, the people, with their respective social groups and forms of subsistence, appeared to be mixed (see, Gurukul, 1994: 23; also Jaiswal, 1998: 7–8). These were dominated by the tribal chiefdoms (Champakalakshmi, 1975: 269). Besides the ecological and resultant material aspects, the ancient Tamil heroic poems, representing a people and their culture and social organizations as well as relations, were recited by a number of poets as a part of oral tradition of that period. Then, an academy of scholars collected and compiled these poems into ten anthologies, known as Sangam Literature, during 300 BC to 300 AD. According to Gurukul (1995: 242), these anthologies about the five *tinais* have also been accepted as efforts made towards "mechanical compartmentalization of nature into five divisions, symbolically denoting the historical evolution from the primitive to the civilized in south India". What is interesting to note here is that the people inhabited in the *tinais* were divided into several occupational groups and were dependent on kins, except *Brahmin* households (which were different from the Brahman households of the Brahmanic tradition transplanted much later in South India) for production of agricultural and other goods. Not only the production of these goods overlapped in several *tinais* but there were also frequent movements and social interactions of people of one *tinai* to the other.

With regard to the origin and growth of caste in these *tinais*, it is said that four *kutis* (castes) of *panam*, *paraiyan*, *tutiyan* and *katampan* existed in a *tinai* during the period of Sangam literature but is has also been mentioned that a *kuti*, in reality, meant a settlement of people or a family of people, and not a caste. It has further been stated that the four castes of *parpar* (seers), *aracar* (kings), *itaiyar* (cowherds) and *kuruvar* (hunters), and not the four stated above, were living in the *tinai*. Yet, at another place, other names of the four castes as *antanar, aracar, vanikar* and *velalar* have been mentioned. Even then, it has been clearly stated that these four castes were entirely different from the four castes and classes or *varnas* of the *varna* Brahmanic ideology in the North India (for details, see Gurukul, 1995: 245–46).

Finally, the last view on the origin and growth of castes and caste system in South India derives its strength from the adaptation process. This means, the Brahmanical version of castes and caste system were adapted, from the north, in South India during the post-Sangam literature period. This was, in other words, operative during the period of 400–600 AD and during 600–900 AD—the period of the dynastic rules of the Pallavas and Pandyas, respectively.

Then, there were three specific mechanisms through which such adaptation was carried out. One, the earlier undertaken visits, from the north of the Jaina Shramanas and later of the Buddhist monks through the routes of the eastern coast, were directed towards spread of the message of *ahimsa* (non-violence) but these also resulted in their cultural interaction with the people of the south. According to Thapar (1998: 132), visits of the Buddhist monks and cultural interaction between them and the people of south were possible during the rein of Ashoka (268–232 BC), the Maurayan ruler. Since both the Jaina Shramans and the Buddhist monks were largely opposed to the Brahmanical caste system in the north, it was out of question of their carrying caste system with them to the south for the purpose of its induction there, though they had their establishments (*mathas, viharas*) there. But it is also stated that several traders from the north travelled later, through this route, to the south and carried castes and the caste system with them and transplanted these over there through their interaction with the local people. Both castes and the caste system in South India subsequently got legitimacy by the local chieftains or rulers of the local regions.

The same or similar trade and commerce mechanism of the origin and growth of castes and the caste system in South India was through the route of the *Dakshinapatha* to the south during this period. This southern trade route of the *Dakshinapatha* was stretched from Magadha (in Bihar), the capital of the Mauryan empire, in the north upto Paithan at the north of the river Godavari in Deccan, in the south via Kashi (Banaras or Varanasi), Ujjaini (present Ujjain) and Maheshwar at the bank of the river Narmada, Bhilsa (now a district) in Madhya Pradesh. More specifically, Paithan, the southern end of the *Dakshinapatha*, was located in the southern part of present Maharashtra bordering north of Karnataka. But interestingly, the *Dakshinapatha* never touched the south—rather southern Karnataka and deep south, the Tamil country. According to Thapar (1999: 120), "The route was not only a channel of communication between north and south but also the vanguard of the exploration of the (southern) peninsula by the states of the north, intensified under the Mauryas". Also, through this route, the trades in shells, diamonds, precious stones, pearls and gold were carried out (Ray, 1995: 143). However, for the purpose of the present discussion, the *Dakshinapatha* was important in terms of penetration of the Brahmanical form of caste, along with its systematic arrangements, culture, customs and rituals, and religious legitimacy during the Maurya regimes, as mentioned above. In other words, the traders from the north were castemen and believers of the Brahmanical caste and religious ideology. Hence, they had played significant role in induction of the Brahmanical caste system in the south. It first got its anchorage in the Kanarese country (the present-day Karnataka) from where it spread to Tamil country consisting of major part of the present Tamil Nadu, southern part of Kerala in west, and the west of Andhra Pradesh in the north-west. Besides the trades reached to South India through both the routes, a few Brahmins from the north were also persuaded by the local rulers to travel over there during this period perhaps initially to perform certain religious rituals and later to introduce the caste system with the Brahmanic ideology under the state patronage. Thus, the Brahmanical form of castes and caste system had reached there through both the east coast and the *Dakshinapatha* during this period and got crystallized there up to the beginning the medieval period.

The second mechanism of adaptation of the Brahmanical caste system in South India was rooted in the Hindu religious sects and cults formed and practised in the north. According to Kosambi

(1962: 82–109), specially the Mother-Goddess cult has spread though the primitive tracks (hilly regions and forests) of the *Dakshinapatha* and the trade routes. The forms or names were obviously different from those in North India but the forms of their reverence and worship were, more or less, similar everywhere. But his analysis is more about the north than the south, and in the case of south it goes utmost to the Deccan, through the *Dakshinapatha*—the southern trade route, and not beyond that. However, a number of Shaivite and even Vaishnavite sects already spread by that time over major parts of South India, and the Virasaivas of Karnataka, adopted obviously from the north, had attacked the Jaina Sharmanas, the images of Mahavira Jaina, and the establishments set in his name from the 7th century onwards (Thapar, 1999: 73). This was equally true in the case of the images of the Buddha, and the *Viharas* set up for the Buddhist monks during that period. The Brahmins, travelled from the north to the south, had also started *yajnas* (sacrifices of animals and forest produces) on the Rigvedic patterns. All these together were instrumental in introduction and adaptation of the Brahmin form of the castes and the caste system, first in the northern part and then in the entire South India during the 300–600 AD and even till the period, as stated earlier.

The third and final mechanism through which the caste system spread throughout South India is related to the Aryan or Hindu religious scriptures, especially the epics like *Ramayana*, written in the major vernacular languages of region, during the early period of the first millennium AD. These scriptures were mainly supportive of the Brahmanic philosophical tradition(s), culture, religious rituals and rites, vegetarianism, etc. Moreover, these legitimized and installed the Brahmanic system of castes and *varnas* with well-knit ideology and hierarchy of pure and impure as well as of superior and inferior or higher and lower ranks of both *varnas* and castes, enthroning obviously the Brahmins at the top and the Shudras, including untouchables, at the bottom of the vertical scale. It may, however, not be agreed that the scheme of ranking of the local population on the North Indian model was a smooth sailing there without any dissention or resentment, as stated earlier. Yet, the ideological induction of *varnas* and castes was well accepted which continues even in the present times, of course, with regional specification of ranks or ordering of statuses of different castes and their sub-castes.

Tribe-Caste Continuum

Keeping aside the pre-tribe and post-caste special formations, the focus of our discussion, in this section, is on the process of continuous change, along with change in the nature of the process itself from tribe to caste over the passage of the historical evolution of the society, specially in South India. The continuum hypothesis, opposed to that of the dichotomy, proceeds with the premise that the two extreme poles or points or stages on a given scale remain constant, and the continuous change occurs from one stage to the other without any abruption. Such changes also occur along the consistent parameters broadly drawn from the socio-cultural attributes or characteristics of the societies supposedly prevalent at both the extreme stages and poles. Another important point to mention here is that it is assumed in the continuum hypothesis, that through the passage of the continuous changes, the society, with its distinct socio-cultural attributes or characteristics, of the first stage foregoes completely its existence and is replaced by another advance form of society evolved at the subsequent stage. But, the gradation of change or form of changes at the stages located in between the two extreme stages is continuous, i.e., every subsequent grade or form of change is necessarily superior or advance to the previous one. Anyway, without going into the critically or validity vis-à-vis invalidity of the hypothesis, which emphasizes change in the unilinear direction, we may accept it at its face value but subscribe to the view that some socio-cultural attributes or characteristics of the first stage are always present through the continuum process and are distinctively visible along with those found at every subsequent pole or stage, irrespective of whether these are viewed significant or insignificant. It is, however, equally true that through the passage, these characteristics or attributes themselves undergo both qualitative and quantitative changes or alterations to the degree of their permeability and acceptability at the extreme or 'last' stage.

In the previous section, we have discussed, in detail, the formation of caste from tribe, specially in the ancient South India. Since the focus of our discussion has been on the formation of castes and caste system from tribe, we have undermined the presence of certain attributes or characteristics or elements of tribe in the caste, and have also not ascertained the side by side existence of the tribe there. Yet, as our immediate concern, in this section, is to trace the tribe-caste continuum not in the ancient past but in the immediate present-day society and culture in general and among the SCs in particular, we shall accept the latter as an example to verify the validity of the tribe-caste continuum hypothesis. More specifically, we shall examine how the various SCs in South India live, even today, with certain socio-cultural attributes or characteristics of tribe, in spite of their being an integral part of the Hindu caste society, though placed at the lowest rank of its hierarchy. But, before doing that, it would be necessary to have an overview of the validity of this hypothesis in the larger context of the continuum of tribal elements in the caste as perceived by a few social scientists in India. Also, contrary to the two extreme stages being polar opposite or the separate monolithic hole, we have to accept them as being diversified at their existential levels, though this latter one may not be relevant for the present discussion.

For the present discussion, both tribe and caste, having separate social and cultural institutions and systemic arrangements, may be placed at the two extreme poles or stages of the continuum hypothesis. There are a few sociological, social anthropological and historical studies on the relationship between tribe and caste in India. Some have talked about change or transformation of tribe or tribe clan, as a unit, into caste (Beteille, 1997: 57–58; Klass 1998) but through transformation to lineage to hereditary occupations (Gurukul, 1993–1994) in ancient period, absorption as well as hierarchy consisting of higher and lower ranks (Bose, 1994), tribe-caste interaction, tribe in transition (Majumdar, 1961), tribals as backward Hindus (Ghurye, 1963), tribe-caste convergence (Bara, 2002), etc. Without explaining the merits and demerits or strong and weak points of these formulations, we may state here that these indirectly endorse, either fully or partially, the continuum hypothesis, though not referring to it. Yet, the point relevant here is that those tribes or their segments, who were absorbed especially at the lower or lowest level in the caste system through the passage of historical evolution, have not asserted for reviving their tribal identity or even elements of that unlike those tribes who have remained out of the caste-fold. Moreover, the former ones have formally been absorbed in the caste system but they substantially retain some attributes or characteristics of tribes along with those of castes, even after thousands of years of their leaving the tribal-fold. Thus, the tribe-caste continuum hypothesis is fully 'valid' in these cases, yet its full validity would be proved only when the socio-cultural attributes of tribes such as the structure of social control and the rituals and belief systems are completely absent among the castes.

The above point can easily be substantiated by giving examples of a few SCs from South India. Almost all the SCs there maintain the traditional caste panchayat (council) headed by the elderly members of the respective castes. The caste panchayat, in its structural organization and functions, resembles with the tribal panchayat whose membership is obligatory or is accorded by birth for men of the respective caste or tribe. Such panchayat has traditionally been an effective mechanism for exerting social control especially over those members who violate the caste norms or indulge in such activities which bring disgrace to the caste. Yet, the forms of social control imposed by the caste panchayat over the deviants are temporal and worth compliance, and some of these are temporary excommunication or social boycott—throwing away from the caste but revoking that after paying the imposed fine, undergoing purification ceremony and hosting the caste or community feast. It is also a fact that the caste panchayat has traditionally been operative as an effective mechanism of social control among the SCs as well as the Shudra castes or the OBCs. Since it has proved to be less or even least effective mechanism among the younger educated generation of the SCs and also the Shudra castes, who are socially and economically better and more powerful compared to the former ones, it also suggests that even upper castes, not only in south India but all over the country, might have adopted caste panchayat as a mechanism for controlling deviances in the respective caste but discarded it earlier, through the passage of time, to make them distinctive from the castes placed at the middle and lower ranks in the local caste hierarchy. In other words, the process of casteization from tribe, initiated much earlier among them, may be accepted as complete one compared to that of the lower castes.

Another consistent parameter of the continuum between tribe and caste in the case of SCs in South India is a set of customs related to their life cycle, and their religious beliefs and practices. Some of their customs are related to birth, marriage and death in the family, and their religious beliefs and practices pertain to reverence and worship of local deities, gods and goddesses, ancestors, totems symbolizing clans, etc. While a few sets of customs, and religious beliefs and practices, are those prescribed to the caste and are drawn from the wider Hindu pantheon, others are necessarily anchored in the tribal system though perhaps with their modified forms. For instance, the custom of preparing separate huts by maternal uncle for an elaborate celebration of the first puberty of girls among some SCs. These are remnants of the earlier customs of tribals of the respective areas. In the case of marriage ceremony also, most of the SCs, in South India, follow the customs, rituals and ceremonies which largely resemble those of the erstwhile tribal customs. For instance, payment of nominal bride price, marriage through elopement, widow remarriage, etc. are some of the marriage customs and practices which remained within the confinement of the tribals of the regions and which are still followed by some of the SCs there.

Thus, the religious beliefs and cultural practices, which are remnants of tribes and are presently found among many SCs in South India, are not the outcome of the tribe-caste interaction but of continuum. This simply means that these SCs were initially tribe and got absorbed in the caste system at some later stage. More specifically, some of their religious beliefs and cultural practices, which they adhered to even in the present time, are their reverence and worshipping of village and regional deities like Maramma or Mariamm, a Ponniamma, faith in omens, demon worship, pacification of ghosts and spirits through reverence and worship, devil dances, sacrifices of goats and fowls, playing musical instruments, on festive occasion, made up of animals or forest animals, ancestor worship and so on and so forth. Since they are Hinduized and part and parcel of the Hindu caste system, they are also staunch believers of gods and goddesses of the wider Hindu pantheon. Even they celebrate Hindu festivals of a calendrical year and other auspicious occasions with other caste people of their respective regions.

Untouchability and the Untouchables in South India

Before we attempt to trace the period and involved mechanism of the origin of untouchability in general, and in South India in particular, it is necessary to distinguish, at the conceptual level, between untouchability and impurity or pollution or defilement, which are often mixed up and used synonymously. The notion of pollution or impurity stands opposite to purity and is generally used for the temporary defilement, which can easily be removed through performing some purificatory rituals. Contrary to it, purity is an abstract notion or entity that remains merely a point of reference and exists only in degrees, along with certain defining elements or attributes or substances. Unlike the dominant view attributing to the notion of purity to have ever worked as the guiding principle in situating an object or a person or a group or community in the Indian culture and civilization in general, and in the Hindu caste system in particular, it is the impurity which, in actuality, has all along enjoyed primacy or absolute authority over purity in terms of determining varying degrees of the former. Louis Dumont (1974) also has placed both pure and impure as binary opposites, which simply means that these exist as a paired concepts and the purity is necessarily opposed to impurity. He has stated further that, "... in the setting of the opposition between pure and impure, the religious division of labour goes hand in hand with the permanent attribution to certain professions of a certain level of purity. From this it should not be inferred that the religious division of labour cannot arise in another setting" (ibid.: 49). Thus, the two poles—the Brahmins (pure) and the untouchables (impure)—are equally necessary, though both being located at unequal levels, simply to maintain for others because the execution of impure tasks by some is necessary (ibid.: 55). This implies that the two—the Brahmin (pure) and the untouchable (impure)—being inflexible or rigid extreme poles, for Bailey (1963), are not only necessary but also complementary to each other in terms of their functionality—of course, the former's function being considered superior to that of the latter. This is what Dumont also has called complementarity between pure and impure (1974: 53–53). But his understanding of complementarity of the two is partial and partisan wherein the untouchable takes away the temporary impurity of the Brahmin, who for Dumont is never impure permanently, by removing his dirts, and the Brahmin, in turn, removes the untouchable's notional impurity temporarily by prescribing specific purificatory rituals for him. But as in his scheme of thought the untouchable is permanently impure, removal of his impurity, even temporarily, does not arise. It is the people of the non-Brahmin castes, other than the untouchables, whose temporary impurity or defilement is to be removed through the ritual purification. However, there exists a duality in relationship between the temporary impurity of the pure and the permanent impurity or untouchability of impure in the sense that the touch of the latter to the former makes it impure only temporarily and not permanently, whereas the temporary impurity and the permanent impurity of the latter one is removed only temporarily through undergoing some purificatory rituals prescribed by the former, as stated above. This implies that the existing contradiction between the two needs to be removed.

Thus, in the words of Dumont, "... the (permanent) impurity of the Untouchable is conceptually inseparate from the purity of the Brahmin. They must have been established together, or in any case have mutually reinforced each other, and we must get used to think of them together" (1974: 54). But, as stated above, such relationship does not exist in strict sense of the term; instead, it is some sort of working relationship as the former exists only among the equals or near equals, and not among those who are placed at the two extreme positions in the system—here, caste system. More so, as the Brahmin has an absolute 'repulsion' or repulsive attitude and behaviour towards, as well as, complete 'separation' from the untouchable (for details, see Bougle, 1971), the complementarity between the two is not possible. It may, however, be mentioned here the Dumont's understanding of complementarity between purity and impurity simply explains the presence of the two in which they exist as autonomous entity without their being co-related, i.e., less impurity means more purity. But, in actuality, it is impurity which provides purity to certain object or person by absorbing his/her impurity in itself. Hence, the centre or rallying point is impurity, and not purity, as located in the mindset of the Hindus as well as the social scientists such as Dumont. Contrary to this, in their understanding the central reference in the status ranking of castes in the caste hierarchy is the purity, e.g., the Brahmin, irrespective of his impurity of temporary nature as well as all sorts of vices is taken as a reference for defining and determining the rank position of rest of the castes in the caste system (for details, see Mandelbaum, 1972).

On the other hand, the permanent impurity in the institutionalized form is untouchability, which is hereditarily attached with an individual as well as his/her caste or community. More so, it is attached with a caste or community; and as an individual, in Indian society, especially in the Hindu social system, is an inherent part or a member of it by birth, the untouchability is inevitably transmitted to him or her from generation to generation even if the individual is far away from the ambit of the criteria applied for determining the nature and magnitude of the permanent impurity or untouchability. In other words, once the members of that caste are made to be associated temporarily with impure occupation or to deal with an impure object on some occasion(s), they are considered to be impure forever, unlike the Brahmins and others who remain impure temporarily. Even if they dissociate themselves from that, the stigma of their occasional impurity or untouchability remains forever simply because of their membership with caste labelled as impure and untouchable. This simply means that, it is not the association with impure occupation or touch with an impure object which makes a person an untouchable but it is his/her membership with a caste which is treated as untouchable caste forever. This also means that, unlike the temporary impurity, the permanent impurity or untouchability is not easily removable due to its institutionalized form as a social-religious institution does not easily die down. It is, therefore, to be abolished both legally and socially, and legally it has already been done away with the promulgation of the Constitution of India.

Our intention in doing somewhat elaborate analysis, at the outset of this section, of the purity and impurity, including untouchability, is simply to demonstrate the fact that the ancient society in both north and south India was consisted of the numerous tribes in which there was no sign of permanent impurity or untouchability in the day-to-day life of the people, though the temporary impurity had existed there. Since the caste as well as the caste system had already been emerged and some adoption of that from the north was also made in South India during the later part of the period, untouchability originated and it not only got associated with certain types of occupations and other related practices and customs but also those, who pursued and practiced these, and were classified into separate caste groups and treated as untouchables. To make this simple generalization into somewhat complex analysis, it may be said that the tribals in India practise, even today, some forms of impurity based on violation of certain totems and taboos, customs and rituals, religious practices, observance of purity on various occasions such as birth, menstruation, death, etc. This is not to be constructed as juxtaposition of the present over the past or of caste traits to that in tribe, but such practices had prevailed among the tribals even in the remotest past or the early ancient period in Indian society—both in north and south—as is evident from the interpretations of the archeological excavations and the historiographical explanations of life of the people of that period. Such practices of impurity and purity were both structurally and functionally different from the permanent impurity or untouchability associated with certain groups of people during the later part of the ancient period of evolution and growth of society in South India.

The Dalits or untouchables have a long history of their origin and that of their untouchability and other forms of discrimination, exploitation and subjugation. One may argue that both the untouchables and their untouchability are synonymous and they originated together, though Ambedkar (1990: 237–379; see also Thapar, 1999) differs in this regard. Such argument is certainly attuned to a thesis of the simultaneous origin of four *varnas* or classes or castes from the divine power. Keeping aside the mystic origin of the institution of *varna* or caste or, by extension, even of untouchables and their untouchability, we shall discuss below a few these, which are universally applicable to the origin and mechanism of untouchability both in north and south India. The thesis of Ambedkar, with inherent empirical evidence, of the origin of untouchability, is that it originated sometimes during the 4th century AD, and was an outcome of the last reconciliation arrived at between the settled communities of the Aryans, divided into the four *varnas* or classes of Brahmin, Kshatriya or Rajanya, Vaishya and Shudra, and the broken men, who were primitive tribes and virtually outside the system of the settled communities (see Ambedkar, 1990). That means, there was already a class of people—the broken men or the unsettled communities—who were living as wanderers or people with unsettled life. Because of the unavoidable situational compulsion on part of both the settled communities and the wanderers as well as more vulnerability of the later, the reconciliation took place. This resulted into the subordinated co-option of the broken men and imposition of the various types of ignominies on them by people of the settled communities. Also, they were to live in separate yet nearby settlement and were part-apart of the social arrangement of the already settled communities (ibid.). In other words, they were, in principle, not part of the socio-religious or ritual hierarchy of people of the settled communities but were dependent on them for rendering their labour and earning livelihood from that. Vivekananda Jha (1975: 14–31) has opined that though untouchability began to take "firm and definite shape with respect to a few groups" upto 2nd century AD, it was also present even during the Vedic period. In fact, he has mentioned about four phases in the early history of untouchables: the first phase ending upto 600 BC with a number of tabooed sections of society during the Vedic period; the second phase extending upto 2nd century AD; third phase ended by 600 AD during which the practice of untouchability was intensified but it was also resisted by the untouchables themselves; and the fourth phase extended upto 1200 AD and beyond during which the ranks of the untouchables swelled by incorporating several other castes, and untouchability reached at its peak. But, the trouble with such formulation is that it is all based on the Hindu religious texts, leaving no room for empirical verification except their reinterpretations and reformulation of the thesis as there seems to be absence of unanimity among the early such texts on the subject.

Still another thesis, which could be, in a way, an extended derivation of the first one, is that the Shudras, last or the fourth of the four *varnas*, were divided into *Sat* (with substance or cleanliness) and *Asat* (without substance or uncleanliness) or Shudras and Ati-Shudra classes or categories. Members of the first category were engaged in clean and of the second in unclean types of occupations. Those engaged in the unclean occupations were termed untouchables whereas those with clean occupations as clean castes but below the Brahmins, Kshatriyas and Vaishya or the merchants and traders. Though this thesis is very much in line with the origin of caste or castes from labour or occupation and, hence, the origin of the caste system based on the division of labour, but the trouble with it is that it fails to get ground in event of absence of caste or caste system in non-Hindu society wherein division of labour, in the form of clean and unclean occupations, is inevitably present. It also ignores the fact that religion—in the form of unconditional faith in supernatural power, and the related notion of ritual purity and pollution—has remained the sole basis of binding together the traditional society in India. Secondly, it fails to ascertain the issue of when, why and how the Shudras got divided into *Sat* and *Asat* or Shudra and Ati-Shudra groups or categories, and whether the socio-religious ignominies were imposed on the *Asat* Shudras only or on both the *Sat* and *Asat* Shudras, as prescribed primarily in the *Manusmriti* compiled during the 2nd century AD. Related to this are two different views: one, the socio-religious ignominies were imposed on the Shudras—a category or *varna* of people as such, irrespective of their sub-groups or categories. Two, this view holds ground as there seems to be absence of such categorization at the level of self-conscious assertion before the middle of 19th century. Although during the later part of the 19th century Jyotiba Phule tried to bring both the Shudras and Ati-Shudras or *Sat* and *Asat* Shudras together on account of commonality of their exploitation by clean castes and this categorization has remained distinctive till date in spite of the sporadic efforts made for bringing them to a common political platform. Such efforts manifest, at present, in the form of Dalit Bahujan or Bahujan Samaj, and remain a mere rhetoric or political articulation in absence of socio-cultural intermixing of the Dalit castes and the OBCs. In fact, the distinction between the classes or castes and the untouchables or the SCs or Dalits has sharpened during all these years due to unwanted superimposition of former over the latter. This has happened due to the fact that after acquiring economic and political dominance, the OBCs have undergone transformation through the process of 'sanskritization' (Srinivas, 1966) by claiming their notional ritual superiority and newly acquired economic and political dominance over the Dalit castes. Their economic and political dominance and caste status superiority has often manifested in their practising untouchability, and committing heinous forms of physical violence and atrocities on the Dalits, especially in rural areas.

Retrospectively, the relevant question to be asked here is that why were the various forms of social and religious ignominies imposed on the broken men or the Shudras, specially the *Asat* category of Shudras, after their co-option in the settled life of Aryans? What was responsible for that—was it their impressed need of getting co-opted in the settled life at any cost or was it their vulnerable economic position of living, as a wanderer, with unsettled life? Or, was it the continued risk to their life from the bewilderness or some other reason responsible for that? From the status quoist point of view, since there was functional necessity of some ones to render free labour and perform the most degraded menial jobs for the settled people, the broken men or the Ati-Shudras (of course, this nomenclature emerged much later after their 'co-option' in the system) were co-opted for the purpose at the cost of their getting located them at the reasonable physical and socio-religious distance. But, such a view point does not explain why the various forms of social and religious ignominies or disabilities, practised in the form of untouchability—the severest form of ignominies—were imposed on them once they agreed to get co-opted in the system of the settled people. That means, there could have been some other valid reason for the same. In fact, Ambedkar has provided the most justified reason for it. Accepting both the settled communities and the broken men initially being members of the primitive society and living life of the nomadic tribes and the former getting transformed into settled communities earlier, Ambedkar has stated that:

> When some (nomadic) tribes became settled, the tribes that remained nomadic found more advantageous to concentrate their fight against the settled tribes. It was more paying than a war against other nomadic tribes. The nomadic tribes had come to realize that the settled tribes were doubly wealthy. Like the nomadic tribes, they had cattle. But, in addition to cattle, they had corn which the nomadic tribes had not and which they greatly coveted. The nomadic tribes systematically organized raids on the settled tribes. The third fact is that the settled tribes were greatly handicapped in defending themselves against these raiders. Being engaged in more gainful occupation, the settled tribes could not always convert their ploughs into swords. Nor could they leave their homes (and their lands and crops as well as cattle) and go in pursuit of the raiding tribes. (1990: 275)

Hence, there was a compromise between the tribes: those with the settled life and those with nomadic life. Since the settled tribes wanted to live peaceful life through finding new defenders and the nomadic tribes were also tired of their continuous raids on the settled tribes and wanted to live a settled life, the compromise was beneficial to both of them. But, the latter, being raiders on the former, had to pay the cost in terms of being asked to get settled at a distance from the main settlement and also getting various types of social and religious ignominies imposed on them, including the practice of untouchability against them which came in existence much later. Ambedkar has further stated that the practice of untouchability against these nomadic tribes or broken men, with their late settled life, started sometimes in the 4th century AD because they had accepted Buddhism, opposed to Hinduism, and continued to eat beef—the flesh of the dead cattle—which the earlier settlers—the Hindus—had already left. That means it was contempt of the Hindus against these Buddhists which caused the practice of untouchability against them (Ambedkar, 1990: 311–20).

With the above theoretical explanations, it is imperative here to venture into the origin and growth as well as adopted mechanism(s) of untouchability in South India. More precisely, we wish to probe when and how it originated, grew and got institutionalized there. Whether the same mechanism(s), as suggested by Ambedkar, worked for that or some others were operative, which were entirely different from that in North India. Then, with regard to the origin and mechanism of untouchability in South India, particularly in Tamil society, Subramaniam (1997: 154) makes sweeping narratives by saying that in the process of Dravidianization (with the Dravidians coming from outside the land during the most ancient period) "... the aboriginal tribes, the primitive people, were driven to the hills and the more amenable ones reduced to a state of helotry. The practice of untouchability and habit of treating one part of the society as 'low class' (*ilicinar*) prevailed there as it did in the north. There is no reason to suppose that untouchability was introduced into Tamil Nadu by immigrants from the north; it was a cultivated attitude of supreme snobbery (of the superior towards the inferior ones) which obtained in both places—north and south India. To substantiate his argument, Subramaniam gives the examples of the Kuruvar, Panar, Paraiyar (Pariah), Tutiyar, etc., listed now as the SCs, who were considered the 'low class' people in South India. A point may be mentioned here that as the helotry universally remained an outcome of a considerable degree of resistance and subsequent defeat of a native people to the invaders, the helots or slaves had always to face the contempt of attitude and behaviour of the victorious ones. Hence, it was not the snobbery but contempt of the winners towards the defeated ones in the game, which was in the root of the origin of untouchability in South India. This, in a way, also supports

Ambedkar's thesis (1990) of the origin of untouchability sometimes during the 4th century AD but not in the too remote period of evolution of society in south India, as suggested by Subramaniam. This is supported even by Thapar's brief mention about untouchability in south India in her relating it to the persecution of the Jaina *Shramans* and the Buddhist monks, since the 7th century AD onwards, by the Saivites. In her own words, "Untouchability was also a form of religious persecution (like persecution of the Broken Men or some primitive tribes—the Buddhists in Ambedkar's thesis), for this exclusion was common to Brahmanism as well to some Sramanic sects, the candala (Chandala) being a category apart" (Thapar, 1999: 74). With whatever period and the involved mechanism of its origin, the untouchability had got institutionalized even in rural Tamil Nadu and other parts of south India during the period of Rajaraja I, the Chola king, who had ruled the Chola-Mandalam, the territory from the Kaveri delta to the extreme south of the Indian peninsula, from 985 to 1016 AD (Karashima, 1997: 21–30).

We may enquire, at this stage, into the question whether both the untouchables and their untouchability in South India originated simultaneously or the former had originated earlier and the latter got associated with them afterward. We will deal with this question by examining, first, their origin in Indian society as such and, then, attempt to trace that in the case of South India. The reference may again be made here of Ambedkar's (1990) thesis of the broken men who had existed in the form of a section of the primitive tribes since the early age. They were not only Buddhist in their faith but were also eating beef (flesh of the dead animals), which the settled tribes had already left. Since both the broken men and people of the settled tribes reconciled due to their situational compulsion, the latter developed hatred and contempt against the former, who had not accepted initially the faith and the cultural practices of the settled tribes. Rather, a large section of the broken men continued to eat beef even after the reconciliation not because of their habit but simply because of lack of a stable source of their earning and utter poverty. Needless to say, they had to face the highest degree of hatred and contempt of the settled tribes for their continuing beef-eating and belief in Buddhism.

At the regional level, particularly in the case of South India, Subramaniam (1997: 198–206) has stated that the local purohitars (Purohits), rulers, merchants and labourers could be roughly equated with the classical four classes or *varnas* of Brahmin, Kshatriya, Vaishya and Shudra of the Aryavarta situated in the north-western part of North India. Then, during the ancient period (300 BC–600 AD) in South India, other communities were the Eyinar (hunters), the Umanar (the salt sellers), the Marawar (the martial community), the Konar, Itaiyar (cow-herds), the Utavar (peasants), the Valainar (fishermen), the Kuyavar (potter) and the Ilicinar (the low-class or low-caste people), besides a few other categories of people who were associated with the low-level unclean occupations or manual works, and the numerous tribes. It is the last category of people—the Ilicinar—whom he has considered the untouchable, who lived in their segregated *cheris* (localities or settlements or hamlets) in both the rural and urban areas. But what is interesting to mention here is that in his entire narratives, Subramaniam does not explain how and exactly when the Ilicinars and their untouchability had originated, except his inference from their association with the unclean occupations.

There seems to be no unanimity among the scholars, specially historians, on the exact or even approximate date and involved mechanism about origin of the untouchables and their untouchability in South India. Hence, we are left with two options: one, since castes and the caste system originated there from the numerous tribes and their social relations over generations during the ancient period, these got crystallized and revitalized at a later stage due to justification from the Brahamanical social order based on the notions of purity-pollution and superior-inferior ranks, adopted from the North India. Accordingly, not only the impurity or defilement was treated as permanent attributes of people of the inferior ranks but all their activities and associated objects were considered to be impure and defiling the pure and the superior ones. This all happened during the periods between 4th and 7th century AD. Then, the second option with us is to accept the thesis that those considered to be impure had not accepted their imposed permanent impurity without showing a considerable degree of resistance to the superior ones with both power and ritual purity. Thus, they became victims of the winners in the game and thereby had to bear the maximum degree of hatred and contempt of the powerful ones. There could be numerous evidences to this effect, both before and after the 4th century AD, but ironically these have not been properly and systematically recorded by the historians, including those from the South India.

The Statutory Position of Scheduled Castes and Criteria for their Scheduling

The Scheduled Castes (SCs), as a nomenclature for the erstwhile depressed classes, appeared, for the first time, in the British Government of India Act, 1935, where it was used for those Hindu castes, and their sections converted to Buddhism, Jainism and Sikhism, who were ostracized and exploited for centuries together. Consequently, the first order named *The Government of India (Scheduled Castes and Scheduled Tribes) Order* was issued in 1936 itself. But in what concrete manner the ostracization as well as exploitation of the depressed classes was spelt out and how many castes from all over the country were included in the schedule or list at that time and in subsequent years is not easily known at this stage. Yet, perhaps the same criteria, along with more emphasis on the practice of untouchability, were adopted in the Constitution of free India, and the list provided by the states was approved by the President of India. The first such order named *The Constitution (Scheduled Castes and Scheduled Tribes) Order,* with the assent of the President, was issued 1950 itself, which was modified as *The Scheduled Castes and Scheduled Tribes Order (Amendment) Act, 1976.* The latest amendment as *The Constitution (Scheduled Castes) Order (Amendment) Act 1990* also includes those SCs who have converted to Buddhism.

At stated above, we may also explore briefly here some of the socio-demographic criteria for inclusion of certain castes in the list of the SCs, particularly in South India. But before that it is necessary to have a look at the number of castes included in the list in South India, consisting of four states of Andhra Pradesh, Karnataka, Kerala and Tamil Nadu, and the union territory of Pondicherry. Going at the face or the mere number, there are 60 castes in Andhra Pradesh, 102 castes in Karnataka, 69 in Kerala, 75 in Tamil Nadu and only 16 in Pondicherry included in the list of the SCs in these states. Thus, the total number of the SCs in South India has remained 322 in 2001. Hardly any new caste(s) from any state or the union territory in South India has been included in the list in the recent years. But it is also true that a number of SCs notified in one state are also notified even in other state(s) and the union territory. For instance, the Adi Andhra and the Adi Dravida, which are originally found in Andhra Pradesh and Tamil Nadu respectively, have been notified in all the four states and the union territory of Pondicherry. Similarly, there are a sizeable number of castes which have been notified as the SCs in all the four states or in three states and in the union territory, a few others only in two states and in the union territory and still a few in two states. Thus, on an average, there are around 295 castes notified separately as SCs in South India, although their exact number is only 112 only due to synonyms of a large number of SCs in these states and the union territory. The total number of persons of these castes, according to 2001 Census, in

Andhra Pradesh is 1,23,39,496, in Karnataka 85,63,930, in Kerala 31,23,941, in Tamil Nadu 1,18,57,504 and in Pondicherry 1,57,771. Hence, the total number of people belonging to SCs in South India is 3,60,42,642 and nearly 80 per cent of them live in rural areas.

Then, going by the socio-demographic criteria for notification of these castes as the SCs in South India, we find that merely the size of population has not been taken into consideration, where a large number of population of a caste perhaps would amount pressure for getting it included in the list of the SCs. It is evident from the fact that the total number of persons belonging to SCs in Karnataka and Kerala is less than those in Andhra Pradesh and Tamil Nadu but the number of castes included in the list of the SCs in the state of Karnataka is higher than that in these latter states. Similarly, if we take untouchability and various other forms of discrimination as the criteria for listing a caste as the SC, then, we also find that all the castes notified as SCs in South India have not suffered from the stigma of untouchability even in the past. Some such castes are Bariki of Andhra Pradesh, Kakkalan of Kerala and Tamil Nadu, Maila and Mavilan of Karnataka, Kerala and Tamil Nadu, Koliyan and Vathiriyan of Tamil Nadu, and several such castes in these states. But, in the case of all these castes, their population size is also less than 10,000 persons in the states where these are found. The majority of the castes smaller in population size (numbering 218), having less than 10,000 persons (large number of them having even less than 1,000 persons), also do not have even effective leadership of their own to articulate the issue of and exert pressure for their inclusion in the list of the SCs. Hence, instead of subscribing to the view of vagueness in the criteria adopted for the purpose, we emphasize here that a complexity of criteria are in operation for identifying and listing a caste as an SCs in a state.

We have already stated in the earlier section that a number of tribes or a section of them had transformed into caste in South India even during later part of the colonial period, which could not be included in the list of the STs. Since they had already Hinduized yet away from the traditional religious system of Hinduism as well as devoid of the practice of untouchability and other forms of discrimination, they largely remained socially and educationally backward. They also remained deprived of the dignified and sustainable self-resource of their livelihood. Had these castes come into closer contact with the caste Hindus, especially in the traditional system of *jajmani* (patron-client) relations, they would have certainly faced the frenzy of untouchability and other forms of discrimination. Hence, a relatively prolonged isolation, and practice of untouchability as well as other forms of discrimination, coupled with socio-economic and educational backwardness, have been the major criteria for notifying and listing a caste as the SC. It is this socio-economic and educational backwardness, which occasionally instigates some sections of caste Hindus or even upper castes to acquire false certificate of an SC and claim for the benefits of the provision of reservations, though they have never experienced any forms of untouchability and other related discriminations.

Ethnic Identity and Origins: Role of Myths

Generally speaking, the ethnicity as a concept has broad connotation, and is inclusive of caste, race (being now discouraged both in principle and in usage), class, religious affiliations, region, political ideology, etc. Being a cultural construct, it thus cuts across the castes, race, class, and religious affiliations, religious, regional and political ideological boundaries and relies largely on the cultural markers like language, customs, food and dress patterns, festivals and alike, besides a strong emotional 'we feeling'. It has its own notional cultural and structural boundary within which members are supposed to pursue the varieties of activity, but in no way violative of its cultural code of conduct or the opinion of its leaders. Initially, an ethnic group or community originates in a particular region, with specific climatic environment, and then it moves out along with movement or migration of its members but it largely retains its cultural markers and interacts as well as integrates with cultures of other host groups and communities. What is more important to mention here is that the members of an ethnic group or community invariably identify themselves with it, hence, their collective identity, though they may cherish a few more identities based on their individual achievements in the secular domain of life. Being originated initially in the European continent sometime during the 1960s and used for the immigrants from several countries, it has travelled since then to India also and is adopted frequently in the academic writings—particularly in a few social sciences like sociology and social anthropology, political science, history, etc. But, in the case of India, it has also been used for castes and tribes where each caste or tribe has its own distinctive identity. Since castes have been arranged as superior and inferior on the basis of their ritual purity and impurity, in a specified hierarchy, there are certainly a number of castes which are stigmatized with their impurity, hence, their stigmatized caste or ethnic identity (Berreman, 1979).

During the recent decades, specially after independence of the country, members of the stigmatized castes or ethnic communities have been striving for overcoming the stigma of their collectivity (caste or ethnic community) as well as of their own. Since they are engaged in looking for alternative self and collective or group (caste) identity, they have been making use of two courses of action, rather than social processes, which have remained in vogue in Indian society: one, making use of achievements in secular domains like education, caste-free occupations or white-collar jobs (economic), and power or authority. But all these three, in actuality, do not replace or obliterate their traditionally stigmatized group or caste identity. This is to be understood in terms of what Ambedkar has said as early as in 1917 (see Ambedkar, 1979) wherein achievement or merit of an individual in the caste system goes along with the merit or demerit of his/her caste. As the lower castes have traditionally been attributed to demerit or non-achievement, the achievement or merit of their members has not yet succeeded in overcoming the stigma of their group or caste. As all the traditionally stigmatized castes have constitutionally been called the SCs, with their traditional nomenclature being intact at the local level, the merit or achievement of their members is considered to be sponsored by the state through its policy of reservation or compensatory discrimination. On the other hand, the merit or achievement of the persons belonging to the non-stigmatized upper and middle level castes is considered to be their individual attribute, yet it has not motivated or inspired them to shelve their caste affiliation. In fact, the self and group or caste or collective identities of people belonging to both the stigmatized and non-stigmatized caste groups go hand in hand, in spite of some apparent changes occurred in the caste system in all these years.

The second option—course of action or process—available to the members of the stigmatized castes or ethnic communities, other than the achievement one, is the myth related to the origin of their castes or communities. It is true that the myths are self-created, but it is equally true that these are interpreted by the people in the manner that suits them. But these take longer time, rather centuries, to get them crystallized and then followed by the large section of population. Broadly speaking, myths are cultural attributes and markers of identity of a person or group or caste, and they play significant role in shaping one's personality as well as providing pride to him/her, besides his/her group (caste). Most of the myths in the caste system are generally anchored in the Hindu mythology and these centre around the personalities or mythological heroes of high origin and their projected achievement. Hence, people of the lower castes also adopt them for the said purpose, though this process cannot be generalized at the universal plank. For instance, a large majority of the people of the lower castes in north, west, central and east India hardly believe in the Hindu myth about their origin or that of their castes. So also, they do not derive any inspiration from these for shaping their personality and targeting their achievement. At the most, they refer to the heroic historic personalities, particularly from their own caste or community, for their immediate gains in the secular domains of life and juxtapose that to their primordial affiliations or castes.

On the contrary, a majority of people of the lower castes (ex-untouchables) in South India have adopted several Hinduized myths to trace the origin of their castes, although their orientation towards secular achievement is hardly guided by that. In few cases, the name of their castes also goes along with these myths. For instance, the Arundhatiyas/Arunthathiyars of Andhra Pradesh, Karnataka, Kerala and Tamil Nadu trace their origin from Arundhati, a female goddess of the Hindu mythology. Similarly, the Jambuvulus of Andhra Pradesh, Karnataka, Tamil Nadu and Pondicherry claim their descent from the *Rishi* (sage) Jambvant of Hindu mythology. Likewise, Pallans or Pallars of Tamil Nadu, where their caste name is also known as Devendrakulathan, claim their ancestry from Devendra, the superior Indra of the Hindu mythology, though they do not do so in Karnataka, Kerala and Pondicherry, where they are in minority or less in number. Besides, a sizeable number of SC people in South India also claim their descent either from goddess Parvati, the wife of Lord Shiva, or from the *Rishi* Jamdagni or Lord Parashurama and a few other personalities of the Hindu mythology. A point may be mentioned here that their claimed ancestry does not go along with their claimed *gotras* who are generally revered at the time of mate selection or solemnization of marriage. But they hardly remember their descent or ancestry in their daily routine. Further, quite a few SCs in all the states in South India also follow the *gotras* and practise totems and taboos, which are either tribal in origin or at least resemble to that. This certainly contradicts their claimed decent from the Hindu mythology, though their belief system and cultural practices are largely drawn from the Hindu pantheon.

Still, one more process has remained at work, in recent years, among the lower castes in South India. Quite a few such castes as Arundhatiya and Jambuvulu of Andhra Pradesh; Arunthathiyar, Chakkiliya, Jambuvulu and Pallan of Karnataka; Arunthathiyar, Chakkiliyan and Pallan of Kerala; Arunthathiyar, Chakkiliyan and Pallan of Tamil Nadu; and Chakkiliyan and Pallan of Pondicherry have started adding a letter or alphabet at the end of their name. Thus, they call themselves Aundhatiyar or Arunthathiyar, Jambuvuluru, Chakkiliyan and Pallar as (or original) name of their castes particularly at the places of the origin. They do this to add respect to their castes like Aiyanagar and Mudaliyar of upper castes; Chettiyar or trading castes; and Nadar, Thevar and Vellalar of the middle level peasant castes of South India, particularly of Tamil Nadu. Such minor addition to the caste's name or change of name of the castes, articulated by their socially and politically conscious members, certainly provides two advantages: one, supposedly it places the caste in relatively higher esteem of respectfulness in the local hierarchy of caste system. But unless it is reinforced by the adequate socio-economic and political dominance as well as mobilization of its members, it does not serve the purpose. Two, it inspires and motivates the members to achieve their worth in the secular domain of their life. However, in both the cases, the traditional low rank or status of caste and the stigmatized caste identity of its members often come in the way of defacing the prejudiced attitude and behaviour of the upper and the middle level castes as well as taking the socio-economic achievement and the assertion of the lower castes to the logical end. Hence, the present continuation of untouchability and infliction of violence vis-à-vis atrocities by the former against the latter in South India and elsewhere in the country, though the state often intervenes ineffectively through its police administration and judiciary.

Social Structure and Social Relations

It is often said that the caste system in South India is more rigid than elsewhere in the country. Though this needs to be empirically verified, a fact, however, may be stated here that the restructuration process of the earlier social system on the line of the Brahmanical system of castes vis-à-vis *varnas* began in South India since the 6th or 7th century AD and continued till the beginning of the colonial rule. As stated earlier, a number of Brahmins from North India were inducted there who, in turn, helped the local rulers in the process by providing the considerable degree of legitimacy and justification through the existing *Dharmashastras* and even creating or writing new sets of Sanskritic literature for the purpose. All this means that as the caste system or the Brahmanical caste system in South India is newer in its origin and structuration than that in North India, its relatively more rigidity is to be there compared to that elsewhere in the country. The caste system has been functioning there through all these years with its 'demonstration effect'. Since our concern here is to look at the nature of the existing social structure, inclusive of economic and political structures, in South India and the type of social relations among people of the various castes there, we shall briefly examine that, especially the one, which has come into being since the mid of the colonial rule in India.

Generally speaking, social structure, being abstract at the conceptual level, manifests concretely in the forms of various institutions, organizations, and roles and relations of their members, besides their status or position either ascribed or achieved one. It also consists of differentiation of roles and statuses or positions in their respective existing hierarchy or the overall system of social stratification. Moreover, social structure is operative at local level, hence, localized social structure, which in many ways exists as a replica of the generalized or even abstract social structure. Needless to say that social structure either in its abstract form or as a living reality is inclusive of economic and political power or authority, cultural and personality structures, with their well-defined regulatory mechanism(s). In the way, it also resembles with social system, though at the conceptual level the latter one is not only different from social structure but even its defining properties are separate from that of the former. For instance, a social system may consist of several structures or social structures and their role-relationships. Since our frame of reference of social structure in India, particularly in South India, is limited to caste system with the explicit hierarchy of castes and of status or rank of each caste in it, and both traditional and modern or present role(s) of its members, their achieved and ascribed statuses as well as their incongruence, their belief system and cultural practices, and their future aspirations of psychic mobility, we shall explain briefly here how the localized social structure has functioned over the last hundred years or so, and what kinds of changes have occurred in it in all these years.

As mentioned above, the social structure in South India, as elsewhere in the country, is localized in the sense of requirements of people in various regions, yet it largely derives inspirations and even dictates, though more at the psychological level, from the religio-philosophical justification from the Sanskritic texts in whatsoever forms these are known or informed to its members—both literati and laity. In such social structure, people of the upper castes like Brahmin had not only enjoyed the superior most rank in the caste hierarchy but they also remained much better in socio-economic and religious positions than the people of the middle and lower castes till the early 20th century. While this was true in the urban areas, the situation had completely changed in the rural areas since the 1970s because of the earlier adopted Land Reforms Act of the 1960s, followed by the imposed ceiling on the size of the landholding per family. Prior to these land-related legislations, almost all land was in the possession of the Brahmins, former princes or rulers, big landlords, etc., and people of both the middle and lower castes, including Dalits or the SCs, were not only associated with land in their capacity of rentiers and landless labourers respectively but they were also under considerable degree of dominance of the former. With the adoption of the stated legislations, the situation became topsy-turvy at least in the case of the middle level castes, who became the owner-cultivators and also increased the size of their landholdings subsequently through their own efforts. So also, due to the manpower available in the family required for cultivation purpose, they flourished financially and captured power at the local as well as state levels because of their numerical dominance (for Andhra Pradesh, see Rao, 1975, Rao, 1998; for Kerala and Tamil Nadu, see Menchar, 1975; for Karnataka, see Srinivas, 1987).

But, the lower castes or Dalits largely remained unaffected by the said legislations, and were pitiably forced to change their master from the Brahmins and other upper castes to the middle level castes. This brought two significant changes in the rural social structure in South India: one, a sizeable number of Brahmins moved to urban areas and got engaged in white-collar jobs. Those who remained in villages, depended, as and when needed, on favour of the middle level castes for their sustenance and well-beings. Two, the landowners of the middle castes became more tyrants or tyrannical to the lower caste agricultural labourers. They became reluctant to pay required wages to the labourers, mostly Dalits, and started practising untouchability and other forms of discrimination, both overtly and covertly, against them in more stringent fashion. However, such practices did not go unchallenged as the lower castes in rural areas started showing considerable degree of resistance (see Mencher, 1975; Rao, 1998; Yagati, 2003; Viswanthan, 2005;

Ramaiah, 2007), resulting into large-scale caste violence and atrocities against them.

The situation has, however, remained somewhat different in urban areas where the Brahmins and other upper castes, although in numerical minority, continued to occupy the top positions in bureaucracy, various professions, and in religious and political organizations. While the trading castes managed the economy through trades and commerce, the middle and lower castes were engaged in sundry occupations, besides their employment in lower level bureaucratic jobs, professions, vending, in the unorganized sector of economic activities and so forth. It is only since the last few decades, especially the 1970s, people of the middle castes started showing their presence in bureaucracy, politics and various professions as well as in educational institutions. The educational achievement, employment in white-collar jobs and political participation, in case of the lower castes or SCs in urban areas, are mostly state sponsored through its policy of protective discrimination or reservation, which of course has reached a small section of their population living in both rural and urban areas. A point may be mentioned here that a relatively flexible social structure has emerged in urban areas during all these years, but it has not shelved completely its relation with the traditional social structure based on caste and communal considerations.

On the whole, some fluidity is visible in the structure of society and culture in South India, though crystals of the traditional social structure are definitely found even in day-to-day social interaction of the people drawn specially from the Brahmin and other upper castes as well as from the middle level castes with those of the SCs. These are seen in the attitude and behaviour of both educated and uneducated, rich and poor. But, the fluid social structure as well as social relations among the various castes are found more in urban than in rural areas, where social classes or status groups exist along the achievable attributes like education, occupation and power or authority positions, income and consumption, etc., though these generally do not transcend the traditional caste and communal or community lines in close interaction among the people, as stated above. On the contrary, some flexibility in agrarian social structure has also occurred, but that is confined mostly to the upper and lower castes, as stated earlier. A few classes like upper and lower castes, as classes, along the size of landholding and income level, have emerged in the agrarian social structure, but these again are within the upper and middle level castes where caste still remains a cementing barrier in brining these two caste groups together along their similarity in the class position (Beteille, 1965). Though a large majority of the Dalits or SCs in rural areas fit in the lower class, there is hardly any class affinity between them and others placed in the same class as caste again comes in their way in establishing same class identity, commensal relations and other such close interaction. However, it is mostly the socially and politically conscious people of the SCs who have been striving for bringing some quantitative and qualitative changes in the existing social structure in rural areas by articulating the idioms of social equality, liberty and fraternity, besides that of self-respect, dignity, and social justice—the very dictum of the Constitution for a free society in independent India.

Social Change and Mobility

Being a neutral or value-free term, social change moves in forward or backward direction and has both positive and negative attributes, though in the general usage the former enjoys primacy over the latter. At the concrete level, both development—inclusive of social, economic, political and cultural as well as of human personality—and social structural and cultural modernization, besides cooperation and conflict, are forms of social change. Then, at the social relational level, change in interpersonal and inter-groups relationships is also termed as social change, both in the narrow and broad senses, respectively. In either case, change or social change is both time and space specific, i.e., both quantity and quality of change is visible distinctly at two different times and spaces. Similarly, social mobility as a concept simply means shift from one status or social status to the other either in vertical or horizontal direction. Although social mobility is examined in a given system of social statuses, which is further examined in a given nature, it has also been analyzed extensively along a single status, or unit of status, like occupation, in the western societies, which are relatively open in nature and where occupation plays the most significant role in determining one's income, expenditure pattern, authority, lifestyle, and in a way, social class position. But, in Indian society, it is caste or other such primordial unit that has ever enjoyed the sole primacy in determining one's social status in the system of given social stratification, and occupation and other units of status or position are only the additional inputs to it. Hence, social mobility in the western sense is possible, in Indian society, only in the case of shift of these status units or positions but such society mobility is only *partial* and not *total* (for details, see Ram, 1988), unless the entire group or corporate status group like caste or caste-like primordial unit moves either vertically or horizontally. It is not out of context to mention here that either vertical or horizontal move/mobility of an individual also does not help much as he/she is necessarily an inherent part of a caste or such primordial unit. Yet, mobility or social mobility in his/her case takes place along a single or even multiple status units, and it has also drawn attention of a few social scientists, especially sociologists and social anthropologists, historians, etc., in their study of present as well as past society in India, though some studies of social mobility of the entire corporate status group are also available.

There are two more interesting aspects of social mobility in Indian society, particularly the Hindu caste system: one, social mobility through social movement and, two, through the state sponsorship, the former being operative since the early times and the latter, of course, being the creation of the post-independent period. Since the early period of the colonial rule in India, a few untouchable castes, like Izhava of Kerala and Shanan of Tamil Nadu, had organized strong social movement for their elevation in the hierarchy of caste system in the respective states. As the frame of reference of their upward social mobility happened to be the caste system, they succeeded in getting them elevated to the level of middle castes. Consequently, the Shanan adopted the nomenclature of Nadar but the Izhava retained the same nomenclature, though with the higher rank in the caste hierarchy. Besides, there have been several other castes traditionally middle ranked like Kamma and Reddy in Andhra Pradesh; Lingayat and Vokaligga in Karnataka; Nayar in Kerala; and Thevar, Vannier and Vellala in Tamil Nadu, which have claimed their status or rank at par with the traditional Kshatriya caste (which had never existed in South India) due to their economic, political and numerical dominance in the respective states. But, such claim, if there was any, of majority of the untouchable castes or the SCs had never succeeded due to their traditional impure status as well as their economic and political vulnerability. Interestingly, the social reformers of the medieval period as well as the political leaders and ideologues of the colonial period had always condemned the caste system and emphasized social equality through the fair and equalitarian deal in the secular domains like education, employment, political power or authority, and social interaction and social relations with others. For the purpose, they had organized numerous social movements and made several petitions and submitted memorandums to the government. Needless to say that they succeeded to some extent, but looking at the huge population size of the untouchable castes, and the limitations of resources and the various types of social constraints of the government, their efforts could not produce the desired results. Moreover, the counter-forces or the status quoists resisted to any meaningful initiatives towards the required radical change or shift, in the then existing social order, to produce the desired results. All such initiatives yet paved the way for realizing limited upward social mobility within the frame of socio-economic status or loosely termed as class or social class, which in itself is problematic at the operative level, not being exclusive of caste or such other primordial unit, as stated earlier.

However, the limited upward social mobility, in the case of SCs, STs and now the OBCs within the framework of socio-economic status or social class, has been sponsored by the state, through the policy of reservation, as stated above. But such social mobility is confined only to a tiny section of the entire SCs all over the country, although the size of such section of the upwardly mobile SCs varies from region to region and from one SC to the other. In fact, the binary concept of sponsored and contest social mobility is distinctively visible as intertwined, rather, overlapping in the case of the upwardly mobile SCs where for the state's sponsorship of limited positions or status sets, there is contest among thousands of persons of these castes. The sponsorship is based on the individual's achievable attributes or merits, which could have proved them to be upwardly mobile even without the state's sponsorship, provided there was fair chance. Also, the upward social mobility of the SCs, at both the individual and group levels, is definitely inspired by the positive references of upwardly mobile individuals as well as groups drawn from the same or other such social background. It is also reinforced, though distantly, by several social movements organized for the purpose in the past. Then, both social change and social mobility together contribute significantly to bring about change in the social relations at micro-as well as macro-level social structure by making the latter relatively fluid.

Then, social change and mobility among the SCs or Dalits in South India is to be analyzed within the social structure operative at both the micro and macro levels. Within the micro or village level social structure, it may be said that not much significant change has occurred among them over the last hundred years or so. For instance, their traditionally low status continues to exist in the local caste hierarchy in villages. The practice of untouchability and other forms of discrimination in their day-to-day interaction and social relations with people of the other castes and communities still exist in rural areas and small towns, though their conditions are, in some ways, better in cities. Not much qualitative and quantitative change is seen in the agrarian wage structure, and consequently the greater number of younger generation of SCs or Dalits has become urban oriented during all these years. At the social relational level, greater degree and amount of tension and conflict has emerged between the SCs and non-SCs as is evident from the large number of caste conflict between them and the atrocities inflicted on the former in rural areas. Such change or social change is to be perceived as a corollary of the growing nature and amount of social consciousness and awareness, and also their assertion for dignity, self-respect and social justice among the SCs or Dalits on one hand, and intolerance and suppression of the non-SCs towards the former on the other, in rural south India, as stated earlier. However, a fact may be mentioned here that such form of social change is witnessed among only those SCs whose number or population size is large and who are more oriented towards achieving upward social mobility in the given social structure in rural areas. By implication, they also intend to alter or bring about qualitative change in that, which is resistibly retained by the non-SCs.

The social structure is also to be understood in terms of intra-caste arrangement where each SC has been regulating its internal affairs through the mandatory caste panchayat. The caste panchayat has all along exerted its control over the deviant behaviour of caste members through assigning punishment either in the form of cash or kind or community feast as well as temporary boycott or ex-communication of offender from the caste, depending upon the nature and degree of offence. The caste membership of the offender used to be restored after fulfilling or meeting out the punishment. Sometimes, the caste panchayat has also mobilized the members to forgo the customary practice and bring about social reform among them. As the caste panchayat used to be constituted either hereditarily or by elderly persons of the caste, irrespective of level of their education and social consciousness, the younger generation started, in modern time, looking at it as oriented towards backwardness of the caste; hence, they invariably flouted its decision or arbitration, resulting into its irrelevance or absence among majority of the SCs in rural South India. Hence, the contemporary social structure among the SCs in South India, particularly in villages, remains amorphous, though traditional structural attributes are still present in preponderance and their relevance may not last long. The emergence of new social structure or restructuration of the existing one in rural South India in general, and among the SCs in particular, which is forcefully resisted by the upper and middle level castes, is a time-consuming process, and its concrete nature and form lies only in future. Needless to say that the initiation of such process has been made by younger generation of the SCs as it improve their life chances vis-à-vis social status in both social and caste hierarchies at the macro and micro levels.

Finally, limited social mobility has taken place among the SCs, both in rural and urban areas in South India, through both sponsorship, including contest, and social movement—the former being available in more systematic form since the independence of the country and the latter remaining a continuous process at least since the beginning of the 20th century. Without going into details of these two processes, it may be surmised here that both intra- and inter-generational social mobility is visible among them more in urban than rural areas. It is found in the forms of educational achievement, white-collar and other non-traditional employment, and limited amount of power or authority. Not only their income level is relatively improved, but they have also acquired greater degree of awareness and consciousness, besides their being assertive and more identity conscious. In rural areas, the limited upward social mobility is witnessed in the form of their being conscious and aware of the individual as well as collective identity, its suppression, oppression and exploitation and so forth, irrespective of their educational level and sources of livelihood. However, their consciousness vis-à-vis psychic or psychological mobility has not sailed without unequivocal resistance from the upper and middle level castes. Their such psychological mobility, yet, continues to draw inspiration from their better-off brethren in urban areas and an overall awareness and consciousness emerged in all these years in Indian society as a whole in which the state initiatives, along with the existing socio-political leadership as well as of civil society or voluntary organizations, have also contributed to some extent.

REFERENCES

Ambedkar, B.R. 1979. "Castes in India: Their Mechanism, Genesis and Development" (first published in 1917), in *Dr. Babasaheb Ambedkar: Writings and Speeches*, Vol. 1, Government of Maharashtra, Bombay.

———. 1990. "The Untouchables: Who Were They and Why They Became Untouchables?" (first published in 1948), in *Dr. Babasaheb Ambedkar: Writings and Speeches*, Vol. 7, Government of Maharashtra, Bombay.

Bailey, F.G. 1963. "Closed Social Stratification in India", *European Journal of Sociology,* 4(1), pp. 107–24.

Bara, Joseph. 2002. "Tribe-Beast or Man: Case for a New Concept of Tribe", *Social Action,* Vol. 51, pp. 121–33.

Berreman, G.D. 1979. "Self, Situation and Escape from Stigmatised Ethnic Identity" in his *Caste and Other Inequalities*, Meerut: Folklore Institute, Meerut. pp. 164–77.

Beteille, Andre. 1965. *Caste, Class and Power*. Delhi: Oxford University Press.

——. 1997. "The Concept of Tribe with Special Reference to India", in his *Society and Politics in India: Essays in a Comparative Perspective*. Delhi: Oxford University Press, pp. 57–78.

Bose, N.K. 1994. *The Structure of Hindu Society*. New Delhi: Orient Longman.

Bougle, Celestin. 1971. *Essays on the Caste System in India.* Cambridge: Cambridge University Press.

Champakalakshmi, R. 1975. "State and Economy: South India Circa A.D. 400–1300", in Romila Thapar (ed.), *Recent Perspectives of Early Indian History*. Bombay: Popular Prakashan, pp. 266–308.

Dumont, Louis. 1970, 1974. *Homo Hierarchicus: The Caste System and Its Implication*. Chicago: The University of Chicago Press.

Dutt, N.K. 1984. *Origin and Growth of Caste in India*. Calcutta: Firma KLM Private Ltd.

Ghurye, G.S. 1963. *The Scheduled Tribes*. Bombay: Popular Prakashan.

Gupta, Dipankar. 1993. "Continuous Hierarchies and Discrete Castes", in his (ed.), *Social Stratification*. New Delhi: Oxford University Press, pp. 110–42.

Gurukul, Rajan. 1995. "The Beginnings of the Historic Period: The Tamil South" in Romila Thapar (ed.), *Recent Perspectives of Early Indian History*. Bombay: Popular Prakashan.

Jaiswal, Suvira. 1990. *Caste: Origin, Function and Dimensions of Change.* New Delhi: Manohar.

Jha, Vivekanand. 1975. "Stages in the History of Untouchable", *Indian Historical Review*, Vol. 2

Karashima, N. 1997. "The Untouchables in Tamil Inscriptions and other Historical Sources in Tamil Nadu", in H. Kotani (ed.), *Caste System, Untouchability and the Depressed*, New Delhi: Manohar, pp. 21–30.

Klass, Morton. 1998. *Caste: The Emergence of South Asian Social System*. Manohar, New Delhi: Manohar.

Kosambi, D.D. 1953. "The Brahman Clans", *American Journal of Orientalist Society*, Vol. 73, pp. 202–08.

——. 1956. *An Introduction to the Study of Indian History*. Bombay: Popular Prakashan.

——. 1962. *Myth and Reality: Studies in the Formation of Indian Culture*. Bombay: Popular Prakashan.

——. 1965. *The Culture and Civilization of Ancient India in Historical Outline*. New Delhi: Vikas Publishing House Pvt. Ltd.

Levi-Strauss, Claude. 1963. "The Bear and the Barber", *The Journal of the Royal Anthropological Institute of Great Britain and Ireland,* 93(1), pp. 1–11

Majumdar, D.N. 1961. *Races and Cultures of India*. New York: Asia Publishing House.

Mandelbaum, David. 1972. *Society in India*. Bombay: Popular Prakashan.

Mencher, J.P. 1974. "Cases System Upside Down: The not-so Mysterious East", *Current Anthropology*, Vol. 12, pp. 191–209.

——. 1975. "Agricultural Labour Movement in their Socio-Political and Ecological Context: Tamil Nadu and Kerala", in B.N. Nair (ed.), *Culture and Society*. Delhi: Thompson Press (India) Limited, pp. 240–66.

Muller, Max. 1883. *India, What Can it Teach Us?* London: Longman, Green and Co.

Nagaraju, S. 1995. "Emergence of Regional Identity and Beginnings of Vernacular Literature: A Case Study of Telugu", *Social Scientist*, Vol. 23. Nos. 10–12, pp. 8–23.

Ram, Nandu. 1988. *The Mobile Scheduled Castes: Rise of a New Middle Class*. Delhi: Hindustan Publishing Corporation.

Ramaiah, A. 2007. *Laws for Dalit Rights and Dignity*. Jaipur: Rawat Publications.

Rao, B.S.S. 1975. "The Land Reforms and their Impact: Study of a Coastal Andhra Village", in B.N. Nair (ed.), *Culture and Society*. Delhi: Thompson (India) Ltd., pp. 370–23.

Rao, N. Sudhakar. 1998. *Organised Power and Unorganised Resistance*. New Delhi: Aravali Books International.

Ray, H.P. 1975. "Trade and Contacts", in Romila Thapar (ed.), *Recent Perspectives of Early Indian History*. Bombay: Popular Prakashan, pp. 142–75.

Risely, H.H. 1908. *The People of India*. Calcutta: Thacker, Spink and Company.

Srinivas, M.N. 1966. *Social Change in Modern India*. Berkeley: University of California Press.

——. 1987. *The Dominant Caste and Other Essays*. New Delhi: Oxford University Press.

Subramaniam, N., 1997. *Tamil Social History*. Vol. 1, Chennai: Institute of Asian Studies.

Thapar, Romila. 1998. *Asoka and the Decline of the Mauryas*. New Delhi: Oxford University Press.

——. 1999. *Interpreting Early India*. New Delhi: Oxford University Press.

Viswanathan, S. 2005. *Dalits in Dravidian Land*. Chennai: Navayana Publishing.

Weber, Max. 1958. *The Religion of India*. Glencoe: Free Press.

Yagati Chinna Rao. 2003. *Dalits' Struggle for Identity: Andhra and Hyderabad 1990–1950*. New Delhi: Kanishka Publishers & Distributors.

14

Scavenging and Scavengers in the State of Haryana: A Study

B.K. NAGLA

The scavengers in Haryana are called Valmiki/Balmiki, Chuhra, Bhangi, Lalbegi and Khaqrobe. Chaudhary and Jamadar are two titles of this community; the latter is normally used for the working class. Locally, they are called Chuhra. They claim to be the descendants of Saint Balmiki, one of the Chuhra *gurus* (teachers), originally a hunter from the Karnal district, who later became a holy *Rishi*, and eventually wrote the epic, *The Ramayana*. Their other *Guru* is Lalbeg and it is after this *guru* that they are also called Lalbegi; and they still call their priests Lalgurus (Ibbetson, 1974: 294).

The Scavenger Castes

Ibbetson (1974) included Chuhra, Dhanak and Khatik among the scavenger castes. These castes are numerically and economically the most important in the province. Though the Jats, Rajputs and Brahmins exceed in number, the Chuhras occupy a very prominent position among the agricultural labourers of Punjab. But socially they are the lowest of the low, even lower perhaps than the vagrant Sansi and the gypsy Nats, and, as a rule, can hardly be said to stand even at the foot of the social ladder, though some sections of the clan have mounted the first one or two rungs. Their hereditary occupation is scavenging, sweeping the houses and streets, carrying manure to the fields, and in cities and in village houses where the women are strictly secluded, removing night soil. They keep 'impure' animals as pigs and fowls and eat the flesh of dead animals. They also eat jackals, lizards, tortoises and pigs. Many of them have abandoned scavenging and have taken to leatherwork and even to weaving, and by doing so, have acquired higher status in society. Together with the vagrants and gypsies they are the hereditary workers in grass and reeds, from which they make winnowing pans and other articles used in agriculture.

Bhangi

The term 'Bhangi' is derived from the Sanskrit word, 'Bhangi' meaning hemp which seems to be a reference to their drinking habits. The Bhangi was described as a representative of the Chandala, by Manu, who is said to have descended from the union of Sudra with a Brahmin woman. The Bhangi were traditionally associated with scavenging, sweeping, basket making, etc. In the colonial period they were brought into urban areas to perform the first two roles and thus became an urban community. With the widespread use of septic latrines and other modes of public conveniences, the practice of carrying night soil on the head has perceptibly declined in many parts of urban India. The National Scheme of Liberation and Rehabilitation of Scavengers and their Dependants (1991–92) seeks to liberate them from their existing "hereditary obnoxious and inhuman occupations of manually removing night soil and filth" and to provide for and engage them in 'alternative and dignified occupations' over a period of five years (Annual Report 1991–92, Ministry of Welfare, Government of India, New Delhi). The Bhangis have now taken to other occupations as well.

Chuhra

The Chuhra or Bhangi of Hindustani is the sweeper and scavenger *par excellence* of the United Punjab and the present Haryana and is found throughout the province. They are also called Churha, Chruhe, Bhangi, and Khakrobe. The major occupation of the Churhas is the removal of dead animals, carrying night soil and scavenging. Of late, some of them have acquired land and taken to agriculture. A few of them are also engaged in sharecropping. Traditionally, the Chuhras are linked to other communities through economic relationships. They used to receive polluted clothes at the time of birth or death and on ceremonial or ritual occasions like the solar and lunar eclipses. They are also given the leftover food while begging for alms. They accept both *kachcha* and *pucca* food from other communities, but no other community accepts any food from them. In urban centres, there are no restrictions on the sharing of common water sources. The Chuhras' attitude towards various development programmes is positive. They avail of educational and medical facilities.

Lalbegi

Lalbegi is a class of Mohammedan sweepers supposed to have come from upper India—some with sepoy regiments, others as wanderers in search of work. Though styled Mohammedans, they neither practise circumcision nor abstain from pork. The Lalbegis were employed as sweepers in European households, and were always addressed as *jamadar* by the other servants. They ate the leftovers of the Europeans, and drank any sort of wine or spirit.

The religious rites of the Lalbegis are partly Hindu, partly Muhammadan. As with Mussulmans generally, marriages are arranged by an old woman who acts as a matchmaker. No marriage settlement is drawn up, but an *ikrair* or bond is executed, in which both promise to love each other and the bridegroom undertakes not to bring a second wife into his house. The Khanduri ceremony as well as other Muhammadan customs are observed on the previous day of wedding; but the services of the *Acharji* Brahman are not required. In case the marriage is celebrated in the bridegroom's house, a fee of twenty annas is paid to the panchayat; if the same is held in the bride's house, only five annas are paid.

A few of the Lalbegis keep fast of Ramzan, although they dare not enter a public mosque. Their funeral ceremonies are peculiar. The dead may not be buried in Mussulman cemetery, but in some abandoned and jungly spot. The corpse is wrapped in five shrouds, a handkerchief is placed under each arm and in each hand, a *kasawa* or napkin is bound round the head and a *khirqa* or blouse is put on the body. After the grave has been filled in, a cloth cover (*phul ka chadar*) is laid over it, while four pieces of *'agar'* wood are inserted at the corners and set fire to. The rest of the funeral ceremonies are strictly Mohammedan. For four days after the death fire is not allowed to be lit in the house of the deceased. The family, in the meantime, receives food from their neighbours. On the fifth day, a tray laden with betelnuts and adorned with flowers is placed in front of the hut, and sumptuous meal is served to the whole tribe.

The Lalbegis follow many Hindu customs, observing the Diwali and the Holi being the greatest festivals of the year. On these occasions a earthen image of a mosque with five domes is made, supposed to be a model of one still existing at Ghazni, in Kabul, which belonged to Lal Beg, the eponymous ancestor of the tribe. In front of the image a cock is sacrificed and offerings of *pulao, sherbet* and sweetmeats are made in his name. Lal Beg is identified by Sir H. Elliot (Supplemental Glossary, I, 32) with Lal Guru, the same as the Raksha Aronakarat; but in Benares (Sherring, *Hindu Tribes of Benares*: 397) he is confounded with Pir Zahr, perhaps the famous Chishtiya saint Sayyid Shah Zuhur. In Punjab, again, Mihtars adore Lal Pir or Baba Faqir, as the dyers do Pir Ali Rangrez, and the blacksmiths Hazrat Daud. It seems not only improbable, therefore, that the Lalbegis, like many other tribes, have converted to Mohammedanism, have adopted a Mohammedan saint as their common ancestor (Risley, 1891: 3–4).

Thus, the word 'Lalbegi' is derived from Lalbeg, 'the eponymous ancestor of the tribe' (Risley, 1891). Their surnames are Begi and Balmiki. They are found in Bihar, Uttar Pradesh, Arunachal Pradesh, Delhi, Meghalaya and Mizoram. The Lalbegis are landless. Most men, women and grown-up children work in municipalities as sweepers. Their oral traditions recall that they were earlier Balmikis, but after taking initiation from Saint Kabir, have become Lalbegis. They also claim that their original homeland was Rajasthan.

Practice of Scavenging

Scavenger is one who is partially or wholly engaged in the obnoxious practice of manually removing night soil and filth. The scavenger community is spread all over the country. In Haryana, they are scattered all over the state. According to the 1981 Census, they numbered about 4,88,649 including all the sub-groups (2,58,827 males and 2,29,822 females). Though they are primarily a rural-based community, 19.16 per cent of their population hailed from urban areas.

Scavengers in Haryana

As per a survey conducted in 1997–98 by the Haryana Harijan Kalyan Nigam to identify the scavengers and their dependents, 16,545 families consisting of 36,362 scavengers/dependents have been found to engage in scavenging work in the state. The district-wise number of scavengers in Haryana and their dependents identified under SLRS (1998–99) is given in Table 1. Their literacy rate is low, i.e., 14.31 per cent. The female literacy rate is 5.35 per cent whereas the male literacy rate is 22.26 per cent. They speak Haryanvi within their group and also with others. Hindi is the common link language. They use devanagari script for writing.

Table 1

District-wise Number of Scavengers and their Dependents Identified under SLRS (1998–99) in Haryana

District	*No. of Families*	*No. of Scavengers*	*No. of Dependents*	*Total*
Ambala	1241	1378	12	2090
Bhiwani	1097	1560	619	2170
Faridabad	1057	1388	715	2103
Gurgoan	1155	1155	1590	2745
Hisar	986	986	898	1884
Jhajjar	303	303	564	867
Jind	1060	1060	1667	2727
Kaithal	1144	1283	1896	3179
Karnal	1714	1690	706	2396
Kurukshetra	1128	1172	1046	2218
Mahender Garh	301	301	499	800
Panchkula	174	186	175	361
Panipat	1325	1375	1570	2945
Rewari	793	798	761	1559
Rohtak	719	719	1334	2053
Sirsa	376	402	651	1053
Sonepat	583	583	1207	1790
Yamuna Nagar	1057	1057	1470	2527
Fatehabad	332	380	506	886
Total	16545	17776	18586	36362

Source: National Scheme of Liberation and Rehabilitation of Scavengers and their Dependents.

The scavengers earn their livelihood by scavenging, working in the fields and at the construction sites. They are also engaged in animal husbandry, poultry and piggery. A few of them also have land. The community's traditional primary occupation is scavenging including removal of night soil from the houses and offices. Their secondary occupations include manual work, playing the band, petty trade, hawking, vending of fruits and vegetables, selling meat and eggs. Some also own small tea stalls and restaurants. They depend on the local market for their day-to-day needs. In towns and cities they transact business in cash, but in villages, there is barter system. However, now, in the villages of Haryana, we do not find scavenging work. Some families engage scavengers for the care of animals. In small towns, Brahmin, Baniya, Punjabi (ethnic community) employ some persons for their scavenging work. In the old areas of the cities, we still find pit latrines in the houses where scavengers are employed for cleaning the latrine pit. They carry human excreta on their heads and throw at the garbage centre where corporation personnel come to transport it.

Scavengers are mostly landless, hence they work as labourers in agriculture, plantations and industries. Many of them have to try their luck with the old traditional low yielding occupations such as leather work, flaying dead cattle, scavenging, weaving, dyeing, bamboo craft, fishery, wild herbs and fruit gathering. These occupations, being in the unorganized sector, require more labour; full day's work and the total employment of the family with low returns. Their social status is considered low because of the involvement in unclean work. Children below the age of 15 years also do the scavenging work. They get their payment in cash or kind.

Working hours of scavengers vary in formal and informal organizations. They work eight hours a day in formal organizations like municipalities, hospitals, schools, colleges, universities, banks and other government organizations. Generally, females do sweeping of roads and males clean gutters as assigned by the municipalities. They work from 6.00 to 11.00 am in the morning and from 2.00 to 5.00 pm in the evening. Normally, they get a salary of Rs 3,000 to 4,000 per month in formal organizations. The scale of a safai-worker is equivalent to the class IV employee, i.e., Rs 2,550–55–2,650-EB–60–3,200 in municipality and other government organizations. However, every one gets DA, medical allowance, HRA, conveyance allowance, CCA, uniform and washing allowance along with the basic pay. In the unorganized sector, they work generally from 7.00 to 11.00 am and in exceptional situations up to 4.00 pm. They visit 30–40 houses daily for cleaning and sweeping work. Their tools of scavenging are broom (small and big), mops (duster on a big stick), bamboo basket, shallow pan, shovel, ash etc.

Scavenging-related Tensions

Ninety-five per cent scavengers are either in private or public jobs. There is no problem of getting jobs for scavengers because there is no competition from other communities. Traditionally, this work is meant only for them because no person of upper caste involves in such occupations. For example, if there is something wrong in the septic tank or sewerage, it will be repaired only by the scavengers. Therefore, they will have always extra earnings. Moreover, all the members of the family are engaged in the work. Nevertheless, they quarrel with their own community members regarding division of households in the area.

Generally, women scavengers do household work. They take help of their daughters in scavenging because ultimately daughters have to do the same work. Earlier, women scavengers used to do only scavenging work in the household. Now, they do other works like cleaning the utensils, cloths etc. They neither have leave nor rest. They work every day even if they are ill because of the fear of losing their work due to irregularity. Often their owners threaten them saying that they themselves would do the work if they (scavengers) are not regular. On the contrary, owners generally complain that women scavengers miss their work for 4 to 8 days work in a month by giving various kinds of excuses. They also give them something in kind occasionally besides their monthly salary. Scavengers quarrel sometimes with their employers for timely payment or when they do not get suitable gifts as desired on certain occasions like marriage, birth of a child or on festivals like Holi, Diwali etc.

Though the traditional occupation of women is scavenging, they are also engaged in other occupations as agriculture, animal husbandry, poultry, piggery, playing musical instruments in a concert, vending fruits, vegetables, meat, eggs, etc.

According to 1981 Census, 29.37 per cent of them have returned as workers (48.62% males and 7.69% females). Of them, 56.63 per cent have returned as agricultural labourers and only 3.1 per cent as cultivators. A total of 3.4 per cent of the workers are engaged in rearing livestock and 23.2 per cent in 'other services' which indicates their traditional occupation of scavenging, and the remaining 13.67 per cent workers are engaged in household or other-than-household industries, construction, trade and commerce.

However, this community has few entrepreneurs, scholars or creative artists or administrators. Some members of the community work as teachers, engineers, and doctors. Some have white-collar jobs. Some members also serve in defence, police and railway services. Political leadership has emerged only at the village level.

Lifestyles of Scavengers

Scavengers live in *kachha* or *pucca* houses but not in slums. Drinking water is available in their localities through taps, handpumps and wells. Facilities like approach roads, electricity, cinema, radio, television are available to them. They use firewood, cowdung cakes, coal, kerosene or liquefied petroleum for fuel and gas for cooking. They also use organic manure. They make use of chemical fertilizers and insecticides. Integrated Child Development Schemes are available and facilities of public distribution system also exist. They get sugar, kerosene, rice and coarse cloth through the fair price shops. However, scavengers complain that they do not have other facilities except reservation in jobs.

Social Inter-mixing

Caste Hindus do not accept water from the scavengers. Many Scheduled Caste communities accept water from the scavengers if they are in a good personal equation. Similarly, *kachha* or *pucca* food is not accepted from them. They accept *sidha* food from all the communities except Sikligars and Dehas. Putative kinship-based relationships exist. They share wells with *Chamars* and the *Dhanaks*. Road facilities are shared with others and so are railways, schools and cremation grounds. But sometimes they also have their separate cremation grounds. They share *panchayat ghars* (community halls) with all other communities. *Jajmani* system has been reported to exist. Community members working as scavengers in some areas get one and a half or two quintals of cereals and some cash biannually.

Food Habits and Use of Intoxicants

The scavengers eat non-vegetarian food almost regularly. They eat pork, chicken, fish and mutton. They consume wheat, rice, *jowar* (minor millet), *bajra,* maize and barley. They prefer *roti* to rice. Among pulses, they eat gram, *urad* (black gram), *moong* (green gram), peas, *moth* (lentil) and *arhar* (red gram). Ghee or mustard oil is used for cooking purposes. Among the scavengers, onion, garlic and egg-eaters are considered vegetarians. They consume all seasonal vegetables and fruits. They are fond of sugar cane juice, tea, milk, coffee, fruit juice and milk products. They are equally fond of alcoholic drinks, even though liquor is considered a vice. They buy liquor from the local market.

Beating their wives is common after drinking. When women go out for work men start playing cards and most of the time, they play in the temple lest the police go after them. They also have the habit of gambling and involve in quarrels on small issues. Many of them are also drug addicts. Children do learn such habits from the elders.

Customs and Rituals

Since the scavengers are Hindus, they share major religious centres and centres of pilgrimages with other Hindu communities. Besides, they have their separate temples, known as the Balmiki temples. They are also staunch believers of Mata Masani. This deity can be worshipped anywhere, but is normally worshipped at some road crossings. There are also holy men in this community and some of them have opened *ashrams.* One such *ashram* is at Modinagar in Uttar Pradesh. There are religious specialists who are also exorcists. They perform *pooja* (worship) and preach on religion. They also perform birth, marriage and death rituals. There is another *ashram* at Rohtak known as 'Sadanath ka Dera'. *Bhajans* and *kirtans* (religious songs) are sung by them. With the income of *ashrams* schools are run. The *gaddi* (enthroning) system is also followed by them. Generally, the disciples inherit the *gaddi*. They celebrate all festivals of the Hindus and have fairs in common with them. They celebrate Balmiki's birthday with great zeal. Festivals are of economic, social and religious importance.

Their old traditions are similar to those of other communities. Both men and women sing folk songs. Folk tales are also recited but only few remember them. The common musical instruments are *damroo, dhol, dholak, ek tara,* harmonium, *banjo, chimta* and *khartal.* Both sexes take part in dance. The scavengers speak the Haryanvi dialect in different parts of the state, in their homes and with other communities. They also speak Hindi with other communities. The community members wear the common attire of the state; that is, men wear *dhoti-kurta* or *kurta-pyjama* and *khes* (blanket) in winter. Elderly men also wear a turban. Women wear *lehnga, kurta* and *odhni;* the young wear *salwar-kameez* and *chunni*.

Marriage

The Balmikis are divided into social divisions known as *gotras* but the exact number of Balmiki *gotras* is not available. However, about two dozen *gotras* are identified and they are: Pihwal, Dugalgach, Tank Saudde, Baid Marholia, Tanwar, Chauhan, Pathak, Rajput Chauhan, Jingalia, Panche, Kunjinwal, Gaichand, Bagdi, Lohat, Luchare, Lohaye, Chandalia, Athwal, Khekhra and Bhooranda.

Marriage rituals are performed both at the bride's and bridegroom's residences. The bride's parents give a feast. Marriage is consummated at the house of the bridegroom. They generally marry by taking *pheras.* Marriage between the same *gotra* is prohibited. One cannot marry within one's mother's or paternal grandmother's *gotras*. The community has a number of exogamous clans (*gotras*) like Pihwal, Tonk, Baid, Tanwar, Jingalia, Chindalia, etc. Their clan names, which are also used as surnames, have transformed into decent surnames. For example, Dugalgach to Duggalm, Chanwaria to Chawla, Sudde to Sood, Chandalia to Chaddha and Pihwal to Panwar.

Some scavenger community members consider themselves inferior to other Hindu communities, while affluent ones consider themselves to be of equal status. They do not recognize the *varna* system, because they think that it leads to untouchability. They also do not consider their place in the Sudra category.

The scavengers are an endogamous community having village and *gotra* exogamy. In cities and towns, they marry in different *mohallas* (localities). *Dewar-bhabhi* (husband's younger brother and elder brother's wife) and *jija-sali* (sister's husband and wife's sister) can marry. *Jeth* (husband's elder brother) may also keep his younger brother's wife after her husband's death or on his becoming invalid. One may also marry wife's elder sister, if she is a widow and gives her consent.

Though adult and negotiated marriage is the norm, there are also a few child marriages. The normal age of marriage for boys is 20 years and for girls 18 years. The boy and the girl do not meet each other before marriage. Monogamy is the rule but there are certain exceptions. *Sindur*, cosmetics and glass bangles are considered marriage symbols. Brideprice, though prevalent 40 to 50 years ago, now has almost disappeared. If any one is found accepting a brideprice, he/she is excommunicated. Brideprice has transformed to dowry which is given both in cash and kind and according to the bride's parent's capacity. Patrilocal form of residence is practised. Frequency of divorce is very low. Mostly it is the *biradari panchayat* that deals with the cases of divorce. It is always in writing. Sometimes a marriage is dissolved through judicial approval and in such cases compensation to the wife is decided by the court of law. When a marriage is dissolved with the intervention of *biradari panchayat* the divorcing husband has to return the dowry to his wife. Both husband and wife can divorce. Children are the father's responsibility, but small children can live with their mother. Common grounds of divorce are adultery, impotency and maladjustment. The widow or widower can remarry. A widow can undergo *phera* ceremony again. Such *pheras* are called *punna pheras* and these consist of two and a half *pheras*. Men or women who are divorced can also get remarried. The marriage age has increased and marriage symbols are observed strictly. Adult and negotiated marriages are in vogue. Levirate and sorrorate are permitted. Sometimes two and a half rounds around the sacred fire (*punna pheras*) are performed in the case of the marriage of a widow.

Family

Among the scavengers, extended families still exist, but they are breaking into nuclear ones. Usually, relations between family members are cordial, but sometimes conflicts and confrontations arise. These are on account of property, restriction on the freedom of youngsters and challenge to the authority of elders. It can also be due to lack of adjustment on the part of the daughters-in-law. Conflicts and confrontations are resolved through a familial compromise, or *biradari panchayat*, failing which the parties seek redress with the court of law. They rarely go to court. Daughters do not take a share in the property of their father, in spite of the provisions in the existing law of the state. In the absence of brothers, they may leave their share in the ancestral property to their cousin and nephew, who in turn discharges their social obligations towards their cousins. The eldest son succeeds as the head of the family on the death of the father. Inter-family linkages are strong as much as they cooperate with each other in happy times as also in adversities.

Status of Women

The scavengers claim to ensure equal status to women. Women have an important role in agricultural operations. They have a role in social functions like rituals or religious functions, and political activities such as canvassing during elections. The women bring potable water and collect fuel and fodder. Some women also contribute to the family income by way of doing scavenging work.

Birth

After birth, *sutak* (pollution) is observed, which runs for one-and-a-quarter months. The mother is first bathed on the third day of her delivery. On *chhathi* (sixth day of post-natal pollution) pudding is cooked and *bemata* (the goddess) is worshipped. New clothes are worn by the newborn and a *tagri* (black thread) is tied round its waist. The woman is also given normal food to eat on the sixth day. Before this, she is fed special food prepared with ghee and *gur* (jaggery). Dry ground coconut is given for five days. On the tenth day, the child and mother are bathed and the house is cleaned. A *havan* is performed for purification. Rice and pudding are cooked. Five, seven or eleven young girls are invited and fed. The *Pundit* of the same community is also fed who sometimes names the child. *Dasuthan* is observed on completion of one-and-a-quarter months. This is observed on the birth of a male child, but some people also observe it on the birth of a female child. On the occasion of *dasuthan,* relatives and community members are invited for a feast. The maternal uncle of the newborn, at times, gives *bhat* (gifts). *Mundan* (tonsure) is held at Gurgoan in April. It is observed when the child is six months or one year old. *Suchche bal* (first crop of hair) is immersed in the tank at Gurgoan.

Death Ceremony

The scavengers bury their dead keeping the face downwards following the customs of the villagers whom they serve. The dead is cremated, but children up to the age of three years are buried. Mourning period runs for thirteen days. On the thirteenth day, thirteen Brahmans are fed with plain rice. On the death of an old man, *pucca* food is cooked. *Mahina* (one month after death) ritual is observed. A dog or cat is fed with milk for three or four days. *Chhamahi* (six months after death) *barsi* rituals are observed both for the death of young and the old. The Brahmins are fed and presented with utensils, clothes and some cash. The burnt bones are immersed in the Ganga at Haridwar or in the Yamuna at Delhi. They observe *kanagat* (ancestor worship) ritual also by cooking *pucca* food for their ancestors. Now, the rituals are becoming shorter because they are expensive.

Caste Panchayat and Other Associational Activities

The Balmiki community panchayats, such as the Balmiki Harijan Seva Samiti at Najafgarh in Delhi, Bahadurgarh and Ballabgarh in Haryana also exist. These are composed of the chairman, Pradhan, secretary, treasurer and eleven members. Funds to run these panchayats are raised as and when required. The function of such a community is to settle disputes, promote welfare activities and provide help in the time of marriage. Caste panchayat does not interfere in family affairs. It arranges games and sports and distributes prizes. However, statutory Gram Panchayats are there with the usual composition and functions. After independence, caste councils have become less effective in the wake of statutory Gram Panchayats.

Political Pressure Groups

Political pressure groups mobilize the scavengers during the elections. Municipal Councillor listens to the *Lamberdars* (influential person of the ward). They are purchased by distributing liquor. Males dominate the families and the females do according to the dictates of the males. These scavengers are generally Congress supporters. However, leaders of every party cajole them for votes.

The formal organizational activities of the scavengers are to be seen in their political movement. The scavengers and their network of institutional structure from the *mohalla* (residential area) to all India level show caste associations in the modernizing adoptive context (Shyamlal, 1984). Scavengers use political means to enhance their status. There are many associations which function for the welfare of scavengers such as Safai Mazdoor Union, Mehtar Sudhar Sabha, Harijan Sewak Sangh, Dalit Varg Sangh and Anusuchit Jati Seva Sangh.

Civic Bodies

There is no regular provision for public amenities. Municipalities or Municipal Corporations receive grants from time to time for such amenities from the government. In turn, they provide facilities for public amenities in slum areas. There is always a problem of getting space for the construction of toilets in different localities. Municipality has framed by-laws relating to toilets in residential houses. Accordingly, every household has to construct a septic tank inside the residential house or to link the toilet to sewer.

Safai-karamcharis (scavengers) get baskets, broomsticks, shovel, wheelbarrow, handcart and rickshaw from the sanitation department of the municipality for scavenging.

Scavengers and Development

There have been many efforts by the government to improve the conditions of scavengers. These include education, training and other means of rehabilitation.

Conversion of Dry Latrines

Once there was a scheme of central government for low cost sanitation to convert dry latrines to prevent manual scavenging. This scheme provided 50 per cent subsidy to construct septic tank or to link the toilet in the sewer. The beneficiaries met the remaining 50 per cent expenses. Consequently, carrying of night soil as head-load has been stopped to a large extent.

Education

The Government of India has been trying to make opportunities for education increasingly equal for all citizens of the country and, therefore, special facilities have been provided for the Scheduled Castes (SCs) and Scheduled Tribes (STs) and for all those who come from backward classes. It is not unfortunate that these facilities are not fully utilized.

Now, the scavenging community has started showing interest in favour of children's education. The boys study up to the tenth or twelfth class. They often drop out due to poverty. The girls study up to the seventh or eighth class and they also drop out due to poverty, household chores and social reasons. Only a few children go for higher education.

Health

Scavengers do not favour indigenous traditional medicinal system and accept modern medicines. Though they marry early, they do not use family planning methods. Consequently, they have a large number of children. They also have a wrong notion that with higher the number of children, they would have higher income. Attitude of educated persons towards family planning is favourable. They also use modern methods of family planning. Generally, women get sterilized. They generally prefer two or three children.

National Scheme of Liberation and Rehabilitation of Scavengers

The main objective of the National Scheme of Liberation and Rehabilitation of Scavengers is to liberate them from their existing hereditary and obnoxious occupation of manually removing night soil and filth and to provide for and engage them in alternative and dignified occupations within a period of five years. As such, the unit, in respect of this scheme, is not the family but each scavenger and each dependent of the scavengers.

The input of training for acquisition/upgradation of skills for rehabilitating the scavengers and their dependents is an essential prerequisite for the rehabilitation programme. The scheme would cover primarily all scavengers belonging to SCs and other communities. It would cover scavengers in urban areas, semi-urban areas and rural areas. The age prescribed for the training is from 15 to 50 years. It is recognized that after certain age the competence to horizontally move to other alternative occupation becomes difficult. Therefore, scavengers below 50 years were selected. The training lasted from one month to six months depending on the type of trade. The training was provided through training institutions set up by the State Government and NGOs. A stipend of Rs 500 per month per trainee was provided.

In this scheme, funding per project was up to Rs 50,000 per beneficiary and margin money of 15 per cent of the project cost at 4 per cent interest was also provided. Another 20 per cent was subsidy and the remaining was obtained from the bank as loan.

Harkalyan Binders and Printers, Panchkula

This centre was set up in 1976 to manufacture exercise and answer books out of controlled paper allotted to the State Level Paper Distribution Committee, Education Department, Haryana, Chandigarh. The aim was to provide training-cum-employment to SC youth as well as to supply exercise books to the students of schools and colleges at consessional rates. Consequent upon the discontinuation of supply of paper by State Level Paper Distribution Committee, the unit was compelled to diversify its activities towards printing and binding work. This unit has been declared as an approved agency for printing and binding work for all government departments/boards/corporations. About 37 workers have been engaged in this centre on regular basis after providing preliminary training in printing and binding work. The centre has its own building at Panchkula.

This unit is functioning well and there is a lot of scope for its expansion. In 1998–99, the turnover was Rs 55.75 lakhs and the profit Rs 8.24 lakhs. It is proposed to instal another stop cylinder letter printing machine so that the centre can generate additional resources for the SCs.

Common Facility Centre, Ambala

The Common Facility Centre was established in Industrial Area, Ambala Cantonment in March 1987, with a view to provide training to SC youth to raise their standard of living by providing them work with better wages. During the years 1995–96 and 1996–97, training to 23 and 31 persons respectively was provided.

During the year 1997–98, 19 candidates in electrical trade and eight candidates in carpentry were trained and they are being given financial assistance to earn their livelihood by running their own enterprise. The Centre has provided jobs to 24 electrical and 22 carpentry trade trainees in 1999.

Grants and Loans

The scavengers have been getting jobs under various rural employment programmes such as Integrated Rural Development Programme. District Rural Development Agency has been giving loans for piggery, buying buffaloes, poultry, buying carts and *tongas*. Matriculates are given loans under employment guarantee schemes for auto-rickshaws or for opening provision shops. Such loans are given for scavengers' welfare under Haryana Harijan Kalyan Nigam (HHKM). For every loan there is subsidy of 33 per cent to maximum of Rs 10,000 and the margin money of 15 per cent will be contributed by HHKM, which is repayable with a nominal rate of interest of 4 per cent. The banks make the balance amount available which has to be returned in 50 instalments.

It is observed that more than 50 per cent of the loan accounts become sick. Recovery by the bank is very poor, as there is no guarantee. Banks have the right to write off such accounts after three to five years. The loans are given under compulsion because of certain schemes. Secondly, many times people do not require loans because they are not in a position to repay. Thirdly, other people apply for loans in the name of scavengers. There are also instances where people who do not have any space to keep buffaloes, have been buying them. Sometimes loan is availed for a certain activity but it is not used for that purpose. Thus, there is no proper use of loans.

Conclusion

The scavengers have suffered a lot. They were forced to live in sub-human conditions till recently and were denied social interaction with the rest of the community. They lived in isolation, servitude and poverty. The chief reason for their backwardness has been that they were denied education for a long time.

In Haryana, now, there is no manual scavenging. Efforts have been made for the elimination of the manual scavenging in towns and cities. Almost all the dry latrines have been converted into wet latrines. However, there is a need to bring the scavengers into the mainstream of social life. Education is the most important aspect in the elevation of the status of scavengers.

We find that there is a lack of awareness among the SCs and STs about the facilities available for them such as free tuition, textbooks and mid-day meals and in some states even free uniforms. Therefore, programmes for the enhancement of such awareness could be designed through the use of personal contacts, involvement of voluntary organizations and the utilization of mass media. Adult education, non-formal education and continuing education can go a long way in accelerating the process of improving their awareness level. They could also be educated on saving habits.

REFERENCES

Annual Action Plan. Haryana Harijan Kalyan Nigam, Chandigarh, 1997–98.

Cohn, B.S. (ed.). 1955. "The Changing Status of Depressed Caste" in *Village India.* Chicago: Chicago University Press.

Crooke, W. 1896. *The Tribes and Castes of N.W.P. and Oudh.* Vol. I, Calcutta: Office of Superintendent, Government Printing Press.

Ibbetson, Denzil. 1974. *Punjab Castes.* Delhi: BR Publishing Corporation.

Risley, H.H. 1891. *The Tribes and Castes of Bengal*. Calcutta: Bengal Secretariat Press, Vol. II.

Sharma, M.L. and Bhatia, A.K. (eds.) and Singh, K.S. (General Editor). 1994. *People of India: Haryana*. Vol. XXIII, Anthropological Survey of India, New Delhi: Manohar Publishers, pp.33–37.

Shyamlal. 1984. *The Bhangis in Transition.* New Delhi: Inter-India Publications.

Singh, K.S. 1993. *People of India.* National Series Vol. II, Anthropological Survey of India, New Delhi: Oxford University Press.

Yadav, S.K.1983. *Harijan Awareness of Educational Schemes*. Gurgaon: The Academic Press.

15

Kudubis of Karnataka

A Case for Reservation

Y. RAVINDRANATH RAO

The tribes constitute an important segment of Indian society. They are a distinct ethnic group having their own indigenous identity. The tribal societies, like other societies, have been changing, though slowly, compared to other complex societies. While integration into the mainstream of India's population has been an excruciatingly painful experience for these societies, it has been all the more so for the non-Scheduled Tribes like Kudubis. Thanks to the humanitarian policies adopted by the farsighted leaders like Pandit Nehru that the impact of the onslaught of 'civilization' on the Scheduled Tribes (STs) has been softened to a great extent by providing constitutional succour to them. But this cannot be said of the so-called non-STs like Kudubis. Deprived of this constitutional protection they are subjected to the ravages of unmitigated economic, political, social and cultural exploitation. As a result, the 'born-free' people, who were once the proud inheritors of a rich and multi-hued culture, are now in hiding and are forced to the ignominy of accepting the status of the most backward caste.

Kudubis mostly live in the west coast of India. Though the social and economic conditions of Kudubis are as poor as the other STs of Karnataka, nevertheless, they had been included in group 'B' by the Government of Karnataka till 1973. They were re-classified as the 'most backward caste' in 1994 as per the recommendations of the Chinnappa Reddy Commission. However, the Kunbi of Goa has been declared as ST by the government in 2003 after struggling for years to achieve this status (Kankar, 2006: 77). This paper is the result of an intense study of Kudubis of coastal Karnataka in terms of their society, culture, social institutions and social change. The study elucidates the structure, change and problems of the Kudubi community in Karnataka. The case is also made for their inclusion in the list of STs in Karnataka.

The Concept of a Tribe

The English word 'tribe' is derived from the Latin *Tribus*, one of the three political divisions or patrician orders of ancient Rome. According to the Oxford Dictionary, the term refers to a race of people, now applied especially to a primary aggregate of people in a primitive, backward or barbarous condition under a headman or a chief. At present, there is no agreement even among the anthropologists and sociologists regarding the definition of a tribe. Desai points out, "there is controversy among the scholars, reformers and administrators with regard to an adequate terminology for describing these people" (1977: 17). Risley (1908), Elwin (1943) and Thakkar (1941) have described the tribes as 'aborigines', Hutton (1961) calls them 'primitive tribes' and Ghurye (1963) describes them as the 'so-called aborigines' or as 'backward Hindus'. Some scholars and reformers call them *adivasis.* Today, the most common administratively used term in India is 'Scheduled Tribes'. It refers to those communities that have been 'scheduled' or listed for special treatment in compliance with the provisions of the Constitution of India.

According to the report of the Commissioner for Scheduled Castes and Tribes (1952) eight features of tribes have been listed. They are: (1) They live away from the civilized world in the inaccessible parts of the forests and hills. (2) They belong to one of the three racial stocks—Negroids, Austroloids and Mongoloids. (3) They speak the same tribal dialect. (4) They profess primitive religion known as 'animism', in which they worship ghosts and spirits as the most important element. (5) They follow primitive occupations, such as gleaning, hunting and gathering of forest products. (6) They are largely carnivorous or flesh and meat-eaters. (7) They are either naked or semi-naked using tree barks or leaves for clothing. (8) They have nomadic habits and are fond of drinking and dancing.

Tribal Development

After independence, the Government of India adopted a two-fold strategy to deal with the tribal population, i.e., of reservation and socio-economic development. The impact of tribal development programmes is not uniform among all the tribal communities. Of all the communities, the tribes in India have been the most neglected by the agencies of development. They lead a hard life and a majority of them live below the subsistence level. We may classify tribes in India as 'tribes' and 'Scheduled Tribes'. It is important to note that the scholarly studies on tribes in India are generally restricted to STs only. The tribes which are not scheduled are also the weaker sections of India's population like the Scheduled Castes (SCs).

However, the condition of the tribes began to change after independence. The rapid development of transport and communication, industrialization and urbanization, the spread of education and health care, the introduction of democratic political processes and institutions and schemes implemented through five-year plans have affected even the remotest tribes at least to some extent. Hence, they are no more totally isolated. Majumdar has pointed out, "there is no social group today which may be said to mark zero point of cultural contact" (1968: 378). Besides various modern forces, the contact of the tribes with the non-tribes has also changed their condition. Some of these factors are Hinduization, Sanskritization and emergence of tribe-caste continuum and tribal social movements.

Kudubis in Karnataka

In Karnataka, 49 communities have been included in the list of STs. According to 1991 census, in Karnataka, the tribal population is 19,15,691, constituting 4.26 per cent of the population. The concentration of the tribes is high in the districts of Bellary, Chitradurga, Kodagu, Kolar, Mysore and Tumkur, where their percentage to the respective population of the districts varies between 4 and 14. Among the 49 communities listed in the ST category, Naikada or Naiks constitute 69 per cent, followed by Kadu Kuruba 11 per cent, Marati Naik 4 per cent, Gonds 3 per cent, and Kolidar, Jenu Kurubas and Koya 2 per cent each. Yerava, Meda, Soliga, Koraga and Hasalaru constitute 1 per cent each.

Kudubis are predominantly found in Kundapur and Mangalore talukas and a few of them are found in Udupi, Karkala and Bantwal talukas in Dakshina Kannada and Udupi districts of Karnataka state. They are the migrants from Goa. So far, no systematic empirical study has been conducted on Kudubis. Thurston (1909) presents a brief description of Kudubis. Sturrock, in Madras District Manuals, South Canara (1894), has presented a brief account of Kudubis under the chapter 'Forest and Hill Tribes'. Nanjundayya and Iyre (1928) made a brief study on one of the sub-divisions of Kudubis known as Are Kudubis (also listed as Kunbi

Marhattas). The Karnataka government has published a brief account of life and cultural practices of Kudubis in the form of reports in South Kanara District Gazetteers (1973, ed. by K. Abhishankar) and in Karnataka Backward Classes Commission, Vol. II (1975, under the chairmanship of L.G. Havanur) describing them as "a nomadic hill tribe living in isolation".

Peer and Heggade (1992), in their evaluation reports on the impact of various developmental programmes implemented during the decade 1980–90 for the social and economic development of tribal population in Karnataka, have briefly highlighted the conditions of Kudubis. There are also several articles and write-ups on life and conditions of Kudubis written in regional languages in dailies, weeklies and monthlies apart from a few short monographs. Although these are neither scientific nor exhaustive, they indicate that the Kudubi tribe has attracted attention of several people, writers and journalists.

Society and Culture

The data pertaining to the Kudubis of coastal Karnataka reveal that they migrated from Goa in the 16th century AD. One of the key factors, which forced the Kudubis to move into coastal Karnataka and Malabar, was the oppression and the proselytizing movement initiated by the then Portuguese. When the Portuguese captured Goa, a significant majority of them left Goa permanently. Thurston (1909) has also acknowledged this. Those who could not escape were forcibly converted by the Portuguese. Consequently, there are a good number of Kudubis turned Christians today in Goa. Gomes (1987) opines that the aboriginal stock in Goa is known as the 'Gavdi'. The Christian convert of the 'Gavdi' aboriginal was termed 'Kunbi'. This study shows that the original endonym 'Kunbi' has become 'Kudubi' in Karnataka after the migration. Mascarenhas (1987) reports that Kudubis belong to the Munda Astroid race. They are divided into six sub-divisions known as Goa-Kudubi, Kareya-Kudubi, Are-Kudubi, Jogi-Kudubi, Nada-Kudubi and Jati-Kudubis. Thurston (1909) lists the following sections, viz., Are, Goa, Jogi, Kodiyal or Kareya Kudubis.

Kudubis live in villages but these villages cannot be called tribal villages, because almost all the settlements of Kudubis are mixed in character. However, they have formed their own compact settlements and hutments within the village, which resemble a small Kudubi village. Generally, each Kudubi hutment will be under the control of *Gurikara* or tribal chieftain. A Kudubi house is called *Ghar,* which is usually made of thatched roofs. Wood and bamboo are also used to construct houses. Except a very few ancestral houses, the houses are generally small in size and rectangular in shape. The walls are made of mud or bricks. Today, a few tile-roofed houses can also be seen.

The Kudubis speak a dialect of Konkani. Many Kannada and Tulu words are used in their dialect due to the influence of regional language. In the past, Kudubis did not know Kannada due to illiteracy and lack of contact with other people. However, today, almost all Kudubis are able to speak in Kannada. Kannada and Tulu languages have influenced Kudubi so much that today, songs composed in Kannada and Tulu languages are sung by them frequently on auspicious occasions like marriage, Holi festival etc. They have also borrowed certain kinship terminologies from Kannada and Tulu, for instance, *Appayya* (father), *Amma* (mother), *Anna* (brother), *Akka* (sister), *Ajja* (grandfather) and *Ajji* (grandmother).

The staple food of the Kudubis is boiled rice. It is eaten as *'ganji'* or *'pej'* (gruel) or strained after boiling with curries and vegetables. Their usual food also comprises *ragi (Eleusine coracana)* and fish. They use coconut and a variety of spices such as cumin seeds, garlic, onion, chili, etc., for cooking. Spices, salt and tamarind are added to vegetables or meat according to taste. Usually, earthen pots and aluminium vessels are used for cooking. Water is drawn from the well or nearby ponds or rivers. In the morning they take gruel with chutney or pickles. The mid-day meal consists of rice and vegetable curry. In the evening meals are taken with leftover curry or occasionally, fish curry. The leftover food articles are eaten the next morning. These food items fulfil their dietary requirements to some extent but they are not prepared hygienically.

Kudubis grow and eat both leafy and root vegetables, such as cow pea (*vigna unguiculate*), lady's finger, cluster beans, sweet melon, bittergourd, cucumber, brinjal, ash gourd taro, spinach, sweet potato, tapioca etc. They are very fond of the curry made out of taro. Other than leaves, its tuber is widely used as an important vegetable. According to Thurston (1909), it is the Kudubis who brought sweet potato, cashew nut, Indian spinach and *Chrysanthemum indicum* from Goa to South Canara.

There are certain restrictions regarding food habits, owing to different beliefs, superstitions and food taboos. Many foods among the Kudubis are prohibited from consumption. The use of milk and milk products such as ghee, butter, butter milk etc. is found to be very negligible. Milk is used only for tea. Though Kudubis are non-vegetarian, it is surprising to note that they do not eat the flesh of reared animals such as fowl, sheep, goat, pig etc. In this sense, they claim to be superior to other SCs/STs of the district. Rearing of fowl is strictly prohibited. The contact with fowl or its droppings results in pollution. However, animals which are hunted for food are considered sacred and venerated.

Generally, the animals hunted for food are wild pig, porcupine, rabbit, small mouse deer (*Tragulus Meminna*), monitor lizard (*Varamus Moniter*), squirrel, wild fowl, etc. However, certain species of animals and birds are avoided. These include snake, bear, vulture, eagle, monkey, wild cat, rat, Indian bison, peacock and parrot.

Tea is the main beverage now popular among Kudubis. Use of liquor was prohibited among them in olden days. They neither make alcoholic drinks nor offer it to deities like many other tribes of India. But some of them now drink liquors frequently. They use both country made liquor and that sold in the wine shop. Some Kudubis have admitted that alcoholic drinks are now prepared by themselves at home, especially in Kodiyala sub-division.

Use of betel leaves and nuts is also popular among them. Both men and women chew it with tobacco and lime. Some even use catechu along with betelnut as a scented ingredient. *Beedi* is also popular among menfolk. It is observed that many young men start smoking at a very early age.

Ill-health has been a major problem among the Kudubis. This is due to several reasons such as unhygienic conditions in which they live; lack of access to clean, potable water; poverty and malnutrition; lack of medical knowledge and information and superstitions. Incidences of asthma and tuberculosis are common. A few cases of leprosy, malaria, jaundice and cancer were also identified.

A large number of Kudubi houses are either insufficiently ventilated or overcrowded without having any facilities of sanitation or hygiene. It is these conditions that have led to various diseases among them. Moreover, Kudubis are more dependent on the magic performed by medicinemen or *Gadya*. Some of the Kudubis themselves use local herbal medicines or seek the expertise of *Gadya*. Majority of them do not admit their pregnant women to hospitals for delivery. A woman during her confinement is kept for 11 days in an outhouse, usually in a shed intended for cattle or sometimes, in a separate shed attached to the cattleshed. Such habitation tends to result in serious illness or sometimes even death.

Educationally, the Kudubis are the most backward, the major reasons being poverty, lack of motivation and encouragement, depressing home/environmental conditions and non-availability of benefits extended to the tribes. On account of these, a significant majority of the Kudubi children drop out from the schools at so early a stage that they almost revert to illiteracy. In the present study, the literacy rate among the Kudubis was found to be only 30 per cent. The aspirations of the parents regarding the education of their children are also not high. Interaction with others, specially the urban dwellers, is very limited.

Dress is one of the social necessities, which assesses the status of an individual. It is also an expression of one's personality. There is a also a shift with regard to the dresses worn by tribes today. In olden days, Kudubi men wore loin cloth. In course of time, they began to use a short towel-like cloth, which covered their waist and leaving the rest of the body naked. Later, they started wearing hand-stitched vests. Today, the normal dress of a Kudubi male is a *dhoti* draped around the waist. Kudubi men sometimes wear half *dhoti* or even full *dhoti* or shirt depending upon the occasion. Sometimes, a short cloth or a towel is thrown over the shoulder by some old men even today. The head is sometimes covered with a piece of cloth or an ordinary turban. Recently, the young men like to wear trousers and modern shirts.

In olden days, practically, all the male Kudubis, irrespective of sub-division, used to grow a long tuft of hair at the back of the head, and they strictly adhered to this practice. The long tuft was also regarded as the symbol of their tribe. The cutting off or trimming a tuft was prohibited. If any one violated the tradition/custom, he had to pay the fine at the tribal court. They were also prohibited from having a hair cut. They used to shave their beard by themselves with the help of *kop* (a kind of knife used as razor). It was sharpened with a stone. Men did not wear chappals earlier. The contact of leather chappals with body parts was supposed to result in pollution.

The womenfolk dress in primitive style. They cover their bust and loin with *sari* and both ends are tied up on the chest. This mode of wearing *sari* is called *Gente.* Some women wear *sari* in this style only at home. Whenever they go out, it is worn in usual Indian style. Blouses were unknown to them till recently. Even today, blouse is not worn by many orthodox women of older generation. This feature of their dress is attributed to the belief that since their goddess *(Amba* or *Adishakti)* wears a blouse on her upper part of the body, therefore, a Kudubi woman is prohibited from wearing a blouse. However, Kudubi bride wears the blouse on the wedding day only as she is believed to be the symbol of mother deity. Some women of Kodiyala sub-division in olden days also wore the *sari* in the *Kacche* style.

Girls and young women of today wear colourful synthetic *saris* and blouses owing to the influences of women of other neighbouring communities. They also wear fashionable vermilion mark on their forehead. They apply oil on their head and comb it. Flowers are a passion with the womenfolk. They are fond of *Aboli* or unarmed organdie and nail dye (*Crossandra undulaefolia*). However, wearing of *Aboli* by an unmarried girl (also boy) is forbidden. They either weave their hair into one large plait or it is tied behind into a knot and fastened with a pin. But hair knot is quite common. Like men, women also wear *muttale* whenever they work outside.

Women also wear a variety of ornaments of different designs and sizes. They are fond of gold and silver ornaments. However, they use ornaments made of aluminium, beads, coins, copper etc. They wear ornaments on different parts of the body such as ear, nose, head, neck, hand, fingers and ankles. It is surprising to note that the ornaments such as *mangalasutra* (necklace of tiny black beads) and toe-ring are worn by unmarried girls though in Hindu society only married women are allowed to wear them. However, this practice is gradually disappearing today.

Family Organization

Family is a basic institution of any society. Vidyarthi and Rai (1977) hold a view that the clan and family are more popular social units among the tribes of South India. They have also observed that monogamous family with a nuclear structure is the main feature of the Indian tribes. However, one can also observe a good number of joint as well as extended families among them. They have further observed that in South India, the tribes of both patriarchal and matriarchal family forms are in great number.

Among the Kudubis, the family is the unit of social organization. Though the dominant form of family among the Kudubis is joint and extended, it has been transforming itself into the nuclear one in the present times. These families are mostly patriarchal and patrilineal in character. A male head manages the entire family matters, such as budget, expenditure, celebration of festivals, feasts, arrangements of marriages and other family functions. Even though the Kudubi joint family is in transition, there are a few houses where several nuclear families live. In such nuclear households the land is cultivated separately but it is not legally divided. However, in some cases, the land was divided among the brothers off the record with an oral agreement. Many such families are found especially among the Goa Kudubis. Due to backwardness and illiteracy, they cannot afford to move outside and construct their own houses. Therefore, their ancestral houses are partitioned and brothers form their own nuclear families and remain separately after they get married. If the houses are too small and cannot be partitioned, then only sons may go little away as a last resort to have a separate house. Consequently, such newly formed nuclear families are also seen around the ancestral house.

Kudubis have a well-organized lineage system, which is called *kutumbo.* The entire Kudubi tribal community is divided into several *kutumbos.* Each *kutumbo* consists of several families or kin groups, all related by blood. Thus, a *kutumbo* is naturally larger than the family and household. In this sense, it may also be understood as an extension of the joint family in a wider area.

The eldest male of the kinship group becomes the head of the *kutumbo.* He enjoys a considerable amount of power and respect in all matters relating to lineage organization. The ancestral house of Kudubis becomes the centre for all the activities of *kutumbo.* The regular life activity of every Kudubi is regulated by the *kutumbo* system. An individual is also dependent on and attached to the lineage system.

The Kudubi lineage system is also associated with their political organization. Several *kutumbos* and households of both joint and nuclear types become important while forming political organization. The political organization among Kudubis is based on lineage and family, which is called *vodow*. *Vodow* is also called *kudukattu* or *gaovu* or *wade.* Normally, each *vodow* consists of families ranging from 10 to 250. Sometimes, the eldest man of the lineage may also function as the head of *vodow.* The ancestral house is normally regarded as the house of *kutumbo* where the eldest man of the *kutumbo* lives. It is said that all the tribal customs, festivals and worships of family deity are strictly observed at the ancestral house.

The work of men is generally confined to outdoor activities. Agriculture and hunting operations are done by men exclusively. They also work as agricultural labourers in other fields in the village. They engage themselves in making purchases from village shops as well as in making hunting equipments, nets, fish traps, baskets, *gummate* (a musical instrument), sticks and poles for dancing purpose. Women generally do their household duties, such as cooking, tending cattle, looking after children, threshing paddy during harvesting seasons, milking cattle, cattle feeding and collecting grass, firewood and dry leaves from the hills and forests. They also engage themselves in the cultivation of vegetables, mat making, carrying water for drinking, and selling vegetables and mats in nearby weekly market. They also assist their menfolk in agricultural operations, such as preparing natural manure, sowing, transplanting, harvesting, threshing and husking of paddy.

Like lineage, kinship also plays an important role in family life of Kudubis. They depend much upon their kinsmen in observing religious rites and rituals, arranging marriages etc. Therefore, family bonds and kinship obligations are comparatively stronger among the rural folk and tribes. A person may expect help only from his kinsmen in times of distress. However, in modern times, the kinship bonds and obligations are weakening. Such changes are also evident in the kinship organization of the Kudubis.

Kudubis practise endogamy. They are divided into several endogamous groups and sections, such as *Jati, Kodiyala, Goa, Jogi, Nada and Are*, which do not intermarry. They also practise a kind of territorial endogamy. For instance, Kodiyala Kudubis do not marry the girls of their own group living in Kundapura region. It is because the Kodiyala Kudubis of Kundapura region are regarded as inferior. Fuchs has rightly pointed out that "the reason for this prohibition is generally the varying degree of Hinduization. More Hinduized tribal sections consider themselves superior and refuse intermarriage with the less Hinduized tribal groups" (1973: 149). Besides the rule of endogamy, Kudubis also practise clan exogamy.

The clan is an important part of tribal organization. It is constituted by all the kinsmen of either the father's or the mother's lineage and all the offspring of one ancestor. One of the main functions of the clan is to regulate marriage relationships, as all marriages must be contracted outside the clan. The Kudubis are divided into a number of clans, known as *Balis*, which are exogamous. That is why, it may be called monometric in structure. Sturrock (1894) has pointed out that each section among Kudubis is further divided into *wargs* or exogamous sects, such as *Ambalakar, Dondikar, Kanchalikar* and *Savant*.

Anantha Krishna Iyer (1935), while discussing the typology of totems, has reported that clan totems are regarded as the most common form of totems. The names of totemistic clans are those of the prominent animals, the sun, the moon, trees and plants, which are held sacred by the people. The animal totems among Kudubis include the names of animals, birds, reptiles and fish such as rat, snake, tiger, fish, wild pig, dog, elephant, rabbit, peacock etc. The plant totems include the names of certain flowers, fruits, vegetables, trees, and their products, such as cashew, mango, arecanut, coconut, pumpkin etc., and various kinds of objects, such as basket, mist, husk, stone, cane, yoke, coconut, fish trap, comb, grass hood, etc.

There are a few clans among Kudubis which are further grouped as clusters of clans. This system resembles the unit of phratry. They call it *Hodbod,* which means big or main clan. It reveals that phratries are not uncommon among South Indian tribes.

Descent among Kudubis is patrilineal. Inheritance too is in the male line. The predominance of the male line is very strong and strictly enforced. The rules pertaining to descent and inheritance are common to all the sub-divisions, viz., *Goan, Are, Kodiyala, Jogi, Nada* and *Jati*. No significant changes have taken place in the rules governing the process of partition and inheritance. Women, though have right over their ornaments, have to give them to their husbands if demanded by them under certain circumstances.

The practice of brideprice, widow remarriage and their high participation in domestic and economic activities, such as cultivation, basket-making, sale of articles in the weekly market etc., may support the view that the status of Kudubi women is better than their non-tribal counterparts. But, due to the influence of Hinduization, in the form of taboos to be observed during menstruation, increase in dowry and restriction on widow remarriage, the status of women has severely affected.

Marriage among Kudubis is considered obligatory. It is called *Vaddig, Vardik* or *Horod.* They generally observe tribal endogamy. However, marriage between Kudubi sub-divisions is prohibited. Thus, a system of sub-tribe endogamy is also observed. In Kudubi society, monogamy is predominant; polygyny and polyandry are strictly prohibited. In the olden days, anyone practising polygamy was expelled from the tribe. However, according to Campbell (1883), it was allowed and practised among the Kudubis of Kanara district of Presidency. Premarital and extramarital relationships are not common among them. As stated earlier, they are divided into exogamous clans, known as *Balis,* which were originally totemic. *Bali* exogamy and often village exogamy are observed among various sub-divisions in Kudubi society. Similarly, as regards marriage, cross-cousin marriage is preferred. For selecting their life partners, certain specific ways, such as marriage arranged by parents (marriage by settlement), marriage by purchase, marriage by exchange, marriage by trial or test and marriage by Hindu rites, have been found among the Kudubis.

Marriage among the Kudubis cannot be celebrated without paying brideprice. The brideprice is determined on engagement day. Generally, the payment of brideprice is traditionally fixed in the form of money, gifts and articles, although, there is some variation in it. Divorce is rare since brideprice is an important aspect of the marriage contract. Like many other tribes, the girl is considered an essential working member and a potential child bearer among the Kudubis. Therefore, the loss is compensated through the payment of brideprice. Besides, the imbalanced sex ratio, i.e., lower number of females, and widespread poverty have also encouraged them to practise brideprice.

As stated above, among Kudubis, cross-cousin marriage is preferred, particularly between a boy and a daughter of his mother's brother. However, the preference for a daughter of one's father's sister is not rare among them. Though sororate is found, levirate is rare. Earlier widow remarriage was permitted among Kudubis. As Aiyappan observes, "widow remarriage is allowed, but as a custom, the widow will not marry a man of the sect to which her deceased husband belonged. Widow remarriage is not accompanied by elaborate ceremonial as in the case of that of a virgin"(1948 :11).

Religious Organization

Like many tribes of India, Kudubis practise a religion, which can be described as animism. According to Fuchs, "animism is the doctrine that inanimate objects as well as living beings are endowed with indwelling spirits of various kinds" (1973: 65). They believe that their life is controlled and guided by some sort of supernatural, spiritual and magical power. Certain elements of their religion also suggest their early totemism. In the present times, their religion has been much influenced by the religion of the Hindus living around them.

Kudubis worship both male and female deities. The head of the family worships the deity, who resides in the house. They believe that the deities may cause trouble to them and their livestock if they are annoyed. The important deities worshipped by almost all the Kudubis are Lord

Mallikarjuna and Goddess Durga, whom they call Goan deities. These deities reside in Goa and worship is offered to them every year, which clearly indicates the spread of Hinduization among the Kudubis.

Kudubis worship different deities, spirits and ghosts. They call spirits and ghosts *Bhootas*. The *Bhootas* are often offered sacrifices through various acts of witchcraft in order to get rid of troubles and diseases. The ghosts or spirits are believed to be the souls of their deceased ancestors. The important deities and spirits propitiated by Kudubis are as follows: *Beejalu Bhoota* (power of spirit in seedlings), *Aduge Bhoota* (spirit at places of cooking), *Padi Kudi Bhoota* (spirit in rice), *Kempanna* (a practice of hunting a wild pig is believed to be a worship offered to this deity—also called a God of hunting, *Jalimi* (a worship of the buffalo of the 'buffalo race' is believed to be a worship offered to this deity), *Siddadevaru, Mallikar Betedevaru* (God of hunting—normally worship offered before hunting rabbits), *Jogiboota, Ranamaru* (gigantic spirit), *Ganas* (deities which protect people from evil spirits) and *Raanboot* (forest-deity). These deities are worshipped by offering non-vegetarian food, particularly fish curry and rice or *roti* (rice bread).

Besides, propitiating and worshipping their own personal deities and spirits, they have also adopted some spirits and ghosts from local Hindus. For example, Chavandi, Dengule, Panjurli, Satyadevata, Jettiga, Mariyamma, Ammargudde, Raktheshwari, Kallukuttika, Yakshe, Jarandaya, Haiguli (Nandi-keshwara), Gadikaiboota, Gulige and Pilchendi, which are recognized as the popular deities in the pantheon cult of Dakshina Kannada district.

Besides having faith in animism, the Kudubis also practise Hinduism by venerating Hindu mythological gods like Rama, Krishna, Parvathi, Narasimha and other deities like Goddess Kali, Lord Venkateshwara of Tirupathi, Goddess Mahalasa of Goa, Siddeshwara of Kodachadri Hills, Kalabyra, Mookambika of Kollur, Manjunatha of Dharmasthala, Guru Raghavendra, Ayyappa and other local deities.

Kudubis also worship different trees and animals, which indicates dendrolatry and zoolatry among them. Lighting a lamp near the *Tulsi* plant is done by the males among Goan Kudubis. However, in other sub-divisions, it is the women who worship *Tulsi* regularly by lightening up sacred lamp.

Kudubis also venerate Nagabana (sacred grove) with Cobra idols installed in it. Such Nagabanas are found in every village in Udupi and Dakshina Kannada districts. Besides, the study on the Kudubi clans named after gods has also revealed a number of deities worshipped by them, such as *Bettalakunte* (a female Bettale deity), Devas, Jatkar (Jettiga or Lord Shiva), Sirimanki (identified with Lord Narayana or Vishnu) Shivagan etc.

Kudubis do not have a well-organized priesthood. The head of the family or the *Gurikara* acts as a priest. The *Gurikara* has two assistants, viz., *Gadya* and *Raibari*, who help him in all social and religious matters. *Gadya* is an important religious person, who acts as a witchdoctor, exorciser and astrologer for Kudubis. *Gadya* has to lead a highly disciplined life. On festivals like Holi *Gurikara* may act in the capacity of *Gadya*. However, today, under the influence of Hinduism, a few Brahmin priests are also found at the temples constructed by Kudubis.

It is hard to find animal sacrifices amongst the Kudubis since they do not eat the flesh of the animals reared in the household, except on special occasions when they give away the slaughtered animal to the neighbouring lower-caste Hindus. All the same, *mari* (Goddess of Cholera and Small Pox) is propitiated with bloody animal sacrifices amongst Jogi and Are Kudubis.

While ancestral worship can be regarded as an important form of animism, it forms an integral part of Kudubi religion and their religious beliefs. Being afraid of the spirits of the dead, they feel they are protected through the worship to the deceased. These ancestral spirits are invoked (called *Kandi, Kule* or *Jakkani)* and worshipped annually or once in two years in some parts. The death anniversary is very well marked and is called *Malakarya*, which is the corrupt form of *Mahalaya.* After taking bath and cleaning the house, the cooked rice and dishes are offered to dead ancestors. They keep cooked rice and water outside the house after offering some share to the cows. Three months after death, the dead ancestors are invoked to the house with an offering of two coconuts to their deities.

Magic has an important place in Kudubis' religious life. They believe that evil spirits may harm them if they are offended and deprived of the offerings due to them. The *Gadyas,* also called *Gadiga,* who act as magicians, witchdoctors, diviners, soothsayers and herbal medicine men, are consulted on such occasions.

The religion of Kudubi tribe is well marked by the characteristic of totemism. M.J. Herskovits observes that "totemism is a belief that a mystical relationship exists between a group of human beings who make up a kinship unit and a species of plant or animal or less commonly, some natural phenomenon" (1974: 175). The totem of Kudubis is an animal, a plant or tree or any other inanimate object. They hold these clan totems sacred. The study on Kudubi clan organization revealed that a large number of clans are totemistic. Clan totems include animal totems, plant totems, individual totems, clan deity and other inanimate object totems. Totemism with predominant inanimate totems is another significant element of Kudubi clan organization. However, next to inanimate totems, the predominance of animal totems can also be observed.

Kudubis observe different types of prenatal and childhood rituals, which are almost similar to the rituals of upper caste Hindus. The most common rituals observed among them are puberty ritual, ritual of first pregnancy, birth rituals such as childbirth, naming ceremony, ear piercing and death ritual. A pregnancy ritual is also observed similar to that of caste Hindus. It is called *Seemantha* among Kodiyala Kudubis and *Bayake* among Jogi Kudubis.

The use of *Panchanga* through Brahmin priest is also found in a few Kudubi families. M.N. Srinivas asserts: "Astrology may be regarded as a sanskritizing agent, and the more a tribe, local group, or caste resorts to astrology the more does its beliefs become sanskritized. Sanskritic Hinduism is Hinduism which transcends provincial barriers and is common to the whole of India" (1978: 75).

The festivals play an important role in the religious life of the Kudubis. Various rites, rituals, dances and festivals observed collectively bring unity and solidarity in Kudubi society. Most of the festivals celebrated by Hindus are celebrated by the Kudubis also. The prominent among them are *Holi, Vanabhojana, 'Nayejecche' (Nayejevan), Yugadi, Shivarathri, Ashada, (Ati-amavasye*-celebrated in July), *Mahalaya Amavasye.* Of all these festivals Holi is of prime importance.

Economic Organization

Kudubis have a mixed economy. Like many Indian tribes, the economic life of Kudubis is characterized by agriculture, hunting, food gathering, animal husbandry, handicrafts etc. Traditionally, Kudubis were forest dwellers. Forest has been a source of livelihood for them for a long time. They collected minor forest products like fruits, roots, herbs etc. It also provided them wood, bamboo, fruits, roots, leaves, tubers, lac, wax, bark, fibre, creepers, flowers, honey, medicinal herbs etc. Thus, the forest served as a major source of livelihood for the Kudubis. They derived their economic goods and other requirements from the forest around them by way of shifting cultivation and food gathering. The forest also provided them materials such as fuelwood, agricultural implements, housing materials, materials for musical instruments etc. Kudubis also used to hunt animals in the forest.

Initially, some of the Kudubis were shifting cultivators and this cultivation was known as *kumri*. Thurston reports: "the main occupation of Kudubis is shifting (Kumri) cultivation. Some however are employed in the preparation of *Cutch* (Catechu) from the wood of *Acacia Catechu*" (1909: 102). Of late, the Kudubis are slowly alienated from the forest and settled in hilly and plain regions in the villages. They have transformed from the food gathering stage to settled agricultural stage.

Among Kudubis, particularly of Kodiyala sub-division, selling medicinal herbs is an important occupation. Many among Kudubis also live as traditional medicine men. The herbs, roots, bark, stems of different medicinal plants and tress collected by men are sold, after drying, usually by their women in the market.

Hunting and fishing, though they cannot be regarded as their main occupations now, do supplement their food to some extent. Hunting is known as *bowndi* in their dialect. Kudubis everywhere are recognized as experts in hunting. Their skill of locating and shooting an animal is great. Their hunting weapons and implements include spears, axe, rope, nets, sticks etc. They use nets and sticks to trap hares. They catch birds by using indigenous ropes. They use both nets and bamboo or wooden sticks of different sizes to trap wild pigs.

Besides hunting, the Kudubis participate in fishing operations. However, fishing is usually done by households independently. Moreover, it is not a regular means of livelihood for Kudubis. People participate in fishing activities in the nearby rivers and streams particularly during rainy seasons. The trap used for fishing is named as *Guli* (a bamboo trap), nets made of fibre for catching fish and crab. They use variety of nets in different sizes depending upon the size and quantity of fish. Creepers and fibres are used for making fishing nets.

In the past Kudubis were engaged in different types of crafts such as wooden chappal-making (out of bark), *kalembi*-making (used for storing articles), making raincoats from leaves and strips of creepers and bamboo, *kalese*-making (a boat shaped wooden material used for drawing water from the pond) etc. But these primitive crafts have perished today.

Mat-making is entirely a woman's job among Kudubis. However, both men and women collect raw materials for making mats. Basket work consists of bamboo and creeper baskets of various sizes and shapes, like cylindrical shaped baskets used for carrying dry leaves from the hills or forests to the house, large circular baskets used for carrying manure to the field or for carrying other articles, and small baskets for storing grains, roots and other edibles. They also make ladle, cradle, tray, sieve from bamboo strips and creepers collected from the forest. The finished goods are sold either to their own people in the village or non-tribes in weekly markets.

The Kudubis settled in hilly and plain regions are engaged in agriculture as tenants or landowners. The data on possession of land reveal that majority (90%) of them possess land which includes both wet (arable and cultivable) and dry (non-arable) land. It is observed that the implementation of Land Reforms Act of 1961 in Karnataka has enabled many Kudubi tenants to acquire land from their masters. A few of them were given a small plot of land for cultivation by their landlords to avoid filing of declaration for the entire land under cultivation. In some other places, the Kudubis could not get land under Land Reforms Act from their landlords owing to fear of landlords, illiteracy and extreme poverty.

Kudubis are hard working and skilled in agricultural operations. All those who have become settled agriculturists are predominantly dependent on plough cultivation. Their common agricultural crops are paddy and pulses. The pulses generally include black gram, horse gram, green gram etc. They also grow sweet potatoes *(Ipemoea batatas), Kyane* or wild elephant yam *(Amorphophallus paeoniifulius),* taro *(Colocasia esculenta), kanaki (bamboo)* and Indian spinach (*Basella rubra*). Recently, certain cash crops like sugarcane, turmeric, chilies, ginger, coconut, and areca nut are also grown in some villages.

It is observed that in almost every village there is an acute problem of water, both for drinking and agricultural purposes. Their farm operations thus depend on the monsoon. However, some use well water or nearby rivers or ponds. Consequently, the income from such agricultural practices is highly uncertain. C.B. Damle opines that excessive dependence on rains and the use of primitive agricultural implements are the causes for low income from agriculture in Dakshina Kannada district (1989: 61).

Further, there is a direct relationship between the practice of settled agriculture and domestication of cattle. Rearing and keeping livestock is a part of Kudubi economy. Almost every house has livestock. Domestication of cattle, particularly cows, helps them in getting organic manure and milk. Kudubis are good breeders of he-buffaloes. Well-reared and good quality he-buffaloes are used for the buffalo races, which is one of the important tournaments of this district conducted after the first crop. Bullocks are used for agricultural operations like ploughing and manuring. However, it is observed in many poor families the domestic animals are poorly kept. Majority of them are not aware of the financial assistance and subsidy for the purchase of livestock.

Kudubis use earthen pots and bowls for cooking. Earthen utensils are also used for storage. These earthen pots are made by the local potters. They have begun using aluminium utensils, bowls for cooking, stainless steel tumblers, plates, spoons, plastic mugs, wooden and iron chairs, tables, benches, transistors, radios, pumpsets etc. Certain wooden articles are also used for storage. Earthen pitchers and iron or plastic buckets are used for carrying water from the well or pond. They also possess pitchers of different sizes for storing water in the house. Almost all houses possess grinding stone. It is usually kept in the open verandah. Since electricity has not reached majority of their houses, they use open kerosene tin lamps for keeping the house lighted after it gets dark.

Majority of the Kudubis (94%) live in their own houses while remaining 6 per cent live in rented houses. It is observed that even landless tenants have constructed their own houses in their master's land and rest of them in barren unirrigated government land. Though most of the Kudubis own houses, most houses are sub-standard and poorly constructed. Among these only two (1%) have RCC houses, 49 per cent have tile-roofed houses and the remaining have thatched houses. Their poor economic condition is reflected from the facts that only 21 per cent houses are electrified and 94 per cent of them depend on firewood for cooking. Their annual family income is Rs 9,262 which further indicates their poor economic status.

Political Organization

Kudubis have a governing body or a council within their community, which is called by different names such as *Vodow, Vadi, Valya, Valthule, Kudukattu* etc. The term *Vodow* appears to be the most common. A *Vodow* is constituted by several *Kutumbos* (lineages), *Balis* (clans) and families of both joint and nuclear types. *Vodow* usually functions at the village level and very rarely it may include a group of villages. Generally, each *Vodow* consists of families ranging from 10 to 250. There are about 40 *Vodows* among Kudubis functioning at present in different villages throughout the districts of Dakshina Kannada and Udupi. The elder male member of each *Kutumbo* functions as a representative of *Vodow.*

Each *Vodow* has a headman or chieftain called *Gurikara* whose office is hereditary. In case there is no direct male descendent for the office of *Gurikara,* the new successor is chosen from amongst his agnates. Sturrock has stated that "in every village where these Kudubis dwell, there is a headman called *Gowda* who has authority to enquire into their tribal disputes and to impose and levy fines according to the gravity of the offence" (1894: 178). The *Gurikara* regulates all internal relationships within the *Vodow.* He represents the rudimentary organization of justice.

There are two subordinates under *Gurikara,* viz., *Raibari* and *Gadya,* who assist in all social and religious matters. The presence of *Gurikara* at every Kudubi marriage, within his jurisdiction, is very essential. Besides, his presence is also necessary during a funeral ritual in his *Vodow.* If *Gurikara* is not able to attend such rituals for some reason, then the *Raibari* attends, as a representative of *Gurikara. Gurikara* also leads hunting expeditions organized by the members of his *Vodow.* He also usually leads the touring dance troupe on the occasion of Holi festival.

The *Vodow* is constituted for controlling and directing the behaviour and activities of its members. Kudubi life is generally governed by religion, customs and traditions. The function of *Vodow* is not to formulate laws and regulations but to see that their religious rites, customs, traditions, festivals and rituals are followed. Mann has asserted, "systems of social control in tribal societies vary from simple to complex ones. It varies from hamlet leadership to chieftainship and from village council to regional one. The decision-making processes vary. But, certain common elements do underline various kinds of councils and the way the conflicting matters are resolved. Such elements are in the form of sanctions, mostly having religious roots" (1984: 263).

There are variations in punishments imposed on the offenders. In case of adultery, an offender will be expelled from the *Vodow* after which he and the members of his family will not be invited for any function arranged by the *Vodow.* However, these days, it is not taken so seriously. If a man indulges in adultery, he is not excommunicated; instead, he receives equal respect like others. But, if a woman indulges in such an act, it is considered a heinous act and she is excommunicated and expelled from her house. She is not allowed to participate in any of the activities relating to *Vodow.* In the case of inter-caste or inter-tribal marriages, the culprits, whether male or female, are also excommunicated resulting in the loss of their position as members of their community.

Consuming prohibited food, particularly flesh of fowl, using bazaar meat or eating cooked food at the hands of other tribes and castes except Brahmins is regarded as an offence and the culprit is fined for such violations of traditional rules of food. Such violators are also seriously criticized by the members of *Vodow*. Selling meat of an animal, hunted from the jungle, is also regarded as an offence. If anyone violates this rule, enquiry is made immediately and fine or punishment is decided in the meeting.

All the members of *Vodow* are expected to participate in the Holi festival, dance and other allied activities. Their non-participation in these occasions is taken seriously and such cases are referred to the *Kudukattu*. The absentee has to state the reason for his/her absence before the *Gurikara* who punishes the offenders. A fine (*kanike*), in the form of coconut, will have to be offered to *Kudukattu* at the meeting itself. The coconut is later used for the feast during Holi festival. Many a time, the person committing an offence has to arrange a feast for all the members of *Vodow*.

While awarding punishments, different types of evidences are called for in deciding cases, particularly criminal cases. The offender has to take an oath in the name of Goan deity during a criminal trial. All disputes and problems are decided and settled in the meeting at the *Gurikara's* house. The nature of the offence will have to be brought to the notice of *Vodow* and a meeting of three prominent local leaders is held and the offender is fined. The fine ranges from Rs 10 to Rs 20. The fine is offered to God and then used for the expenses of Holi festival. For any type of offence, if an offender tells a lie, it is believed that the anger of God will punish him/her within three years. They also strongly believe that a culprit will come and submit the facts before *Gurikara* if he/she experiences any trouble or problem whatsoever.

The behaviour and activities of the members of the group are regulated not only through the method of punishments but also by praising and rewarding right conduct and involvement in the day-to-day affairs of the group. A person continues to retain his membership in the *Vodow* is treated with special respect. Similarly, a person who knows their traditional dance forms, viz., *Gumte, Toni* and *Dorinach,* is accorded great respect in the community. On the contrary, those who have severed relationship with *Vodow,* or have been expelled from it, do not receive any respect in their society.

In the modern Kudubi society, a few enlightened and educated Kudubis have formed new organizations at different villages with different names, similar to the new organizations formed by different caste groups among the Hindus. Some of these organizations are: Dakshina Kannada Jilla Kudubi Samaja Seva Sangha (Regd.), Sri Rama Kudubi Samaja Seva, Kudubi Samaja Seva Sangha, Vivekananda Kudubi Samaja Seva Sangha, Kudubi Samajoddaraka and Kudubi Jananga Shreyobivriddi Sangha. In 2008, some of the Kudubi Seva Sanghas got together and formed a Federation of Kudubi Sanghas. The political awareness of the Kudubis is restricted to voting in general elections.

A Case for Reservation

Kudubis are not recognized as STs in Karnataka although they are a district ethnic group having their own indigenous identity. They are the aboriginal stocks of Goa. Having settled down in coastal Karnataka, its neighbouring areas and some parts of Kerala and Maharashtra, Kudubis have established themselves as an important tribe in South India.

While Stephen Fuchs (1973) calls Kudubis as one of the food gathering tribes of South India, Havanur (1975) reported that they are a hill tribe living in isolation in the forests. Various social anthropologists, historians, ethnographers and editors of District Gazetteers like Olivinho J.F. Gomes (1987), Ananta Krishna Iyer (1928), P. Gururaja Bhatta (1963), Thurston (1909), Sturrock (1895) and Abhishankar (1973), in their studies and reports, describe Kudubis variously as 'hunting tribes', 'interesting tribes', 'shifting-cultivating forest tribe', 'landless labourers of aboriginal stock', etc. James M. Cambell (1883) calls them as 'Konkan Kudubis' and this name is supported by the relation which they maintain with the Kudubis of south-west Goa. They live in huts in isolated villages near forests. Aiyappan (1948), in the report on the socio-economic conditions of the aboriginal tribes in the province of Madras, included Kudubis in the list of tribes of South Kanara along with other tribes, viz., Male Kudias, Koragas and Maratis. Further, it is interesting to note that from 1941 to 1956, i.e., till the reorganization of states on linguistic basis, the Kudubis were included in the category of 'Scheduled Castes' in Madras province under the Madras Provincial and Subordinate Services Record (1941, Rule 3, Part II: 183) and Madras State and Subordinate Services Schedule II (1941, Part A, Rule 2: 61).

Economically, Kududis are the most backward. They are one of the weaker sections leading a hard and miserable life. Earlier, Kududis were living a nomadic life. The shifting cultivation, which was widely practised among them, was uneconomic and wasteful. When they migrated from Goa and settled down in coastal Karnataka, they largely occupied the forest regions and lived in almost isolation for a long time. They were also employed in the cashew plantations in the forest regions. Today, they are settled agriculturists. However, the method adopted for agricultural operations is primitive. The agricultural income is also supplemented by handicrafts, hunting, selling of dried medical leaves and roots etc. They also work as labourers on farms, construction workers or seasonal workers. A few landless Kududis even work as servants or labourers for high caste landlords. Some Kududi families have also adopted beedi rolling as a source of livelihood. Owing to poverty, many women also work as domestic servants, farm labourers, sellers, coolies etc., outside home, which has affected their traditional basket and mat weaving works.

It is observed today that a large number of Kududis own land, which they got under land reforms programmes. However, they suffer from lack of irrigational facilities. Today, most of them depend on primary sector of agriculture including cattle breeding and it is very difficult for them to earn their livelihood from agriculture exclusively due to several problems. In their villages and settlements, the opportunities for employment in other sectors are limited. Besides the use of liquor, smoking, age-old practices, food taboos, heavy expenses on festivities, particularly 'Holi' and marriage celebrations, ignorance, poverty, superstition, illiteracy etc., are also contributing to their socio-economic backwardness. Though a few of them could have better earnings today, they do not have saving habits. On account of miserable conditions and lack of specialized skills, Kududis are incapable of getting easy employment. The increasing amount of brideprice and the practice of dowry system also have an adverse effect on the economy of the Kududis. In order to improve their living conditions, certain developmental programmes have been started by local banks, cooperative sector and other organizations in some Kududis settlements and villages in Udupi taluk. These have however not been extended to other areas of Udupi and Dakshina Kannada district. Moreover, the government, banks and voluntary organizations have not launched any programmes so far in developing entrepreneurship among Kududis.

The process of political development is also very slow in the Kududi society. Although a few new organizations, similar to those of Hindu caste organizations, have been formed in different villages in different names, they are not functioning effectively due to lack of leadership and motivation, absence of proper education and financial constraints. They are slowly becoming politically conscious and organized. The study reveals that, though majority of Kududis are aware of different governmental programmes, some of them still are not aware of their needs, problems and the reasons for their backwardness. Thus, there is a need to develop local leadership among them and also consceintizing them.

Educationally, Kududis are backward. Poverty, lack of motivation and encouragement, depressing home/environmental conditions, non-availability of reservation facility etc., are the prime causes of their educational backwardness. On account of these factors, a significant majority of the Kududi children drop out from the schools at an early stage and almost revert to illiteracy. The study on the parental aspirations for children's education reveals that, though the outlook of the members of the Kududi tribe with regard to education is changing, their aspirations for their children's education are not high. Ill-health has been one of the major problems among the Kududis. The study shows that there are some who suffer from fatal diseases caused by unhygienic living conditions. Lack of access to clean water, malnutrition and consumption of alcohol have affected the health of many Kududis and caused certain infectious diseases. It is observed that the number of people suffering from tuberculosis is more among the Kududis than among other caste and religious groups in their villages. A large number of Kudubis today consult both religious specialists and modern doctors for the treatment of diseases and believe that the diseases are mainly due to the influence of supernatural elements and evil spirits. Thus, there is a need to make Kududis aware of the importance of education, health and hygiene, and nutrition. There is also a need to motivate and sensitize Kududi children to go to schools regularly.

The views and supporting evidences provided by various scholars, ethnographers, sociologists, historians, anthropologists and the findings of the empirical study conducted by this author prove that the Kududis are the most backward and weakest group found in Karnataka state. They deserve constitutional benefits and safeguards by including them in the category of ST. On this basis, this paper argues that today the Kudubis of Karnataka is a strong case for reservation.

Though Kudubis have been left out from ST position at the transitional stage of reorganization of states. The earlier Governor of Karnataka had realized and was convinced that there is a need to designate Kudubis as ST. Various political leaders, present and earlier, scholars and writers express their views in favour of including them in the category of STs. The Kudubis in Karnataka are still struggling and mobilizing for recognition as ST, whereas the Kudubis of Goa achieved this status recently after struggling for years. However, this has created a regional inequality and confusion due to error in this kind of scheduling process.

Conclusion

The development of tribals and their mainstreaming like any other deprived section of the society has been accepted as an important postulate of the state policy. Tribals have to be integrated into a common whole, where all diverse cultures of the country, along with various populations and geographical regions, are brought together in a secular and democratic set-up provided by its constitution.

The study shows the extreme backwardness of Kudubis—both economically and educationally. Their average annual family income indicates their economic status below the poverty line. The deficiency in their economy is mainly due to lack of education, lack of knowledge about modern agricultural methods and partly due to possession of non-cultivable dry land and more significantly non-availability of benefits extended to STs. Today, poverty, ignorance, superstitions, illiteracy and ill-health are the major problems among Kudubis along with the non-recognition as ST. The struggle of Kudubis for recognition in Karnataka is not as severe as the struggle by Santals in Assam. Earlier this author (2006) had proposed this as a form of tribal movement, viz., "Movement for Constitutional Recognition or Scheduled Tribe Status" and preferred to designate this phenomenon as a 'new tribal movement' operating both in North and South India. The paper reveals that the Kudubis are in the state of transition as well as turmoil. In the changing situations, there is need to preserve some of their indigenous rituals and practices which are positive and healthy and change those that are detrimental through decisive and planned action. The paper also suggests that there is an urgent need on the part of policy makers, administrators and NGOs to pay immediate attention and initiate suitable remedial measures for the welfare and development of Kudubis by extending them the recognition as ST.

REFERENCES

Bhatt, Gururaja P. 1963. *Tulunadu*. Udupi: Bhavyavani Publications.

Damle, C.B. 1989. Land Reforms and Changing Agrarian Relations in Dakshina Kannada District. Ph.D. Thesis, Department of Sociology, University of Poona.

Desai, A.R. 1977. "Tribes in Transition", in Ramesh Thapar (ed.). *Tribe, Caste and Religion in India*. Delhi: Macmillan India Ltd.

Elwin, Verrier. 1943. *The Aboriginals*. Bombay: Oxford University Press.

Fuchs, Stephen. 1973. *The Aboriginal Tribes of India*. Delhi: MacMillan.

Gomes, Olivino J.F. 1987. *Village Goa* (A Study of Goan Social Structure and Change). New Delhi: S. Chand & Co.

Government of Karnataka. 1973. South Kanara District Gazetteer. Bangalore: Government Press.

——. 1975 and 1986. Report of the Second Karnataka Backward Classes Commission. Vol. II (Population and Education), Bangalore: Government Press.

Government of India. 1952. Report of the Commissioner for Scheduled Caste and Tribes. New Delhi.

Government of Bombay. 1883. Gazetteer of the Bombay Presidency, Kanara District. Vol. XV, Part I, James M. Campbell (ed.), Bombay: Government Central Press.

Government of Madras. 1948. Report of the Socio-Economic Conditions of the Aboriginal Tribes in the Province of Madras. by A. Aiyappan, Secretary, Aboriginal Tribes Welfare Enquiry Committee. Madras: Government Press.

——. 1894. Madras District Manuals, South Canara. Vol. I (Compiled by J. Sturrock) Madras: Government Press.

——. 1941. Madras Provincial and Subordinate Services. Rule 3, Part II, p. 183, Madras: Government Press.

——. 1941. Madras Provincial Schedule II. Part A, Rule 2, p. 61, Madras: Government Press.

Ghurye, G.S. 1963. *The Mahadev Kolis (A Scheduled Tribe)*. Bombay: Popular Prakashan.

Herskovits, Melville J. 1974. *Cultural Anthropology*. New Delhi: Oxford & IBH.

Hutton, J.H. 1980 (Reprinted). *Caste in India*. Bombay: Oxford.

Iyer, Anantha Krishna L.K. 1935. *The Mysore Tribals and Castes*. Vol. 1, Mysore: The University of Mysore.

Kankar, Pratap Singh Velip. 2006. *The Kurmis: Kurmis of India*. Margoa: Pritam Prakashan.

Mann R.S. 1984. *Anthropological and Sociological Theory: Approaches and Applications*. Jaipur: Rawat Publications.

Majumdar, D.N. 1968. *Races and Cultures of India*. Bombay: Asia.

Mascarenhas, Antonio. 1987. *"The Kudubis" Goa from Pre-Historic Times*. Vasco, pp. 20–29.

Nanjundayya and Iyre. 1928, *The Mysore Tribes And Castes*. Vol. II, The University of Mysore.

Peer, Mohammed and Heggade, O.D. 1992. Tribal Development Programmes: A Case Study of Karnataka. An Evaluation Report Submitted to the Government of India, Dept. of Sociology, Mangalore University.

Rao, Ravindranath Y. 2003. *Tribal Tradition and Change: A Study of Kudubis of South India*. Mangalore: Mangala Publications.

——. 2006. Trends in Tribal Movements in North and South India: A Comparative Analysis. XIV World Congress, Durban (S. Africa): ISA and Kwazulu Natal University.

Risley, H. 1908. *The People of India*. Calcutta: Secretariat Press.

Srinivas, M.N. 1978 (Reprinted). *Religion and Society among the Coorgs of South India*. London: J.K. Publishers.

Thakkar, A.V. 1941. *The Problem of Aborigines in India*. Poona: Gokhale Institute.

Thurston, Edger. 1909. *Caste and Tribes of South India*. Vol. I to VII, Madras: Government Press.

Vidyarthi, L.P. and Rai, B.K. 1977. *The Tribal Culture of India*. Delhi: Concept.

16

Caste, Religion and Social Exclusion

VINAY RAJATH D.

Social inequality is the fact of social life. In every society, based on the possession of social, economic and political advantages, and physical and psychological capacities and attributes, individuals and groups of individuals are conceived as higher or lower and superior or inferior. In line with this system of inequality, Indian society is stratified on the basis of caste, religion, language, culture, race, wealth and so on. However, caste has been the typical and most prominent system that arranges groups in terms of high and low statuses. The concept of purity and pollution is central to the idea of caste and this principle is so pervasive that not only individuals are ranked higher or lower but also occupations, food and such other objects. This peculiar character of caste and its other characteristics have drawn the attention of a large number of scholars both from India and abroad.

Social exclusion and discrimination are the direct consequences of the practice of caste. In the sense, in its rigidity, certain sections or castes are systematically excluded from the privileges and life chances. Caste system from the beginning has excluded the lower sections of society, i.e., the Shudras and the untouchables, commonly referred as Dalits today, from most of the benefits and privileges that a normal citizen would deserve. The system of religious beliefs justified the existing inequality and exploitation and convinced people the conditions of life they were living was the right one which they received through the doctrine of *karma*. Among the many theories of the origin of caste, the Divine Origin Theory or Religious Theory is important as it justifies the interplay between caste, religion and social exclusion.

Social Exclusion

The concept of social exclusion characterizes contemporary forms of social disadvantages. The concept relates to the processes wherein entire communities are systematically blocked from rights, opportunities, resources and necessities as housing, employment, health care, civic engagement, democratic participation, etc. that are normally available to an average citizen, and which are important for social integration. The concept of social exclusion has been defined as "the process through which individuals or groups are wholly or partially excluded from full participation in the society within which they live. In this sense, it is the opposite of social integration" (Haan, 1999). The concept is also related to the concepts of alienation, separation, deprivation and even refers to disenfranchisement of certain people within a society. Social exclusion is often related to a person's social class, educational status and living standards and the access to various opportunities. It is sometimes perceived as the inability of the society to provide the individuals and groups the rewards or to realize their full potential.

To be socially excluded is to be deprived from social recognition and social value. In the sphere of politics, social recognition is obtained by full citizenship; in the economic sphere, it means being paid enough to be able to participate fully in the life of the community. Social exclusion is the result of lack of social integration of some sections of society due to poverty, professional exclusion or marginalization, social and civic disenfranchisement, absence or weakening of support networks and frequent inter-cultural conflicts. In turn, it may result in crime, social movements, agitations, etc. As a result, the disadvantaged minority groups may face arrests, convictions and imprisonment.

The consequences of social exclusion involve the denial of access to resources, civil and other rights and common facilities or benefits that others have. It certainly impoverishes the lives of individuals from excluded groups. From the human rights perspective, it essentially means the denial of certain basic human rights, that is, rights to freedom, equality and dignity. The consequences of exclusion, however, depend crucially on how institutions function and how exclusionary and discriminatory they are (Thorat et al., 2009: 2–3).

Social Exclusion in Indian Society

Social exclusion and isolation is a unique feature of Indian society, particularly Hindu society. Exclusion here involves social processes that exclude, discriminate, isolate and deprive some groups on the basis of caste, ethnicity and religion. These excluded groups include former untouchables or Dalits, *Adivasis* and some religious minorities. Although these social groups experienced exclusion and isolation that caused deprivation and poverty, there are differences in sources and process of deprivation. The source of poverty among these groups is rooted not only in the economic structure but in the process of social exclusion as well.

The Dalits suffered grievously from exclusion and discrimination in economic and social spheres based on caste and untouchability. Traditionally, they were excluded from access to property rights, economic rights, civil, religious and other rights. Disabilities of untouchables became more severe as they were also physically and socially segregated from the rest of the Hindu society through the institution of untouchability. It is this institutionalized, comprehensive and multiple exclusion of the Dalits that has a severe consequence on their deprivation.

Exclusion in political participation and in governance affects the capacity of the excluded group to use the political institutions and the state apparatus to their advantage. Our vision of strong and developed India has to be measured not only in terms of raising income but also and more so to what extent the excluded groups also have an equal share in the increased income. Similarly, the strength of the political parties needs to be measured not only in terms of number of seats in legislature alone but by the share of excluded groups. And, the success of governance will have to be measured by the extent the excluded groups participate in decision-making and administration.

In India caste is so pervasive that it has entered the boundaries of other religions too. Hindu religion, the foundation of which rests on caste structures, provides a religious explanation to caste differentiation and justifies it through Vedic principles.

Caste Exclusion in Christian Community

Caste, according to Dumont (1970), can be understood in the light of an ideology of purity and pollution forming the basis of an emphatic distinction between power and status. This ideology is inherently Hindu and cannot be expounded without constant reference to Hindu beliefs. However, in India, we find the non-Hindu groups also, which operate as castes while rejecting the Hindu beliefs at the same time. For example, Forrester (1980) points out that in Kerala, the Syrian Christian community operates very much as a caste-like group in relation to other communities around. But among themselves they do not observe the Hindu rules of pollution, and have in their belief system no real justification for regarding some people as inherently pure and others as inherently polluting. Therefore, a non-Hindu group is also treated as a caste though rejecting the ideology of caste.

Christianity that believes in the fatherhood of God and brotherhood of mankind dogmatically denounces inequality in any form. However, in some parts of India, it is the fact that the Christians are stratified by sects, locations and the castes of their predecessors. This is specially noticed among Catholics. In this regard, many Dalit Catholics have spoken out against discrimination against them by the Catholic Church, specially in the south. According to *Wikipedia Encyclopedia,* in India, more than 70 per cent of Catholics/Christians are Dalits, but the higher caste Catholics (30% estimated) control 90 per cent of the churches' administrative jobs. Out of the 156 Catholic Bishops, only six are from the lower castes. Although Dalits form the majority in all these churches, their influence is minimal or even insignificant. Their presence is totally eclipsed by the power of the upper castes. This is all the more true in the case of the Catholic churches where such discrimination is strongly felt.

In Goa, during the Portuguese rule in 16th century, the Hindu converts retained their caste practices and continued practising the caste system. There was no deliberate effort to do away with the caste system. The original Hindu Brahmins in Goa became Christian Bammon and the Kshatriyas became Christian noblemen called Chardos. The Christian clergy became almost exclusively Bammon. Likewise, the Vaishyas converted to Christianity became Gauddo and the Shudras, Sudir. The Dalits or untouchables converted to Christianity became Maharas and Chamers. Thus, the caste system was effectively mapped into Catholic society in the region.

In Kerala, the Syrian Christians derive their high caste status from the tradition that they were converted from Namboodiri caste. The converts from the fisher-folk community are attributed to a lower status. The Syrian Christians tend to be endogamous and not to intermarry with other Christian castes. The intermarriage between Latin-Rite Christians and new Christians, converted in 16th and 19th centuries respectively, is very rare.

Churches in India were largely controlled by upper caste Catholic priests and nuns. Lower-caste/Dalit Catholics were discriminated against by upper-caste Catholics. There are instances of separate seats, communion cups, burial grounds and churches for lower-caste Catholics. Dalit boys were not allowed to be altar boys or lectors. Very few Catholic Dalits are in the administrative services of churches.

Many low castes among Hindus were attracted to Christianity, especially in Tamil Nadu and Kerala, due to the egalitarian principles; hence, they got themselves converted to Christian faith. However, conversion to Christianity did not redeem Dalit Christians from social discrimination and untouchability. It has only added to their misery. Conversion disqualifies a Dalit Christian to a whole lot of constitutionally guaranteed protection and privileges. The Dalits accepted the new faith with some hope that they would regain their lost humanity and they would be considered as human beings. But, in reality, it was only a dream. They continued to suffer and live all human misery both in the society and in the church.

A Dalit sociologist, Antony Raj (1992), reports discrimination against Dalits within the churches in Tamil Nadu. The study reports the following discriminatory practices:

- Construction of two separate chapels, one for non-Dalits and the other for the Dalits. In some parishes liturgical services are conducted separately.
- Separate seating arrangements within the same chapel. Even if there are benches or chairs, Dalits are required only to be seated on the floor.
- The existence of two separate cemeteries and two separate hearses to carry the dead.
- The operation of two separate queues to receive the communion. In some places, Dalits are required to receive communion only after the non-Dalits.
- Dalit boys are not allowed to be altar boys and lectors at the sacred liturgy.
- Non-Dalits restrict the Corpus Christi procession, Palm Sunday procession and other processions to the limits of their streets.
- Dalits are not invited to participate in the ceremony of washing of feet on Monday and Thursday.
- For fear of claiming equal participation in the celebration of the feast of the parish patron saint, Parish Councils decide not to collect financial contribution from Dalits.
- The feast of the village patron saint is celebrated separately.

The Dalit Christians suffer the same socio-educational and economic disabilities like the Dalits of other faiths. The change of religion does not change their social, economical and educational status. It is evident that the Dalit Christians are subject to atrocities, violence and disabilities solely because they suffer the stigma of the untouchability. Most of the Dalits, whether they are Hindus or Christians, often live together side by side, while the other caste people live separately. The upper-caste Christians do not treat the Dalit Christians as equals. Though the Dalit Christians undergo the same unjust caste discrimination as Dalits in other religions, the Christian Dalits are deprived of the privileges of Protection of Civil Rights Act and Prevention of Atrocities Act, 1989. The Indian Constitution grants to the President of India power to designate certain disadvantaged groups referred to as the 'Scheduled Castes', who are now to receive special rights to compensate for the disadvantages they have been suffering in the past. The Indian government has refused to include Christian Dalits in the list of the Scheduled Castes, thus denying the rights that are appropriate to them under the Constitution. This way the Dalit Christians are twice discriminated both by the state and the church. The politicians have made sweet-coated promises to the Dalit Christians in order to win their votes, but once in power, they have turned their back. On the whole, the resultant social position exhibits economic deprivation, educational discrimination and powerlessness.

Roman Catholic missions in India, from the beginning, appear to have regarded the caste system as the given social structure of Indian society. Within this structure evangelization was carried out without detaching from social context of individuals or of whole caste groups. Therefore, Christianity in general and Catholics in particular can be seen as neither threatening nor undermining the caste system. But, rather working within it and accommodating to the norms of caste.

The Christian theology in general affirms egalitarian values and does not recognize or accept the principle of caste as it is practised in India. The Bible so emphatically puts across the ideology of equality in the spirit of Catholicism, i.e., the fatherhood in God and brotherhood of fellow Christians. The message 'love one another' is all-pervasive in different verses of the Bible. Even the later Christian writings also emphasize this oneness and unity, and teaches the obligation to love one another. It directs to live a life controlled by love. On the whole, the Christian teachings do not justify any inequality or discrimination, especially in line with ethnic origin. But, in Indian context, the egalitarian aspect of Christianity did not seem to have much immediate effect on the way of life of people who got converted to Christianity. The ethnic identity seems to be cutting across the ideology of equality as we observe the caste-like groups among the Catholics. Therefore, the practice of caste in social life continued among the Catholics also even after their conversion.

Caste among Roman Catholics: A Case of Catholics of Coastal Karnataka

Overtly, the Roman Catholic community of coastal Karnataka appears to be a homogeneous community. In economic standards, they are rather comfortable, especially those living in urban centres. Some are basically rich due to their ancestral land holdings and a sizeable population has created a neo-rich class due to their Gulf earnings. However, a vast majority of the Catholic population living in rural belt is poor.

The Catholics of coastal Karnataka belong to a major division of Christianity—Roman Catholics. They follow the Latin-Rite Roman Catholicism. The study was conducted in the diocese of Mangalore which covers Dakshina Kannada and Udupi districts of Karnataka and Kasargod district of Kerala. The Catholic community is visible because it is numerically significant as it constitutes about 8 per cent of the population of the diocese area with its numerical schools and educational institutions.

In coastal Karnataka the Konkani-speaking Roman Catholics are treated as a single *jati* or caste group. But actually they are not a monolithic block. They have internal divisions which they call in Konkani either *zath* (from *jati* in Sanskrit) or *kuli* (from *kula* in Sanskrit). Therefore, in spite of considering them one *jati*, all the Roman Catholics of coastal Karnataka do not constitute a single compact group as far as ethnic feeling is concerned. Instead, they kept up the same caste-like divisions that they had in Goa, before their conversion. There are historical evidences and reasons to believe that the ancestors of the greater section of present Catholic population of coastal Karnataka migrated from Goa; the chief *zaths* among Catholics of coastal Karnataka are Bammon, Charodi, Sudir and Gowdi. There are other sub-castes but they still can be included in these four groupings. Catholics belonging to these different castes are spread over the whole area. Even today, the Catholic community with its different caste-like groups still makes efforts to cling on to the age-old customs based on caste differences.

Although there are many similarities between the castes among Hindus and the castes among Catholics, a major difference is that there is no association between caste and occupation among the catholics as is in the case of Hindus. Certain castes continued their traditional occupation but no definite occupation was assigned to a particular caste group after their conversion. For example, Catholic Bammon does not constitute a priestly caste since priesthood among Catholics is a matter of 'vocation' or 'calling'. There are Bammon among cultivators, agricultural labourers, traders, masons and cooks, while there are Sudir or Gowdi also among the cultivators, traders and agricultural labourers.

Caste among Konkani Catholics

The study (Rajath, 2000) identifies the following important caste groups among Catholics of coastal Karnataka:

1. *Bammon:* Bammon, tracing their origin from Goa, are the converts to Catholicism from the Brahmin community of Shenvi. For various reasons like wars and inquisition they migrated to coastal Karnataka (then known as Canara). Some still retain their old surnames like Prabhu, Pai, Kamath, Nayak, Shenvi, etc. Even today, we find similarities between the Bammon and the Gaud Saraswath Brahmins in respect of language, marriage practices and other cultural practices. Traditionally, the Bammon did not accept food from others, and endogamy was strictly practised. On special occasions like weddings, the lower caste Catholics were served food along with Bammon but not in parallel rows, but at right angle rows, to mark the caste differentiation.

2. *Charodi:* Charodi are generally believed to have converted from the Hindu Kshatriya caste. According to George Moreas, Charodi are the descendants of Kshatriya caste converted to Christianity (Saldanha, 1938). At the same time, there are scholars who hold the view that they were converted from Brahmin community but from different region and therefore they derive a different name. According to D'Souza (1983), the Charodi are the descendants of the migrants from Karad (Maharashtra). Originally, they are of Brahmin stock but termed as Karadis (from Karad). However, the Portuguese spelt it as 'charadi' since there is no use of 'K' in Portuguese and pronounced as 'tcharadi' or 'tsaradi' which eventually came to be Charodi. Therefore, the Bammon and Charodi fight for supremacy in social status ranking. Actually, Charodi is also a dominant section in Catholic community in some areas, while in other areas they just make their significance felt.

3. *Sudir/Sudra:* Sudir have a visible lower socio-economic status compared to the other two castes, viz., Bammon and Charodi. Sudir were

workers and agricultural labourers and were also engaged in the service professions. Generally, all craftsmen came under the title 'Sudir' and none of them belonged to the class of landlords. They were also treated as an inferior class. They are not a single group but comprise of several sub-groups, which were mostly endogamous and based on occupation. For example, *sonar* (goldsmith), *kamar* (blacksmith), *sutar* (carpenter) *pidrer* (mason), *kumbar* (potter), *ghannekar* (oil presser), *mhali* (gardener), *alfiad* (tailor), *kharvi* (fisherman), *modval* (washerman) and *render* (toddy taper).

4. *Gowdi:* Gowdi in coastal Karnataka generally reside along the riversides or seashores. Like Sudir, Gowdi also have lower socio-economic status and usually are endogamous. It is quite possible to surmise that they are converts from fisher-folk. But there are four different explanations about their origin. First, they are believed to be the descendants of Kunbi community of Goa (Silva, 1961). Second, Gowdi are the descendants of the Gowdi migrated from Bardes region of Goa. Third, they are the converts from the Hindu Vanni-Vaishya castes of Goa, migrated to Canara (Saldanha, 1938) and fourth, they are of the converts of native origin (D'Souza, 1983).

5. *New Catholics:* Apart from the above four, there is another section that stands apart significantly from the rest of the Catholic community for different reasons. In Konkani they are known as *'Nove Christanvu'* meaning 'New Christians'. They are the Catholics converted during the early decades of 20th century and later. Besides tribals, these converts include mostly from the lowest sections of the local Hindu community, i.e., the Scheduled Castes, commonly termed as Harijans and the Koragas. After their conversion it was found difficult to integrate them into the stream of traditional Catholics and, at the same time, people of their caste who were not converted could not accommodate them. Therefore, it was felt necessary to rehabilitate them by establishing new colonies. Such colonies today are located at Naravi (near Kudremukh), Arva (about 9 km from Naravi), Alangar (Moodubidri), Badyar, Belthangadi, Madanthyar, Pavoor, Manjeshwar, Jeppu and other places. The New Catholics also faced some difficulties. First, on conversion to Catholicism, the convert was ex-communicated from the caste. Neither he could intermarry nor take part in any of their social functions. Secondly, out of ignorance and other motives, the traditional Catholics had prejudices against the converts. They considered them as lower in social status. Hence, they did not mix with them freely and were unwilling to intermarry. As a result, the spiritual and moral condition of the New Christians

was very low, especially in villages. So conversion, instead of solving their problems, increased them.

Thus, due to the above mentioned caste differences, we cannot consider the Catholic community of coastal Karnataka as a monolithic block. We witness in them the caste-like groupings. Moreover, this caste differentiation is not obvious all the time and in all spheres of life. Generally, it gives an impression that all Catholics who belong to different caste groups as mentioned above live in harmony and cooperation. On the other hand, there are situations where the different sections are hostile to each other. In fact, we can observe a dual life situations—first, life in church matters and second, the social life.

Caste Consciousness

Some of the important areas where the caste consciousness is made explicit are:

1. *Intra-caste marriage:* Traditionally, all castes were endogamous. Recently, we find people giving less importance to caste in the marriage alliances due to the factors such as wealth, education and modern occupations. Though we find the incidents of inter-caste marriages, the general trend is not towards any caste. The Bammon may seek a marriage alliance with a Charodi or vice versa but not with Sudir or Gowdi, which proves that social segregation still exists even today.

2. *Dietary habits:* Each caste has its own dietary habits and the consumption of delicacies. Though all were non-vegetarians and rice eaters, they differed in delicacies. For instance, while pork and *sanna* (rice cake) were the delicacies among the Bammon, rice and *payasam* (*vorn*) were among the Charodi and fish curry among the Gowdi.

3. *Family structures and family norms:* Family structures and family norms also showed variation when viewed in terms of castes. The variables that can be measured are authority in the family, rules of residence, status of female in the family etc.

4. *Involvement in church activities:* Involvement in church activities differed very much when related to castes. The lower castes (Sudir, Gowdi, and new Catholics) showed lot of diffidence and were given lesser chances in church activities when compared to the higher castes. Although there were learned and educated among the Sudir, Gowdi or new Catholics, generally, the position of leaders at different levels was occupied either by Bammon or Charodi. Exceptions to this were found only when the Gowdi or new Catholics were in absolute majority in a particular locality. A significant change in this area is observed today when

people showed greater social mobility by acquiring higher education, wealth, job security and lucrative employment.

5. *Language:* Language was another factor that made the caste grouping obvious. Though Konkani is the mother tongue of all the caste groups, it is spoken differently in terms of terminology, usage and articulation.

The caste situation among the Catholics of coastal Karnataka cannot be directly equated with *varna* or *jati* concept among the Hindus. Caste is given importance in terms of social differentiation and to prove social superiority. But, the same is not directly attributed to the concept of purity and pollution or the occupational association. Another significant fact that can be observed here is that there is no multiplication of caste groups. Inter-caste marriages do take place but usually the children are affiliated to the caste of the father or to the caste of the mother if she is of higher caste status than her husband. Therefore, no new castes are created.

In recent years lots of changes have taken place in the caste observances. As a result, there is also a shift in caste consciousness among the Catholics of coastal Karnataka. Of the attributes that have been reported as prominent to make the caste consciousness explicit, the present study shows an interesting feature. In certain attributes such as language, modes of behaviour, religious participation etc., the caste feeling is not weakening, rather it subtly gets recognized whereas in areas such as

Table 1
Modes of Caste Behaviour

Attributes	***Overt***	***Latent***	***Same***	***Weakened***	***Strengthened***
Marriage alliance	20.00	80.00	04.45	84.44	11.11
Church leadership	12.00	88.00	02.67	91.11	06.22
Religious devotion	51.11	48.89	05.44	25.33	69.33
Language	84.67	13.33	06.67	14.22	79.11
General behaviour	80.00	20.00	08.00	24.00	68.00
Family structure	20.00	80.00	04.45	47.11	48.44
Dietary habits	18.00	82.00	04.44	92.89	02.67
Occupation	13.00	87.00	05.78	84.44	09.78

Note: Figures are in percentages.

dietary habits, church leadership and marriage alliances, the caste seems to have weakened its hold. One significant fact is that though we find a trend of diminished role of caste in certain areas, we find the caste feeling is at work in latent form in other spheres of social life. Further, due to the new set of values of modernized, literate society, they are not expressed or made overt very emphatically. Table 1 gives a short glimpse of this trend. Further, it illustrates the attributes that are indicated as weakened have in fact become latent and still continue to be prominent. The fact that an attribute is not overt can not suggest that is has weakened the caste identity; it is still felt strong in spite of varied influences and expressions.

Therefore, it is observed that the Catholics of coastal Karnataka are still cognisant of caste or ethnic feeling. The social differentiation is contextual. In matters concerned with church life such as rituals, rites, sacraments, services and so on, all are considered equal. Moreover, at the social context, we find differentiation as superior or inferior and even discrimination on such basis. Categorization and discrimination on the basis of caste origin and ascription of superior or subordinate social position is the noted practice. The ascriptive position accorded to the Gowdi, Sudir and the New Catholics is also significant.

Caste Segregation

Some of the areas where lower castes are excluded are:

1. *Marriage alliance:* Traditionally, Bammon and Charodi occupied the higher ranking and were occasionally fighting between themselves for supremacy. The others generally occupied the lower social ranking. Marriage would be contracted only within the same caste. However, the incidents of inter-caste marriages seem to have been reported between the Bammon and Charodi and between Gowdi and Sudir. The New Catholics usually married among themselves. The situation does not seem very much different today. There are incidents of marriages between the Gowdi and the Bammon or Charodi. However, the cases are not frequent. As a matter of fact, they are not arranged with the consent of the elders, but are based on 'self-choice' or 'love marriage'. These trends do not seem to be successful in uprooting the caste elements. They only overshadow with modern attributes such as wealth, education and job. Therefore, the exclusion of Gowdi and, especially New Catholics, is evident.

2. *Participation in church activities:* Caste was made explicit in the activities of the church. The church leaders were mostly from the high

castes—Bammon and Charodi. The Gowdi were not given an opportunity to prove their merit. The ward (*wado)* leaders or *Gurkars* were selected or elected mostly from amongst the Bammon or Charodi.

Different castes formerly had their own influence in church matters. The dominant castes usually dominated in the parish affairs. When there is any congregational worship or mass in progress, traditionally, only the high castes could sit on the benches. In certain parishes, the benches were marked for castes or families. Caste position was said to be the criterion or eligibility to take initiative in handling responsibility at the parish level. This tendency, coupled with the advantage the high caste had of education and economic background, enabled them to occupy the leadership positions. Therefore, many of the leaders were found to be from the Bammon or Charodi castes giving not many chances to the Gowdi. It is due to their higher status that high castes dominated at the *'junta'* (parish council meetings). The dominance of the Bammon and Charodi in parish activities brought about decisions favouring upper sections.

The choice of leaders from particular caste was deliberate in certain areas. However, in some areas, it was situational, because different wards or parishes were dominated by a particular caste. In such cases, a leader was elected from amongst the majority caste. Therefore, there were leaders and *Gurkars* among the Gowdi in the places, ward or parishes where Gowdis were in majority. Generally, the Bammon and Charodi felt confident and participated in church activities quite freely, while the Gowdi community showed good deal of diffidence, fear and shyness. As a result, their presence was not noticed at any occasion.

3. *Priesthood and religious life:* Traditionally, the priests were predominantly from the Bammon caste. Non-Bammon candidates for priesthood were known to have often received discouragement in the seminaries. The membership in the prestigious priestly orders and religious congregations in coastal Karnataka was restricted only to the upper castes, i.e. Bammon and Charodi. The aspirants from the lower sections as Gowdi, Sudir and New Catholics were either discouraged or convinced that they are incapable of studying for priesthood or religious life. Even if they were accepted for priesthood or religious life their chances of further education and holding responsible and prestigious positions as teachers, superiors, etc. were far less.

In the past the parish priests were appointed mostly from the Bammon or Charodi caste. Therefore, they preferred their own caste men as leaders to hold responsibility at parishes. The traditional punishments at church level such as *Kulpa* (beating on the palm by a wooden spatula), *Khandi-Kuris* (carrying the cross), etc., were decided and executed by the Bammon and Charodi castes. Even today, the Bammon and Charodi have upper hand. The domineering position of Bammon and Charodi had its effect on the church life too. The lower sections such as Gowdi, Sudir and New Catholics were hardly given any chances for leadership. They always remained as subordinates. However, today, the situation is somewhat different.

4. *Educational opportunities:* Most of the schools and the educational institutions were located in the residential areas of the upper castes. This created difficulty for the lower castes to avail education.

5. *Areas of residence:* The origin of the Catholic community in coastal Karnataka is attributed to the waves of migration from Goa. The migrants settled down generally on the basis of caste. To cite a few examples—Bammon settled down in Mangalore and Udupi city areas and parts of Kinnigoli, Bajpe, Belman and Karkala generally preferring close to the city centres. The Charodi in the adjacent interior belts, comparatively in developing, or agriculturally promising areas as Suratkal, Katipalla, Kallianpur, Barkur, Puttur, Sullia and other places. The Gowdis are located generally along the riversides—Kulur, Bajal, Ranipura, Bantwal, and such other areas. The New Catholics found support by living in separate colonies. This association of a caste with the place is found even today.

6. *Social interaction:* Social interaction among the Catholics of coastal Karnataka also shows attitudes and sometimes the prejudices against the other groups within the community. This is based on categorization and differentiation on the basis of the origin of caste and also on the basis of superior or subordinate social position. Table 2 shows the attitude of Bammons towards Gowdi and New Catholics and Table 3 shows the attitudes of Charodi towards Gowdi and New Catholics. The variables taken to measure the social distance are: economic relations, social interaction, inter-dining, and marriage alliance. In fact, they are placed in the increasing order in terms of closeness or intimacy in social relations and interactions. Economic relations measure the basic social relations expected to live with, including mutual tolerance and trust. Social interaction measures the willingness to reside in one locality, share common customs and practices, cooperation and social participation in different activities. Inter-dining is extended to account for freedom to share a meal, eat together and follow same dietary habits, freedom to accommodate one

in the house and a sense of feeling of belongingness. The variable—marriage alliance—concentrates on the highest degree of social intimacy measuring the areas as acceptance to share life, readiness to give and take members in marriage into one's household etc., which exhibits least social barriers between the sections.

Tables 2 and 3 show that the preference and desirability of Bammon and Charodi, who are generally considered as high castes, is very marginal towards the Gowdi and the New Catholics for different variables. Much of the responses centre on to indicate the attitude of 'comfortable' for variables such as 'economic relations', 'social interactions' and 'inter-dining'. However, the responses to the variable, 'marriage alliances', are rather negative indicating either 'not comfortable' or 'reject'. This attitudinal position indicates the superiority-inferiority feelings that are carried on in the community. Though the Catholics consider equal among themselves as a community, the inequality is explicit in terms of social living.

Table 2
Attitudes of Bammon towards the Gowdi and the New Catholics

Variables	*Prefer*	*Desire*	*Comfortable*	*Not-comfortable*	*Reject*
Economic relations	01.00	01.33	86.33	09.67	01 67
Social interactions	01.33	03.67	17.33	78.00	00.33
Inter-dining	—	01.00	87.00	11.33	00.67
Marriage alliance	—	00.67	07.33	65.33	26.67

Table 3
Attitudes of Charodi towards the Gowdi and the New Catholics

Variables	*Prefer*	*Desire*	*Comfortable*	*Not-comfortable*	*Reject*
Economic relations	—	—	92.87	06.22	00.89
Social interactions	—	—	37.33	62.67	—
Inter-dining	—	01.78	60.87	36.43	—
Marriage alliance	—	—	05.33	92.43	01.73

Discrimination against the New Catholics in the history has detached them into a separate group. It is an accepted fact that the community ascribed a different identity for the New Catholics, whether in the social life or in the church or parish life activities. They were segregated and considered separately in the past, the influence of this practice prevails even today. Though some of the Gowdi and New Catholics have good features and complexion, they are also treated low due to their cultural origin, occupation, association with local cults, and association with liquor, either in terms of brewing or drunkenness. The New Catholics too do not feel very comfortable with the rest of the Catholics while participating in social as well as religious functions.

The study by Rajath (2000) observes certain remarks made by the respondents with regard to the interrelations between the castes. A respondent from Bammon caste is comfortable with a Hindu GSB Brahmin in marriage alliance, if took place, though a member of Bajrang Dal than a lower section. In another case the respondent is comfortable to invite non-Catholics for the church feast dinner, but positively keep away members of other sections within Catholic fold. Yet another respondent is comfortable to attend 'Ganesh Utsav' and other *jatra* but not comfortable to attend the feast at the neighbouring parish that belongs to the other caste section.

The factors for feeling discomfort on the part of the New Catholics and social exclusion on part of the rest of the Catholics are:

(i) *Language:* Though some of the New Catholics speak Konkani, it sounds quite different than that of the rest in pronunciation and intonation. At times they tend to speak Tulu, a language spoken by them before conversion.

(ii) *Source of origin:* They originally do not belong to the Catholic community but converted from the lower sections of Hindu community.

(iii) *Caste:* They were converted from the lowest sections of the coastal Karnataka Hindu society. They are the converts from Koragas and Harijans.

(iv) *Income:* Traditionally, their financial background was not very sound. It took several decades for them to gain some economic base. Even today, not many are economically well placed.

(v) *Culture and practices:* They are generally considered culturally low. One can observe the prevalence of some of the Hindu practices, as spirit worship (*Bhutharadhane*), ancestor worship etc. among them, which are generally disapproved by the popular Catholic community.

(vi) *Low educational background and achievement:* The older generation is not much educated due to lack of opportunities and existing caste discrimination. Even today, the general attitude towards higher education is rather low.

(vii) *Harsh and rude behaviour:* Harsh and rude behaviour due to drunkenness and other vices are reported among them.

(viii) *Low occupation:* They are involved in low occupations as daily wagers, agriculture, brewing of liquor etc.

Effect of Caste Segregation on Community

This discrimination had its far-reaching effects on the community of Catholics. To mention a few:

1. Non-participation in the community activities that are deliberately planned at the parish level.
2. Groupism within the community.
3. Issue-based conflicts.
4. Attraction to other sects as Syrian Orthodox Church and the New Life Community.
5. Separation or division into different parish units.
6. Lowering the image of Catholics in the society in general.
7. Strict regulations on endogamous marriage alliances.
8. Practice of the local cults that are not strictly accepted by the Catholic principles or teachings.

The significant event of 'Kallianpur Schism' which took place around 1930s in the history of the diocese of Mangalore can be referred to illustrate the division into different parish units. Strong affiliation to their respective castes as Bammon or Charodi had two consequences—first, the division of the parish into Milagres church at Kallianpur, known as lower church and Mount Rosary church, known as the upper church. Of course, the division has pontifical reasons also, but the separation was strongly based on caste lines. The Bammon joined the upper church though they reside in the area covered by the lower church; and the same case with the Charodi who joined the lower church. Secondly, a large section of Catholics in the area left the Roman Catholic community and joined the Syrian Orthodox Church; a parish unit situated at Brahmavar, about six kilometers away from Kallianpur. The schism is attributed both to religion and caste status.

Moreover, this trend is not so consistent today. Today the situation is different. Thanks to the modernizing effects in the society and the widespread attraction for education among the Catholics. What is interesting to note today is that the fact remains the same but the incidents are different, that is, the age-old practices of discrimination on the basis of caste are not overtly emphasized today, but the fact of caste consciousness is still very strong and it is expressed quite differently, mostly in subtle ways.

With this study we can make some observations that can be meaningful to understand the present caste reality:

1. The caste identity is still felt strong, may not be under the traditional label but in the line of same ethnic origin.
2. The younger generation does not seem to be aware of their caste name or ethnic origin but definitely is aware of the different caste-like groups and the differentiation made between these groups on the basis of such factors as language, area of residence, parental origin, etc.
3. Today people in society express their ethnic feeling or identity in different modes. Caste is one such expression. Religion and language can be others.
4. The cultural items in Indian society including caste are influenced by various factors such as education, economy, polity, urbanization, globalization and so on, from within and from outside. Hence, caste hides its prominent hood when faced with modern challenges and sets of values. It only takes subtle ways to express and does not die out.
5. The emphasis on different attributes of caste as it is made explicit varies due to the varied ideology and the spread of new secular mind. Therefore caste is not emphatic in attributes such as dietary habits, dress patterns, religious or ritual significance etc., but in certain other aspects like inter-marriages, dialect, family norms and so on.

Therefore, it becomes obvious that the ethnic identity, ethnic feeling, ethnic consciousness or ethnic unity persists in spite of the social, economic, ideological and structural changes. The Konkani-speaking Roman Catholic community of coastal Karnataka is a witness to this fact. Social exclusion is a social fact, quite well rooted in social life. India is no exception to this in its practices of caste system, no matter what region, language or religions. However, something glaring and significant is that it still continues its hold in spite of the modern developments and high standards of educational attainment.

REFERENCES

Dumont, Louis. 1970. *Homo Hierarchicus: The Caste System and its Implications*. London: Weidenfeld and Nicolson.

D'Souza, A.L.P. 1983. *History of the Catholic Community in South Kanara*. Mangalore: Preethi Books.

Forrester, Duncan B. 1980. *Caste and Christianity*. London: Curzon Press.

Gomes, Olivinho. 1987. *Village Goa*. New Delhi: S. Chand and Company.

Haan, Arjan. 1999. Poverty and Social Exclusion: A Comparison of Debates on Deprivation. Working Paper No. 2, Brighton: Poverty Research Unit, Sussex University.

Miranda, Rockey V. *Caste, Religion and Dialect Differentiation in the Konkani Area*. Mangalore: Institute of Konkani, St Aloysius College.

Power, Wilson A.W.J. 2000. *Social Exclusion and the Future of Cities*. London. Centre for Analysis of Social Exclusion, London School of Economics.

Raj, Antony. 1992. "Discrimination among Dalit Christians in Tamil Nadu", in *SAR News*, September 19–25, Mumbai.

Rajath, Vinay. 2000. Social Structure and Stratification among the Catholics of Dakshina Kannada. Unpublished Ph.D. Thesis, Department of Sociology, Mangalore University, Mangalore.

Saldanha, Jerome A. 1905. *The Indian Castes*. Vol. I, Konkani and Goan Castes, Sirsi.

——. 1938. *Origin and Growth of Konkani Language and Goan Communities*. Mangalore.

Silva, Severine. 1961. *History of Christianity in Canara*. Bombay: Hindi Sanskrit Sangam.

Silva, Severine and Fuchs, Stephen. 1965. *The Marriage Customs of the Christians in South Canara, India*. Bombay: Publications of the Indian Branch of the Anthropos Institute.

Thorat, Sukhadeo et al. 2009. *Social Justice Philanthropy*. Jaipur: Rawat Publications.

Contributors

Rose Veera D'Souza, Reader and Head, Department of Political Science, St. Aloysius College, Mangalore.

K. Gopal, Professor (Retired) of Sociology, Meerut University, Meerut.

M. Gurulingaiah, Professor of Sociology, Kuvempu University, Shimoga, Karnataka.

R. Indira, Professor of Sociology, Mysore University, Mysore.

Jagan Karade, Lecturer in Sociology, Tilak Maharashtra University, Pune.

M.H. Makwana, Professor and Head, Department of Sociology, Gujarat University, Ahmedabad.

Parthasarathi Mondal, Assistant Professor, Tata Institute of Social Sciences, Mumbai.

B.K. Nagla, Professor (Retired) of Sociology, M.D. University, Rohtak, Haryana.

Richard Pais, Professor and Head, Department of Sociology, St. Aloysius College, Mangalore.

Vinay Rajath D., Reader in Sociology, Milagres College, Kallianpur, Udupi District.

Nandu Ram, Professor of Sociology, Jawaharlal Nehru University, New Delhi.

Y. Ravindranath Rao, Professor and Head, Department of Sociology, St. Mary's Syrian College, Brahmavar, Udupi District.

H.M. Vasanthamma, Professor (Retired) of Sociology, Maharaja's College, Mysore.

D. Venkateswarlu, Professor of Sociology, Sri Venkateshwara University, Tirupati.

Jag Mohan Singh Verma, Professor (Retired) of Sociology, Lucknow University, Lucknow.

Index